THE MESSAGE OF THE GITA

The Message of the Gita

WITH TEXT, TRANSLATION AND NOTES

as interpreted by
SRI AUROBINDO

edited by
ANILBARAN ROY

SRI AUROBINDO ASHRAM
PONDICHERRY

First Edition 1938
Fifth Edition 1993
Second Impression 1999

(Typeset in 11/13 pt. Times)

ISBN 81-7058-305-5

© Sri Aurobindo Ashram Trust 1993
Published by Sri Aurobindo Ashram Publication Department
Printed at Sri Aurobindo Ashram Press, Pondicherry 605 002
PRINTED IN INDIA

Preface

The Gita is a great synthesis of Aryan spiritual culture and Sri Aurobindo's luminous exposition of it, as contained in his *Essays on the Gita*, sets out its inner significances in a way that brings them home to the modern mind. I have prepared this commentary summarising its substance with the permission of Sri Aurobindo. The notes have been entirely compiled from the *Essays on the Gita* and arranged under the *slokas* in the manner of the Sanskrit commentators.

ANILBARAN

Sri Aurobindo Ashram,
Pondicherry,
21st February, 1938.

CONTENTS

Preface	v
Conspectus	ix
Introduction	xv

First Chapter
    I. Kurukshetra   1

Second Chapter
    I. The Creed of the Aryan Fighter   14
    II. The Yoga of the Intelligent Will   27

Third Chapter
    I. Works and Sacrifice   49
    II. The Determinism of Nature   61

Fourth Chapter
    I. The Possibility and Purpose of Avatarhood   69
    II. The Divine Worker   77
    III. The Significance of Sacrifice   82

Fifth Chapter
    I. Renunciation and Yoga of Works   90

Sixth Chapter
    I. Nirvana and Works in the World   101

Seventh Chapter
    I. The Two Natures   115
    II. The Synthesis of Devotion and Knowledge   124

Eighth Chapter
    I. The Supreme Divine   132

Ninth Chapter
    I. Works, Devotion and Knowledge   142

Tenth Chapter
    I. The Supreme Word of the Gita   157
    II. God in Power of Becoming   163

Eleventh Chapter
    I. Time the Destroyer   173
    II. The Double Aspect   183

Twelfth Chapter
    I. The Way and the Bhakta   191

Thirteenth Chapter
    I. The Field and Its Knower   199

Fourteenth Chapter
    I. Above the Gunas   211

Fifteenth Chapter
    I. The Three Purushas   223

Sixteenth Chapter
    I. Deva and Asura   232

Seventeenth Chapter
    I. The Gunas, Faith and Works   241

Eighteenth Chapter
    I. The Gunas, Mind and Works   252
    II. Swabhava and Swadharma   266
    III. Towards the Supreme Secret   273
    IV. The Supreme Secret   281

Appendix I.
    The Story of the Gita   292

Appendix II.
    The Historicity of Krishna   294

Appendix III.
    Some Psychological Presuppositions   296

    Glossary   302
    Index   306

CONSPECTUS

FIRST CHAPTER

Kurukshetra – Arjuna, the representative man of his age, is overcome with dejection and sorrow at the most critical moment of his life on the battle-field of Kurukshetra, and raises incidentally the whole question of human life and action; the whole exposition of the Gita revolves and completes its cycle round this original question of Arjuna.   1-13

SECOND CHAPTER

The answer of the Teacher proceeds upon two different lines:

I. *The Creed of the Aryan Fighter* (1-38)
First, a brief reply founded upon the philosophic and moral conceptions of Vedanta and the social idea of duty and honour which formed the ethical basis of Aryan Society.   14-26

II. *The Yoga of the Intelligent Will* (39-72)
Another reply founded on a more intimate Knowledge, opening into deeper truths of our being, which is the real starting-point of the teaching of the Gita. The Gita lays the first foundation by subtly unifying Sankhya, Yoga and Vedanta.   27-48

THIRD CHAPTER

I. *Works and Sacrifice* (1-26)
Arjuna, the pragmatic man, is perplexed by metaphysical thought and asks for a simple rule of action. The Gita begins to develop more clearly its positive and imperative doctrine of works, – of works done as a sacrifice to the Divine.   49-60

II. *The Determinism of Nature* (27-43)
Arjuna is told that he must act always by the law of his nature. "All existences follow their nature and what shall coercing it avail?"   61-68

FOURTH CHAPTER

I. *The Possibility and Purpose of Avatarhood* (1-15)
The Divine Teacher, the Avatar, gives his own example, his own standard to Arjuna. In India the belief in the reality of the Avatar, the descent into form, the revelation of the Godhead in humanity, has grown up and persisted as a logical outcome of the Vedantic view of life and taken firm root in the consciousness of the race.   69-76

II. *The Divine Worker* (16-23)
Equality, impersonality, peace, joy and freedom — these are the signs which distinguish a divine worker; they are all profoundly subjective and do not depend on so outward a thing as doing or not doing works.   77-81

III. *The Significance of Sacrifice* (24-42)
The Gita brings out the inner meaning of the Vedic sacrifice, interpreting the secret symbolism of the ancient Vedic mystics.   82-89

FIFTH CHAPTER

Renunciation and Yoga of Works — The Gita, after speaking of the perfect equality of the Brahman-knower who has risen into the Brahman-consciousness, develops in the last nine verses of this chapter its idea of Brahmayoga and of Nirvana in the Brahman.   90-100

SIXTH CHAPTER

Nirvana and Works in the World — This chapter is a full development of the idea of the closing verses of the fifth, — that shows the importance which the Gita attaches to them.   101-114

SEVENTH CHAPTER

The seventh to the twelfth chapters lay down a large metaphysical statement of the nature of the Divine Being and on that foundation closely relate and synthetise knowledge and devotion, just as the first part of the Gita related and synthetised works and knowledge in giving the primary basis of its teachings.

I. *The Two Natures* (1-14)

The Gita makes the distinction between the two Natures, the phenomenal and the spiritual. Here is the first new metaphysical idea of the Gita which helps it to start from the notions of the Sankhya philosophy and yet exceed them and give to their terms a Vedantic significance. 115-123

II. *The Synthesis of Devotion and Knowledge* (15-30)

The Gita is not a treatise of metaphysical philosophy. It seeks the highest truth for the highest practical utility. Thus it turns the philosophic truth given in the opening section of this chapter into a first starting-point for the unification of works, knowledge and devotion. 124-131

EIGHTH CHAPTER

The Supreme Divine — We have here the first description of the Supreme Purusha, — the Godhead who is even more and greater than the Immutable and to whom the Gita gives subsequently (as in the fifteenth chapter) the name of *Purushottama*. The language here is taken bodily from the Upanishads. 132-141

NINTH CHAPTER

Works, Devotion and Knowledge — What the Gita now proceeds to say is the most secret thing of all. It is the knowledge of the whole Godhead which the Master of his being has promised to Arjuna (VII. -I). To direct the whole self Godwards in an entire union is the way to rise out of a mundane into a divine existence. 142-156

TENTH CHAPTER

I. *The Supreme Word of the Gita* (1-11)

The divine Avatar declares, in a brief reiteration of the upshot of all that he has been saying, that this and no other is his supreme word. 157-162

II. *God in Power of Becoming* (12-42)

This section enumerates examples of Vibhutis or

forms in which the Divine manifests its power in the world. It leads up to the vision of the World-Purusha in the next chapter.   163-172

ELEVENTH CHAPTER

I. *Time the Destroyer* (1-34)   173-182

II. *The Double Aspect* (35-55)

The Time figure of the Godhead is now revealed and from the million mouths of that figure issues the command for the appointed action to the liberated Vibhuti. This vision of the universal Purusha is one of the most powerfully poetic passages in the Gita.   183-190

TWELFTH CHAPTER

The way and the Bhakta – In the eleventh chapter the original object of the teaching has been achieved and brought up to a certain completeness. What remains still to be said turns upon the difference between the current Vedantic view of spiritual liberation and the larger comprehensive freedom which the teaching of the Gita opens to the spirit. The twelfth chapter leads up to this remaining knowledge and the last six that follow develop it to a grand final conclusion.   191-198

THIRTEENTH CHAPTER

The Field and its Knower – The distinctions between Purusha and Prakriti, Soul and Nature, rapidly drawn in this chapter in the terms of the Sankhya Philosophy, are the basis on which the Gita rests its whole idea of the liberated being made one in the conscious law of its existence with the Divine.   199-210

FOURTEENTH CHAPTER

Above the Gunas – The Gita now proceeds to work out its ideas of the action of the gunas, of the ascension beyond the gunas and of the culmination of desireless works in knowledge where knowledge coalesces with bhakti, – knowledge, works and love made one, – and it rises thence to its great finale, the supreme secret of self-surrender to the Master of Existence.   211-222

FIFTEENTH CHAPTER

The Three Purushas – The entire doctrine of the Gita converges, on all its lines and through all the flexibility of its turns, towards one central thought – the idea of a triple consciousness, three and yet one, present in the whole scale of existence. All that is now brought together into one focus of grouping vision.

This chapter opens with a description of cosmic existence in the Vedantic image of the *ashwattha* tree. 223-231

SIXTEENTH CHAPTER

Deva and Asura – The Gita now proceeds to give the psychological discipline by which our human and earthly nature can be transmuted. But first it prefaces the consideration of this enlightening movement by a distinction between two kinds of being, the Deva and the Asura. 232-240

SEVENTEENTH CHAPTER

The Gunas, Faith and Works – The Gita next gives an analysis of action in the light of the fundamental idea of the three gunas and the transcendence of them by a self-exceeding culmination of the highest sattwic discipline. In this chapter it lays special stress on Faith, *shraddha*, the will to believe and to be, know, live and enact the Truth as the principal factor. 241-251

EIGHTEENTH CHAPTER

I. *The Gunas, Mind and Works* (1-39)

The Gita enters into a summary psychological analysis of the mental powers before it proceeds to its great finale, the highest secret which is that of a spiritual exceeding of all *dharmas*. 252-265

II. *Swabhava and Swadharma* (40-48)

In this section the Gita deals with an incidental question of great importance – the ancient social idea of *chaturvarnya*, which was a very different thing from the present day caste system. 266-272

III. *Towards the Supreme Secret* (49-56)
In this section the Gita re-states the body of its message.   273-280

IV. *The Supreme Secret* (57-78)
The essence of the teaching and the Yoga has thus been given to the disciple and the divine Teacher now proceeds to apply it to his action. Attached to a crucial example, spoken to the protagonist of Kurukshetra, the words bear a much wider significance and are a universal rule for all who are ready to ascend above the ordinary mentality and to live and act in the highest spiritual consciousness.   281-291

INTRODUCTION

It may be useful in approaching an ancient Scripture, such as the Veda, Upanishads or Gita to indicate precisely the spirit in which we approach it and what exactly we think we may derive from it that is of value to humanity and its future. First of all, there is undoubtedly a Truth one and eternal which we are seeking, from which all other truth derives, by the light of which all other truth finds its right place, explanation and relation to the scheme of knowledge. But precisely for that reason it cannot be shut up in a single trenchant formula, it is not likely to be found in its entirety or in all its bearings in any single philosophy or scripture or uttered altogether and for ever by any one teacher, thinker, prophet or Avatar. Nor has it been wholly found by us if our view of it necessitates the intolerant exclusion of the truth underlying other systems; for when we reject passionately, we mean simply that we cannot appreciate and explain. Secondly, this Truth, though it is one and eternal, expresses itself in Time and through the mind of man; therefore every Scripture must necessarily contain two elements, one temporary, perishable, belonging to the ideas of the period and country in which it was produced, the other eternal and imperishable and applicable in all ages and countries. Moreover, in the statement of the Truth the actual form given to it, the system and arrangement, the metaphysical and intellectual mould, the precise expression used must be largely subject to the mutations of Time and cease to have the same force; for the human intellect modifies itself always, continually dividing and putting together it is obliged to shift its divisions continually and to re-arrange its synthesis; it is always leaving old expression and symbol for new or, if it uses the old, it so changes its connotation or at least its exact content and association that we can never be quite sure of understanding an ancient book of this kind precisely in the sense and spirit it bore to its contemporaries. What is of entirely permanent value is that which besides being universal has been experienced, lived and seen with a higher than the intellectual vision.

We hold it therefore of small importance to extract from the Gita its exact metaphysical connotation as it was understood by the men of the time, – even if that were accurately possible. That it is not possible, is shown by the divergence of the original commentaries which have been and are still being written upon it; for they all agree in each disagreeing with all the others, each finds in the Gita its own system of metaphysics and trend of religious thought. Nor will even the most painstaking and disinterested scholarship and the most luminous theories of the historical development of Indian philosophy save us from inevitable error. But what we can do with profit is to seek in the Gita for the actual living truths it contains, apart from their metaphysical form, to extract from it what can help us or the world at large and to put it in the most natural and vital form and expression we can find that will be suitable to the mentality and helpful to the spiritual needs of our present-day humanity. No doubt in this attempt we may mix a good deal of error born of our own individuality and of the ideas in which we live, as did greater men before us, but if we steep ourselves in the spirit of this great Scripture and, above all, if we have tried to live in that spirit, we may be sure of finding in it as much real truth as we are capable of receiving as well as the spiritual influence and actual help that, personally, we were intended to derive from it. And that is after all what Scriptures were written to give; the rest is academical disputation or theological dogma. Only those Scriptures, religions, philosophies which can be thus constantly renewed, relived, their stuff of permanent truth constantly reshaped and developed in the inner thought and spiritual experience of a developing humanity, continue to be of living importance to mankind. The rest remain as monuments of the past, but have no actual force or vital impulse for the future.

The thought of the Gita is not pure Monism although it sees in one unchanging, pure, eternal Self the foundation of all cosmic existence, nor Mayavada although it speaks of the Maya of the three modes of Prakriti omnipresent in the created world; nor is it qualified Monism although it places in the One his eternal supreme Prakriti manifested in the form of the Jiva and lays most stress on dwelling in God rather than dissolution as the supreme state of spiritual consciousness; nor is it Sankhya although it explains the created world by the double principle of Purusha and Prakriti; nor is it Vaishnava Theism although it presents to us Krishna, who is the Avatar of Vishnu according to the Puranas, as the supreme Deity and allows no essential difference nor any actual superiority of the status of the indefinable relationless Brahman over that of this Lord of beings who is the Master of the universe and the Friend of all creatures. Like the earlier spiritual synthesis of the Upanishads this later synthesis at once spiritual and intellectual avoids naturally every such rigid determination as would injure its universal comprehensiveness. Its aim is precisely the opposite to that of the polemist commentators who found this Scripture established as one of the three highest Vedantic authorities and attempted to turn it into a weapon of offence and defence against other schools and systems. The Gita is not a weapon for dialectical warfare; it is a gate opening on the whole world of spiritual truth and experience and the view it gives us embraces all the provinces of that supreme region. It maps out, but it does not cut up or build walls or hedges to confine our vision.

There have been other syntheses in the long history of Indian thought. We start with the Vedic synthesis of the psychological being of man in its highest flights and widest rangings of divine knowledge, power, joy, life and glory with the cosmic existence of the gods, pursued behind the symbols of the material universe into those superior planes which are hidden from the physical sense and the material mentality. The crown of this synthesis was in the experience of the Vedic Rishis something divine, transcendent and blissful in whose unity the increasing soul of man and the eternal divine fulness of the cosmic godheads meet perfectly and fulfil themselves. The Upanishads take up this crowning experience of the earlier seers and make it their starting-point for a high and profound synthesis of spiritual knowledge; they draw together into a great harmony all that had been seen and experienced by the inspired and liberated knowers of the Eternal throughout a great and fruitful period of spiritual seeking. The Gita starts from this Vedantic synthesis and upon the basis of its essential ideas builds another harmony of the three great means and powers, Love, Knowledge and Works, through which the soul of man can directly approach and cast itself into the Eternal. There is yet another, the Tantric,[1] which though less subtle and spiritually profound, is even more bold and forceful than the synthesis of the Gita, – for it seizes even upon the obstacles to the spiritual life and compels them to become the means for a richer spiritual conquest and enables us to embrace the whole of Life in our divine scope as the Lila[2] of the Divine; and in some directions it is more immediately rich and fruitful, for it brings forward into the foreground along with divine knowledge, divine works and an enriched devotion of divine Love, the secrets also of the Hatha and Raja Yogas, the use of the body and of mental askesis for the opening up of the divine life on all its planes, to which the Gita gives only a passing and perfunctory attention. Moreover it grasps at that idea of the divine perfectibility of man, possessed by the Vedic Rishis but thrown into the background by the intermediate ages, which is destined to fill so large a place in any future synthesis of human thought, experience and aspiration.

We of the coming day stand at the head of a new age of development which must lead to such a new and larger synthesis. We are not called upon to be orthodox Vedantins

---

[1] All the Puranic tradition, it must be remembered, draws the richness of its contents from the Tantra.
[2] The cosmic Play.

of any of the three schools or Tantrics or to adhere to one of the theistic religions of the past or to entrench ourselves within the four corners of the teaching of the Gita. That would be to limit ourselves and to attempt to create our spiritual life out of the being, knowledge and nature of others, of the men of the past, instead of building it out of our own being and potentialities. We do not belong to the past dawns, but to the noons of the future. A mass of new material is flowing into us; we have not only to assimilate the influences of the great theistic religions of India and of the world and a recovered sense of the meaning of Buddhism, but to take full account of the potent though limited revelations of modern knowledge and seeking; and, beyond that, the remote and dateless past which seemed to be dead is returning upon us with an effulgence of many luminous secrets long lost to the consciousness of mankind but now breaking out again from behind the veil. All this points to a new, a very rich, a very vast synthesis; a fresh and widely embracing harmonisation of our gains is both an intellectual and a spiritual necessity of the future. But just as the past syntheses have taken those which preceded them for their starting-point, so also must that of the future, to be on firm ground, proceed from what the great bodies of realised spiritual thought and experience in the past have given. Among them the Gita takes a most important place.

Our object, then, in studying the Gita will not be a scholastic or academical scrutiny of its thought, nor to place its philosophy in the history of metaphysical speculation, nor shall we deal with it in the manner of the analytical dialectician. We approach it for help and light and our aim must be to distinguish its essential and living message, that in it on which humanity has to seize for its perfection and its highest spiritual welfare.

First Chapter

KURUKSHETRA

धृतराष्ट्र उवाच —
धर्मक्षेत्रे कुरुक्षेत्रे समवेता युयुत्सवः ।
मामकाः पाण्डवाश्चैव किमकुर्वत सञ्जय ॥१॥

1. Dhritarashtra[1] **said:–** On the field of Kurukshetra, the field of the working out of the Dharma[2], gathered together, eager for battle, what did they, O Sanjaya, my people and the Pandavas?

[1] The peculiarity of the Gita among the great religious books of the world is that it does not stand apart as a work by itself, the fruit of the spiritual life of a creative personality like Christ, Mohammed or Buddha or of an epoch of pure spiritual searching like the Veda and Upanishads, but is given as an episode in an epic history of nations and their wars and men and their deeds and arises out of a critical moment in the soul of one of its leading personages face to face with the crowning action of his life, a work terrible, violent and sanguinary, at the point when he must either recoil from it altogether or carry it through to its inexorable completion. The teaching of the Gita must therefore be regarded not merely in the light of a general spiritual philosophy or ethical doctrine, but as bearing upon a practical crisis in the application of ethics and spirituality to human life.

[2] We might symbolically translate the phrase as the field of human action which is the field of the evolving Dharma. The Gita takes for its frame such a period of transition and crisis as humanity periodically experiences in its history, in which great forces clash together for a huge destruction and reconstruction, intellectual, social, moral, religious, political, and these in the actual psychological and social stage of human evolution culminate usually through a violent physical convulsion of strife, war or revolution. The Gita proceeds from the acceptance of the necessity in Nature for such vehement crises and it accepts not only the moral aspect, the struggle between righteousness and unrighteousness, between the self-affirming law of Good and the forces that oppose its progression, but also the physical aspect, the actual armed war or other vehement physical strife between the human beings who represent the antagonistic powers. A day may come, must surely come, we will say, when humanity will be ready spiritually, morally, socially for the reign of universal peace; meanwhile the aspect of battle and the nature and

सञ्जय उवाच —

दृष्ट्वा तु पाण्डवानीकं व्यूढं दुर्योधनस्तदा ।
आचार्यमुपसङ्गम्य राजा वचनमब्रवीत् ॥२॥

2. **Sanjaya said:**— Then the prince Duryodhana, having seen the army of the Pandavas arrayed in battle order, approached his teacher and spoke these words:—

पश्यैतां पाण्डुपुत्राणामाचार्य महतीं चमूम् ।
व्यूढां द्रुपदपुत्रेण तव शिष्येण धीमता ॥३॥

3. "Behold this mighty host of the sons of Pandu, O Acharya, arrayed by Drupada's son, thy intelligent disciple.

अत्र शूरा महेष्वासा भीमार्जुनसमा युधि ।
युयुधानो विराटश्च द्रुपदश्च महारथः ॥४॥
धृष्टकेतुश्चेकितानः काशिराजश्च वीर्यवान् ।
पुरुजित् कुन्तिभोजश्च शैब्यश्च नरपुङ्गवः ॥५॥
युधामन्युश्च विक्रान्त उत्तमौजाश्च वीर्यवान् ।
सौभद्रो द्रौपदेयाश्च सर्व एव महारथाः ॥६॥

4-6. Here in this mighty army are heroes and great bowmen who are equal in battle to Bhima and Arjuna; Yuyudhana, Virata and Drupada of the great car, Dhrishtaketu, Chekitana and the valiant prince of Kashi, Purujit and Kuntibhoja, and Shaibya, foremost among men; Yudhamanyu, the strong, and Uttamauja, the victorious; Subhadra's son (Abhimanyu) and the sons of Draupadi; all of them of great prowess.

अस्माकं तु विशिष्टा ये तान्निबोध द्विजोत्तम ।
नायका मम सैन्यस्य संज्ञार्थं तान् ब्रवीमि ते ॥७॥

---

function of man as a fighter have to be accepted and accounted for by any practical philosophy and religion. The Gita, taking life as it is and not only as it may be in some distant future, puts the question how this aspect and function of life, which is really an aspect and function of human activity in general, can be harmonised with the spiritual existence.

7. On our side also know those who are the most distinguished, O best of the twice-born, the leaders of my army; these I name to thee for thy special notice.

भवान् भीष्मश्च कर्णश्च कृपश्च समितिञ्जयः ।
अश्वत्थामा विकर्णश्च सौमदत्तिस्तथैव च ॥८॥
अन्ये च बहवः शूरा मदर्थे त्यक्तजीविताः ।
नानाशस्त्रप्रहरणाः सर्वे युद्धविशारदाः ॥९॥

8-9. Thyself and Bhishma and Karna and Kripa, the victorious in battle, Ashvatthama, Vikarna, and Saumadatti also; and many other heroes have renounced their life for my sake, they are all armed with diverse weapons and missiles and all well-skilled in war.

अपर्याप्तं तदस्माकं बलं भीष्माभिरक्षितम् ।
पर्याप्तं त्विदमेतेषां बलं भीमाभिरक्षितम् ॥१०॥

10. Unlimited is this army of ours and it is marshalled by Bhishma, while the army of theirs is limited, and they depend on Bhima.

अयनेषु च सर्वेषु यथाभागमवस्थिताः ।
भीष्ममेवाभिरक्षन्तु भवन्तः सर्व एव हि ॥११॥

11. Therefore all ye standing in your respective divisions in the different fronts of the battle, guard Bhishma."

तस्य सञ्जनयन् हर्षं कुरुवृद्धः पितामहः ।
सिंहनादं विनद्योच्चैः शङ्खं दध्मौ प्रतापवान् ॥१२॥

12. Cheering the heart of Duryodhana, the mighty grand-sire (Bhishma), the Ancient of the Kurus, resounding the battlefield with a lion's roar, blew his conch.

ततः शङ्खाश्च भेर्यश्च पणवानकगोमुखाः ।
सहसैवाभ्यहन्यन्त स शब्दस्तुमुलोऽभवत् ॥१३॥

13. Then conchs and kettledrums, tabors and drums and horns, suddenly blared forth, and the clamour became tremendous.

ततः श्वेतैर्हयैर्युक्ते महति स्यन्दने स्थितौ ।
माधवः पाण्डवश्चैव दिव्यौ शङ्खौ प्रदध्मतुः ॥१४॥

14. Then, seated in their great chariot[1]; yoked to white horses, Madhava (Sri Krishna) and the son of Pandu (Arjuna) blew their divine conchs.

[1] Arjuna is the fighter in the chariot with divine Krishna as his charioteer. There is a method of explaining the Gita in which not only this episode but the whole Mahabharata is turned into an allegory of the inner life and has nothing to do with our outward human life and action, but only with the battles of the soul and the powers that strive within us for possession. That is a view which the general character and the actual language of the epic does not justify and, if pressed, would turn the straightforward philosophical language of the Gita into a constant, laborious and somewhat puerile mystification. The language of the Veda and part at least of the Puranas is plainly symbolic, full of figures and concrete representations of things that lie behind the veil, but the Gita is written in plain terms and professes to solve the great ethical and spiritual difficulties which the life of man raises, and it will not do to go behind this plain language and thought and wrest them to the service of our fancy. But there is this much of truth in the view, that the setting of the doctrine, though not symbolical, is certainly typical, as indeed the setting of such a discourse as the Gita must necessarily be if it is to have any relation at all with that which it frames.

There are indeed three things in the Gita which are spiritually significant, almost symbolic, typical of the profoundest relations and problems of the spiritual life and of human existence at its roots; they are the divine personality of the Teacher, his characteristic relations with his disciple and the occasion of his teaching. The teacher is God himself descended into humanity; the disciple is the first, as we might say in modern language, the representative man of his age, closest friend and chosen instrument of the Avatar, his protagonist in an immense work and struggle the secret purpose of which is unknown to the actors in it, known only to the incarnate Godhead who guides it all from behind the veil of his unfathomable mind of Knowledge; the occasion is the violent crisis of that work and struggle at the moment when the anguish and moral difficulty and blind violence of its apparent movements forces itself with the shock

पाञ्चजन्यं हृषीकेशो देवदत्तं धनञ्जयः ।
पौण्ड्रं दध्मौ महाशङ्खं भीमकर्मा वृकोदरः ॥१५॥
अनन्तविजयं राजा कुन्तीपुत्रो युधिष्ठिरः ।
नकुलः सहदेवश्च सुघोषमणिपुष्पकौ ॥१६॥

15-16. Hrishikesha (Krishna) blew his Panchajanya and Dhananjaya (Arjuna) his Devadatta (god-given); Vrikodara of terrific deeds blew his mighty conch, Paundra; the King Yudhishthira, the son of Kunti, blew Anantavijaya; Nakula and Sahadeva, Sughosha and Manipushpaka.

(Yudhishthira, Vrikodara, Nakula and Sahadeva are the four brothers of Arjuna.)

काश्यश्च परमेष्वासः शिखण्डी च महारथः ।
धृष्टद्युम्नो विराटश्च सात्यकिश्चापराजितः ॥१७॥
द्रुपदो द्रौपदेयाश्च सर्वशः पृथिवीपते ।
सौभद्रश्च महाबाहुः शङ्खान् दध्मुः पृथक् पृथक् ॥१८॥

17-18. And Kashya of the great bow, and Shikhandi of the great chariot, Dhrishtadyumna and Virata and Satyaki, the unconquered, Drupada, and the sons of Draupadi, O Lord of earth, and Saubhadra, the mighty-armed, on all sides their several conchs blew.

स घोषो धार्तराष्ट्राणां हृदयानि व्यदारयत् ।
नभश्च पृथिवीं चैव तुमुलो व्यनुनादयन् ॥१९॥

19. That tumultuous uproar resounding through earth and sky tore the hearts of the sons of Dhritarashtra.

अथ व्यवस्थितान् दृष्ट्वा धार्तराष्ट्रान् कपिध्वजः ।
प्रवृत्ते शस्त्रसंपाते धनुरुद्यम्य पाण्डवः ॥२०॥
हृषीकेशं तदा वाक्यमिदमाह महीपते ।

---

of a visible revelation on the mind of its representative man and raises the whole question of the meaning of God in the world and the goal and drift and sense of human life and conduct.

20. Then, beholding the sons of Dhritarashtra standing in battle order, and the flight of missiles having begun[1], the son of Pandu (Arjuna), whose emblem is an ape, took up his bow and spoke this word to Hrishikesha, O Lord of earth:

अर्जुन उवाच —
सेनयोरुभयोर्मध्ये रथं स्थापय मेऽच्युत ॥२१॥
यावदेतान्निरीक्षेऽहं योद्धुकामानवस्थितान् ।
कैर्मया सह योद्धव्यमस्मिन् रणसमुद्यमे ॥२२॥
योत्स्यमानानवेक्षेऽहं य एतेऽत्र समागताः ।
धार्तराष्ट्रस्य दुर्बुद्धेर्युद्धे प्रियचिकीर्षवः ॥२३॥

21-23. Arjuna[2] said: O Achyuta (the faultless, the immovable), stay my chariot between the two armies, so that I

---

[1] The symbolic companionship of Arjuna and Krishna, the human and the divine soul, is expressed elsewhere in Indian thought in the heavenward journey of Indra and Kutsa seated in one chariot, in the figure of the two birds upon one tree in the Upanishad, in the twin figures of Nara and Narayana, the seers who do *tapasyā* together for the knowledge. But in all three it is the idea of the divine knowledge in which, as the Gita says, all action culminates that is in view; here it is instead the action which leads to that knowledge and in which the divine Knower figures himself. Arjuna and Krishna, this human and this divine, stand together not as seers in the peaceful hermitage of meditation, but as fighter and holder of the reins in the clamorous field, in the midst of the hurtling shafts, in the chariot of battle. The Teacher of the Gita is therefore not only the God in man who unveils himself in the word of knowledge, but the God in man who moves our whole world of action, by and for whom all our humanity exists and struggles and labours, towards whom all human life travels and progresses. He is the secret Master of works and sacrifice and the friend of the human peoples.

[2] The Gita starts from action and Arjuna is the man of action and not of knowledge. It is typical of the pragmatic man that it is through his sensations that he awakens to the meaning of his action. He has asked his friend and charioteer to place him between the two armies, not with any profounder idea, but with the proud intention of viewing and looking in the face these myriads of the champions of unrighteousness whom he has to meet and conquer and slay "in this holiday of fight" so that the right may prevail. It is as he gazes that the revelation of the meaning of a civil and domestic war comes home to him, a war in which not only men of the

may view these myriads standing, longing for battle, whom I have to meet in this holiday of fight, and look upon those who have come here to champion the cause of the evil-minded son of Dhritarashtra.

सञ्जय उवाच —
एवमुक्तो हृषीकेशो गुडाकेशेन भारत ।
सेनयोरुभयोर्मध्ये स्थापयित्वा रथोत्तमम् ।।२४।।
भीष्मद्रोणप्रमुखतः सर्वेषां च महीक्षिताम् ।
उवाच पार्थ पश्यैतान् समवेतान् कुरूनिति ।।२५।।

24-25. Sanjaya said: Thus addressed by Gudakesha (one that has overcome sleep, Arjuna), Hrishikesha, O Bharata, having stayed that best of chariots between the two armies, in front of Bhishma, Drona and all the princes of earth, said: "O Partha, behold these Kurus gathered together."

तत्रापश्यत् स्थितान् पार्थः पितॄनथ पितामहान् ।
आचार्यान् मातुलान् भ्रातॄन् पुत्रान् पौत्रान् सखींस्तथा ।
श्वशुरान् सुहृदश्चैव सेनयोरुभयोरपि ।।२६।।

26. Then saw Partha standing upon opposite sides, uncles and grandsires, teachers, mother's brothers, cousins, sons and grandsons, comrades, fathers-in-law, benefactors.

---

same race, the same nation, the same clan, but those of the same family and household stand upon opposite sides. All whom the social man holds most dear and sacred, he must meet as enemies and slay, all these social ties have to be cut asunder by the sword. It is not that he did not know these things before, but he has never realised it all; obsessed by his claims and wrongs and by the principles of his life, the struggle for the right, the duty of the Kshatriya to protect justice and the law and fight and beat down injustice and lawless violence, he has neither thought out deeply nor felt it in his heart and at the core of his life. And now it is shown to his vision by the divine charioteer, placed sensationally before his eyes, and comes home to him like a blow delivered at the very centre of his sensational, vital and emotional being.

तान् समीक्ष्य स कौन्तेय: सर्वान् बन्धूनवस्थितान् ।
कृपया परयाविष्टो विषीदन्निदमब्रवीत् ।।२७।।

27. Seeing all these kinsmen thus standing arrayed, Kaunteya, invaded by great pity, uttered this in sadness and dejection:

अर्जुन उवाच —
दृष्ट्वेमं स्वजनं कृष्ण युयुत्सुं समुपस्थितम् ।
सीदन्ति मम गात्राणि मुखं च परिशुष्यति ।।२८।।
वेपथुश्च शरीरे मे रोमहर्षश्च जायते ।
गाण्डीवं स्रंसते हस्तात्त्वक् चैव परिदह्यते ।।२९।।

28-29. Arjuna said: Seeing these my own people, O Krishna, arrayed for battle, my limbs collapse[1] and my mouth is parched, my body shakes and my hair stands on end; Gandiva (Arjuna's bow) slips from my hand, and all my skin seems to be burning.

न च शक्नोम्यवस्थातुं भ्रमतीव च मे मन: ।
निमित्तानि च पश्यामि विपरीतानि केशव ।।३०।।

30. I am not able to stand and my mind seems to be whirling; also I see evil omens, O Keshava.

---

[1] The first result is a violent sensational and physical crisis which produces a disgust of the action and its material objects and of life itself. He rejects the vital aim pursued by egoistic humanity in its action, – happiness and enjoyment; he rejects the vital aim of the Kshatriya, victory and rule and power and the government of men. What after all is this fight for justice when reduced to its practical terms, but just this, a fight for the interests of himself, his brothers and his party, for possession and enjoyment and rule? But at such a cost these things are not worth having. For they are of no value in themselves, but only as a means to the right maintenance of social and national life and it is these very aims that in the person of his kin and his race he is about to destroy. And then comes the cry of the emotions.

FIRST CHAPTER

न च श्रेयोऽनुपश्यामि हत्वा स्वजनमाहवे ।
न काङ्क्षे विजयं कृष्ण न च राज्यं सुखानि च ॥३१॥

31. Nor do I see any good in slaying my own people in battle; O Krishna, I desire not victory, nor kingdom, nor pleasures.

किं नो राज्येन गोविन्द किं भोगैर्जीवितेन वा ।
येषामर्थे काङ्क्षितं नो राज्यं भोगाः सुखानि च ॥३२॥
त इमेऽवस्थिता युद्धे प्राणांस्त्यक्त्वा धनानि च ।
आचार्याः पितरः पुत्रास्तथैव च पितामहाः ॥३३॥
मातुलाः श्वशुराः पौत्राः श्यालाः सम्बन्धिनस्तथा ।
एतान्न हन्तुमिच्छामि घ्नतोऽपि मधुसूदन ॥३४॥
अपि त्रैलोक्यराज्यस्य हेतोः किं नु महीकृते ।
निहत्य धार्तराष्ट्रान्नः का प्रीतिः स्याज्जनार्दन ॥३५॥

32-35. What is kingdom to us, O Govinda, what enjoyment, what even life? Those for whose sake we desire kingdom, enjoyments and pleasures, they stand here in battle, abandoning life and riches – teachers, fathers, sons, as well as grandsires, mother's brothers, fathers-in-law, grandsons, brothers-in-law, and other kith and kin; these I would not consent to slay, though myself slain, O Madhusudana, even for the kingdom of the three worlds; how then for earth? What pleasures can be ours after killing the sons of Dhritarashtra, O Janardana?

पापमेवाश्रयेदस्मान् हत्वैतानाततायिनः ।
तस्मान्नार्हा वयं हन्तुं धार्तराष्ट्रान् स्वबान्धवान् ।
स्वजनं हि कथं हत्वा सुखिनः स्याम माधव ॥३६॥

36. Sin[1] will take hold of us in slaying them, though they

---

[1] The whole thing is a dreadful sin, – for now the moral sense awakens to justify the revolt of the sensations and the emotions. It is a sin, there is no right nor justice in mutual slaughter; especially are those who are to be slain the natural objects of reverence and of love, those without whom one would not care to live, and to violate these sacred feelings can be no

are the aggressors. So it is not fit that we kill the sons of Dhritarashtra, our kinsmen; indeed how may we be happy, O Madhava, killing our own people?

यद्यप्येते न पश्यन्ति लोभोपहतचेतसः ।
कुलक्षयकृतं दोषं मित्रद्रोहे च पातकम् ॥३७॥
कथं न ज्ञेयमस्माभिः पापादस्मान्निवर्तितुम् ।
कुलक्षयकृतं दोषं प्रपश्यद्भिर्जनार्दन ॥३८॥

37-38. Although these, with a consciousness clouded with greed, see no guilt in the destruction of the family, no crime in hostility to friends, why should not we have the wisdom to draw back from such a sin, O Janardana, we who see the evil in the destruction of the family?

कुलक्षये प्रणश्यन्ति कुलधर्माः सनातनाः ।
धर्मे नष्टे कुलं कृत्स्नमधर्मोऽभिभवत्युत ॥३९॥

39. In the annihilation of the family the eternal traditions of the family are destroyed; in the collapse of traditions, lawlessness overcomes the whole family.

अधर्माऽभिभवात्कृष्ण प्रदुष्यन्ति कुलस्त्रियः ।
स्त्रीषु दुष्टासु वार्ष्णेय जायते वर्णसंकरः ॥४०॥

40. Owing to predominance of lawlessness, O Krishna,

---

virtue, can be nothing but a heinous crime. Granted that the offence, the aggression, the first sin, the crimes of greed and selfish passion which have brought things to such a pass came from the other side; yet armed resistance to wrong under such circumstances would be itself a sin and crime worse than theirs because they are blinded by passion and unconscious of guilt, while on this side it would be with a clear sense of guilt that the sin would be committed. And for what? For the maintenance of family morality, of the social law and the law of the nation? These are the very standards that will be destroyed by this civil war.

the women of the family become corrupt; women corrupted, O Varshneya, the confusion of the *varnas*[1] arises.

संकरो नरकायैव कुलघ्नानां कुलस्य च ।
पतन्ति पितरो ह्येषां लुप्तपिण्डोदकक्रियाः ।।४१।।

41. This confusion leads to hell the ruiners of the family, and the family; for their ancestors fall, deprived of *pinda* (rice offering) and libations.

दोषैरेतैः कुलघ्नानां वर्णसंकरकारकैः ।
उत्साद्यन्ते जातिधर्माः कुलधर्माश्च शाश्वताः ।।४२।।

42. By these misdeeds of the ruiners of the family leading to the confusion of the orders, the eternal laws of the race and moral law of the family are destroyed.

उत्सन्नकुलधर्माणां मनुष्याणां जनार्दन ।
नरकेऽनियतं वासो भवतीत्यनुशुश्रुम ।।४३।।

43. And men whose family morals are corrupted, O Janardana, live for ever in hell. Thus have we heard.

अहो बत महत्पापं कर्तुं व्यवसिता वयम् ।
यद्राज्यसुखलोभेन हन्तुं स्वजनमुद्यताः ।।४४।।

44. Alas! we were engaged in committing a great sin, we who were endeavouring to kill our own people through greed of the pleasures of kingship.

यदि मामप्रतीकारमशस्त्रं शस्त्रपाणयः ।
धार्तराष्ट्रा रणे हन्युस्तन्मे क्षेमतरं भवेत् ।।४५।।

45. It is more for my welfare that the sons of Dhrita-

---

[1] *Varna* is usually translated as caste, but the existing caste system is a very different thing from the ancient social idea of *caturvarna*, the four clear-cut orders of the Aryan community, and in no way corresponds with the description of the Gita. See Ch. XVIII.

rashtra armed should slay me unarmed and unresisting. (I will not fight.)

सञ्जय उवाच —
एवमुक्त्वार्जुनः सङ्ख्ये रथोपस्थ उपाविशत् ।
विसृज्य सशरं चापं शोकसंविग्नमानसः ॥४६॥

46. Sanjaya said: Having thus spoken on the battlefield, Arjuna sank down on the seat of the chariot, casting down the divine bow and the inexhaustible quiver (given to him by the gods for that tremendous hour), his spirit overwhelmed with sorrow.[1]

इति श्रीमद्भगवद्गीतासूपनिषत्सु ब्रह्मविद्यायां योगशास्त्रे
श्रीकृष्णार्जुनसंवादेऽर्जुनविषादयोगो नाम प्रथमोऽध्यायः ।

[1] Although Arjuna is himself concerned only with his own situation, his inner struggle and the law of action he must follow, yet the particular question he raises, in the manner in which he raises it does really bring up the whole question of human life and action, what the world is and why it is and how possibly, it being what it is, life here in the world can be reconciled with life in the spirit. And all this deep and difficult matter the Teacher insists on resolving as the very foundation of his command to an action which must proceed from a new poise of being and by the light of a liberating knowledge. But what, then, is it that makes the difficulty for the man who has to take the world as it is and act in it and yet would live, within, the spiritual life? What is this aspect of existence which appals his awakened mind and brings about what the title of the first chapter of the Gita calls significantly the Yoga of the dejection of Arjuna, the dejection and discouragement felt by the human being when he is forced to face the spectacle of the universe as it really is with the veil of the ethical illusion, the illusion of self-righteousness torn from his eyes, before a higher reconciliation with himself is effected? It is that aspect which is figured outwardly in the carnage and massacre of Kurukshetra and spiritually by the vision of the Lord of all things as Time arising to devour and destroy the creatures whom it has made. The outward aspect is that of world-existence and human existence proceeding by struggle and slaughter; the inward aspect is that of the universal Being fulfilling himself in a vast creation and a vast destruction. Life is a battle and a field of death, this is Kurukshetra; God the Terrible, this is the vision that Arjuna sees on that field of massacre.

We must acknowledge Kurukshetra; we must submit to the law of Life by Death before we can find our way to the life immortal; we must open our eyes, with a less appalled gaze than Arjuna's, to the vision of our Lord of Time and Death and cease to deny, hate or recoil from the universal Destroyer.

Thus in the Upanishad sung by the Lord, the science of Brahman, the scripture of Yoga, the dialogue between Sri Krishna and Arjuna, ends the first chapter entitled "The Yoga of the Dejection of Arjuna".

Second Chapter

I. THE CREED OF THE ARYAN FIGHTER

सञ्जय उवाच —
तं तथा कृपयाविष्टमश्रुपूर्णाकुलेक्षणम् ।
विषीदन्तमिदं वाक्यमुवाच मधुसूदनः ॥१॥

1. Sanjaya said: To him thus by pity[1] invaded, his eyes full and distressed with tears,[2] his heart overcome by depression and discouragement, Madhusudana spoke these words.

श्रीभगवान् उवाच —
कुतस्त्वा कश्मलमिदं विषमे समुपस्थितम् ।
अनार्यजुष्टमस्वर्ग्यमकीर्तिकरमर्जुन ॥२॥

2. The Blessed Lord said: Whence[3] has come to thee this dejection, this stain and darkness of the soul in the hour of difficulty and peril, O Arjuna? This is not the way cherished by the Aryan man; this mood came not from heaven nor can it lead to heaven, and on earth it is the forfeiting of glory.

---

[1] This pity of Arjuna is quite different from the godlike compassion mentioned later on in the Gita, which observes with an eye of love and wisdom and calm strength the battle and the struggle, the strength and weakness of man, his virtues and sins, his joy and suffering, his knowledge and his ignorance, and enters into it all to help and to heal. Arjuna's pity is a form of self-indulgence; it is the physical shrinking of the nerves from the act of slaughter, the egoistic emotional shrinking of the heart from the destruction of the Dhritarashtrians because they are "one's own people" and without them life will be empty.

[2] Invaded by the self-indulgent pity Arjuna has lapsed into unheroic weakness which first draws a strongly worded rebuke from the divine Teacher.

[3] This question points to the real nature of Arjuna's deviation from his heroic qualities. The Gita is not a mere gospel of war and heroic action, a Nietzschean creed of power and high-browed strength which holds pity to be a weakness. There is a divine compassion which descends to us from on high and for the man whose nature does not possess it, is not cast in its

कलैब्यं मा स्म गमः पार्थ नैतत्त्वय्युपपद्यते ।
क्षुद्रं हृदयदौर्बल्यं त्यक्त्वोत्तिष्ठ परन्तप ॥३॥

3. Fall not from the virility of the fighter and the hero, O Partha! It is not fitting in thee.[1] Shake off this paltry faint-heartedness! Stand up, Parantapa (Scourge of the foes)!

अर्जुन उवाच —
कथं भीष्ममहं सङ्ख्ये द्रोणं च मधुसूदन ।
इषुभिः प्रतियोत्स्यामि पूजार्हावरिसूदन ॥४॥

4. Arjuna said: How, O Madhusudana, shall I strike Bhishma and Drona with weapons in battle, they who are worthy of worship, O Slayer of foes?

गुरूनहत्वा हि महानुभावान् श्रेयो भोक्तुं भैक्ष्यमपीह लोके ।
हत्वार्थकामांस्तु गुरूनिहैव भुञ्जीय भोगान् रुधिरप्रदिग्धान् ॥५॥

5. Better in this world to live even on alms than to slay these high-souled Gurus. Slaying these Gurus, I should taste of blood-stained enjoyments even in this world.

---

mould, to pretend to be the superman is a folly and an insolence, for he alone is the superman who most manifests the highest nature of the Godhead in humanity. But such is not the compassion which actuates Arjuna in the rejection of his work and mission. That is not compassion but an impotence full of a weak self-pity, a recoil from the mental suffering which his act must entail on himself, and of all things self-pity is among the most ignoble and un-Aryan of moods.

[1] Arjuna's pity is a weakness of the mind and senses, — a weakness which may well be beneficial to men of a lower grade of development, who have to be weak; because otherwise they will be hard and cruel. But this way is not for the developed Aryan man who has to grow not by weakness, but by an ascension from strength to strength. Not this was fitting in the son of Pritha, not thus should the champion and chief hope of a righteous cause abandon it in the hour of crisis and peril or suffer the sudden amazement of his heart and senses, the clouding of his reason and the downfall of his will to betray him into the casting away of his divine weapons and the refusal of his God-given work.

न चैतद्विद्मः कतरन्नो गरीयो यद्वा जयेम यदि वा नो जयेयुः ।
यानेव हत्वा न जिजीविषामस्तेऽवस्थिताः प्रमुखे धार्तराष्ट्राः ॥६॥

6. Nor do I know which for us is better, that we conquer them or they conquer us, – before us stand the Dhritarashtrians whom having slain we should not care to live.

कार्पण्यदोषोपहतस्वभावः पृच्छामि त्वां धर्मसंमूढचेताः ।
यच्छ्रेयः स्यान्निश्चितं ब्रूहि तन्मे शिष्यस्तेऽहं शाधि मां त्वां प्रपन्नम् ॥७॥

7. It is poorness of spirit that has smitten away from me my (true heroic) nature[1], my whole consciousness is bewildered[2] in its view of right and wrong. I ask thee which

---

[1] Arjuna is the man of action and not of knowledge, the fighter, never the seer or the thinker. In the Gita he typifies the human soul of action brought face to face through that action in its highest and most violent crisis with the problem of human life and its apparent incompatibility with the spiritual state or even with a purely ethical ideal of perfection. The nature of the crisis which he undergoes is an all-embracing inner bankruptcy which he expresses when he says that his whole conscious being, not the thought alone but heart and vital desires and all, are utterly bewildered and can find nowhere the *dharma*, nowhere any valid law of action. That for the soul of action in the mental being is the worst possible crisis, failure and overthrow. For this alone he takes refuge as a disciple with Krishna; give me, he practically asks, that which I have lost, a true law, a clear rule of action, a path by which I can again confidently walk. He does not ask for the secret of life or of the world, the meaning and purpose of it all, but for a *dharma*. Yet it is precisely this secret for which he does not ask, or at least so much of the knowledge as is necessary to lead him into a higher life, to which the divine Teacher intends to lead his disciple; for he means him to give up all *dharma*s except the one broad and vast rule of living consciously in the Divine and acting from that consciousness.

Dharma means literally that which one lays hold of and which holds things together, the law, the norm, the rule of nature, action and life.

[2] It is a mistake to interpret the Gita from the standpoint of the mentality of today and force it to teach us the disinterested performance of duty as the highest and all-sufficient law. For the whole point of the teaching, that from which it arises, that which compels the disciple to seek the Teacher, is an inextricable clash of the various related conceptions of

may be the better – that tell me decisively. I take refuge as a disciple with thee; enlighten me.

न हि प्रपश्यामि ममापनुद्याद् यच्छोकमुच्छोषणमिन्द्रियाणाम् ।
अवाप्य भूमावसपत्नमृद्धं राज्यं सुराणामपि चाधिपत्यम् ॥८॥

8. I see not what shall thrust from me the sorrow that dries up the senses, even if I should attain rich and unrivalled kingdom on earth or even the sovereignty of the gods.

सञ्जय उवाच —
एवमुक्त्वा हृषीकेशं गुडाकेशः परन्तपः ।
न योत्स्य इति गोविन्दमुक्त्वा तूष्णीं बभूव ह ॥९॥

9. Sanjaya said: Gudakesha, terror of his foes, having thus spoken to Hrishikesha, and said to him, "I will not fight!" became silent.

तमुवाच हृषीकेशः प्रहसन्निव भारत ।
सेनयोरुभयोर्मध्ये विषीदन्तमिदं वचः ॥१०॥

10. To him thus depressed and discouraged, Hrishikesha, smiling as it were, O Bharata, spoke these words between the two armies.

(Arjuna in his reply to Krishna admits the rebuke even while he strives against and refuses the command. He is aware of his weakness and yet accepts subjection to it. He attempts still to justify his refusal on ethical and rational grounds, but merely cloaks by words of apparent rationality

---

duty ending in the collapse of the whole useful intellectual and moral edifice erected by the human mind. The Gita does not teach the disinterested performance of duties but the following of the divine life, the abandonment of all dharmas, *sarvadharmān*, to take refuge in the Supreme alone.

the revolt of his ignorant and unchastened emotions. It is these claims of Arjuna's egoistic being that Krishna sets out first to destroy in order to make place for the higher law which shall transcend all egoistic motives of action.)

श्रीभगवान् उवाच —
अशोच्यान्वन्वशोचस्त्वं प्रज्ञावादांश्च भाषसे ।
गतासूनगतासूंश्च नानुशोचन्ति पण्डिताः ॥११॥

11. The Blessed Lord said: Thou grievest for those that should not be grieved for, yet speakest words of wisdom. The enlightened man does not mourn either for the living or for the dead.

(The answer of the Teacher proceeds upon two different lines, first, a brief reply founded upon the highest ideas of the general Aryan culture in which Arjuna has been educated, secondly, another and larger founded on a more intimate knowledge, opening into deeper truths of our being, which is the real starting-point of the teaching of the Gita. This first answer relies on the philosophic and moral conceptions of the Vedantic philosophy and the social idea of duty and honour which formed the ethical basis of Aryan Society.)

न त्वेवाहं जातु नासं न त्वं नेमे जनाधिपाः ।
न चैव न भविष्यामः सर्वे वयमतः परम् ॥१२॥

12. It is not true that at any time I was not, nor thou, nor these kings of men; nor is it true that any of us shall ever cease to be hereafter.

देहिनोऽस्मिन् यथा देहे कौमारं यौवनं जरा ।
तथा देहान्तरप्राप्तिर्धीरस्तत्र न मुह्यति ॥१३॥

13. As the soul passes physically through childhood and youth and age, so it passes on to the changing of the body.

The self-composed[1] man does not allow himself to be disturbed and blinded by this.

मात्रास्पर्शास्तु कौन्तेय शीतोष्णसुखदुःखदाः ।
आगमापायिनोऽनित्यास्तांस्तितिक्षस्व भारत ॥१४॥

14. The material touches, O son of Kunti, giving cold and heat, pleasure and pain, things transient which come and go, these learn to endure, O Bharata.

यं हि न व्यथयन्त्येते पुरुषं पुरुषर्षभ ।
समदुःखसुखं धीरं सोऽमृतत्वाय कल्पते ॥१५॥

15. The man whom these do not trouble nor pain, O lion-hearted among men, the firm and wise who is equal in pleasure and suffering, makes himself apt for immortality.[2]

नासतो विद्यते भावो नाभावो विद्यते सतः ।
उभयोरपि दृष्टोऽन्तस्त्वनयोस्तत्त्वदर्शिभिः ॥१६॥

---

[1] The calm and wise mind, the *dhīra*, the thinker looks beyond the apparent facts of the life of the body and senses to the real fact of his being and rises beyond the emotional and physical desires of the ignorant nature to the true and only aim of the human existence. What is that real fact? that highest aim? This, that human life and death repeated through the aeons in the great cycles of the world are only a long progress by which the human being prepares and makes himself fit for immortality.

[2] By immortality is meant not the survival of death, – that is already given to every creature born with a mind, – but the transcendence of life and death. It means that ascension by which man ceases to live as a mind-informed body and lives at last as a spirit and in the Spirit. Whoever is subject to grief and sorrow, a slave to the sensations and emotions, occupied by the touches of things transient cannot become fit for immortality. These things must be borne until they are conquered, till they can give no pain to the liberated man, till he is able to receive all the material happenings of the world whether joyful or sorrowful with a wise and calm equality, even as the tranquil eternal Spirit secret within us receives them.

16. That[1] which really is, cannot go out of existence, just as that which is non-existent cannot come into being. The end of this opposition of 'is' and 'is not' has been perceived by the seers of essential truths.

अविनाशि तु तद्विद्धि येन सर्वमिदं ततम् ।
विनाशमव्ययस्यास्य न कश्चित् कर्तुमर्हति ॥१७॥

17. Know that to be imperishable by which all this is extended. Who can slay the immortal spirit?

अन्तवन्त इमे देहा नित्यस्योक्ताः शरीरिणः ।
अनाशिनोऽप्रमेयस्य तस्माद्युध्यस्व भारत ॥१८॥

18. Finite bodies have an end, but that which possesses and uses the body, is infinite, illimitable, eternal, indestructible. Therefore fight, O Bharata.

य एनं वेत्ति हन्तारं यश्चैनं मन्यते हतम् ।
उभौ तौ न विजानीतो नायं हन्ति न हन्यते ॥१९॥

19. He who regards this (the soul) as a slayer, and he who thinks it is slain, both of them fail to perceive the truth. It does not slay, nor is it slain.

न जायते म्रियते वा कदाचिन्नायं भूत्वा भविता वा न भूयः ।
अजो नित्यः शाश्वतोऽयं पुराणो न हन्यते हन्यमाने शरीरे ॥२०॥

20. This is not born, nor does it die, nor is it a thing that comes into being once and passing away will never come

---

[1] The soul is and cannot cease to be, though it may change the forms through which it appears. This opposition of 'is' and 'is not', this balance of being and becoming which is the mind's view of existence, finds its end in the realisation of the soul as the one imperishable self by whom all this universe has been extended.

into being again. It is unborn, ancient, sempiternal; it is not slain with the slaying of the body.

वेदाविनाशिनं नित्यं य एनमजमव्ययम् ।
कथं स पुरुषः पार्थ कं घातयति हन्ति कम् ॥२१॥

21. Who knows it as immortal eternal imperishable spiritual existence, how can that man slay, O Partha, or cause to be slain?

वासांसि जीर्णानि यथा विहाय नवानि गृह्णाति नरोऽपराणि ।
तथा शरीराणि विहाय जीर्णान्यन्यानि संयाति नवानि देही ॥२२॥

22. The embodied soul casts away old and takes up new bodies as a man changes worn-out raiment for new.

नैनं छिन्दन्ति शस्त्राणि नैनं दहति पावकः ।
न चैनं क्लेदयन्त्यापो न शोषयति मारुतः ॥२३॥

23. Weapons cannot cleave it, nor the fire burn, nor do the waters drench it, nor the wind dry.

अच्छेद्योऽयमदाह्योऽयमक्लेद्योऽशोष्य एव च ।
नित्यः सर्वगतः स्थाणुरचलोऽयं सनातनः ॥२४॥

24. It is uncleavable, it is incombustible, it can neither be drenched nor dried. Eternally stable, immobile, all-pervading, it is for ever and for ever.

अव्यक्तोऽयमचिन्त्योऽयमविकार्योऽयमुच्यते ।
तस्मादेवं विदित्वैनं नानुशोचितुमर्हसि ॥२५॥

25. It is unmanifest[1], it is unthinkable, it is immutable, so

[1] Not manifested like the body, but greater than all manifestation, not to be analysed by the thought, but greater than all mind, not capable of change and modification like the life and its organs and their objects, but beyond the changes of mind and life and body, it is yet the Reality which all these strive to figure.

it is described (by the Srutis); therefore knowing it as such, thou shouldst not grieve.

अथ चैनं नित्यजातं नित्यं वा मन्यसे मृतम् ।
तथापि त्वं महाबाहो नैवं शोचितुमर्हसि ॥२६॥

26. Even if thou thinkest of it (the self) as being constantly subject to birth and death, still, O mighty-armed, thou shouldst not grieve.

जातस्य हि ध्रुवो मृत्युर्ध्रुवं जन्म मृतस्य च ।
तस्मादपरिहार्येऽर्थे न त्वं शोचितुमर्हसि ॥२७॥

27. For certain is death for the born, and certain is birth for the dead; therefore what is inevitable[1] ought not to be a cause of thy sorrow.

अव्यक्तादीनि भूतानि व्यक्तमध्यानि भारत ।
अव्यक्तनिधनान्येव तत्र का परिदेवना ॥२८॥

28. Beings are unmanifest in the beginning, manifest in the middle, O Bharata, unmanifest likewise are they in disintegration. What is there to be grieved at?

आश्चर्यवत्पश्यति कश्चिदेनमाश्चर्यवद्वदति तथैव चान्यः ।
आश्चर्यवच्चैनमन्यः शृणोति श्रुत्वाप्येनं वेद न चैव कश्चित् ॥२९॥

[1] Constant subjection to birth and death is an inevitable circumstance of the soul's self-manifestation. Its birth is an appearing out of some state in which it is not non-existent but unmanifest to our mortal senses, its death is a return to that unmanifest world or condition and out of it it will again appear in the physical manifestation. The to-do made by the physical mind and senses about death and the horror of death whether on the sick-bed or the battlefield, is the most ignorant of nervous clamours. Our sorrow for the death of men is an ignorant grieving for those for whom there is no cause to grieve, since they have neither gone out of existence nor suffered any painful or terrible change of condition, but are beyond death no less in being and no more unhappy in circumstance than in life.

29. One sees it as a mystery or one speaks of it or hears of it as a mystery, but none knows it. That (the Self, the One, the Divine) we look on and speak and hear of as the wonderful beyond our comprehension, for after all our learning from those who have knowledge, no human mind has ever known this Absolute.[1]

देही नित्यमवध्योऽयं देहे सर्वस्य भारत ।
तस्मात्सर्वाणि भूतानि न त्वं शोचितुमर्हसि ॥३०॥

30. This dweller in the body of everyone is eternal and indestructible, O Bharata; therefore thou shouldst not grieve for any creature.

स्वधर्ममपि चावेक्ष्य न विकम्पितुमर्हसि ।
धर्म्याद्धि युद्धाच्छ्रेयोऽन्यत् क्षत्रियस्य न विद्यते ॥३१॥

31. Further[2], looking to thine own law of action thou

[1] It is this which is here veiled by the world, the master of the body; all life is only its shadow; the coming of the soul into physical manifestation and our passing out of it by death is only one of its minor movements. When we have known ourselves as this, then to speak of ourselves as slayer or slain is an absurdity. One thing only is the truth in which we have to live, the Eternal manifesting itself as the soul of man in the great cycle of its pilgrimage with birth and death for milestones, with worlds beyond as resting-places, with all the circumstances of life happy or unhappy as the means of our progress and battle and victory and with immortality as the home to which the soul travels.

[2] But how does this self-knowledge justify the action demanded of Arjuna and the slaughter of Kurukshetra? The answer is that this is the action required of Arjuna in the path he has to travel; it has come inevitably in the performance of the function demanded of him by his *svadharma**, his social duty, the law of his life and the law of his being. This world, this manifestation of the Self in the material universe is not only a cycle of inner development, but a field in which the external circumstances of life have to be accepted as an environment and an occasion for that development. It is a world of mutual help and struggle; not a serene and peaceful gliding through easy joys is the progress it

(* The Kshatriya ideal, the ideal of the four orders is here placed in its social aspect, not as afterwards in its spiritual meaning.)

shouldst not tremble; there is no greater good for the Kshatriya than righteous battle.

यदृच्छया चोपपन्नं स्वर्गद्वारमपावृतम् ।
सुखिनः क्षत्रियाः पार्थ लभन्ते युद्धमीदृशम् ॥३२॥

32. When such a battle comes to them of itself like the open gate of heaven, happy[1] are the Kshatriyas then.

अथ चेत्त्वमिमं धर्म्यं संग्रामं न करिष्यसि ।
ततः स्वधर्मं कीर्तिं च हित्वा पापमवाप्स्यसि ॥३३॥

33. But if thou dost not this battle for the right,[2] then hast thou abandoned thy duty and virtue and thy glory, and sin shall be thy portion.

---

allows us, but every step has to be gained by heroic effort and through a clash of opposing forces. Those who take up the inner and the outer struggle even to the most physical clash of all, that of war, are the Kshatriyas, the mighty men; war, force, nobility, courage are their nature; protection of the right and an unflinching acceptance of the gage of battle is their virtue and their duty.

[1] The Teacher turns aside for a moment to give another answer to the cry of Arjuna over the sorrow of the death of kindred which will empty his life of the causes and objects of living. What is the true object of the Kshatriya's life and his true happiness? Not self-pleasing and domestic happiness and a life of comfort and peaceful joy with friends and relatives, but to battle for the right is his true object of life and to find a cause for which he can lay down his life or by victory win the crown and glory of the hero's existence is his greatest happiness.

[2] There is continually a struggle between right and wrong, justice and injustice, the force that protects and the force that violates and oppresses, and when this has once been brought to the issue of physical strife, the champion and standard-bearer of the Right must not shake and tremble at the violent and terrible nature of the work he has to do. His virtue and his duty lie in battle and not in abstention from battle; it is not slaughter, but non-slaying which would here be the sin.

अकीर्तिं चापि भूतानि कथयिष्यन्ति तेऽव्ययाम् ।
संभावितस्य चाकीर्तिर्मरणादतिरिच्यते ।।३४।।

34. Besides, men will recount thy perpetual disgrace, and to one in noble station, dishonour is worse than death.

भयाद्रणादुपरतं मंस्यन्ते त्वां महारथाः ।
येषां च त्वं बहुमतो भूत्वा यास्यसि लाघवम् ।।३५।।

35. The mighty men will think thee fled from the battle through fear[1], and thou, that wast highly esteemed by them, wilt allow a smirch to fall on thy honour.

अवाच्यवादांश्च बहून् वदिष्यन्ति तवाहिताः ।
निन्दन्तस्तव सामर्थ्यं ततो दुःखतरं नु किम् ।।३६।।

36. Many unseemly words will be spoken by thy enemies, slandering thy strength; what is worse grief than that?

हतो वा प्राप्स्यसि स्वर्गं जित्वा वा भोक्ष्यसे महीम् ।
तस्मादुत्तिष्ठ कौन्तेय युद्धाय कृतनिश्चयः ।।३७।।

37. Slain thou shalt win Heaven, victorious thou shalt enjoy the earth; therefore[2] arise, O son of Kunti, resolved upon battle.

---

[1] To give the example of a hero among heroes whose action lays itself open to the reproach of cowardice and weakness and thus to lower the moral standard of mankind, is to be false to himself and to the demand of the world on its leaders and kings.

[2] Indian ethics has always seen the practical necessity of graded ideals for the developing moral and spiritual life of man. This, says Krishna in effect, is my answer to you if you insist on joy and sorrow and the result of your actions as your motive of action. I have shown you in what direction the higher knowledge of self and the world points you; I have now shown you in what direction your social duty and the ethical standard of your order point you, *svadharmam api cāvekṣya*. Whichever you consider, the result is the same. But if you are not satisfied with your social duty and the

सुखदुःखे समे कृत्वा लाभालाभौ जयाजयौ ।
ततो युद्धाय युज्यस्व नैवं पापमवाप्स्यसि ॥३८॥

38. Make grief and happiness, loss and gain, victory and defeat equal to thy soul and then turn to battle; so thou shalt not incur sin[1].

---

virtue of your order, if you think that leads you to sorrow and sin, then I bid you rise to a higher and not sink to a lower ideal. Hence the next verse.

[1] Put away all egoism from you, disregard joy and sorrow, disregard gain and loss and all worldly results; look only at the cause you must serve and the work that you must achieve by divine command; "so thou shalt not incur sin." Thus Arjuna's plea of sorrow, his plea of the recoil from slaughter, his plea of the sense of sin, his plea of the unhappy results of his action, are answered according to the highest knowledge and ethical ideals to which his race and age had attained.

II. THE YOGA OF THE INTELLIGENT WILL

(In the moment of his turning from this first and summary answer to Arjuna's difficulties and in the very first words which strike the keynote of a spiritual solution, the Teacher makes at once a distinction which is of the utmost importance for the understanding of the Gita, – the distinction of Sankhya and Yoga. The Gita is in its foundation a Vedantic work; it is one of the three recognised authorities for the Vedantic teaching. But still its Vedantic ideas are throughout and thoroughly coloured by the ideas of the Sankhya and the Yoga way of thinking and it derives from this colouring the peculiar synthetic character of its philosophy. It is in fact primarily a practical system of Yoga that it teaches and it brings in metaphysical ideas only as explanatory of its practical system.

What, then, are the Sankhya and Yoga of which the Gita speaks? They are certainly not the systems which have come down to us under these names as enunciated respectively in the Sankhya Karika of Ishwara Krishna and the Yoga aphorisms of Patanjali. Still, all that is essential in the Sankhya and Yoga systems, all in them that is large, catholic and universally true, is admitted by the Gita, even though it does not limit itself by them like the opposing schools. Its Sankhya is the catholic and Vedantic Sankhya such as we find it in its first principles and elements in the great Vedantic synthesis of the Upanishads and in the later developments of the Puranas. Its idea of Yoga is that large idea of a principally subjective practice and inner change, necessary for the finding of the Self or the union with God, of which the Raja-Yoga[1] is only one special application and not the most important and vital. The Gita insists that Sankhya and Yoga are not two different, incompatible and discordant systems but one in their principle and aim; they differ only in their method and starting-point.

[1] The Yoga system of Patanjali is a purely subjective method of Raja-Yoga.

But what are the truths of Sankhya? The philosophy drew its name from its analytical process. Sankhya is the analysis, the enumeration, the separative and discriminative setting forth of the principles of our being of which the ordinary mind sees only the combinations and results of combination. It did not seek at all to synthetise. Its original standpoint is in fact dualistic, not with the very relative dualism of the Vedantic schools which call themselves by that name, Dwaita, but in a very absolute and trenchant fashion. For it explains existence not by one, but by two original principles whose inter-relation is the cause of the universe, – Purusha, the inactive, Prakriti, the active. Purusha is the Soul, not in the ordinary or popular sense of the word, but of pure conscious Being immobile, immutable and self-luminous. Prakriti is Energy and its process. Purusha does nothing, but it reflects the action of Energy and its processes; Prakriti is mechanical, but by being reflected in Purusha it assumes the appearance of consciousness in its activities, and thus there are created those phenomena of creation, conservation, dissolution, birth and life and death, consciousness and unconsciousness, sense-knowledge and intellectual knowledge and ignorance, action and inaction, happiness and suffering which the Purusha under the influence of Prakriti attributes to itself although they belong not at all to itself but to the action or movement of Prakriti alone.

For Prakriti is constituted of three *guṇa*s or essential modes of energy; sattwa, the seed of intelligence, conserves the workings of energy; rajas, the seed of force and action, creates the workings of energy; tamas, the seed of inertia and non-intelligence, the denial of sattwa and rajas, dissolves what they create and conserve. When these three powers of the energy of Prakriti are in a state of equilibrium, all is in rest, there is no movement, action or creation and there is therefore nothing to be reflected in the immutable luminous being of the conscious Soul. But when the equilibrium is disturbed, then the three gunas fall into a state of inequality in which they strive with and act upon each other and the whole inextricable business of ceaseless creation, conservation and dissolution begins, unrolling the phenomena of the cosmos. This continues so long as the Purusha consents to reflect the disturbance which obscures his eternal nature and attributes to it the nature of Prakriti; but when he withdraws his consent, the gunas fall into equilibrium and the Soul returns to its eternal, unchanging immobility; it is delivered from phenomena. So the Sankhya explains the existence of the cosmos.

But whence then come this conscious intelligence and conscious will which we perceive to be so large a part of our being and which we commonly and instinctively refer not to the Prakriti, but to the Purusha? According to the Sankhya this intelligence and will are entirely a part of the mechanical energy of Nature and are not properties of the soul; they are the principle of Buddhi, one of the twenty-four *tattva*s, the twenty-four cosmic principles. (See Chap. III, Sl. 42 and Chap. XIII, Sl. 5.) If we find it difficult to realise how intelligence and will can be properties of the mechanical Inconscient and themselves mechanical (*jaḍa*), we have only to remember that modern Science itself has been driven to the same conclusion. But Sankhya explains what modern Science leaves in obscurity, the process by which the mechanical and inconscient takes on the appearance of consciousness. It is because of the reflection of Prakriti in Purusha; the light of consciousness of the Soul is attributed to the workings of the mechanical energy. To get rid of this delusion is the first step towards the liberation of the soul from Nature and her works.

What we do not seize at first is why Sankhya should bring in an element of pluralism into its dualism by affirming one Prakriti, but many Purushas. It would seem that the existence of one Purusha and one Prakriti should be sufficient to account for the creation and procession of the universe. But the Sankhya was bound to evolve pluralism by its rigidly analytical observation of the principles of things. First, actually, we find that there are many conscious beings in the world and each regards the same world in his own way and has his independent experience of its subjective and objective things, his separate dealings with the same perceptive and reactive processes. If there were only one Purusha, there would not be this central independence and separativeness, but all would see the world in an identical fashion and with a common subjectivity and objectivity. There is another difficulty quite as formidable. Liberation is the object set before itself by this philosophy as by others. This liberation is effected, we have said, by the Purusha's withdrawal of his consent from the activities of Prakriti which she conducts only for his pleasure; but, in sum, this is only a way of speaking. The Purusha is passive and the act of giving or withdrawing consent cannot really belong to it, but must be a movement in Prakriti itself. If we consider, we shall see that it is, so far as it is an operation, a movement of reversal or recoil in the principle of Buddhi, the discriminative will. Buddhi arrives by the process of discriminating things at the acid and dissolvent realisation that the identity of the Purusha and the Prakriti is a delusion. Buddhi, at once intelligence and will, recoils from the falsehood which it has been supporting and the Purusha, ceasing to be bound, no longer associates himself with the interest of the mind in the cosmic play. But if there were only the one Purusha and this recoil of the discriminating principles from its delusions took place, all cosmos would cease. As it is, we see that nothing of the kind happens. A few beings among innumerable millions attain to liberation, the rest are in no way affected, nor is cosmic Nature in her play with them one whit inconvenienced by this summary rejection which should be the end of all her processes. Only by the theory of many independent Purushas can this fact be explained.

The Gita starts from this analysis and seems at first, even in its setting forth of Yoga, to accept it almost wholly. It accepts Prakriti and her three gunas and twenty-four principles; accepts the attribution of all action to the Prakriti and the passivity of the Purusha; accepts the multiplicity of conscious beings in the cosmos; accepts the dissolution of the identifying ego-sense[1], the discriminating action of the intelligent will and the transcendence of the action of the three modes of energy as the means of liberation. The Yoga which Arjuna is asked to practise from the outset is Yoga by the Buddhi, the intelligent will. But there is one deviation of capital importance, – the Purusha is regarded as one, not many; for the free, immaterial, immobile, eternal, immutable Self of the Gita, but for one detail, is a Vedantic description of the eternal, passive, immobile, immutable Purusha of the Sankhyas. But the capital difference is that there is One and not many. This brings in the whole difficulty which the Sankhya multiplicity avoids and necessitates a quite different solution. This the Gita provides by bringing into its Vedantic Sankhya the ideas and principles of Vedantic Yoga.

The first important new element we find is in the conception of Purusha itself. Prakriti conducts her activities for the pleasure of Purusha; but how is that pleasure determined? In the strict Sankhya analysis it can only be by a passive consent of the silent Witness. Passively the Witness consents to the action of the intelligent will and the ego-sense, passively he consents to the recoil of that will from the ego-sense. He is Witness, source of the consent, by reflection upholder of the work of Nature, *sākṣī anumantā bhartā*, but nothing more. But the Purusha of the Gita is also the lord of Nature; he is Ishwara (see Chap. XIII, Sl. 22). If the operation of the intelligent will belongs to Nature, the origination and power of the will proceed from the conscious Soul; he is the Lord of Nature. If the act of intelligence of the Will is the act of Prakriti, the source and light of the intelligence are actively contributed by the Purusha; he is not only the Witness, but the Lord and Knower, master of knowledge and will, *jñātā īśvaraḥ*. He is the supreme cause

---

[1] The ego-sense (Ahankara) is a principle of Nature which induces the Purusha to identify himself with Prakriti.

of the action of Prakriti, the supreme cause of its withdrawal from action. In the Sankhya analysis, Purusha and Prakriti in their dualism are the cause of the cosmos; in this synthetic Sankhya, Purusha by *his* Prakriti is the cause of the cosmos. We see at once how far we have travelled from the rigid purism of the traditional analysis.

But what of the one self immutable, immobile, eternally free, with which the Gita began? That is free from all change or involution in change, *avikārya*, unborn, unmanifested, the Brahman, yet it is that "by which all this is extended." Therefore it would seem that the principle of the Ishwara is in its being; if it is immobile, it is yet the cause and lord of all action and mobility. But how? And what of the multiplicity of conscious beings in the cosmos? They do not seem to be the Lord, but rather very much not the Lord *anīśa*, for they are subject to the action of the three gunas and the dualism of the ego-sense, and if, as the Gita seems to say, they are all the one self, how did this involution, subjection and delusion come about or how is it explicable except by the pure passivity of the Purusha? And whence the multiplicity? or how is it that the one self in one body and mind attains to liberation while in others it remains under the delusion of bondage? These are difficulties which cannot be passed by without a solution.

The Gita answers them in its later chapters by an analysis of Purusha and Prakriti which brings in new elements very proper to a Vedantic Yoga, but alien to the traditional Sankhya. It speaks of three Purushas or rather a triple status of the Purusha. The Upanishads in dealing with the truths of Sankhya seem sometimes to speak only of two Purushas. There is one unborn of three colours, says a text, the eternal feminine principle of Prakriti with its three gunas, ever creating; there are two unborn, two Purushas, of whom one cleaves to and enjoys her, the other abandons her because he has enjoyed all her enjoyments. In another verse they are described as two birds on one tree, eternally yoked companions, one of whom eats the fruits of the tree, – the

Purusha in Nature enjoying her cosmos, – the other eats not, but watches his fellow, – the silent Witness, withdrawn from the enjoyment; when the first sees the second and knows that all is his greatness, then he is delivered from sorrow. The point of view in the two verses is different, but they have a common implication. One of the birds is the eternally silent, unbound Self or Purusha by whom all this is extended and he regards the cosmos he has extended, but is aloof from it; the other is the Purusha involved in Prakriti. The first verse indicates that the two are the same, represent different states, bound and liberated, of the same conscious being, – for the second Unborn has descended into the enjoyment of Nature and withdrawn from her; the other verse brings out what we would not gather from the former, that in its higher status of unity the self is for ever free, inactive, unattached, though it descends in its lower being into the multiplicity of the creatures of Prakriti and withdraws from it by reversion in any individual creature to the higher status. This theory of the double status of the one conscious soul opens a door; but the process of the multiplicity of the One is still obscure.

To these two the Gita, developing the thought of other passages in the Upanishads, adds yet another, the supreme, the Purushottama, the highest Purusha, whose greatness all this creation is. Thus there are three, the Kshara, the Akshara, the Uttama. Kshara, the mobile, the mutable is Nature, *svabhāva*, it is the various becoming of the soul; the Purusha here is the multiplicity of the divine Being; it is the Purusha multiple not apart from, but in Prakriti. Akshara the immobile, the immutable, is the silent and inactive self, it is the unity of the divine Being witness of Nature, but not involved in its movement; it is the inactive Purusha free from Prakriti and her works. The Uttama is the Lord, the supreme Brahman, the supreme Self, who possesses both the immutable unity and the mobile multiplicity. It is by a large mobility and action of His nature, His energy, His will and power that He manifests himself in the world and by a greater stillness and immobility of His being that He[1] is aloof from it; yet is He as Purushottama above both the aloofness from Nature and the attachment to Nature. This idea of the Purushottama, though continually implied in the Upanishads, is disengaged and definitely brought out by the Gita and has exercised a powerful influence on the later developments of the Indian religious consciousness. It is the foundation of the highest Bhakti-Yoga which claims to exceed the rigid definitions of monistic philosophy; it is at the back of the philosophy of the devotional Puranas.

The Gita is not content, either, to abide within the Sankhya analysis of Prakriti; for that makes room only for the ego-sense and not for the multiple Purusha, which is there not a part of Prakriti, but separate from her. The Gita affirms on the contrary that the Lord by His nature becomes the Jiva. How is that possible, since there are only the twenty-four principles of the cosmic Energy and no others? Yes, says the divine Teacher in effect, that is a perfectly valid account for the apparent operations of the cosmic Prakriti with its three gunas, and the relation attributed to Purusha and Prakriti there is also quite valid and of great use for the practical purposes of the involution and the withdrawal. But this is only the lower Prakriti of the three modes, the inconscient, the apparent; there is a higher, a supreme, a conscient and divine Nature, and it is that which has become the individual soul, the Jiva. In the lower Nature each being appears as the ego, in the higher he is the individual Purusha. In other words, multiplicity is part of the spiritual nature of the One. This individual soul is myself, in the creation it is a partial manifestation of me, *mamaiva aṁśaḥ*, and it possesses all my powers; it is witness, giver of the sanction, upholder, knower, lord. It descends into the lower nature and thinks itself bound by action, so to enjoy the lower being: it can draw back and know itself as the passive Purusha free from all action. It can rise above the

---

[1] *Puruṣa ... akṣarāt parataḥ paraḥ*, – although the Akshara is supreme, there is a supreme Purusha higher than it, says the Upanishad.

three gunas and, liberated from the bondage of action, yet possess action, even as I do myself, and by adoration of the Purushottama and union with him it can enjoy wholly its divine nature.)

एषा तेऽभिहिता साङ्ख्ये बुद्धिर्योगे त्विमां शृणु ।
बुद्ध्या युक्तो यया पार्थ कर्मबन्धं प्रहास्यसि ॥३९॥

39. Such[1] is the intelligence (the intelligent knowledge of things and will) declared to thee in the Sankhya, hear now this in the Yoga, for if thou art in Yoga by this intelligence, O son of Pritha, thou shalt cast away the bondage of works.

नेहाभिक्रमनाशोऽस्ति प्रत्यवायो न विद्यते ।
स्वल्पमप्यस्य धर्मस्य त्रायते महतो भयात् ॥४०॥

40. On this path no effort is lost, no obstacle prevails; even a little of this dharma delivers from the great fear[2].

---

[1] I have declared to you the poise of a self-liberating intelligence in Sankhya. I will now declare to you another poise in Yoga. You are shrinking from the results of your works, you desire other results and turn from your right path in life because it does not lead you to them. But this idea of works and their result, desire of result as the motive, the work as a means for the satisfaction of desire, is the bondage of the ignorant who know not what works are, nor their true source, nor their real operation, nor their high utility. My Yoga, says the divine Teacher to Arjuna, will free you from all bondage of the soul to its works.

[2] Arjuna is seized with the great fear which besieges humanity, its fear of sin and suffering now and hereafter, its fear in a world of whose true nature it is ignorant, of a God whose true being also it has not seen and whose cosmic purpose it does not understand. My Yoga, says the divine Teacher to him, will deliver you from the great fear and even a little of it will bring deliverance. When you have once set out on this path, you will find that no step is lost; every least movement will be a gain; you will find there no obstacle that can baulk you of your advance. A bold and absolute promise and one to which the fearful and hesitating mind beset and stumbling in all its paths cannot easily lend an assured trust.

व्यवसायात्मिका बुद्धिरेकेह कुरुनन्दन ।
बहुशाखा ह्यनन्ताश्च बुद्धयोऽव्यवसायिनाम् ॥४१॥

41. The fixed and resolute intelligence[1] is one and homogeneous, O joy of the Kurus; many-branching and multifarious is the intelligence of the irresolute.

यामिमां पुष्पितां वाचं प्रवदन्त्यविपश्चितः ।
वेदवादरताः पार्थ नान्यदस्तीति वादिनः ॥४२॥
कामात्मानः स्वर्गपरा जन्मकर्मफलप्रदाम् ।
क्रियाविशेषबहुलां भोगैश्वर्यगतिं प्रति ॥४३॥

42-43. This flowery[2] word which they declare who have not clear discernment, devoted to the creed of the Veda, whose creed is that there is nothing else, souls of desire, seekers of Paradise, – it gives the fruits of the works of birth, it is multifarious with specialities of rites, it is directed to enjoyment and lordship as its goal.

[1] Buddhi, the word used, means, properly speaking, the mental power of understanding, but it is evidently used by the Gita in a large philosophic sense for the whole action of the discriminating and deciding mind which determines both the direction and use of our thoughts and the direction and use of our acts; thought, intelligence, judgment, perceptive choice and aim are all included in its functioning: for the characteristic of the unified intelligence is not only concentration of the mind that knows, but especially concentration of the mind that decides and persists in the decision, *vyāvasāya*, while the sign of the dissipated intelligence is not so much even discursiveness of the ideas and perceptions as discursiveness of the aims and desires, therefore of the will. Will, then, and knowledge are the two functions of the Buddhi. The unified intelligent will is fixed in the enlightened soul, it is concentrated in inner self-knowledge; the many-branching and multifarious, busied with many things, careless of the one thing needful is, on the contrary, subject to the restless and discursive action of the mind, dispersed in outward life and works and their fruits.

[2] In the first six chapters the Gita lays a large foundation for its synthesis of works and knowledge, its synthesis of Sankhya, Yoga and Vedanta. But first it finds that *karma*, works, has a particular sense in the language of the Vedantins; it means the Vedic sacrifices and ceremonies or at most that and the ordering of life according to the Grihyasutras in

भोगैश्वर्यप्रसक्तानां तयाऽपहृतचेतसाम् ।
व्यवसायात्मिका बुद्धिः समाधौ न विधीयते ॥४४॥

44. The intelligence of those who are misled by that (flowery word), and cling to enjoyment and lordship, is not established in the self with concentrated fixity.

which these rites are the most important part, the religious kernel of the life. By works the Vedantins understood these religious works, the sacrificial system, the *yajña*, full of a careful order, *vidhi*, of exact and complicated rites, *kriyāviśeṣa bahulam*. But in Yoga works had a much wider significance. The Gita insists on this wider significance; in our conception of spiritual activity all works have to be included, *sarva-karmāṇi*. At the same time it does not, like Buddhism, reject the idea of the sacrifice, it prefers to uplift and enlarge it. Yes, it says in effect, not only is sacrifice, *yajña*, the most important part of life, but all life, all works should be regarded as sacrifice, are *yajña*, though by the ignorant they are performed without the higher knowledge and by the most ignorant not in the true order, *avidhi-pūrvakam*. Sacrifice is the very condition of life; with sacrifice as their eternal companion the Father of creatures created the peoples. But the sacrifices of the Vedavadins are offerings of desire directed towards material rewards, desire eager for the result of works, desire looking to a larger enjoyment in Paradise as immortality and highest salvation. This the system of the Gita cannot admit; for that in its very inception starts with the renunciation of desire, with its rejection and destruction as the enemy of the soul. The Gita does not deny the validity even of the Vedic sacrificial works; it admits them, it admits that by these means one may get enjoyment here and Paradise beyond; it is I myself, says the divine Teacher (Ch. IX, Sl. 24), who accept these sacrifices and to whom they are offered, I who give these fruits in the form of the gods since so men choose to approach me. But this is not the true road, nor is the enjoyment of Paradise the liberation and fulfilment which man has to seek. It is the ignorant who worship the gods, not knowing whom they are worshipping ignorantly in these divine forms; for they worshipping, though in ignorance, the One, the Lord, the only Deva, and it is He who accepts their offering. To that Lord must the sacrifice be offered, the true sacrifice of all the life's energies and activities, with devotion, without desire, for His sake and for the welfare of the peoples. It is because the Vedavada obscures this truth and with its tangle of ritual ties man down to the action of the three gunas that it has to be so severely censured and put roughly aside; but its central idea is not destroyed; transfigured and uplifted, it is turned into a most important part of the true spiritual experience and of the method of liberation.

त्रैगुण्यविषया वेदा निस्त्रैगुण्यो भवार्जुन ।
निर्द्वन्द्वो नित्यसत्त्वस्थो निर्योगक्षेम आत्मवान् ॥४५॥

45. The action of the three gunas is the subject-matter of the Veda; but do thou become free from the triple guna, O Arjuna; without the dualities, ever based in the true being, without gettting[1] or having, possessed of the self.

यावानर्थ उदपाने सर्वतः संप्लुतोदके ।
तावान् सर्वेषु वेदेषु ब्राह्मणस्य विजानतः ॥४६॥

46. As much use as there is in a well with water in flood on every side, so much is there in all the Vedas for the Brahmin who has the knowledge.

कर्मण्येवाधिकारस्ते मा फलेषु कदाचन ।
मा कर्मफलहेतुर्भूर्मा ते सङ्गोऽस्त्वकर्मणि ॥४७॥

47. Thou hast a right to action[2], but only to action, never to its fruits; let not the fruits[3] of thy works be thy motive,

---

[1] What gettings and havings has the free soul? Once we are possessed of the Self, we are in possession of all things. And yet he does not cease from work and action. There is the originality and power of the Gita, that having affirmed this static condition, this superiority to Nature, this emptiness even of all that constitutes ordinarily the action of Nature for the liberated soul, it is still able to vindicate for it, to enjoin on it even the continuance of works and thus avoid the great defect of the merely quietistic and ascetic philosophies, – the defect from which we find them today attempting to escape.

[2] The whole range of human action has been decreed by me with a view to the progress of man from the lower to the higher nature, from the apparent undivine to the conscious Divine. The whole range of human works must be that in which the God-knower shall move. Let no one cut short the thread of action before it is spun out, let him not perplex and falsify the stages and gradations of the ways I have hewn.

[3] But "let not the fruits of thy works be thy motive." Therefore it is not the works practised with desire by the Vedavadins, it is not the claim for the satisfaction of the restless and energetic mind by a constant activity, the claim made by the practical or the kinetic man, which is here enjoined.

neither let there be in thee any attachment to inactivity.

योगस्थः कुरु कर्माणि सङ्गं त्यक्त्वा धनञ्जय ।
सिद्ध्यसिद्ध्योः समो भूत्वा समत्वं योग उच्यते ॥४८॥

48. Fixed in Yoga[1] do thy actions, having abandoned attachment, having become equal in failure and success; for it is equality that is meant by Yoga.

दूरेण ह्यवरं कर्म बुद्धियोगाद्धनञ्जय ।
बुद्धौ शरणमन्विच्छ कृपणाः फलहेतवः ॥४९॥

49. Works are far inferior to Yoga of the intelligence, O Dhananjaya; desire rather refuge in the intelligence; poor and wretched souls are they who make the fruit of their works the object of their thoughts and activities.

बुद्धियुक्तो जहातीह उभे सुकृतदुष्कृते ।
तस्माद्योगाय युज्यस्व योगः कर्मसु कौशलम् ॥५०॥

50. One whose intelligence has attained to unity, casts[2] away from him even here in this world of dualities both good

---

[1] It is because he acts ignorantly, with a wrong intelligence and therefore a wrong will in these matters, that man is or seems to be bound by his works; otherwise works are no bondage to the free soul. It is because of this wrong intelligence that he has hope and fear, wrath and grief and transient joy; otherwise works are possible with a perfect serenity and freedom. Therefore it is the Yoga of the Buddhi, the intelligence, that is first enjoined on Arjuna. To act with right intelligence and, therefore, a right will, fixed in the One, aware of the one self in all and acting out of its equal serenity, not running about in different directions under the thousand impulses of our superficial mental self, is the Yoga of the intelligent will.
  Action is distressed by the choice between a relative good and evil, the fear of sin and the difficult endeavour towards virtue? But this is true only of the action of the ordinary man, not of a Yogin.
[2] For he rises to a higher law beyond good and evil, founded in the liberty of self-knowledge. Such desireless action can have no decisiveness,

doing and evil doing; therefore strive to be in Yoga; Yoga is skill in works.

कर्मजं बुद्धियुक्ता हि फलं त्यक्त्वा मनीषिणः ।
जन्मबन्धविनिर्मुक्ताः पदं गच्छन्त्यनामयम् ॥५१॥

51. The sages who have united their reason and will with the Divine renounce the fruit which action yields and, liberated from the bondage of birth, they reach the status¹ beyond misery.

यदा ते मोहकलिलं बुद्धिर्व्यतितरिष्यति ।
तदा गन्तासि निर्वेदं श्रोतव्यस्य श्रुतस्य च ॥५२॥

52. When thy intelligence shall cross beyond the whirl of delusion, then shalt thou become indifferent² to Scripture heard or that which thou hast yet to hear.

श्रुतिविप्रतिपन्ना ते यदा स्थास्यति निश्चला ।
समाधावचला बुद्धिस्तदा योगमवाप्स्यसि ॥५३॥

---

no effectiveness, no efficient motive, no large or vigorous creative power? Not so; action done in Yoga is not only the highest but the wisest, the most potent and efficient even for the affairs of the world; for it is informed by the knowledge and will of the Master of works: "Yoga is the true skill in works."

¹ But all action directed towards life leads away from the universal aim of the Yogin which is by common consent to escape from bondage to this distressed and sorrowful human birth? Not so, either; the sages who do works without desire for fruits and in Yoga with the Divine are liberated from the bondage of birth and reach that other perfect status (*brāhmī sthiti*) in which there are none of the maladies which afflict the mind and life of a suffering humanity.

² The Vedas and the Upanishads are declared to be unnecessary for the man who knows (Sl. 46). Nay, they are even a stumbling-block; for the letter of the Word – perhaps because of its conflict of texts and its various and mutually dissentient interpretations – bewilders the understanding, which can only find certainty and concentration by the light within.

53. When thy intelligence which is bewildered by the Sruti[1], shall stand unmoving and stable in Samadhi, then shalt thou attain to Yoga.

अर्जुन उवाच —
स्थितप्रज्ञस्य का भाषा समाधिस्थस्य केशव ।
स्थितधीः किं प्रभाषेत किमासीत व्रजेत किम् ॥५४॥

54. Arjuna said: What is the sign of the man in Samadhi whose intelligence is firmly fixed in wisdom? How does the sage of settled understanding speak, how sit, how walk?

(Arjuna, voicing the average human mind, asks for some outward, physical, practically discernible sign of Samadhi. No such signs[2] can be given, nor does the Teacher attempt to supply them; for the only possible test of its possession is inward and that there are plenty of hostile psychological forces to apply. Equality is the great stamp of the liberated soul and of that equality even the most discernible signs are still subjective).

श्रीभगवान् उवाच —
प्रजहाति यदा कामान् सर्वान् पार्थ मनोगतान् ।
आत्मन्येवात्मना तुष्टः स्थितप्रज्ञस्तदोच्यते ॥५५॥

---

[1] Sruti is a general term for the Vedas and the Upanishads. This criticism of the Sruti is so offensive to conventional religious sentiment that attempts are naturally made by the convenient and indispensable human faculty of text-twisting to put a different sense on some of these verses, but the meaning is plain and hangs together from beginning to end. It is confirmed and emphasised by a subsequent passage in which the knowledge of the knower is described as passing beyond the range of Veda and Upanishad, *śabdabrahmativartate* (Ch. VI, Sl. 44). At the same time, as we have already seen, the Gita does not treat such important parts of the Aryan Culture in a spirit of mere negation and repudiation.

[2] The sign of the man in Samadhi is not that he loses consciousness of objects and surroundings and of his mental and physical self and cannot be recalled to it even by burning or torture of the body, – the ordinary idea of the matter; trance is a particular intensity, not the essential sign.

55. The Blessed Lord said: When a man expels,[1] O Partha, all desires from the mind, and is satisfied in the self by the self, then is he called stable in intelligence.

दुःखेष्वनुद्विग्नमनाः सुखेषु विगतस्पृहः ।
वीतरागभयक्रोधः स्थितधीर्मुनिरुच्यते ॥५६॥

56. He whose mind is undisturbed[2] in the midst of sorrows and amid pleasures is free from desire, from whom liking and fear and wrath have passed away, is the sage of settled understanding.

---

[1] The test of Samadhi is the expulsion of all desires, their inability to get at the mind, and it is the inner state from which this freedom arises, the delight of the soul gathered within itself with the mind equal and still and high-poised above the attractions and repulsions, the alternations of sunshine and storm and stress of the external life. It is drawn inward even when acting outwardly; it is concentrated in self even when gazing out upon things; it is directed wholly to the Divine even when to the outward vision of others busy and preoccupied with the affairs of the world.

[2] The Stoic self-discipline calls desire and passion into its embrace of the wrestler and crushes them between its arms, as did old Dhritarashtra in the epic the iron image of Bhima. The Gita, making its call on the warrior nature of Arjuna, starts with this heroic movement. It calls on him to turn on the great enemy desire and slay it. Its first description of equality is that of the Stoic philosopher. But the Gita accepts this Stoic discipline, this heroic philosophy, on the same condition that it accepts the tamasic recoil, – it must have above it the sattwic vision of knowledge, at its root the aim at self-realisation and in its steps the ascent to the divine nature. A Stoic discipline which merely crushed down the common affections of our human nature, – although less dangerous than a tamasic weariness of life, unfruitful pessimism and sterile inertia, because it would at least increase the power and self-mastery of the soul, – would still be no unmixed good, since it might lead to insensibility and an inhuman isolation without giving the true spiritual release. The Stoic equality is justified as an element in the discipline of the Gita because it can be associated with and can help to the realisation of the free immutable self in the mobile human being, *param dṛṣṭvā*, and to status in that new self-consciousness, *eṣā brāhmī sthitiḥ*.

यः सर्वत्रानभिस्नेहस्तत्तत्प्राप्य शुभाशुभम् ।
नाभिनन्दति न द्वेष्टि तस्य प्रज्ञा प्रतिष्ठिता ॥५७॥

57. Who in all things is without affection though visited by this good or that evil and neither hates nor rejoices, his intelligence sits firmly founded in wisdom.

यदा संहरते चायं कूर्मोऽङ्गानीव सर्वशः ।
इन्द्रियाणीन्द्रियार्थेभ्यस्तस्य प्रज्ञा प्रतिष्ठिता ॥५८॥

58. Who draws[1] away the senses from the objects of sense, as the tortoise draws in his limbs into the shell, his intelligence sits firmly founded in wisdom.

विषया विनिवर्तन्ते निराहारस्य देहिनः ।
रसवर्जं रसोऽप्यस्य परं दृष्ट्वा निवर्तते ॥५९॥

59. If one abstains[2] from food, the objects of sense cease

---

[1] The first movement must be obviously to get rid of desire which is the whole root of the evil and suffering; and in order to get rid of desire, we must put an end to the cause of desire, the rushing out of the senses to seize and enjoy their objects. We must draw them back when they are inclined thus to rush out, draw them away from their objects into their source, quiescent in the mind, the mind quiescent in the intelligence, the intelligence quiescent in the soul and its self-knowledge, observing the action of Nature, but not subject to it, not desiring anything that the objective life can give.

It is not an external asceticism, the physical renunciation of the objects of sense that I am teaching, suggests Krishna immediately to avoid a misunderstanding which is likely at once to arise; I speak of an inner withdrawal, a renunciation of desire.

[2] The embodied soul, having a body, has to support it normally by food for its normal physical action; by abstention from food it simply removes from itself the physical contact with the objects of sense, but does not get rid of the inner relation which makes that contact hurtful. It retains the pleasure of the sense in the object, the *rasa*, the liking and disliking, – for *rasa* has two sides; the soul must, on the contrary, be capable of enduring the physical contact without suffering inwardly this sensuous reaction (see Sl. 64).

to affect, but the affection itself of the sense, the *rasa*, remains; the *rasa* also ceases when the Supreme is seen.

यततो ह्यपि कौन्तेय पुरुषस्य विपश्चितः ।
इन्द्रियाणि प्रमाथीनि हरन्ति प्रसभं मनः ॥६०॥

60. Even the mind of the wise[1] man who labours for perfection is carried away by the vehement insistence of the senses, O son of Kunti.

तानि सर्वाणि संयम्य युक्त आसीत मत्परः ।
वशे हि यस्येन्द्रियाणि तस्य प्रज्ञा प्रतिष्ठिता ॥६१॥

61. Having brought all the senses under control, he must sit firm in Yoga, wholly given up to Me; for whose senses are mastered[2], of him the intelligence is firmly established (in its proper seat).

---

[1] Certainly self-discipline, self-control is never easy. All intelligent human beings know that they must exercise some control over themselves and nothing is more common than this advice to control the senses; but ordinarily it is only advised imperfectly and practised imperfectly in the most limited and insufficient fashion. Even, however, the sage, the man of clear, wise and discerning soul who really labours to acquire complete self-mastery finds himself hurried and carried away by the senses.

[2] This cannot be done perfectly by the act of the intelligence itself, by a merely mental self-discipline; it can only be done by Yoga with something which is higher than itself and in which calm and self-mastery are inherent. And this Yoga can only arrive at its success by devoting, by consecrating, by giving up the whole self to the Divine, "to Me", says Krishna; for the Liberator is within us, but it is not our mind, nor our intelligence, nor our personal will, – they are only instruments. It is the Lord in whom, as we are told in the end, we have utterly to take refuge. And for that we must at first make him the object of our whole being and keep in soul-contact with him. This is the sense of the phrase "he must sit firm in Yoga, wholly given up to Me"; but as yet it is the merest passing hint after the manner of the Gita, three words only which contain in seed the whole gist of the highest secret yet to be developed. *Yukta āsīta matparaḥ.*

ध्यायतो विषयान् पुंसः सङ्गस्तेषूपजायते ।
सङ्गात् सञ्जायते कामः कामात्क्रोधोऽभिजायते ॥६२॥

62. In him whose mind dwells on the objects of sense with absorbing interest, attachment to them is formed; from attachment arises desire; from desire anger comes forth.

क्रोधाद् भवति संमोहः संमोहात्स्मृतिविभ्रमः ।
स्मृतिभ्रंशाद् बुद्धिनाशो बुद्धिनाशात्प्रणश्यति ॥६३॥

63. Anger[1] leads to bewilderment, from bewilderment comes loss of memory; and by that the intelligence is destroyed; from destruction of intelligence he perishes.

रागद्वेषवियुक्तैस्तु विषयानिन्द्रियैश्चरन् ।
आत्मवश्यैर्विधेयात्मा प्रसादमधिगच्छति ॥६४॥
प्रसादे सर्वदुःखानां हानिरस्योपजायते ।
प्रसन्नचेतसो ह्याशु बुद्धिः पर्यवतिष्ठते ॥६५॥

64-65. It is by ranging[2] over the objects with the senses, but with senses subject to the self, freed from liking and disliking, that one gets into a large and sweet clearness of soul and temperament in which passion and grief find no place; the intelligence of such a man is rapidly established (in its proper seat).

[1] By passion the soul is obscured, the intelligence and will forget to see and be seated in the calm observing soul, there is a fall from the memory of one's true self, and by that lapse the intelligent will is also obscured, destroyed even. For, for the time being, it no longer exists to our memory of ourselves, it disappears in a cloud of passion; we become passion, wrath, grief and cease to be self and intelligence and will.

[2] But how is this desireless contact with objects, this unsensuous use of the senses possible? It is possible, *param dṛṣṭvā*, by the vision of the Supreme, – *param*, the Soul, the Purusha, – and by living in the Yoga, in union or oneness of the whole subjective being with that, through the Yoga of the intelligence. Then, free from reactions, the senses will be delivered from the affections of liking and disliking, escape the duality of positive and negative desire, and calm, peace, clearness, happy tranquil-

नास्ति बुद्धिरयुक्तस्य न चायुक्तस्य भावना ।
न चाभावयतः शान्तिरशान्तस्य कुतः सुखम् ॥६६॥

66. For one who is not in Yoga, there is no intelligence, no concentration of thought; for him without concentration there is no peace, and for the unpeaceful how can there be happiness?

इन्द्रियाणां हि चरतां यन्मनोऽनुविधीयते ।
तदस्य हरति प्रज्ञां वायुर्नावमिवाम्भसि ॥६७॥

67. Such of the roving senses as the mind follows, that carries away the understanding, just as the winds carry away a ship on the sea.

तस्मादस्य महाबाहो निगृहीतानि सर्वशः ।
इन्द्रियाणीन्द्रियार्थेभ्यस्तस्य प्रज्ञा प्रतिष्ठिता ॥६८॥

68. Therefore, O mighty-armed, one who has utterly restrained the excitement of the senses by their objects, his intelligence sits firmly founded in calm self-knowledge.

या निशा सर्वभूतानां तस्यां जागर्ति संयमी ।
यस्यां जाग्रति भूतानि सा निशा पश्यतो मुनेः ॥६९॥

69. That (higher being) which is to all creatures a night, is to the self-mastering sage his waking (his luminous day of true being, knowledge and power); the life of the dualities

---

lity, *ātmaprasāda*, will settle upon the man. That clear tranquillity is the source of the soul's felicity; all grief begins to lose its power of touching the tranquil soul; the intelligence is rapidly established in the peace of the self; suffering is destroyed. It is this calm, desireless, griefless fixity of the buddhi in self-poise and self-knowledge to which the Gita gives the name of Samadhi.

The culmination of the Yoga of the intelligent will is in the Brahmic status, *brāhmī sthiti*. It is a reversal of the whole view, experience, knowledge, values, seeings of earth-bound creatures.

which is to them their waking (their day, their consciousness, their bright condition of activity) is a night (a troubled sleep and darkness of the soul) to the sage who sees.

आपूर्यमाणमचलप्रतिष्ठं समुद्रमापः प्रविशन्ति यद्वत् ।
तद्वत्कामा यं प्रविशन्ति सर्वे स शान्तिमाप्नोति न कामकामी ॥७०॥

70. He attains peace, into whom all desires enter as waters into the sea (an ocean of wide being and consciousness) which is ever being filled, yet ever motionless – not he who (like troubled and muddy waters) is disturbed by every little inrush of desire.

विहाय कामान् यः सर्वान् पुमांश्चरति निःस्पृहः ।
निर्ममो निरहङ्कारः स शान्तिमधिगच्छति ॥७१॥

71. Who abandons all desires and lives and acts free from longing, who has no "I" or "mine" (who has extinguished his individual ego in the One and lives in that unity), he attains to the great peace.

एषा ब्राह्मी स्थितिः पार्थ नैनां प्राप्य विमुह्यति ।
स्थित्वाऽस्यामन्तकालेऽपि ब्रह्मनिर्वाणमृच्छति ॥७२॥

72. This is *brāhmī sthiti* (firm standing in the Brahman), O son of Pritha. Having attained thereto one is not bewildered; fixed in that status at his end, one can attain to extinction in the Brahman[1].

इति श्रीमद्भगवद्गीतासूपनिषत्सु ब्रह्मविद्यायां योगशास्त्रे श्रीकृष्णार्जुनसंवादे
साङ्ख्ययोगो नाम द्वितीयोऽध्यायः ।

---

[1] Nirvana is not the negative self-annihilation of the Buddhists, but the great immergence of the separate personal self into the vast reality of the one infinite impersonal Existence. Throughout the first six chapters the Gita quietly substitutes the still immutable Brahman of the Vedantins, the One without a second immanent in all cosmos, for the still immutable but multiple Purusha of the Sankhyas. It accepts throughout these chapters

knowledge and realisation of the Brahman as the most important, the indispensable means of liberation, even while it insists on desireless works as an essential part of knowledge. It accepts equally Nirvana of the ego in the infinite equality of the immutable, impersonal Brahman as essential to liberation; it practically identifies this extinction with the Sankhya return of the inactive immutable Purusha upon itself when it emerges out of identification with the actions of Prakriti.

Such, subtly unifying Sankhya, Yoga and Vedanta, is the first foundation of the teaching of the Gita. It is far from being all, but it is the first indispensable practical unity of knowledge and works with a hint already of the third crowning intensest element in the soul's completeness, divine love and devotion.

Third Chapter

I. WORKS AND SACRIFICE

अर्जुन उवाच —
ज्यायसी चेत्कर्मणस्ते मता बुद्धिर्जनार्दन ।
तत्किं कर्मणि घोरे मां नियोजयसि केशव ॥१॥

1. Arjuna said: If thou holdest the intelligence to be greater[1] than works, O Janardana, why then dost thou, O Keshava, appoint me to a terrible work?

व्यामिश्रेणेव वाक्येन बुद्धिं मोहयसीव मे ।
तदेकं वद निश्चित्य येन श्रेयोऽहमाप्नुयाम् ॥२॥

2. Thou seemest to bewilder my intelligence with a confused and mingled speech; tell me then decisively that one thing by which I may attain to my soul's weal.

---

[1] The Yoga of the intelligent will and its culmination in the Brahmic status, which occupies all the close of the second chapter, contains the seed of much of the teaching of the Gita, – its doctrine of desireless works, of equality, of the rejection of outward renunciation, of devotion to the Divine; but as yet all this is slight and obscure. What is most strongly emphasised as yet is the withdrawal of the will from the ordinary motive of human activities, desire, from man's normal temperament of sense-seeking thought and will with its passions and ignorance, and from its customary habit of troubled many-branching ideas and wishes to the desireless calm unity and passionless serenity of the Brahmic poise. So much Arjuna has understood. He is not unfamiliar with all this; it is the substance of the current teaching which points man to the path of knowledge and to the renunciation of life and works as his way of perfection. Krishna seems quite to admit the orthodox philosophic doctrine (Vedantic Sankhya) when he says that works are far inferior to the Yoga of the intelligence (Ch. II, Sl. 49). And yet works are insisted upon as part of the Yoga so that there seems to be in the teaching a radical inconsistency. It is in answer to this objection that the Gita begins at once to develop more clearly its positive and imperative doctrine of works.

श्रीभगवान् उवाच —
लोकेऽस्मिन् द्विविधा निष्ठा पुरा प्रोक्ता मयानघ ।
ज्ञानयोगेन साङ्ख्यानां कर्मयोगेन योगिनाम् ॥३॥

3. The Blessed Lord said: In this world twofold is the self-application of the soul (by which it enters into the Brahmic condition), as I before said, O sinless one: that of the Sankhyas by the Yoga of knowledge, that of the Yogins by the Yoga of works[1].

[1] The whole object of the first six chapters of the Gita is to synthetise in a large frame of Vedantic truth of two methods, ordinarily supposed to be diverse and even opposite. Whatever the precise distinctions of their metaphysical ideas, the practical difference between Sankhya and Yoga as developed by the Gita is the same as that which now exists between the Vedantic Yogas of knowledge and of works, and the practical results of the difference are also the same. The Sankhya proceeded like the Vedantic Yoga of knowledge by the Buddhi, by the discriminating intelligence; it arrived by reflective thought, *vicāra*, at right discrimination, *viveka*, of the true nature of the soul and of the imposition on it of the works of Prakriti through attachment and identification, just as the Vedantic method arrives by the same means at the right discrimination of the true nature of the Self and of the imposition on it of cosmic appearances by mental illusion which leads to egoistic identification and attachment. In the Vedantic method Maya ceases for the soul by its return to its true and eternal status as the one Self, the Brahman, and the cosmic action disappears; in the Sankhya method the working of the *guṇa*s falls to rest by the return of the soul to its true and eternal status as the inactive Purusha and the cosmic action ends. The Brahman of the Mayavadins is silent, immutable and inactive; so too is the Purusha of the Sankhya; therefore for both ascetic renunciation of life and works is a necessary means of liberation. But for the Yoga of the Gita, as for the Vedantic Yoga of works, action is not only a preparation but itself the means of liberation; and it is the justice of this view which the Gita seeks to bring out with such an unceasing force and insistence, – an insistence, unfortunately, which could not prevail in India against the tremendous tide of Buddhism, was lost afterwards in the intensity of ascetic illusionism (made popular by Shankara) and the fervour of world-shunning saints and devotees and is only now beginning to exercise its real and salutary influence on the Indian mind. Renunciation is indispensable, but the true renunciation is the inner rejection of desire and egoism; without that the outer physical abandoning of works is a thing unreal and ineffective, with

THIRD CHAPTER

न कर्मणामनारम्भान्नैष्कर्म्यं पुरुषोऽश्नुते ।
न च संन्यसनादेव सिद्धिं समधिगच्छति ॥४॥

4. Not by abstention from works does a man enjoy actionlessness[1], nor by mere renunciation (of works) does he attain to his perfection (to *siddhi*, the accomplishment of the aims of his self-discipline by Yoga).

न हि कश्चित् क्षणमपि जातु तिष्ठत्यकर्मकृत् ।
कार्यते ह्यवशः कर्म सर्वः प्रकृतिजैर्गुणैः ॥५॥

5. For none stands even for a moment not doing work,

---

it it ceases even to be necessary, although it is not forbidden. Knowledge is essential, there is no higher force for liberation, but works with knowledge are also needed; by the union of knowledge and works the soul dwells entirely in the Brahmic status not only in repose and inactive calm, but in the very midst and stress and violence of action. Devotion is all-important, but works with devotion are also important; by the union of knowledge, devotion and works the soul is taken up into the highest status of the Ishwara to dwell there in the Purushottama who is master at once of the eternal spiritual calm and the eternal cosmic activity. This is the synthesis of the Gita.

[1] *Naiṣkarmya*, a calm voidness from works, is no doubt that to which the soul, the Purusha has to attain; for it is Prakriti which does the work and the soul has to rise above involution in the activities of the being and attain to a free serenity and poise watching over the operations of Prakriti, but not affected by them. That, and not cessation of the work of Prakriti, is what is really meant by the soul's *naiṣkarmya*.

But if the works of Prakriti continue, how can the soul help being involved in them? How can I fight and yet in my soul not think or feel that I the individual am fighting, not desire victory nor be inwardly touched by defeat? This is the teaching of the Sankhyas that the intelligence of the man who engages in the activities of Nature, is entangled in egoism, ignorance and desire and therefore drawn to action; on the contrary, if the intelligence draws back, then the action must cease with the cessation of the desire and the ignorance. Therefore the giving up of life and works is a necessary part, an inevitable circumstance and an indispensable last means of the movement to liberation. This objection of a current logic, the Teacher immediately anticipates. No, he says, such renunciation, far from being indispensable, is not even possible.

everyone is made to do action[1] helplessly by the modes born of Prakriti.

कर्मेन्द्रियाणि संयम्य य आस्ते मनसा स्मरन् ।
इन्द्रियार्थान् विमूढात्मा मिथ्याचार: स उच्यते ॥६॥

6. Who controls the organs of action, but continues in his mind[2] to remember and dwell upon the objects of sense, such a man has bewildered himself with false notions of self-discipline.

यस्त्विन्द्रियाणि मनसा नियम्यारभतेऽर्जुन ।
कर्मेन्द्रियै: कर्मयोगमसक्त: स विशिष्यते ॥७॥

7. He who controlling the senses by the mind, O Arjuna, without attachment engages with the organs of action in Yoga of action, he excels.

नियतं कुरु कर्म त्वं कर्म ज्यायो ह्यकर्मण: ।
शरीरयात्रापि च ते न प्रसिद्ध्येदकर्मण: ॥८॥

[1] The strong perception of the great cosmic action and the eternal activity and power of the cosmic energy which was so much emphasised afterwards by the teaching of the Tantric Shaktas who even made Prakriti or Shakti superior to Purusha, is a very remarkable feature of the Gita. Although here an undertone, it is still strong enough, coupled with what we might call the theistic and devotional elements of its thought, to bring in that activism which so strongly modifies in its scheme of Yoga the quietistic tendencies of the old metaphysical Vedanta. Man embodied in the natural world cannot cease from action, not for a moment, not for a second; his very existence here is an action; the whole universe is an act of God, mere living even is His movement.

[2] It is not our physical movements and activities alone which are meant by works, by *karma*; our mental existence also is a great complex action, it is even the greater and more important part of the works of the unresting energy, – subjective cause and determinant of the physical. We have gained nothing if we repress the effect but retain the activity of the subjective cause.

Since the mind is the instrumental cause, since inaction is impossible, what is rational, necessary, the right way is a controlled action of the subjective and objective organism.

THIRD CHAPTER

8. Do[1] thou do controlled[2] action, for action is greater than inaction; even the maintenance of thy physical life cannot be effected without action.

यज्ञार्थात्कर्मणोऽन्यत्र लोकोऽयं कर्मबन्धनः ।
तदर्थं कर्म कौन्तेय मुक्तसङ्गः समाचर ॥९॥

9. By doing works otherwise than for sacrifice, this world of men is in bondage to works; for sacrifice[3] practise works, O son of Kunti, becoming free from all attachment.

[1] Do action thus self-controlled, says Krishna: I have said that knowledge, the intelligence, is greater than works, *jyāyasi karmaṇo buddhiḥ*, but I did not mean that inaction is greater than action; the contrary is the truth, *karma jyāyo akarmaṇaḥ*. For knowledge does not mean renunciation of works, it means equality and non-attachment to desire and the objects of sense; and it means the poise of the intelligent will in the Soul free and high-uplifted above the lower instrumentation of Prakriti and controlling the works of the mind and the senses and body in the power of self-knowledge and the pure objectless self-delight of spiritual realisation, *niyatam karma*. Buddhiyoga is fulfilled by Karma-yoga; the Yoga of the self-liberating intelligent will finds its full meaning by the Yoga of desireless works. Thus the Gita founds its teaching of the necessity of desireless works, *niṣkāma karma*, and unites the subjective practice of the Sankhyas – rejecting their merely physical rule – with the practice of Yoga.

But still there is an essential difficulty unsolved. How, our nature being what it is and desire the common principle of its action, is it possible to institute a really desireless action? For what we call ordinarily disinterested action is not really desireless; it is simply replacement of certain smaller personal interests by other large desires which have only the appearance of being impersonal, virtue, country, mankind. How is true desirelessness to be brought about? By doing all works with sacrifice as the only object, is the reply of the divine Teacher.

[2] We cannot accept the current interpretation of *niyatam karma* as if it meant fixed and formal works and were equivalent to the Vedic *nitya-karma*, the regular works of sacrifice, ceremonial and the daily rule of Vedic living. Surely, *niyata*, simply takes up the *niyamya* of the last verse. Not formal works fixed by an external rule, but desireless works controlled by the liberated *buddhi*, is the Gita's teaching.

[3] It is evident that all works and not merely sacrifice and social duties can be done in this spirit; any action may be done either from the ego-

सहयज्ञाः प्रजाः सृष्ट्वा पुरोवाच प्रजापतिः ।
अनेन प्रसविष्यध्वमेष वोऽस्त्विष्टकामधुक् ॥१०॥

10. With sacrifice the Lord of creatures of old created creatures and said, By this shall you bring forth (fruits or offspring), let this be your milker of desires.

देवान् भावयतानेन ते देवा भावयन्तु वः ।
परस्परं भावयन्तः श्रेयः परमवाप्स्यथ ॥११॥

11. Foster by this the gods and let the gods foster you; fostering each other, you shall attain to the supreme good.

इष्टान् भोगान् हि वो देवा दास्यन्ते यज्ञभाविताः ।
तैर्दत्तानप्रदायैभ्यो यो भुङ्क्ते स्तेन एव सः ॥१२॥

12. Fostered by sacrifice the gods shall give you desired enjoyments; who enjoys their given enjoyments and has not given to them, he is a thief.

यज्ञशिष्टाशिनः सन्तो मुच्यन्ते सर्वकिल्बिषैः ।
भुञ्जते ते त्वघं पापा ये पचन्त्यात्मकारणात् ॥१३॥

sense narrow or enlarged or for the sake of the Divine. All being and all action of Prakriti exist only for the sake of the Divine; from that it proceeds, by that it endures, to that it is directed. All life, all world-existence is the sacrifice offered by Nature to the Purusha, the one and secret soul in Nature, in whom all her workings take place; but its real sense is obscured in us by ego, by desire, by our limited, active, multiple personality. So long as we are dominated by the ego-sense we cannot perceive or act in the spirit of this truth, but act for the satisfaction of the ego and in the spirit of the ego, otherwise than for sacrifice. Egoism is the knot of the bondage. By acting Godwards, without any thought of ego, we loosen this knot and finally arrive at freedom.

The Gita's theory of sacrifice is stated in two separate passages; one we find here in the third chapter, another in the fourth; the first gives it in language which might, taken by itself, seem to be speaking only of the ceremonial sacrifice; the second interpreting that into the sense of a large philosophical symbolism, transforms at once its whole significance and raises it to a plane of high psychological and spiritual truth.

13. The good who eat what is left from the sacrifice, are released from all sin; but evil are they and enjoy sin who cook (the food) for their own sake.

अन्नाद्भवन्ति भूतानि पर्जन्यादन्नसम्भवः ।
यज्ञाद्भवति पर्जन्यो यज्ञः कर्मसमुद्भवः ॥१४॥
कर्म ब्रह्मोद्भवं विद्धि ब्रह्माक्षरसमुद्भवम् ।
तस्मात्सर्वगतं ब्रह्म नित्यं यज्ञे प्रतिष्ठितम् ॥१५॥

14-15. From food creatures come into being, from rain is the birth of food, from sacrifice comes into being the rain, sacrifice is born of work; work know to be born of Brahman, Brahman is born of the Immutable; therefore is the all-pervading Brahman established in the sacrifice.

एवं प्रवर्तितं चक्रं नानुवर्तयतीह यः ।
अघायुरिन्द्रियारामो मोघं पार्थ स जीवति ॥१६॥

16. He who follows not here the wheel thus set in movement, evil is his being, sensual is his delight, in vain, O Partha, that man lives[1].

---

[1] In the Gita there is very little that is merely local or temporal and its spirit is so large, profound and universal that even this little can easily be universalised without the sense of the teaching suffering any diminution or violation; rather by giving an ampler scope to it than belonged to the country and epoch, the teaching gains in depth, truth and power. Often indeed the Gita itself suggests the wider scope that can in this way be given to an idea in itself local or limited. Thus it dwells on the ancient Indian system and idea of sacrifice as an interchange between gods and men, – a system and idea which have long been practically obsolete in India itself and are no longer real to the general human mind; but we find here a sense so entirely subtle, figurative and symbolic given to the word "sacrifice" and the conception of the gods is so little local or mythological, so entirely cosmic and philosophical that we can easily accept both as expressive of a practical fact of psychology and general law of Nature and so apply them to the modern conceptions of interchange between life and life and of ethical sacrifice and self-giving as to widen and deepen these and cast over them a more spiritual aspect and the light of a profounder and more far-reaching Truth.

यस्त्वात्मरतिरेव स्यादात्मतृप्तश्च मानवः ।
आत्मन्येव च सन्तुष्टस्तस्य कार्यं न विद्यते ॥१७॥

17. But the man whose delight is in the Self and who is satisfied with the enjoyment of the Self and in the Self he is content, for him there exists no work that needs to be done.

नैव तस्य कृतेनार्थो नाकृतेनेह कश्चन ।
न चास्य सर्वभूतेषु कश्चिदर्थव्यपाश्रयः ॥१८॥

18. He has no object here to be gained by action done and none to be gained by action undone; he has no dependence on all these existences for any object to be gained[1].

तस्मादसक्तः सततं कार्यं कर्म समाचर ।
असक्तो ह्याचरन् कर्म परमाप्नोति पूरुषः ॥१९॥

19. Therefore without attachment perform ever the work that is to be done (done for the sake of the world, *lokasaṅgraha*, as is made clear immediately afterward); for by

---

Having thus stated the necessity of sacrifice, Krishna proceeds to state the superiority of the spiritual man to works.

[1] Here are the two ideals, Vedist and Vedantist, standing as if in all their sharp original separation and opposition, on one side the active ideal of acquiring enjoyments here and the highest good beyond by sacrifice and the mutual dependence of the human being and the divine powers and on the other, facing it, the austerer ideal of the liberated man who, independent in the Spirit, has nothing to do with enjoyment or works or the human or the divine worlds, but exists only in the peace of the supreme Self, joys only in the calm joy of the Brahman. The next verses create a ground for the reconciliation between the two extremes; the secret is not inaction as soon as one turns towards the higher truth, but desireless action both before and after it is reached. The liberated man has nothing to gain by action, but nothing also to gain by inaction, and it is not at all for any personal object that he has to make his choice.

doing work without attachment man attains to the highest[1].

कर्मणैव हि संसिद्धिमास्थिता जनकादयः ।
लोकसंग्रहमेवापि संपश्यन् कर्तुमर्हसि ॥२०॥

20. It was even by works[2] that Janaka and the rest attained to perfection. Thou shouldst do works regarding also the holding together of the peoples.

यद्यदाचरति श्रेष्ठस्तत्तदेवेतरो जनः ।
स यत्प्रमाणं कुरुते लोकस्तदनुवर्तते ॥२१॥

[1] It is true that works and sacrifice are a means of arriving at the highest good; but there are three kinds of works, that done without sacrifice for personal enjoyment which is entirely selfish and egoistic and misses the true law and aim and utility of life, *mogham pārtha sa jīvati*, that done with desire, but with sacrifice and the enjoyment only as a result of sacrifice and therefore to that extent consecrated and sanctified, and that done without desire or attachment of any kind. It is the last which brings the soul of man to the highest.

[2] There are few more important passages in the Gita than these seven striking couplets. But let us clearly understand that they must not be interpreted, as the modern pragmatic tendency concerned much more with the present affairs of the world than with any high and far-off spiritual possibility seeks to interpret them, as no more than a philosophical and religious justification of social service, patriotic, cosmopolitan and humanitarian effort and attachment to the hundred eager social schemes and dreams which attract the modern intellect. It is not the rule of a large moral and intellectual altruism which is here announced, but that of a spiritual unity with God and with this world of beings who dwell in Him and in whom He dwells. It is not an injunction to subordinate the individual to society and humanity or immolate egoism on the altar of the human collectivity, but to fulfil the individual in God and to sacrifice the ego on the one true altar of the all-embracing Divinity. The Gita moves on a plane of ideas and experiences higher than those of the modern mind which is at the stage indeed of a struggle to shake off the coils of egoism, but is still mundane in its outlook and intellectual and moral rather than spiritual in its temperament. Patriotism, cosmopolitanism, service of society, collectivism, humanitarianism, the ideal or religion of humanity are admirable aids towards our escape from our primary condition of individual, family, social, national egoism into a secondary stage in which the individual realises, as far as it can be done on

21. Whatsoever the Best[1] doeth, that the lower kind of man puts into practice; the standard he creates, the people follow.

न मे पार्थास्ति कर्तव्यं त्रिषु लोकेषु किञ्चन ।
नानवाप्तमवाप्तव्यं वर्त एव च कर्मणि ॥२२॥

the intellectual, moral and emotional level, – on that level he cannot do it entirely in the right and perfect way, the way of the integral truth of his being, – the oneness of his existence with the existence of other beings. But the thought of the Gita reaches beyond to a tertiary condition of our developing self-consciousness towards which the secondary is only a partial stage of advance.

[1] The rule given here by the Gita is the rule for the master man, the superman, the divinised human being, the Best, not in the sense of any Nietzschean, any one-sided and lop-sided, any Olympian, Apollonian or Dionysian, any angelic or demoniac supermanhood, but in that of the man whose whole personality has been offered up into the being, nature and consciousness of the one transcendent and universal Divinity and by loss of the smaller self has found its greater self, has been divinised.

To exalt oneself out of the lower imperfect Prakriti, *traigunyamayī māyā*, into unity with the divine being, consciousness and nature*, *mādhavam agataḥ*, is the object of the Yoga. But when this object is fulfilled, when the man is in the Brahmic status and sees no longer with the false egoistic vision himself and the world, but sees all beings in the Self, in God, and the Self in all beings, God in all beings, what shall be the action, – since action there still is, – which results from that seeing, and what shall be the cosmic or individual motive of all his works? It is the question of Arjuna (Ch. II. Sl. 54) but answered from a standpoint other than that from which Arjuna had put it. The motive cannot be personal desire on the intellectual, moral, emotional level, for that has been abandoned, – even the moral motive has been abandoned, since the liberated man has passed beyond the lower distinction of sin and virtue, lives in a glorified purity beyond good and evil. It cannot be the spiritual call to his perfect self-development by means of disinterested works, for the call has been answered, the development is perfect and fulfilled. His motive of action can only be the holding together of the peoples, *cikīrṣur lokasaṅgraham*. This great march of the peoples towards a far-off divine ideal has to be held together, prevented from falling into the bewilderment, confusion and utter discord of the understanding which would lead to dissolution and destruction and to which the world moving forward in the night or

(* *Sāyujya*, *sālokya* and *sādṛśya* or *sādharmya*. *Sādharmya* is becoming of one law of being and action with the Divine.)

22. O Son of Pritha, I¹ have no work that I need to do in all the three worlds², I have nothing that I have not gained and have yet to gain, and I abide verily in the paths of action (*varta eva ca karmāṇi, – eva* implying, I abide in it and do not leave it as the sannyasin thinks himself bound to abandon works).

यदि ह्यहं न वर्तेयं जातु कर्मण्यतन्द्रितः ।
मम वर्त्मानुवर्तन्ते मनुष्याः पार्थ सर्वशः ॥२३॥
उत्सीदेयुरिमे लोका न कुर्यां कर्म चेदहम् ।
सङ्करस्य च कर्ता स्यामुपहन्यामिमाः प्रजाः ॥२४॥

23-24. For if I did not abide sleeplessly in the paths of action, men follow in every way my path, these peoples would sink to destruction if I did not work and I should be the creator of confusion and slay these creatures.

---

dark twilight of ignorance would be too easily prone if it were not held together, conducted, kept to the great lines of its discipline by the illumination, by the strength, by the rule and example, by the visible standard and the invisible influence of its Best. But the divinised man is the Best in no ordinary sense of the word and his influence, his example must have a power which that of no ordinary superior man can exercise. In order to indicate more perfectly his meaning, the divine Teacher, the Avatar gives his own example, his own standard to Arjuna.

¹ The giving of the example of God himself to the liberated man is profoundly significant; for it reveals the whole basis of the Gita's philosophy of divine works. The liberated man is he who has exalted himself into the divine nature and according to that divine nature must be his actions. Neither the dynamism of the kinetic man nor the actionless light of the ascetic or quietist, neither the vehement personality of the man of action nor the indifferent impersonality of the philosophic sage is the complete divine ideal. These are the two conflicting standards of the man of this world and the ascetic or the quietist philosopher, one immersed in the action of the Kshara, the other striving to dwell entirely in the peace of the Akshara; but the complete divine ideal proceeds from the nature of the Purushottama which transcends this conflict and reconciles all divine possibilities.

² Physical, vital, mental (including the higher mental worlds).

सक्ताः कर्मण्यविद्वांसो यथा कुर्वन्ति भारत ।
कुर्याद्विद्वांस्तथाऽसक्तश्चिकीर्षुर्लोकसंग्रहम् ॥२५॥

25. As those who know not act with attachment to the action, he who knows should act without attachment, having for his motive to hold together the peoples.

न बुद्धिभेदं जनयेदज्ञानां कर्मसङ्गिनाम् ।
जोषयेत्सर्वकर्माणि विद्वान् युक्तः समाचरन् ॥२६॥

26. He should not create a division of their understanding in the ignorant who are attached to their works; he should set them to all[1] actions, doing them himself with knowledge and in Yoga.

---

[1] The whole range of human works must be that in which the God-knower shall move. All individual, all social action, all the works of the intellect, the heart and the body are still his, not any longer for his own separate sake, but for the sake of God in the world, of God in all beings and that all those beings may move forward, as he has moved, by the path of works towards the discovery of the Divine in themselves. Outwardly his actions may not seem to differ essentially from theirs; battle and rule as well as teaching and thought, all the various commerce of man with man may fall in his range; but the spirit in which he does them must be very different, and it is that spirit which by its influence shall be the great attraction drawing men upwards to his own level, the great lever lifting the mass of men higher in their ascent.

II. THE DETERMINISM OF NATURE

(The passages in which the Gita lays stress on the subjection of the ego-soul to Nature, have by some been understood as the enunciation of an absolute and a mechanical determinism which leaves no room for any freedom within the cosmic existence. Certainly, the language it uses is emphatic and seems very absolute. But we must take, here as elsewhere, the thought of the Gita as a whole and not force its affirmations in their solitary sense quite detached from each other.

We have always to keep in mind the two great doctrines which stand behind all the Gita's teachings with regard to the soul and Nature, – the Sankhya truth of the Purusha and Prakriti corrected and completed by the Vedantic truth of the threefold Purusha and the double Prakriti of which the lower form is the Maya of the three gunas and the higher is the divine nature and the true soul nature. This is the key which reconciles and explains what we might have otherwise to leave as contradictions and inconsistencies. There are, in fact, different planes of our conscious existence, and what is practical truth on one plane ceases to be true, because it assumes a quite different appearance, as soon as we rise to a higher level from which we can see things more in the whole.)

प्रकृतेः क्रियमाणानि गुणैः कर्माणि सर्वशः ।
अहङ्कारविमूढात्मा कर्ताहमिति मन्यते ॥२७॥

27. While the actions are being entirely done by the modes of Nature, he whose self is bewildered by egoism thinks that it is his "I" which is doing them.

तत्त्ववित्तु महाबाहो गुणकर्मविभागयोः ।
गुणा गुणेषु वर्तन्त इति मत्वा न सज्जते ॥२८॥

28. But one, O mighty-armed, who knows the true

principles of the divisions of the modes and of works, realises that it is the modes which are acting and reacting on each other and is not caught in them by attachment.

प्रकृतेर्गुणसंमूढाः सज्जन्ते गुणकर्मसु ।
तान्कृत्स्नविदो मन्दान् कृत्स्नवित्र विचालयेत् ॥२९॥

29. Those who are bewildered by the modes, not knowers of the whole, let not the knower of the whole disturb in their mental standpoint[1].

मयि सर्वाणि कर्माणि संन्यस्याध्यात्मचेतसा ।
निराशीर्निर्ममो भूत्वा युद्ध्यस्व विगतज्वरः ॥३०॥

30. Giving up thy works to Me, with thy consciousness founded in the Self, free from desire and egoism, fight delivered from the fever of thy soul.

[1] Here there is the clear distinction between two levels of consciousness, two standpoints of action, that of the soul caught in the web of its egoistic nature and doing works with the idea, but not the reality of free will, under the impulsion of Nature, and that of the soul delivered from its identification with the ego, observing, sanctioning and governing the works of Nature from above her.

We speak of the soul being subject to Nature; but, on the other hand, the Gita in distinguishing the properties of the soul and Nature affirms that while Nature is the executrix, the soul is always the lord, *īśvara*. It speaks here of the self being bewildered by egoism, but the real Self to the Vedantin is the divine, eternally free and self-aware. What then is this self that is bewildered by Nature, this soul that is subject to her? The answer is that we are speaking here in the common parlance of our lower or mental view of things; we are speaking of the apparent self, or the apparent soul, not of the real self, not of the true Purusha. It is really the ego which is subject to Nature, inevitably, because it is itself part of Nature, one functioning of her machinery; but when the self-awareness in the mind-consciousness identifies itself with the ego, it creates the appearance of a lower self, an ego-self. And so too what we think of ordinarily as the soul is really the natural personality, not the true Person, the Purusha, but the desire-soul in us which is a reflection of the consciousness of the Purusha in the workings of Prakriti: it is, in fact, itself only an action of the three modes and therefore a part of Nature. Thus there are, we may say, two

THIRD CHAPTER 63

ये मे मतमिदं नित्यमनुतिष्ठन्ति मानवाः ।
श्रद्धावन्तोऽनसूयन्तो मुच्यन्ते तेऽपि कर्मभिः ॥३१॥
ये त्वेतदभ्यसूयन्तो नानुतिष्ठन्ति मे मतम् ।
सर्वज्ञानविमूढांस्तान् विद्धि नष्टानचेतसः ॥३२॥

31-32. Who, having faith and not trusting to the critical intelligence, constantly follow this teaching of mine, they too are released from (the bondage of) works. But those who find fault with my teaching and act not thereon, know

---

souls in us, the apparent or desire-soul, which changes with the mutations of the gunas and is entirely constituted and determined by them, and the free and eternal Purusha not limited by Nature and her gunas. We have two selves, the apparent self, which is only the ego, that mental centre in us which takes up this mutable action of Prakriti, this mutable personality, and which says "I am this personality, I am this natural being who am doing these works," – but the natural being is simply Nature, a composite of the gunas, – and the true self which is, indeed, the upholder, the possessor and the lord of Nature and figured in her, but is not itself the mutable natural personality. The way to be free must then be to get rid of the desires of this desire-soul and the false self-view of this ego.

This view of our being starts from the Sankhya analysis of the dual principle in our nature, Purusha and Prakriti. Purusha is inactive, *akartā*; Prakriti is active, *kartrī*: Purusha is the being full of the light of consciousness; Prakriti is the Nature, mechanical, reflecting all her works in the conscious witness, the Purusha. Prakriti works by the inequality of her three modes, gunas, in perpetual collision and intermixture and mutation with each other; and by her function of ego-mind she gets the Purusha to identify himself with all this working and so creates the sense of active, mutable, temporal personality in the silent eternity of the Self. But if this were all, then the only remedy would be to withdraw altogether the sanction, suffer or compel all our nature by this withdrawal to fall into a motionless equilibrium of the three gunas and so cease from all action. But this is precisely the remedy, – though it is undoubtedly a remedy, one which abolishes, we might say, the patient along with the disease, – which the Gita constantly discourages. Especially, to resort to a tamasic inaction is just what the ignorant will do if this truth is thrust upon them; the discriminating mind in them will fall into a false division, a false opposition, *buddhibheda*; therefore the Gita says "fight with all the fever of thy soul passed away from thee."

them to be of unripe mind, bewildered in all knowledge and fated to be destroyed[1].

सदृशं चेष्टते स्वस्याः प्रकृतेर्ज्ञानवानपि ।
प्रकृतिं यान्ति भूतानि निग्रहः किं करिष्यति ॥३३॥

33. All existences follow their nature and what shall coercing[2] it avail? Even the man of knowledge acts according to his own nature.

---

[1] In fact, these higher truths can only be helpful because there only they are true to experience and can be lived, on a higher and vaster plane of consciousness and being. To view these truths from below is to mis-see, misunderstand and probably to misuse them. It is a higher truth that the distinction of good and evil is indeed a practical fact and law valid for the egoistic human life which is the stage of transition from the animal to the divine, but on a higher plane we rise beyond good and evil, are above their duality even as the Godhead is above it. But the unripe mind, seizing on this truth without rising from the lower consciousness where it is not practically valid, will simply make it a convenient excuse for indulging its Asuric propensities, denying the distinction between good and evil altogether and falling by self-indulgence deeper into the morass of perdition, *sarvajñānavimūḍhānstān viddhi naṣṭānacetasaḥ*. So too with this truth of the determinism of Nature; it will be mis-seen and misused, as those misuse it who declare that a man is what his nature has made him and cannot do otherwise than as his nature compels him. It is true in a sense, but not in the sense which is attached to it, not in the sense that the ego-self can claim irresponsibility and impunity for itself in its works; for it has will and it has desire and so long as it acts according to its will and desire, even though that be its nature, it must bear the reactions of its Karma. It is in a net, if you will, a snare which may well seem perplexing, illogical, unjust, terrible to its present experience, to its limited self-knowledge, but a snare of its own choice, a net of its own weaving.

[2] This seems, if we take it by itself, a hopelessly absolute assertion of the omnipotence of Nature over the soul. And on this it founds the injunction to follow faithfully in our action the law of our nature. What is precisely meant by this *svadharma* we have to wait to see until we get to the more elaborate disquisition in the closing chapter about Purusha and Prakriti and the gunas; but certainly it does not mean that we are to follow any impulse, even though evil, which what we call our nature dictates to

इन्द्रियस्येन्द्रियस्यार्थे रागद्वेषौ व्यवस्थितौ ।
तयोर्न वशमागच्छेत्तौ ह्यस्य परिपन्थिनौ ॥३४॥

34. In the object of this or that sense liking and disliking are set in ambush; fall not into their power, for they are the besetters of the soul in its path.

श्रेयान् स्वधर्मो विगुणः परधर्मात् स्वनुष्ठितात् ।
स्वधर्मे निधनं श्रेयः परधर्मो भयावहः ॥३५॥

35. Better is one's own law of works, *svadharma*[1], though in itself faulty, than an alien law well wrought out; death in one's own law of being is better, perilous is it to follow an alien law.

---

us. For between these two verses the Gita throws in this further injunction, "fall not into the power of liking and disliking." There is therefore a distinction to be made between what is essential in the nature, its native and inevitable action, which it avails not at all to repress, suppress, coerce, and what is accidental to it, its wanderings, confusions, perversions, over which we must certainly get control. There is a distinction implied too between coercion and suppression, *nigraha*, and control with right use and right guidance, *samyama*. The former is a violence done to the nature by the will, which in the end depresses the natural powers of the being, *ātmanam avasādayet*; the latter is the control of the lower by the higher self, which successfully gives to those powers their right action and their maximum efficiency, – *yogaḥ karmasu kauśalam*.

[1] Man is not like the tiger or the fire or the storm; he cannot kill and say as a sufficient justification, "I am acting according to my nature," and he cannot do it, because he has not the nature and not, therefore, the law of action, *svadharma*, of the tiger, storm or fire. He has a conscious intelligent will, a *buddhi*, and to that he must refer his actions. If he does not do so, if he acts blindly according to his impulses and passions, then the law of his being is not rightly worked out, *svadharmaḥ su-anuṣṭhitaḥ*, he has not acted according to the full measure of his humanity, but even as might the animal. Man knows more or less imperfectly that he has to govern his rajasic and tamasic by his sattwic nature and that thither tends the perfection of his normal humanity. The Teacher makes this clear in answering the following practical question of Arjuna.

अर्जुन उवाच —
अथ केन प्रयुक्तोऽयं पापं चरति पूरुषः ।
अनिच्छन्नपि वार्ष्णेय बलादिव नियोजितः ॥३६॥

36. Arjuna said: But (if there is no fault in following our Nature) what is this in us that drives a man to sin, as if by force, even against his own struggling will, O Varshneya?

श्रीभगवान् उवाच —
काम एष क्रोध एष रजोगुणसमुद्भवः ।
महाशनो महापाप्मा विद्ध्येनमिह वैरिणम् ॥३७॥

37. The Blessed Lord said: This is desire[1] and its companion wrath, children of rajas, all-devouring, all-polluting, know thou this as the soul's great enemy (which has to be slain).

धूमेनाव्रियते वह्निर्यथादर्शो मलेन च ।
यथोल्बेनावृतो गर्भस्तथा तेनेदमावृतम् ॥३८॥

38. As a fire is covered over by smoke, as a mirror by dust, as an embryo is wrapped by the amnion, so this (knowledge) is enveloped by it.

[1] The kinetic man is not satisfied with any ideal which does not depend upon the fulfilment of this cosmic nature, this play of the three qualities of that nature, this human activity of mind and heart and body. The highest fulfilment of that activity, he might say, is my idea of human perfection, of the divine possibility in man. Each being is bound to his nature and within it he must seek for his perfection. According to our human nature must be our human perfection; and each man must strive for it according to the line of his personality, his *svadharma*, but in life, in action, not outside life and action. Yes, there is a truth in that, replies the Gita; the fulfilment of God in man, the play of the Divine in life is part of the ideal perfection. But if you seek it only in the external, in life, in the principle of action, you will never find it; for you will then not only act according to your nature, which is in itself a rule of perfection, but you will be – and this is a rule of the imperfection – eternally subject to its modes, its dualities of liking and dislike, pain and pleasure and especially to the rajasic mode with its principle of desire and its snare of wrath and grief and longing.

आवृतं ज्ञानमेतेन ज्ञानिनो नित्यवैरिणा ।
कामरूपेण कौन्तेय दुष्पूरेणानलेन च ॥३९॥

39. Enveloped is knowledge, O Kaunteya, by this eternal enemy of knowledge in the form of desire which is an insatiable fire.

इन्द्रियाणि मनो बुद्धिरस्याधिष्ठानमुच्यते ।
एतैर्विमोहयत्येष ज्ञानमावृत्य देहिनम् ॥४०॥

40. The senses, mind and intellect are its seat[1]; enveloping knowledge by these it bewilders the embodied soul.

तस्मात्त्वमिन्द्रियाण्यादौ नियम्य भरतर्षभ ।
पाप्मानं प्रजहि ह्येनं ज्ञानविज्ञाननाशनम् ॥४१॥

41. Therefore, O Best of the Bharatas, controlling first the senses, do thou slay this thing of sin destructive of knowledge (in order to live in the calm, clear, luminous truth of the Spirit).

इन्द्रियाणि पराण्याहुरिन्द्रियेभ्यः परं मनः ।
मनसस्तु परा बुद्धिर्यो बुद्धेः परतस्तु सः ॥४२॥

42. Supreme, they say, (beyond their objects) are the senses, supreme over the senses the mind, supreme over the mind the intelligent will: that which is supreme over the intelligent will, is he (the Purusha)[2].

---

[1] And yet it is within the sense, mind and intellect, this play of the lower nature that you would limit your search for perfection! The effort is vain. The kinetic side of your nature must first seek to add to itself the quietistic; you must uplift yourself beyond this lower nature to that which is above the three gunas, that which is founded in the highest principle, in the soul. Only when you have attained to peace of soul, can you become capable of a free and divine action.

[2] We must remember the psychological order of the Sankhya which the Gita accepts. First in order come Buddhi, discriminative or determinative power evolving out of Nature-force, and its subordinate power of

एवं बुद्धेः परं बुद्ध्वा संस्तभ्यात्मानमात्मना ।
जहि शत्रुं महाबाहो कामरूपं दुरासदम् ॥४३॥

43. Thus awakening by the understanding to the Highest[1] which is beyond even the discerning mind, putting force on the self by the self to make it firm and still, slay thou, O mighty-armed, this enemy in the form of desire, who is so hard to assail.

इति श्रीमद्भगवद्गीतासूपनिषत्सु ब्रह्मविद्यायां योगशास्त्रे श्रीकृष्णार्जुनसंवादे
कर्मयोगो नाम तृतीयोऽध्यायः ।

---

self-discriminative ego. Then as a secondary evolution there arises out of these the power which seizes the discriminations of objects, sense-mind or Manas. As a tertiary evolution out of sense-mind we have the specialising organic senses, ten in number, five of perception, five of action. In the evolution of the soul back from Prakriti towards Purusha, the reverse order has to be taken to the original Nature-evolution, and that is how the Upanishads and the Gita following and almost quoting the Upanishads state the ascending order of our subjective powers.

[1] The Akshara is the self higher than the buddhi – it exceeds even that highest subjective principle of Nature in our being, the liberating intelligence, through which man, returning beyond his restless mobile mental to his calm eternal spiritual self, is at last free from the persistence of birth and the long chain of action, of Karma. Therefore, says the Gita, it is this Purusha, this supreme cause of our subjective life which we have to understand and become aware of by the intelligence; in that we have to fix our will.

Fourth Chapter

I. THE POSSIBILITY AND PURPOSE OF AVATARHOOD

श्रीभगवान् उवाच —
इमं विवस्वते योगं प्रोक्तवानहमव्ययम् ।
विवस्वान् मनवे प्राह मनुरिक्ष्वाकवेऽब्रवीत् ॥१॥

1. The Blessed Lord said: This imperishable Yoga[1] I gave to Vivasvan (the Sun-God), Vivasvan gave it to Manu (the father of men), Manu gave it to Ikshvaku (head of the Solar line).

एवं परम्पराप्राप्तमिमं राजर्षयो विदुः ।
स कालेनेह महता योगो नष्टः परन्तप ॥२॥

2. And so it came down from royal sage to royal sage till it was lost in the great lapse of Time, O Parantapa.

स एवायं मया तेऽद्य योगः प्रोक्तः पुरातनः ।
भक्तोऽसि मे सखा चेति रहस्यं ह्येतदुत्तमम् ॥३॥

3. This same ancient and original Yoga has been today declared to thee by Me, for thou art My devotee and My friend; this is the highest secret.[2]

---

[1] In speaking of this Yoga in which action and knowledge become one, the Yoga of the sacrifice of works with knowledge, in which works are fulfilled in knowledge, knowledge supports, changes and enlightens works and both are offered to the Purushottama, the supreme Divinity who becomes manifest within us as Narayana, Lord of all our being and action seated secret in our hearts for ever, who becomes manifest even in the human form as the Avatar, the divine birth taking possession of our humanity, Krishna declares in passing that this was the ancient and original Yoga which he gave to Vivasvan and is now renewed for Arjuna, because he is the lover and devotee, friend and comrade of the Avatar.

[2] It is superior to all other forms of Yoga, because those others lead to the impersonal Brahman or to a personal Deity, to a liberation in

अर्जुन उवाच —
अपरं भवतो जन्म परं जन्म विवस्वतः ।
कथमेतद्विजानीयां त्वमादौ प्रोक्तवानिति ॥४॥

4. Arjuna said: The Sun-God[1] was one of the first-born of beings (ancestor of the solar dynasty) and Thou art only now born into the world; how am I to comprehend that Thou declaredst it to him in the beginning?

श्रीभगवान् उवाच —
बहूनि मे व्यतीतानि जन्मानि तव चार्जुन ।
तान्यहं वेद सर्वाणि न त्वं वेत्थ परन्तप ॥५॥

5. The Blessed Lord said: Many are my lives that are past, and thine also, O Arjuna; all of them I know, but thou knowest not, O scourge of the foe.

अजोऽपि सन्नव्ययात्मा भूतानामीश्वरोऽपि सन् ।
प्रकृतिं स्वामधिष्ठाय सम्भवाम्यात्ममायया ॥६॥

6. Though I am the unborn, though I am imperishable in my self-existence, though I am the Lord of all existences, yet I stand upon my own Nature and I come into birth by my self-Maya.[2]

---

actionless knowledge or a liberation in absorbed beatitude, but this gives the highest secret and the whole secret; it brings us to divine peace and divine works, to divine knowledge, action and ecstasy unified in a perfect freedom; it unites into itself all the Yogic paths as the highest being of the Divine reconciles and makes one in itself all the different and even contrary powers and principles of its manifested being. Therefore this Yoga of the Gita is not, as some contend, only the Karmayoga, one and the lowest, according to them, of the three paths, but a highest Yoga synthetic and integral directing Godward all the powers of our being.

[1] The practical intelligence of Arjuna is baffled by Krishna's assertion that it was he who in ancient times revealed to Vivasvan this Yoga, since lost, which he is now again revealing to Arjuna, and by his demand for an explanation he provokes the famous and oft-quoted statement of Avatarhood and its mundane purpose.

[2] To the modern mind Avatarhood is one of the most difficult to accept or to understand of all the ideas that are streaming in from the East

यदा यदा हि धर्मस्य ग्लानिर्भवति भारत ।
अभ्युत्थानमधर्मस्य तदात्मानं सृजाम्यहम् ॥७॥

7. Whensoever there is the fading of the Dharma and the uprising of unrighteousness, then I loose myself forth into birth.

परित्राणाय साधूनां विनाशाय च दुष्कृताम् ।
धर्मसंस्थापनार्थाय सम्भवामि युगे युगे ॥८॥

---

upon the rationalised human consciousness. The rationalist objects that if God exists, he is extracosmic or supracosmic and does not intervene in the affairs of the world, but allows them to be governed by a fixed machinery of law; he is pure Spirit and cannot put on a body, infinite and cannot be finite as the human being is finite, the ever unborn creator and cannot be the creature born into the world, – these things are impossible even to his absolute omnipotence. These objections, so formidable at first sight to the reason, seem to have been present to the mind of the Teacher in the Gita when he says that although the Divine is unborn, imperishable in his self-existence, the Lord of all beings, yet he assumes birth by a supreme resort to the action of his Nature and by force of his self-Maya; that he whom the deluded despise because lodged in a human body, is verily in his supreme being the Lord of all; that he is in the action of the divine consciousness the creator of the fourfold Law and the doer of the works of the world and at the same time in the silence of the divine consciousness the impartial witness of the works of his own Nature, – for he is always beyond both the silence and the action, the supreme Purushottama. And the Gita is able to meet all these oppositions and to reconcile all these contraries because it starts from the Vedantic view of existence, of God and the universe. For all here is God, is the Spirit or Self-existence, is Brahman, *ekamevādvitīyam*, – there is nothing else, nothing other and different from it and there can be nothing else, can be nothing other and different from it. Far from the unborn being unable to assume birth, all beings are even in their individuality unborn spirits, eternal without beginning or end, and in their essential existence and their universality all are the one unborn Spirit of whom birth and death are only a phenomenon of the assumption and change of forms. The assumption of imperfection by the perfect is the whole mystic phenomenon of the universe; but the imperfection appears in the form and action of the mind or body assumed, subsists in the phenomenon, – in that which assumes it there is no imperfection, even as in the Sun which illumines all there is no defect of light or of vision, but only in the capacities of the individual organ of vision.

8. For the deliverance of the good, for the destruction of the evil-doers, for the enthroning of the Right, I am born from age to age.

जन्म कर्म च मे दिव्यमेवं यो वेत्ति तत्त्वतः ।
त्यक्त्वा देहं पुनर्जन्म नैति मामेति सोऽर्जुन ॥९॥

9. He who knoweth thus in its right principles my divine birth[1] and my divine work, when he abandons his body, comes not to rebirth, he comes to Me, O Arjuna.

It is notable that with a slight but important variation of language the Gita describes in the same way both the action of the Divine in bringing about the ordinary birth of creatures and his action in his birth as the Avatar. "Leaning upon my own Nature, *prakṛtim svāmadhiṣṭāya*" it will say later "I loose forth variously, *visṛjami*, this multitude of creatures helplessly subject owing to the control of Prakriti, *avaśam prakṛter vaśāt*." "Standing upon my own Nature" it says here, "I am born by my self-Maya, *prakṛtim svāmadhiṣṭāya... ātmamāyayā* I loose forth myself, *ātmanām sṛjāmi*." The action implied in the word *avaṣṭabhya* is a forceful downward pressure by which the object controlled is overcome, oppressed, blocked or limited in its movement or working and becomes helplessly subject to the controlling power, *avaśam vaśāt*: Nature in this action becomes mechanical and its multitude of creatures are held helpless in the mechanism, not lords of their own action. On the contrary the action implied in the word *adhiṣṭāya* is a dwelling in, but also a standing upon and over the Nature, a conscious control and government by the indwelling Godhead, *adhiṣṭhātrī devatā*, in which the Purusha is not helplessly driven by the Prakriti through ignorance, but rather the Prakriti is full of the light and the will of the Purusha.

[1] The language of the Gita shows that the divine birth is that of the conscious Godhead in our humanity and essentially the opposite of the ordinary birth even though the same means are used, because it is not the birth into the Ignorance, but the birth of the knowledge, not a physical phenomenon, but a soul-birth. It is the Soul's coming into birth as the self-existent Being controlling consciously its becoming and not lost to self-knowledge in the cloud of the Ignorance. It is the Soul born into the body as Lord of Nature, standing above and operating in her freely by its will, not entangled and helplessly driven round and round in the mechanism; for it works in the Knowledge and not, as most do, in the Ignorance. It is the secret Soul in all coming forward from its governing secrecy behind the veil to possess wholly in a human type, but as the Divine, the birth

FOURTH CHAPTER

वीतरागभयक्रोधा मन्मया मामुपाश्रिताः ।
बहवो ज्ञानतपसा पूता मद्भावमागताः ॥१०॥

10. Delivered from liking and fear and wrath, full of me, taking refuge in me, many purified by austerity of knowledge have arrived at my nature of being[1] (*madbhāvam*, the divine nature of the Purushottama).

---

which ordinarily it possesses only from behind the veil as the Ishwara while the outward consciousness in front of the veil is rather possessed than in possession because there it is a partially conscious being, the Jiva lost to self-knowledge and bound in its works through a phenomenal subjection to Nature. The Avatar* therefore is a direct manifestation in humanity by Krishna, the Divine Soul, of that divine condition of being to which Arjuna, the human soul, the type of a highest human being, a Vibhuti, is called upon by the Teacher to arise, and to which he can only arise by climbing out of the ignorance and limitation of his ordinary humanity. It is the manifestation from above of that which we have to develop from below; it is the descent of God into that divine birth of the human being into which we mortal creatures must climb; it is the attracting divine example given by God to man in the very type and form and perfected model of our human existence.

(* The word Avatar means a descent; it is a coming down of the Divine below the line which divides the divine from the human world or status.)

[1] We have to remark carefully that the upholding of Dharma in the world is not the only object of the descent of the Avatar, the great mystery of the Divine manifest in humanity; for the upholding of the Dharma is not an all-sufficient object in itself, not the supreme possible aim for the manifestation of a Christ, a Krishna, a Buddha, but is only the general condition of a higher aim and a more supreme and divine utility. For there are two aspects of the divine birth; one is a descent, the birth of God in humanity, the Godhead manifesting itself in the human form and nature, the eternal Avatar; the other is an ascent, the birth of man into the Godhead, man rising into the divine nature and consciousness, *madbhāvamāgatāḥ*; it is the being born anew in a second birth of the soul. It is that new birth which Avatarhood and the upholding of the Dharma are intended to serve. If there were not this rising of man into the Godhead to be helped by the descent of God into humanity, Avatarhood for the sake of the Dharma would be an otiose phenomenon, since mere Right, mere justice or standards of virtue can always be upheld by the divine omnipotence through its ordinary means, by great men or great move-

ये यथा मां प्रपद्यन्ते तांस्तथैव भजाम्यहम् ।
मम वर्त्मानुवर्तन्ते मनुष्याः पार्थ सर्वशः ॥११॥

11. As men approach Me, so I accept them to My love (*bhajāmi*); men follow in every way my path, O son of Pritha.

काङ्क्षन्तः कर्मणां सिद्धिं यजन्त इह देवताः ।
क्षिप्रं हि मानुषे लोके सिद्धिर्भवति कर्मजा ॥१२॥

12. They who desire the fulfilment[1] of their works on earth sacrifice to the gods (various forms and personalities of the one Godhead); because the fulfilment that is born of works (of works without knowledge) is very swift and easy in the human world.

---

ments, by the life and work of sages and kings and religious teachers, without any actual incarnation. The Avatar comes as the manifestation of the divine nature in the human nature, the apocalypse of its Christhood, Krishnahood, Buddhahood, in order that the human nature may by moulding its principle, thought, feeling, action, being on the lines of that Christhood, Krishnahood, Buddhahood transfigure itself into the divine. The law, the Dharma which the Avatar establishes is given for that purpose chiefly; the Christ, Krishna, Buddha stands in its centre as the gate, he makes through himself the way men shall follow. That is why each Incarnation holds before men his own example and declares of himself that he is the way and the gate; he declares too the oneness of his humanity with the divine being, declares that the Son of Man and the Father above from whom he has descended are one, that Krishna in the human body, *mānuṣīṁ tanum āśritam*, and the supreme Lord and Friend of all creatures are but two revelations of the same divine Purushottama, revealed there in his own being, revealed here in the type of humanity.

[1] The other, the divine self-fulfilment in man by the sacrifice with knowledge to the supreme Godhead, is much more difficult; its results belong to a higher plane of existence and they are less easily grasped. Men therefore have to follow the fourfold law of their nature and works and on this plane of mundane action they seek the Godhead through his various qualities.

FOURTH CHAPTER

चातुर्वर्ण्यं मया सृष्टं गुणकर्मविभागशः ।
तस्य कर्तारमपि मां विद्ध्यकर्तारमव्ययम् ॥१३॥

13. The fourfold[1] order was created by Me according to the divisions of quality and active function. Know Me for the doer of this (the fourfold law of human workings) who am yet the imperishable non-doer.

न मां कर्माणि लिम्पन्ति न मे कर्मफले स्पृहा ।
इति मां योऽभिजानाति कर्मभिर्न स बध्यते ॥१४॥

14. Works fix not themselves on Me, nor have I desire for the fruits of action; he who thus knoweth Me[2] is not bound by works.

---

[1] The Gita does not take the fourfold order in the narrow sense in which it is commonly understood, nor does it regard it as an eternal and universal social order (Chapter XVIII). The fourfold order of society is merely the concrete form of a spiritual truth which is itself independent of the form; it rests on the conception of right works as a rightly ordered expression of the nature of the individual being through whom the work is done, that nature assigning him his line and scope in life according to his inborn quality and his self-expressive function.

[2] The giving of the example of God himself to the liberated man is profoundly significant; for it reveals the whole basis of the Gita's philosophy of divine works. The liberated man is he who has exalted himself into the divine nature and according to that divine nature must be his actions. But what is the divine nature? It is not entirely and solely that of the Akshara, the immobile, inactive, impersonal self; for that by itself would lead the liberated man to actionless immobility. It is not characteristically that of the Kshara, the multitudinous, the personal, the Purusha self-subjected to Prakriti; for that by itself would lead him back into subjection to his personality and the lower nature and its qualities. It is the nature of the Purushottama who holds both these together and by his supreme divinity reconciles them in a divine reconciliation which is the highest secret of his being, *rahasyam hyetad uttamam*. He is not the doer of works in the personal sense of our action involved in Prakriti; for God works through his power, conscious nature, effective force, – Shakti, Maya, Prakriti – but yet above it, not involved in it, not subject to it, not unable to lift himself beyond the laws, workings, habits of action it

एवं ज्ञात्वा कृतं कर्म पूर्वैरपि मुमुक्षुभिः ।
कुरु कर्मैव तस्मात्त्वं पूर्वैः पूर्वतरं कृतम् ॥१५॥

15. So knowing was work done by the men of old who sought liberation; do therefore, thou also, work of that more ancient kind done by ancient men.¹

---

creates, not affected or bound by them, not unable to distinguish himself, as we are unable, from the workings of life, mind and body. He is the doer of works who acts not, *kartāram akartāram.*

¹ The inner fruit of the Avatar's coming is gained by those who learn from it the true nature of the divine birth and the divine works and who, growing full of him in their consciousness and taking refuge in him with their whole being, *manmaya mām upāśritāḥ,* purified by the realising force of their knowledge and delivered from the lower nature, attain to the divine being and divine nature, *madbhāvam.* The Avatar comes to reveal the divine nature in man above this lower nature and to show what are the divine works, free, unegoistic, disinterested, impersonal, universal, full of the divine light, the divine power and the divine love. He comes as the divine personality which shall fill the consciousness of the human being and replace the limited egoistic personality, so that it shall be liberated out of ego into infinity and universality, out of birth into immortality. He comes as the divine power and love which calls men to itself, so that they may take refuge in that and no longer in the insufficiency of their human wills and the strife of their human fear, wrath and passion, and liberated from all this unquiet and suffering may live in the calm and bliss of the Divine. Nor does it matter essentially in what form and name or putting forward what aspect of the Divine he comes; for in all ways, varying with their nature, men are following the path set to them by the Divine which will in the end lead them to him, and the aspect of him which suits their nature is that which they can best follow when he comes to lead them; in whatever way men accept, love and take joy in God, in that way God accepts, loves and takes joy in man.

II. THE DIVINE WORKER

(To attain to the divine birth, – a divinising new birth of the soul into a higher consciousness, – and to do divine works both as a means towards that before it is attained and as an expression of it after it is attained, is then all the *Karmayoga* of the Gita. The Gita does not try to define works by any outward signs through which they can be recognisable to an external gaze, measurable by the criticism of the world; it deliberately renounces even the ordinary ethical distinctions by which men seek to guide themselves in the light of the human reason. The signs by which it distinguishes divine works are all profoundly intimate and subjective; the stamp by which they are known is invisible, spiritual, supra-ethical. They are recognisable only by the light of the soul from which they come.)

किं कर्म किमकर्मेति कवयोऽप्यत्र मोहिताः ।
तत्ते कर्म प्रवक्ष्यामि यज्ज्ञात्वा मोक्ष्यसेऽशुभात् ॥१६॥

16. What is action and what is inaction, as to this even the sages are perplexed and deluded. I will declare to thee that action by the knowledge of which thou shalt be released from all ills.

कर्मणो ह्यपि बोद्धव्यं बोद्धव्यं च विकर्मणः ।
अकर्मणश्च बोद्धव्यं गहना कर्मणो गतिः ॥१७॥

17. One has to understand about action as well as to understand about wrong action and about inaction one has to understand; thick and tangled is the way of works.[1]

---

[1] Action in the world is like a deep forest, *gahana*, through which man goes stumbling as best he can, by the light of the ideas of his time, the standards of his personality, his environment, or rather of many times, many personalities, layers of thought and ethics from many social stages all inextricably confused together, temporal and conventional amidst all their claim to absoluteness and immutable truth, empirical and irrational

कर्मण्यकर्म यः पश्येदकर्मणि च कर्म यः ।
स बुद्धिमान् मनुष्येषु स युक्तः कृत्स्नकर्मकृत् ॥१८॥

18. He who in action can see inaction and can see action still continuing in cessation from works, is the man of true reason and discernment among men; he is in Yoga and a many-sided universal worker (for the good of the world, for God in the world).¹

यस्य सर्वे समारम्भाः कामसङ्कल्पवर्जिताः ।
ज्ञानाग्निदग्धकर्माणं तमाहुः पण्डितं बुधाः ॥१९॥

19. Whose inceptions² and undertakings are all free from

---

in spite of their aping of right reason. And finally the sage seeking in the midst of it all a highest foundation of fixed law and an original truth finds himself obliged to raise the last supreme question, whether all action and life itself are not a delusion and a snare and whether cessation from action, *akarma*, is not the last resort of the tired and disillusioned human soul. But, says Krishna, in this matter even the sages are perplexed and deluded. For by action, by works, not by inaction comes the knowledge and the release.

What then is the solution? What is that type of works by which we shall be released from the ills of life, from this doubt, this error, this grief, from this mixed, impure and baffling result even of our purest and best-intentioned acts, from these million forms of evil and suffering?

¹ No outward distinctions need be made, is the reply; no work the world needs, be shunned; no limit or hedge set round our human activities; on the contrary, all actions should be done, but from a soul in Yoga with the Divine. *Akarma*, cessation from action is not the way; the man who has attained to the insight of the highest reason, perceives that such inaction is itself a constant action, a state subject to the workings of Nature and her qualities. The mind that takes refuge in physical inactivity, is still under the delusion that it and not Nature is the doer of works; it has mistaken inertia for liberation; it does not see that even in what seems absolute inertia greater than that of the stone or clod, Nature is at work, keeps unimpaired her hold. On the contrary, in the full flood of action the soul is free from its works, is not the doer, not bound by what is done, and he who lives in the freedom of the soul, not in the bondage of the modes of Nature, alone has release from works.

² The liberated man is not afraid of action, he is a large and universal doer of all works, *kṛtsna-karma-kṛt*; not as others do them in subjection to

the will of desire,¹ whose works are burned up by the fire of knowledge, him the wise have called a sage.

त्यक्त्वा कर्मफलासङ्गं नित्यतृप्तो निराश्रयः ।
कर्मण्यभिप्रवृत्तोऽपि नैव किञ्चित्करोति सः ॥२०॥

20. Having abandoned all attachment to the fruits of his works, ever satisfied² without any kind of dependence, he

Nature, but poised in the silent calm of the soul, tranquilly in Yoga with the Divine. The Divine is the lord of his works, he is only their channel through the instrumentality of his nature conscious of and subject to her Lord. By the flaming intensity and purity of this knowledge all his works are burned up as in a fire and his mind remains without any stain or disfiguring mark from them, calm, silent, unperturbed, white and clean and pure. To do all in this liberating knowledge, without the personal egoism of the doer, is the first sign of the divine worker.

¹ The second sign is freedom from desire; for where there is not the personal egoism of the doer, desire becomes impossible; it is starved out, sinks for want of a support, dies of inanition. Outwardly the liberated man seems to undertake works of all kinds like other men, on a larger scale perhaps with a more powerful will and driving-force, for the might of the divine will works in his active nature; but his works are all free from desire. He has abandoned all attachment to the fruits of his works, and where one does not work for the fruit, but solely as an impersonal instrument of the Master of works, desire can find no place, – not even the desire to serve successfully, for the fruit is the Lord's and determined by him and not by the personal will and effort, or to serve with credit and to the Master's satisfaction, for the real doer is the Lord himself and all glory belongs to a form of his Shakti missioned in the nature and not to the limited human personality. The human mind and soul of the liberated man does nothing, *na kiñcit karoti*; even though through his nature he engages in action, it is the Nature, the executive Shakti, it is the conscious Goddess governed by the divine Inhabitant who does the work.

² Another sign of the divine worker is that which is central to the divine consciousness itself, a perfect inner joy and peace which depends upon nothing in the world for its source or its continuance; it is innate, it is the very stuff of the soul's consciousness, it is the very nature of divine being. The ordinary man depends upon outward things for his happiness; therefore he has desire; therefore he has anger and passion, pleasure and pain, joy and grief; therefore he measures all things in the balance of good fortune and evil fortune. None of these things can affect the divine soul; it is ever satisfied without any kind of dependence, *nityatṛpto nirāśrayaḥ*.

does nothing though (through his nature) he engages in action.

निराशीर्यतचित्तात्मा त्यक्तसर्वपरिग्रहः ।
शारीरं केवलं कर्म कुर्वन्नाप्नोति किल्बिषम् ॥२१॥

21. He has no personal hopes, does not seize on things as his personal possessions; his heart and self are under perfect control; performing action by the body alone, he does not commit sin.[1]

यदृच्छालाभसन्तुष्टो द्वन्द्वातीतो विमत्सरः ।
समः सिद्धावसिद्धौ च कृत्वापि न निबध्यते ॥२२॥

22. He who is satisfied with whatever gain comes to him, who has passed beyond the dualities, is jealous of none, is equal[2] in failure and success, he is not bound even when he acts.

---

[1] The liberated man receives what the divine Will brings him, covets nothing, is jealous of none: what comes to him he takes without repulsion and without attachment; what goes from him he allows to depart into the whirl of things without repining or grief or sense of loss. The action of the liberated man is indeed a purely physical action, *śarīraṁ kevalaṁ karma*; for all else comes from above, is not generated on the human plane, is only a reflection of the will, knowledge, joy of the divine Purushottama. Therefore he does not by a stress on doing and its objects bring about in his mind and heart any of those reactions which we call passion and sin. For sin consists not at all in the outward deed, but in an impure reaction of the personal will, mind and heart which accompanies it or causes it; the impersonal, the spiritual is always pure, *apāpaviddham*, and gives to all that it does its own inalienable purity. This spiritual impersonality is a third sign of the divine worker. The result of this knowledge, this desirelessness and this impersonality is a perfect equality in the soul and the nature. Equality is the fourth sign of the divine worker.

[2] Good happening and evil happening, so all-important to the human soul subject to desire, are to the desireless divine soul equally welcome since by their mingled strand are worked out the developing forms of the eternal good. He cannot be defeated, since all for him is moving towards

गतसङ्गस्य मुक्तस्य ज्ञानावस्थितचेतसः ।
यज्ञायाचरतः कर्म समग्रं प्रविलीयते ॥२३॥

23. When a man liberated,[1] free from attachment, with his mind, heart and spirit firmly founded in self-knowledge, does works as sacrifice, all his work is dissolved.

---

the divine victory in the Kurukshetra of Nature, *dharmakṣetre kurukṣetre*, the field of doings which is the field of the evolving Dharma, and every turn of the conflict has been designed and mapped by the foreseeing eye of the Master of the battle, the Lord of works and Guide of the Dharma.

[1] His liberation does not at all prevent him from acting. Only, he knows that it is not he who is active, but the modes, the qualities of Nature, her triple gunas. This superiority of the calm soul observing its action but not involved in it, this *traiguṇātītya*, is also a high sign of the divine worker. By itself the idea might lead to a doctrine of the mechanical determinism of Nature and the perfect aloofness and irresponsibility of the soul; but the Gita effectively avoids this fault of an insufficient thought by its illumining supertheistic idea of the Purushottama. The reposing of works in the Impersonal is a means of getting rid of the personal egoism of the doer, but the end is to give up all our actions to that great Lord of all, *sarva-bhūta-maheśvara*. "With a consciousness identified with the Self, renouncing all thy actions into Me, freed from personal hopes and desires, from the thought of 'I' and 'mine', delivered from the fever of the soul, fight," work, do my will in the world. The Divine motives, inspires, determines the entire action; the human soul impersonal in the Brahman is the pure and silent channel of his power; that power in the Nature executes the divine movement. Such only are the works of the liberated soul, *muktasya karma*, for in nothing does he act from a personal inception; such are the actions of the accomplished *Karmayogin*. They rise from a free spirit and disappear without modifying it, like waves that rise and disappear on the surface of conscious, immutable depths.

III. THE SIGNIFICANCE OF SACRIFICE

(The Gita now proceeds to give an elaborate explanation of the meaning of *yajña* which leaves no doubt at all about the symbolic use of the words and the psychological character of the sacrifice enjoined by this teaching.)

ब्रह्मार्पणं ब्रह्म हविर्ब्रह्माग्नौ ब्रह्मणा हुतम् ।
ब्रह्मैव तेन गन्तव्यं ब्रह्मकर्मसमाधिना ॥२४॥

24. Brahman is the giving, Brahman is the food-offering, by Brahman it is offered into the Brahman-fire, Brahman is that which is to be attained by samadhi in Brahman-action.[1]

दैवमेवापरे यज्ञं योगिनः पर्युपासते ।
ब्रह्माग्नावपरे यज्ञं यज्ञेनैवोपजुह्वति ॥२५॥

25. Some Yogins follow after the sacrifice which is of the

---

[1] This then is the knowledge in which the liberated man has to do works of sacrifice. It is the knowledge declared of old in the great Vedantic utterances, "I am He", "All this verily is the Brahman, Brahman is this Self." It is the knowledge of the entire unity; it is the One manifest as the doer and the deed and the object of works, knower and knowledge and the object of knowledge. The universal energy into which the action is poured is the Divine; the consecrated energy of the giving is the Divine; whatever is offered is only some form of the Divine; the giver of the offering is the Divine himself in man; the action, the work, the sacrifice is itself the Divine in movement, in activity; the goal to be reached by sacrifice is the Divine. For the man who has this knowledge and lives and acts in it, there can be no binding works, no personal and egoistically appropriated action; there is only the divine Purusha acting by the divine Prakriti in His own being, offering everything into the fire of His self-conscious cosmic energy, while the knowledge and the possession of His divine existence and consciousness by the soul unified with Him is the goal of all this God-directed movement and activity. To know that and to live and act in this unifying consciousness is to be free.

But all even of the Yogins have not attained to this knowledge.

gods; others offer the sacrifice by the sacrifice itself into the Brahman-fire.[1]

श्रोत्रादीनीन्द्रियाण्यन्ये संयमाग्निषु जुह्वति ।
शब्दादीन् विषयानन्य इन्द्रियाग्निषु जुह्वति ॥२६॥

26. Some[2] offer hearing and the other senses into the fires of control, others offer sound and the other objects of sense into the fires of sense.

सर्वाणीन्द्रियकर्माणि प्राणकर्माणि चापरे ।
आत्मसंयमयोगाग्नौ जुह्वति ज्ञानदीपिते ॥२७॥

27. And others offer all the actions of the sense and all the actions of the vital force into the fire of the Yoga of self-control kindled by knowledge.[3]

द्रव्ययज्ञास्तपोयज्ञा योगयज्ञास्तथापरे ।
स्वाध्यायज्ञानयज्ञाश्च यतयः संशितव्रताः ॥२८॥

28. The offering of the striver after perfection may be

---

[1] Those who follow after the sacrifice of the gods, conceive of the Divine in various forms and powers and seek him by various means, ordinances, *dharmas*, laws or, as we might say, settled rites of action, self-discipline, consecrated works; but for those who have the knowledge, the simple fact of sacrifice, of offering whatever work to the Divine itself, of casting all their activities into the unified divine consciousness and energy, is their one means, their one *dharma*.

[2] The means of sacrifice are various; the offerings are of many kinds. There is the psychological sacrifice of self-control and self-discipline which leads to the higher self-possession and self-knowledge. There is the discipline which receives the objects of sense-perception without allowing the mind to be disturbed or affected by its sense-activities, the senses themselves becoming pure fires of sacrifice; there is the discipline which stills the senses so that the soul in its purity may appear from behind the veil of mind-action, calm and still.

[3] There is the discipline by which, when the self is known, all the actions of the sense-perceptions and all the actions of the vital being are received into that one still and tranquil soul.

material and physical (*dravyayajña*, like that consecrated in worship by the devotee to his deity), or it may be the austerity of his self-discipline and energy of his soul directed to some high aim, *tapo-yajña*, or it may be some form of Yoga (like the *prāṇāyāma* of the Raja-yogins and Hatha-yogins, or any other *yoga-yajña*); or it may be the offering of reading and knowledge.

अपाने जुह्वति प्राणं प्राणेऽपानं तथापरे ।
प्राणापानगती रुद्ध्वा प्राणायामपरायणाः ॥२९॥

29. Others again who are devoted to controlling the breath, having restrained the Prana (the outgoing breath) and Apana (the incoming breath) pour as sacrifice Prana into Apana and Apana into Prana.

अपरे नियताहाराः प्राणान् प्राणेषु जुह्वति ।
सर्वेऽप्येते यज्ञविदो यज्ञक्षपितकल्मषाः ॥३०॥

30. Others having regulated the food pour as sacrifice their life-breaths into life-breaths. All these are knowers of sacrifice and by sacrifice have destroyed their sins.[1]

यज्ञशिष्टामृतभुजो यान्ति ब्रह्म सनातनम् ।
नायं लोकोऽस्त्ययज्ञस्य कुतोऽन्यः कुरुसत्तम ॥३१॥

31. They who enjoy the nectar of immortality left over from the sacrifice attain to the eternal Brahman; this world

---

[1] All these tend to the purification of the being; all sacrifice is a way towards the attainment of the highest. The one thing needful, the saving principle constant in all these variations, is to subordinate the lower activities, to diminish the control of desire and replace it by a superior energy, to abandon the purely egoistic enjoyment for that diviner delight which comes by sacrifice, by self-dedication, by self-mastery, by the giving up of one's lower impulses to a greater and higher aim.

is not for him who doeth not sacrifice, how then any other world?¹

एवं बहुविधा यज्ञा वितता ब्रह्मणो मुखे ।
कर्मजान् विद्धि तान् सर्वानेवं ज्ञात्वा विमोक्ष्यसे ॥३२॥

32. Therefore all² these and many other forms of sacrifice have been extended in the mouth of the Brahman (the mouth of that Fire which receives all offerings). Know thou that all these are born of work³ and so knowing thou shalt be free.

श्रेयान् द्रव्यमयाद्यज्ञाज्ज्ञानयज्ञः परन्तप ।
सर्वं कर्माखिलं पार्थ ज्ञाने परिसमाप्यते ॥३३॥

33. The sacrifice of knowledge, O Parantapa, is greater than any material sacrifice. Knowledge is that in which all this action culminates (not any lower knowledge, but the highest self-knowledge and God-knowledge), O Partha!

तद्विद्धि प्रणिपातेन परिप्रश्नेन सेवया ।
उपदेक्ष्यन्ति ते ज्ञानं ज्ञानिनस्तत्त्वदर्शिनः ॥३४॥

34. Learn that by worshipping the feet of the teacher, by questioning and by service; the men of knowledge who have

---

¹ Sacrifice is the law of the world and nothing can be gained without it, neither mastery here, nor the possession of heavens beyond, nor the supreme possession of all.

² They are all means and forms of the one great Existence in activity, means by which the action of the human being can be offered up to That of which his outward existence is a part and with which his inmost self is one.

³ All these proceed from and are ordained by the one vast energy of the Divine which manifests itself in the universal *karma* and makes all the cosmic activity a progressive offering to the one Self and Lord and of which the last stage for the human being is self-knowledge and the possession of the divine or Brahmic consciousness. But there are gradations in the range of these various forms of sacrifice.

seen (not those who know merely by the intellect) the true principles of things, will instruct thee in knowledge.

यज्ज्ञात्वा न पुनर्मोहमेवं यास्यसि पाण्डव ।
येन भूतान्यशेषेण द्रक्ष्यस्यात्मन्यथो मयि ॥३५॥

35. Possessing that knowledge thou shalt not fall again into the mind's ignorance, O Pandava; for by this, thou shalt see all existences without exception in the Self,[1] then in Me.

अपि चेदसि पापेभ्यः सर्वेभ्यः पापकृत्तमः ।
सर्वं ज्ञानप्लवेनैव वृजिनं सन्तरिष्यसि ॥३६॥

36. Even if thou art the greatest doer of sin beyond all sinners, thou shalt cross over all the crookedness of evil in the ship of knowledge.

यथैधांसि समिद्धोऽग्निर्भस्मसात्कुरुतेऽर्जुन ।
ज्ञानाग्निः सर्वकर्माणि भस्मसात्कुरुते तथा ॥३७॥

37. As a fire kindled turns to ashes its fuel, O Arjuna, so the fire of knowledge turns all works to ashes.

---

[1] For the Self is that one, immutable, all-pervading, all-containing, self-existent reality or Brahman hidden behind our mental being into which our consciousness widens out when it is liberated from the ego; we come to see all beings as becomings, *bhūtāni*, within that one self-existence. But this Self or immutable Brahman we see too to be the self-presentation to our essential psychological consciousness of a supreme Being who is the source of our existence and of whom all that is mutable or immutable is the manifestation. He is God, the Divine, the Purushottama. To Him we offer everything as a sacrifice; into His hands we give up our actions; in His existence we live and move; unified with Him in our nature and with all existences in Him, we become one soul and one power of being with Him and with all beings; with His supreme reality we identify and unite our self-being. By works done for sacrifice, eliminating desire, we arrive at knowledge and at the soul's possession of itself; by works done in self-knowledge and God-knowledge we are liberated into the unity, peace and joy of the divine existence.

न हि ज्ञानेन सदृशं पवित्रमिह विद्यते ।
तत्स्वयं योगसंसिद्धः कालेनात्मनि विन्दति ॥३८॥

38. There is nothing in the world equal in purity to knowledge,[1] the man who is perfected by Yoga, finds it of himself[2] in the self by the course of Time.

श्रद्धावांल्लभते ज्ञानं तत्परः संयतेन्द्रियः ।
ज्ञानं लब्ध्वा परां शान्तिमचिरेणाधिगच्छति ॥३९॥

39. Who has faith, who has conquered and controlled the mind and senses, who has fixed his whole conscious being on the supreme Reality, he attains knowledge; and having attained knowledge he goes swiftly to the supreme Peace.

अज्ञश्चाश्रद्दधानश्च संशयात्मा विनश्यति ।
नायं लोकोऽस्ति न परो न सुखं संशयात्मनः ॥४०॥

---

[1] Yoga and knowledge are, in this early part of the Gita's teaching, the two wings of the soul's ascent. By Yoga is meant union through divine works done without desire, with equality of soul to all things and all men, as a sacrifice to the Supreme, while knowledge is that on which this desirelessness, this equality, this power of sacrifice is founded. The two wings indeed assist each other's flight; acting together, yet with a subtle alternation of mutual aid, like the two eyes in a man which see together because they see alternately, they increase one another mutually by interchange of substance. As the works grow more and more desireless, equal-minded, sacrificial in spirit, the knowledge increases: with the increase of the knowledge the soul becomes firmer in the desireless, sacrificial equality of its works.

[2] The knowledge grows within him and he grows into it as he goes on increasing in desirelessness, in equality, in devotion to the Divine. It is only of the supreme knowledge that this can altogether be said; the knowledge which the intellect of man amasses, is gathered laboriously by the senses and the reason from outside. To get this other knowledge, self-existent, intuitive, self-experiencing, self-revealing, we must have self-control and faith (Shraddha).

40. The ignorant who has not faith,[1] the soul of doubt goeth to perdition; neither this world, nor the supreme world nor any happiness is for the soul full of doubts.

योगसंन्यस्तकर्माणं ज्ञानसंछिन्नसंशयम् ।
आत्मवन्तं न कर्माणि निबध्नन्ति धनञ्जय ॥४१॥

41. He who has destroyed all doubt by knowledge and has by Yoga given up all works and is in possession of the Self is not bound by his works,[2] O Dhananjaya.

तस्मादज्ञानसम्भूतं हृत्स्थं ज्ञानासिनात्मनः ।
छित्त्वैनं संशयं योगमातिष्ठोत्तिष्ठ भारत ॥४२॥

42. Therefore, having cut asunder with the sword of knowledge this doubt[3] that has arisen out of ignorance and abides in the heart, resort to Yoga, do thou stand up, O Bharata."

इति श्रीमद्भगवद्गीतासूपनिषत्सु ब्रह्मविद्यायां योगशास्त्रे श्रीकृष्णार्जुनसम्वादे
ज्ञानकर्मसंन्यासयोगो नाम चतुर्थोऽध्यायः

[1] We must have a faith which no intellectual doubt can be allowed to disturb. In fact, it is true that without faith nothing decisive can be achieved either in this world or for possession of the world above, and that it is only by laying hold of some sure basis and positive support that man can attain any measure of terrestrial or celestial success and satisfaction and happiness; the merely sceptical mind loses itself in the void.

[2] When the Gita says that all the totality of work finds its completion in knowledge or that the fire of knowledge turns all works to ashes, it is not at all meant that there is cessation from works. What is meant by the Gita is made clear in this sloka; the man of Yoga and knowledge is not bound by his works.

[3] In the lower knowledge doubt and scepticism have their temporary uses; in the higher they are stumbling-blocks: for there the whole secret is not the balancing of truth and error, but a constantly progressing realisation of revealed truth. It is not a truth which has to be proved, but a truth which has to be lived inwardly, a greater reality into which we have to grow. Finally, it is in itself a self-existent truth and would be self-

evident if it were not for the sorceries of the ignorance in which we live; the doubts, the perplexities which prevent us from accepting and following it, arise from that ignorance, from the sense-bewildered, opinion-perplexed heart and mind, living as they do in a lower and phenomenal truth and therefore questioning the higher realities, *ajñānasambhūtaṁ hṛtstham saṁśayam*. They have to be cut away by the sword of knowledge, says the Gita, by the knowledge that realises, by resorting constantly to Yoga, that is by living out the union with the Supreme whose truth being known all is known, *yasmin vijñate sarvam vijñatam*.

Fifth Chapter

RENUNCIATION AND YOGA OF WORKS

अर्जुन उवाच —
सन्न्यासं कर्मणां कृष्ण पुनर्योगं च शंससि ।
यच्छ्रेय एतयोरेकं तन्मे ब्रूहि सुनिश्चितम् ॥१॥

1. Arjuna said: Thou declarest to me the renunciation of works, O Krishna, and again thou declarest to me Yoga; which one of these is the better way, that tell me with a clear decisiveness.[1]

श्रीभगवान् उवाच —
सन्न्यासः कर्मयोगश्च निःश्रेयसकरावुभौ ।
तयोस्तु कर्मसन्न्यासात्कर्मयोगो विशिष्यते ॥२॥

2. The Blessed Lord said: Renunciation and Yoga of works both bring about the soul's salvation, but of the two the Yoga of works is distinguished above the renunciation of works.

ज्ञेयः स नित्यसन्न्यासी यो न द्वेष्टि न काङ्क्षति ।
निर्द्वन्द्वो हि महाबाहो सुखं बन्धात्प्रमुच्यते ॥३॥

---

[1] Arjuna is perplexed; here are desireless works, the principle of Yoga, and renunciation of works, the principle of Sankhya, put together side by side as if part of one method, yet there is no evident reconciliation between them. For the kind of reconciliation which the Teacher has already given, – in outward inaction to see action still persisting and in apparent action to see a real inaction since the soul has renounced its illusion of the worker and given up works into the hands of the Master of sacrifice, – is for the practical mind of Arjuna too slight, too subtle and expressed almost in riddling words; he has not caught their sense or at least not penetrated into their spirit and reality.

The answer is important, for it puts the whole distinction very clearly and indicates though it does not develop entirely the line of reconciliation.

3. He should be known as always a Sannyasin (even when he is doing action) who neither dislikes nor desires; for free from the dualities he is released easily and happily from the bondage.

साङ्ख्ययोगौ पृथग्बालाः प्रवदन्ति न पण्डिताः ।
एकमप्यास्थितः सम्यगुभयोर्विन्दते फलम् ॥४॥

4. Children speak of Sankhya and Yoga apart from each other, not the wise; if a man applies himself integrally to one, he gets the fruit of both.

यत्साङ्ख्यैः प्राप्यते स्थानं तद्योगैरपि गम्यते ।
एकं साङ्ख्यं च योगं च यः पश्यति स पश्यति ॥५॥

5. The status which is attained by the Sankhya, to that the men of the Yoga also arrive; who sees Sankhya and Yoga as one, he sees.

सन्न्यासस्तु महाबाहो दुःखमाप्तुमयोगतः ।
योगयुक्तो मुनिर्ब्रह्म न चिरेणाधिगच्छति ॥६॥

6. But renunciation, O mighty-armed, is difficult[1] to attain without Yoga; the sage[2] who has Yoga attains soon to the Brahman.

[1] The painful process of outward Sannyasa, *duḥkham āptum,* is an unnecessary process. It is perfectly true that all actions, as well as the fruit of action, have to be given up, to be renounced, but inwardly, not outwardly, not into the inertia of Nature, but to the Lord in sacrifice, into the calm and joy of the Impersonal from whom all action proceeds without disturbing his peace. The true Sannyasa of action is the reposing of all works on the Brahman. (See sloka 10-12)

[2] He knows that the actions are not his, but Nature's and by that very knowledge he is free; he has renounced works, does no actions; though actions are done through him; he becomes the Self, the Brahman, *brahmabhūta,* he sees all existences as becomings (*bhūtāni*) of that self-existent Being, his own only one of them, all their actions as only the development of cosmic Nature working through their individual nature and his own actions also as a part of the same cosmic activity.

योगयुक्तो विशुद्धात्मा विजितात्मा जितेन्द्रियः ।
सर्वभूतात्मभूतात्मा कुर्वन्नपि न लिप्यते ।।७।।

7. He who is in Yoga, the pure soul, master of his self, who has conquered the senses, whose self becomes the self of all existences (of all things that have become), even though he does works, he is not involved in them.

नैव किञ्चित्करोमीति युक्तो मन्येत तत्त्ववित् ।
पश्यञ्शृण्वन्स्पृशञ्जिघ्रन्नश्नन्गच्छन्स्वपञ्श्वसन् ।।८।।
प्रलपन्विसृजन्गृह्णन्नुन्मिषन्निमिषन्नपि ।
इन्द्रियाणीन्द्रियार्थेषु वर्तन्त इति धारयन् ।।९।।

8-9. The man who knows the principles of things thinks, his mind in Yoga (with the inactive Impersonal), "I am doing nothing"; when he sees, hears, tastes, smells, eats, moves, sleeps, breathes, speaks, takes, ejects, opens his eyes or closes them, he holds that it is only the senses acting upon the objects of the senses.

ब्रह्मण्याधाय कर्माणि सङ्गं त्यक्त्वा करोति यः ।
लिप्यते न स पापेन पद्मपत्रमिवाम्भसा ।।१०।।

10. He who, having abandoned attachment, acts reposing[1] (or founding) his works on the Brahman, is not stained by sin even as water clings not to the lotus leaf.

---

[1] The Gita says that the Yoga of works is better than the physical renunciation of works (Sloka 2). That Yoga of works is, we have seen, the offering of all action to the Lord, which induces as its culmination an inner and not an outer, a spiritual, not a physical giving up of works into the Brahman, into the being of the Lord, *brahmaṇi ādhāya karmāṇi, mayi saṁyāsya*. When works are thus "reposed on the Brahman," the personality of the instrumental doer ceases; though he acts, he does nothing; for he has given up not only the fruits of his works, but the works themselves and the doing of them to the Lord. The Divine then takes the burden of works from him; the Supreme becomes the doer and the act and the result.

कायेन मनसा बुद्ध्या केवलैरिन्द्रियैरपि ।
योगिनः कर्म कुर्वन्ति सङ्गं त्यक्त्वात्मशुद्धये ॥११॥

11. Therefore the Yogins do works with the body, mind, understanding, or even merely with the organs of action, abandoning attachment, for self-purification.

युक्तः कर्मफलं त्यक्त्वा शान्तिमाप्नोति नैष्ठिकीम् ।
अयुक्तः कामकारेण फले सक्तो निबध्यते ॥१२॥

12. By abandoning attachment to the fruits of works, the soul in union with Brahman attains to peace of rapt foundation in Brahman, but the soul not in union is attached to the fruit and bound by the action of desire.

सर्वकर्माणि मनसा सन्न्यस्यास्ते सुखं वशी ।
नवद्वारे पुरे देही नैव कुर्वन्न कारयन् ॥१३॥

13. The embodied soul perfectly controlling its nature, having renounced all its actions by the mind (inwardly, not outwardly), sits serenely in its nine-gated[1] city neither doing nor causing to be done.

न कर्तृत्वं न कर्माणि लोकस्य सृजति प्रभुः ।
न कर्मफलसंयोगं स्वभावस्तु प्रवर्तते ॥१४॥

14. The Lord neither creates the works of the world nor the state of the doer nor the joining of the works to the fruit; nature works out these things.

नादत्ते कस्यचित्पापं न चैव सुकृतं विभुः ।
अज्ञानेनावृतं ज्ञानं तेन मुह्यन्ति जन्तवः ॥१५॥

15. The all-pervading Impersonal accepts neither the sin

---

[1] Seven gates in the upper body – the two eyes, the two ears, the two nostrils and the mouth, and the two gates in the lower body for ejection – these are the nine gates.

nor the virtue of any; knowledge is enveloped by ignorance; thereby creatures are bewildered.

ज्ञानेन तु तदज्ञानं येषां नाशितमात्मनः ।
तेषामादित्यवज्ज्ञानं प्रकाशयति तत्परम् ॥१६॥

16. Verily, in whom ignorance is destroyed by self-knowledge, in them knowledge[1] lights up like a sun the supreme Self (within them).

तद्बुद्धयस्तदात्मानस्तन्निष्ठास्तत्परायणाः ।
गच्छन्त्यपुनरावृत्तिं ज्ञाननिर्धूतकल्मषाः ॥१७॥

17. Turning their discerning mind to That, directing their whole conscious being to That, making That their whole aim and the sole object of their devotion, they go whence there is no return, their sins washed by the waters of knowledge.

[1] This knowledge of which the Gita speaks, is not an intellectual activity of the mind; it is a luminous growth into the highest state of being by the outshining of the light of the divine sun of Truth, "that Truth, the Sun lying concealed in the darkness" of our ignorance of which the Rigveda speaks, *tat satyaṁ sūryaṁ tamasi kṣiyantam*. The immutable Brahman is there in the spirit's skies above this troubled lower nature of the dualities, untouched either by its virtue or by its sin, accepting neither our sense of sin or self-righteousness, untouched by its joy and its sorrow, indifferent to our joy in success and our grief in failure, master of all, supreme, all-pervading, *prabhu, vibhu*, calm, strong, pure, equal in all things, the source of Nature, not the direct doer of our works, but the witness of Nature and her works, not imposing on us either the illusion of being the doer, for that illusion is the result of the ignorance of this lower Nature. But this freedom, mastery, purity we cannot see; we are bewildered by the natural ignorance which hides from us the eternal self-knowledge of the Brahman secret within our being. But knowledge comes to its persistent seeker and removes the natural self-ignorance; it shines out like a long-hidden sun and lights up to our vision that self-being supreme beyond the dualities of this lower existence.

The result is, says the Gita, a perfect equality to all things and all persons; and then only can we repose our works completely in the Brahman.

विद्याविनयसम्पन्ने ब्राह्मणे गवि हस्तिनि ।
शुनि चैव श्वपाके च पण्डिताः समदर्शिनः ॥१८॥

18. Sages see with an equal eye[1] the learned and cultured Brahmin, the cow, the elephant, the dog, the outcaste.

इहैव तैर्जितः सर्गो येषां साम्ये स्थितं मनः ।
निर्दोषं हि समं ब्रह्म तस्माद् ब्रह्मणि ते स्थिताः ॥१९॥

19. Even here on earth they have conquered the creation whose mind is established in equality: the equal Brahman[2] is faultless, therefore they live in the Brahman.

न प्रहृष्येत्प्रियं प्राप्य नोद्विजेत्प्राप्य चाप्रियम् ।
स्थिरबुद्धिरसम्मूढो ब्रह्मविद् ब्रह्मणि स्थितः ॥२०॥

20. With intelligence stable, unbewildered, the knower of the Brahman, living in the Brahman, neither rejoices on

---

[1] He has at heart for all the same equal kindliness, the same divine affection. Circumstances may determine the outward clasp or the outward conflict, but can never affect his equal eye, his open heart, his inner embrace of all.

[2] The Brahman is equal, *samaṁ brahma*, and it is only when we have this perfect equality seeing with an equal eye the learned and cultured Brahmin, the cow, the elephant, the dog, the outcaste and knowing all as one Brahman, that we can, living in that oneness, see like the Brahman our works proceeding from the nature freely without any fear of attachment, sin or bondage. Sin and stain then cannot be; for we have overcome that creation full of desire and its works and reactions which belong to the ignorance, *tair jitaḥ sargaḥ*, and living in the supreme and divine nature there is no longer fault or defect in our works; for these are created by the inequalities of the ignorance. The equal Brahman is faultless, beyond the confusion of good and evil, and living in the Brahman we too rise beyond good and evil; we act in that purity, stainlessly, with an equal and single purpose of fulfilling the welfare of all existences. (See sloka 25)

The Gita after speaking of the perfect equality of the Brahman-knower who has risen into the Brahman-consciousness, *brahmavid brahmaṇi sthitaḥ*, develops in nine verses that follow its idea of Brahmayoga and of Nirvana in the Brahman.

obtaining what is pleasant, nor sorrows on obtaining what is unpleasant.

बाह्यस्पर्शेष्वसक्तात्मा विन्दत्यात्मनि यत्सुखम् ।
स ब्रह्मयोगयुक्तात्मा सुखमक्षयमश्नुते ॥२१॥

21. When the soul is no longer attached[1] to the touches of outward things, then one finds the happiness that exists in the Self; such a one enjoys an imperishable happiness, because his self is in Yoga, *yukta*, by Yoga with the Brahman.

ये हि संस्पर्शजा भोगा दुःखयोनय एव ते ।
आद्यन्तवन्तः कौन्तेय न तेषु रमते बुधः ॥२२॥

22. The enjoyments born of the touches of things are causes of sorrow, they have a beginning and an end; therefore the sage, the man of awakened understanding, *budhaḥ*, does not place his delight in these.

शक्नोतीहैव यः सोढुं प्राक् शरीरविमोक्षणात् ।
कामक्रोधोद्भवं वेगं स युक्तः स सुखी नरः ॥२३॥

23. He who can bear here in the body the velocity of wrath and desire, is the Yogin, the happy man.

योऽन्तःसुखोऽन्तरारामस्तथान्तर्ज्योतिरेव यः ।
स योगी ब्रह्मनिर्वाणं ब्रह्मभूतोऽधिगच्छति ॥२४॥

24. He who has the inner happiness and the inner ease

---

[1] The non-attachment is essential, the Gita says, in order to be free from the attacks of desire and wrath and passion, a freedom without which true happiness is not possible. That happiness and that equality are to be gained entirely by man in the body: he is not to suffer any least remnant of the subjection to the troubled lower nature to remain in the idea that the perfect release will come by a putting off of the body; a perfect spiritual freedom is to be won here upon earth and possessed and enjoyed in the human life.

and repose and the inner light, that Yogin becomes the Brahman and reaches self-extinction in the Brahman, *brahmanirvāṇam*.[1]

लभन्ते ब्रह्मनिर्वाणमृषयः क्षीणकल्मषाः ।
छिन्नद्वैधा यतात्मानः सर्वभूतहिते रताः ॥२५॥

25. Sages win Nirvana in the Brahman, they in whom the stains of sin are effaced and the knot of doubt is cut asunder, masters of their selves, who are occupied in doing good to all creatures.

कामक्रोधवियुक्तानां यतीनां यतचेतसाम् ।
अभितो ब्रह्मनिर्वाणं वर्तते विदितात्मनाम् ॥२६॥

26. Yatis (those who practise self-mastery by Yoga and austerity) who are delivered from desire and wrath and have gained self-mastery, for them Nirvana in the Brahman exists all about them, encompasses them, they already live in it because they have knowledge[2] of the Self.[3]

---

[1] Here, very clearly, Nirvana means the extinction of the ego in the higher spiritual inner Self, that which is for ever timeless, spaceless, not bound by the chain of cause and effect and the changes of the world-mutation, self-blissful, self-illumined and for ever at peace. The Yogin ceases to be the ego, the little person limited by the mind and the body; he becomes the Brahman; he is unified in consciousness with the immutable divinity of the eternal Self which is immanent in his natural being. But is this a going in into some deep sleep of samadhi away from all world-consciousness, or is it the preparatory movement for a dissolution of the natural being and the individual soul into some absolute Self who is utterly and for ever beyond Nature and her works, *laya*, *mokṣa*?

[2] That is to say, to have knowledge and possession of the Self is to exist in Nirvana. This is clearly a large extension of the idea of Nirvana. Freedom from all stain of the passions, the self-mastery of the equal mind on which that freedom is founded, equality to all beings, *sarvabhūteṣu*, and beneficial love for all, final destruction of that doubt and obscurity of the ignorance which keeps us divided from the all-unifying Divine and the knowledge of the One Self within us and in all are evidently the conditions of Nirvana which are laid down in these verses of the Gita, go to

स्पर्शान्कृत्वा बहिर्बाह्यांश्चक्षुश्चैवान्तरे भ्रुवोः ।
प्राणापानौ समौ कृत्वा नासाभ्यन्तरचारिणौ ॥२७॥
यतेन्द्रियमनोबुद्धिर्मुनिर्मोक्षपरायणः ।
विगतेच्छाभयक्रोधो यः सदा मुक्त एव सः ॥२८॥

27-28. Having put outside of himself all outward touches and concentrated the vision between the eyebrows and made equal the *prāṇa* and the *apāna* moving within the nostrils, having controlled the senses, the mind and the understanding, the sage devoted to liberation, from whom desire and wrath and fear have passed away, is ever free.[1]

---

constitute it and are its spiritual substance. Thus Nirvana is clearly compatible with world-consciousness and with action in the world. For the sages who possess it are conscious of and in intimate relation by works with the Divine in the mutable universe; they are occupied with the good of all creatures, *sarvabhūtahite*.

[3] By Nirvana in the Brahman must be meant a destruction or extinction of the limited separative consciousness, falsifying and dividing, which is brought into being on the surface of existence by the lower Maya of the three gunas, and entry into Nirvana is a passage into this other true unifying consciousness which is the heart of existence and its continent and its whole containing and supporting, its whole original and eternal and final truth. Nirvana when we gain it, enter into it, is not only within us, but all around, *abhito vartate*, because this is not only the Brahman-consciousness which lives secret within us, but the Brahman-consciousness in which we live. It is the Self which we are within, the supreme Self of our individual being but also the Self which we are without, the supreme Self of the universe, the self of all existences. By living in that self we live in all, and no longer in our egoistic being alone; by oneness with that self a steadfast oneness with all in the universe becomes the very nature of our being and the root status of our active consciousness and root motive of all our action.

[1] Here we have a process of Yoga that brings in an element which seems quite other than the Yoga of works and other even than the pure Yoga of knowledge by discrimination and contemplation; it belongs in all its characteristic features to the system, introduces the psycho-physical askesis of, Rajayoga. There is the conquest of all the movements of the mind, *cittavṛtti-nirodha*; there is the control of the breathing, Pranayama; there is the drawing in of the sense and the vision. All of them are processes which lead to the inner trance of Samadhi, the object of all of

FIFTH CHAPTER

भोक्तारं यज्ञतपसां सर्वलोकमहेश्वरम् ।
सुहृदं सर्वभूतानां ज्ञात्वा मां शान्तिमृच्छति ।।२९।।

29. When a man has known Me as the Enjoyer of sacrifice and tapasya (of all askesis and energisms), the mighty lord of all the worlds, the friend of all creatures, he comes by the peace.[1]

इति श्रीमद्भगवद्गीतासूपनिषत्सु ब्रह्मविद्यायां योगशास्त्रे श्रीकृष्णार्जुनसंवादे
कर्मसंन्यासयोगो नाम पञ्चमोऽध्यायः ।

---

them *mokṣa*, and *mokṣa* signifies in ordinary parlance the renunciation not only of the separative ego-consciousness, but of the whole active consciousness, a dissolution of our being into the highest Brahman. Are we to suppose that the Gita gives this process in that sense as the last movement of a release by dissolution or only as a special means and a strong aid to overcome the outward-going mind? Is this the finale, the climax, the last word? We shall find reason to regard it as both a special means, an aid, and at least one gate of a final departure, not by dissolution, but by an uplifting to the supracosmic existence. For even here in this passage this is not the last word; the last word, the finale, the climax comes in a verse that follows and is the last couplet of the chapter.

[1] The power of the Karmayoga comes in again; the knowledge of the active Brahman, the cosmic supersoul, is insisted on among the conditions of the peace of Nirvana. We get back to the great idea of the Gita, the idea of the Purushottama, — though that name is not given till close upon the end, it is always that which Krishna means by his "I" and "me", the Divine who is there as the one self in our timeless immutable being, who is present too in the world, in all existences, in all activities, the master of the silence and the peace, the master of the power and the action, who is here incarnate as the divine charioteer of the stupendous conflict, the Transcendent, the Self, the All, the master of every individual being. He is the enjoyer of all sacrifice and of all tapasya, therefore shall the seeker of liberation do works as a sacrifice and as a tapasya; he is the lord of all the worlds, manifested in Nature and in these beings, therefore shall the liberated man still do works for the right government and leading on of the peoples in these worlds, *loka-saṁgraha*; he is the friend of all existences, therefore is the sage who has found Nirvana within him and all around, still and always occupied with the good of the creatures, — even as

the Nirvana of Mahayana Buddhism took for its highest sign the works of a universal compassion. Therefore too, even when he has found oneness with the Divine in his timeless and immutable self, is he still capable, since he embraces the relations also of the play of Nature, of divine love for man and of love for the Divine, of bhakti. That this is the drift of the meaning, becomes clearer when we have fathomed the sense of the sixth chapter which is a large comment on and a full development of the idea of these closing verses of the fifth, – that shows the importance which the Gita attaches to them.

Sixth Chapter

NIRVANA AND WORKS IN THE WORLD

श्रीभगवान् उवाच —
अनाश्रितः कर्मफलं कार्यं कर्म करोति यः ।
स सन्न्यासी च योगी च न निरग्निर्न चाक्रियः ।।१।।

1. The Blessed Lord said: Whoever does the work to be done without resort to its fruits, he is the Sannyasin and the Yogin, not the man who lights not the sacrificial fire and does not the works.

यं सन्न्यासमिति प्राहुर्योगं तं विद्धि पाण्डव ।
न ह्यसंन्यस्तसङ्कल्पो योगी भवति कश्चन ।।२।।

2. What they have called renunciation (Sannyasa), know to be in truth Yoga, O Pandava; for none becomes a Yogin who has not renounced the desire-will in the mind.[1]

आरुरुक्षोर्मुनेर्योगं कर्म कारणमुच्यते ।
योगारूढस्य तस्यैव शमः कारणमुच्यते ।।३।।

3. For a sage who is ascending the hill of Yoga, action is the cause;[2] for the same sage when he has got to the top of Yoga self-mastery is the cause.[3]

---

[1] First the Teacher emphasises – and this is very significant – his often repeated asseveration about the real essence of Sannyasa, that it is an inward, not an outward renunciation. Works are to be done, but with what purpose and in what order?

[2] Works are the cause, but of what? The cause of self-perfection, of liberation, of Nirvana in the Brahman; for by doing works with a steady practice of the inner renunciation this perfection, this liberation, this conquest of the desire-mind and the ego-self and the lower nature are easily accomplished.

[3] But when one has got to the top? Then works are no longer the cause; the calm of self-mastery and self-possession gained by works

यदा हि नेन्द्रियार्थेषु न कर्मस्वनुषज्जते ।
सर्वसङ्कल्पसन्न्यासी योगारूढस्तदोच्यते ॥४॥

4. When one does not get attached[1] to the objects of sense or to works and has renounced all will of desire in the mind, then is he said to have ascended to the top of Yoga.

उद्धरेदात्मनात्मानं नात्मानमवसादयेत् ।
आत्मैव ह्यात्मनो बन्धुरात्मैव रिपुरात्मनः ॥५॥

5. By the self thou shouldst deliver the self, thou shouldst not depress and cast down the self (whether by self-indulgence or suppression); for the self is the friend of the self and the self is the enemy.

बन्धुरात्मात्मनस्तस्य येनात्मैवात्मना जितः ।
अनात्मनस्तु शत्रुत्वे वर्तेतात्मैव शत्रुवत् ॥६॥

6. To the man is his self a friend in whom the (lower) self has been conquered by the (higher) self, but to him who is not in possession of his (higher) self, the (lower) self is as if an enemy and it acts as an enemy.

जितात्मनः प्रशान्तस्य परमात्मा समाहितः ।
शीतोष्णसुखदुःखेषु तथा मानापमानयोः ॥७॥

---

becomes the cause. Again, the cause of what? Of fixity in the self, in the Brahman-consciousness and of the perfect equality in which the divine works of the liberated man are done.

[1] That is the spirit in which the liberated man does works; he does them without desire and attachment, without the egoistic personal will and the mental seeking which is the parent of desire. He has conquered his lower self, reached the perfect calm in which his highest self is manifest to him, that highest self always concentrated in its own being, *samāhita*, in Samadhi, not only in the trance of the inward-drawn consciousness but always, in the waking state of the mind as well, in exposure to the causes of desire and of the disturbance of calm, to grief and pleasure, heat and cold, honour and disgrace, all the dualities. This higher self is the Akshara, *kūṭastha*.

7. When one has conquered one's self and attained to the calm of a perfect self-mastery and self-possession, then is the supreme self in a man founded and poised (even in his outwardly conscious human being) in cold and heat, pleasure and pain as well as in honour and dishonour.

ज्ञानविज्ञानतृप्तात्मा कूटस्थो विजितेन्द्रियः ।
युक्त इत्युच्यते योगी समलोष्टाश्मकाञ्चनः ॥८॥

8. The Yogin, who is satisfied with self-knowledge, tranquil and self-poised, master of his senses, regarding alike clod and stone and gold, is said to be in Yoga.[1]

सुहृन्मित्रार्युदासीनमध्यस्थद्वेष्यबन्धुषु ।
साधुष्वपि च पापेषु समबुद्धिर्विशिष्यते ॥९॥

9. He who is equal in soul to friend and enemy and to neutral and indifferent, also to sinner and saint, he excels.

योगी युञ्जीत सततमात्मानं रहसि स्थितः ।
एकाकी यतचित्तात्मा निराशीरपरिग्रहः ॥१०॥

---

[1] The Akshara, the higher self stands above the changes and the perturbations of the natural being; and the Yogin is said to be in Yoga with it when he also is like it, *kūṭastha*, when he is superior to all appearances and mutations, when he is satisfied with self-knowledge, when he is equal-minded to all things and happenings and persons. In other words, to master the lower self by the higher, the natural self by the spiritual is the way of man's perfection and liberation. But this Yoga is after all no easy thing to acquire, as Arjuna indeed shortly afterwards suggests, for the restless mind is always liable to be pulled down from these heights by the attacks of outward things and to fall back into the strong control of grief and passion and inequality. Therefore, it would seem, the Gita proceeds to give us in addition to its general method of knowledge and works a special process of Rajayogic meditation also, a powerful method of practice, *abhyāsa*, a strong way to the complete control of the mind and all its workings.

10. Let the Yogin practise continually union with the Self (so that that may become his normal consciousness) sitting apart and alone, with all desire and idea of possession banished from his mind, self-controlled in his whole being and consciousness.

शुचौ देशे प्रतिष्ठाप्य स्थिरमासनमात्मनः ।
नात्युच्छ्रितं नातिनीचं चैलाजिनकुशोत्तरम् ॥११॥
तत्रैकाग्रं मनः कृत्वा यतचित्तेन्द्रियक्रियः ।
उपविश्यासने युञ्ज्याद्योगमात्मविशुद्धये ॥१२॥

11-12. He should set in a pure spot his firm seat, neither too high, nor yet too low, covered with a cloth, with a deer skin, with sacred grass, and there seated with a concentrated mind and with the workings of the mental consciousness and the senses under control, he should practise Yoga for self-purification.

समं कायशिरोग्रीवं धारयन्नचलं स्थिरः ।
संप्रेक्ष्य नासिकाग्रं स्वं दिशश्चानवलोकयन् ॥१३॥
प्रशान्तात्मा विगतभीर्ब्रह्मचारिव्रते स्थितः ।
मनः संयम्य मच्चित्तो युक्त आसीत मत्परः ॥१४॥

13-14. Holding the body, head and neck erect, motionless (the posture proper to the practice of Rajayoga), the vision drawn in and fixed between eyebrows, not regarding the regions, the mind kept calm and free from fear and the vow of Brahmacharya observed, the whole controlled mentality turned to Me (the Divine), he must sit firm in Yoga, wholly given up to Me (so that the lower action of the consciousness shall be merged in the higher peace).

युञ्जन्नेवं सदात्मानं योगी नियतमानसः ।
शान्तिं निर्वाणपरमां मत्संस्थामधिगच्छति ॥१५॥

15. Thus always putting himself in Yoga by control of his

mind, the Yogin attains to the supreme peace of Nirvana[1] which has its foundation in Me.

नात्यश्नतस्तु योगोऽस्ति न चैकान्तमनश्नतः ।
न चाति स्वप्नशीलस्य जाग्रतो नैव चार्जुन ॥१६॥

16. Verily this Yoga is not for him who eats too much or sleeps too much, even as it is not for him who gives up sleep and food, O Arjuna.

युक्ताहारविहारस्य युक्तचेष्टस्य कर्मसु ।
युक्तस्वप्नावबोधस्य योगो भवति दुःखहा ॥१७॥

17. Yoga destroys all sorrow for him in whom the sleep and waking, the food, the play, the putting forth of effort in works are all *yukta*.[2]

---

[1] Yet the result is not, while one yet lives, a Nirvana which puts away every possibility of action in the world, every relation with beings in the world. It would seem at first that it ought to be so. When all the desires and passions have ceased, when the mind is no longer permitted to throw itself out in thought, when the practice of this silent and solitary Yoga has become the rule, what farther action or relation with the world of outward touches and mutable appearances is any longer possible? No doubt, the Yogin for a time still remains in the body, but the cave, the forest, the mountain-top seem now the fittest, the only possible scene of his continued living and constant trance of Samadhi his sole joy and occupation. But, first, while this solitary Yoga is being pursued, the renunciation of all other action is not recommended by the Gita.

[2] This is generally interpreted as meaning that all should be moderate, regulated, done in fit measure, and that may indeed be the significance. But at any rate when the Yoga is attained, all this has to be *yukta* in another sense, the ordinary sense of the word everywhere else in the Gita. In all states, in waking and in sleeping, in food and play and action, the Yogin will then be in Yoga with the Divine, and all will be done by him in the consciousness of the Divine as the self and as the All and as that which supports and contains his own life and his action. Desire and ego and personal will and the thought of the mind are the motives of action only in the lower nature; when the ego is lost and the Yogin becomes Brahman, when he lives in and is, even, a transcendent and universal consciousness,

यदा विनियतं चित्तमात्मन्येवावतिष्ठते ।
निःस्पृहः सर्वकामेभ्यो युक्त इत्युच्यते तदा ॥१८॥

18. When all the mental consciousness is perfectly controlled and liberated from desire and remains still in the self, then it is said, "He is in Yoga."

यथा दीपो निवातस्थो नेङ्गते सोपमा स्मृता ।
योगिनो यतचित्तस्य युञ्जतो योगमात्मनः ॥१९॥

19. Motionless like the light of a lamp in a windless place is the controlled consciousness (free from its restless action, shut in from its outward motion) of the Yogin who practises union with the Self.

यत्रोपरमते चित्तं निरुद्धं योगसेवया ।
यत्र चैवात्मनात्मानं पश्यन्नात्मनि तुष्यति ॥२०॥

20. That in which the mind becomes silent and still by the practice of Yoga; that in which the Self is seen within in the Self by the Self (seen, not as it is mistranslated falsely or partially by the mind and represented to us through the ego, but self-perceived by the Self, *svaprakāśa*), and the soul is satisfied.

सुखमात्यन्तिकं यत्तद् बुद्धिग्राह्यमतीन्द्रियम् ।
वेत्ति यत्र न चैवायं स्थितश्चलति तत्त्वतः ॥२१॥

21. That in which the soul knows its own true and exceeding bliss,[1] which is perceived by the intelligence and is

---

action comes spontaneously out of that, luminous knowledge higher than the mental thought comes out of that, a power other and mightier than the personal will comes out of that to do for him his works and bring its fruits; personal action has ceased, all has been taken up into the Brahman and assumed by the Divine, *mayi saṁyasya karmāṇi.*

[1] Not that untranquil happiness which is the portion of the mind and the senses, but an inner and serene felicity in which it is safe from the

beyond the senses, wherein established, it can no longer fall away from the spiritual truth of its being.

यं लब्ध्वा चापरं लाभं मन्यते नाधिकं ततः ।
यस्मिन् स्थितो न दुःखेन गुरुणापि विचाल्यते ॥२२॥

22. That is the greatest of all gains and the treasure beside which all lose their value, wherein established he is not disturbed by the fieriest assault of mental grief.

तं विद्याद् दुःखसंयोगवियोगं योगसंज्ञितम् ।
स निश्चयेन योक्तव्यो योगोऽनिर्विण्णचेतसा ॥२३॥

23. It is the putting away of the contact with pain, the divorce of the mind's marriage with grief. The firm winning of this inalienable spiritual bliss is Yoga; it is the divine union. This Yoga is to be resolutely practised without yielding to any discouragement by difficulty or failure (until the release, until the bliss of Nirvana is secured as an eternal possession).

संकल्पप्रभवान् कामांस्त्यक्त्वा सर्वानशेषतः ।
मनसैवेन्द्रियग्रामं विनियम्य समन्ततः ॥२४॥
शनैः शनैरुपरमेद् बुद्ध्या धृतिगृहीतया ।
आत्मसंस्थं मनः कृत्वा न किञ्चिदपि चिन्तयेत् ॥२५॥

24-25. Abandoning without any exception or residue all the desires born of the desire-will and holding the senses by the mind so that they shall not run to all sides (after their usual disorderly and restless habit), one should slowly cease from mental action by a buddhi held in the grasp of fixity,

---

mind's perturbations and can no longer fall away from the spiritual truth of its being.

The main stress here has fallen on the stilling of the emotive mind, the mind of desire and the senses which are the recipients of outward touches and reply to them with our customary emotional reactions; but even the mental thought has to be stilled in the silence of the self-existent being.

and having fixed the mind in the higher Self one should not think of anything at all.

यतो यतो निश्चरति मनश्चञ्चलमस्थिरम् ।
ततस्ततो नियम्यैतदात्मन्येव वशं नयेत् ॥२६॥

26. Whenever the restless and unquiet mind goes forth, it should be controlled and brought into subjection in the Self.

प्रशान्तमनसं ह्येनं योगिनं सुखमुत्तमम् ।
उपैति शान्तरजसं ब्रह्मभूतमकल्मषम् ॥२७॥

27. When the mind is thoroughly quieted, then there comes upon the Yogin stainless, passionless, the highest bliss of the soul that has become the Brahman.

युञ्जन्नेवं सदात्मानं योगी विगतकल्मषः ।
सुखेन ब्रह्मसंस्पर्शमत्यन्तं सुखमश्नुते ॥२८॥

28. Thus freed from stain of passion and putting himself constantly into Yoga, the Yogin easily and happily enjoys the touch of the Brahman which is an exceeding bliss.

सर्वभूतस्थमात्मानं सर्वभूतानि चात्मनि ।
ईक्षते योगयुक्तात्मा सर्वत्र समदर्शनः ॥२९॥

29. The man whose self is in Yoga, sees the self in all beings and all beings in the self, he is equal-visioned everywhere.

यो मां पश्यति सर्वत्र सर्वं च मयि पश्यति ।
तस्याहं न प्रणश्यामि स च मे न प्रणश्यति ॥३०॥

30. He who sees Me[1] everywhere and sees all in Me, to him I do not get lost, nor does he get lost to Me.

---

[1] All that he sees is to him the Self, all is his self, all is the Divine. But is there no danger, if he dwells at all in the mutability of the Kshara, of his

सर्वभूतस्थितं यो मां भजत्येकत्वमास्थितः ।
सर्वथा वर्तमानोऽपि स योगी मयि वर्तते ॥३१॥

31. The Yogin who has taken his stand upon oneness and loves[1] Me in all beings, however and in all ways he lives and acts, lives and acts in Me.

आत्मौपम्येन सर्वत्र समं पश्यति योऽर्जुन ।
सुखं वा यदि वा दुःखं स योगी परमो मतः ॥३२॥

---

losing all the results of this difficult Yoga, losing the Self and falling back into the mind, of the Divine losing him and the world getting him, of his losing the Divine and getting back in its place the ego and the lower nature? No, says the Gita. For this peace of Nirvana, though it is gained through the Akshara, is founded upon the being of the Purushottama, *mat-saṁsthām*, and that is extended, the Divine, the Brahman is extended too in the world of beings and, though transcendent of it, not imprisoned in its own transcendence. One has to see all things as He and live and act wholly in that vision; that is the perfect fruit of the Yoga.

But why act? Is it not safer to sit in one's solitude looking out upon the world, if you will, seeing it in Brahman, in the Divine, but not taking part in it, not moving in it, not living in it, not acting in it, living rather ordinarily in the inner Samadhi? Should not that be the law, the rule, the dharma of this highest spiritual condition? No, again; for the liberated Yogin there is no other law, rule, Dharma than simply this, to live in the Divine and love the Divine and be one with all beings; his freedom is an absolute and not a contingent freedom, self-existent and not dependent any longer on any rule of conduct, law of life or limitation of any kind. He has no longer any need of a process of Yoga, because he is now perpetually in Yoga.

[1] The love of the world spiritualised, changed from a sense experience to a soul experience, is founded on the love of God and in that love there is no peril and no shortcoming. Fear and disgust of the world may often be necessary for the recoil from the lower nature, for it is really the fear and disgust of our own ego which reflects itself in the world. But to see God in the world is to fear nothing, it is to embrace all in the being of God; to see all as the Divine is to hate and loathe nothing, but love God in the world and the world in God.

But at least the things of the lower nature will be shunned and feared, the things which the Yogin has taken so much trouble to surmount? Not this either; all is embraced in the equality of the self-vision.

32. He, O Arjuna, who sees with equality[1] everything in the image of the self whether it be grief or it be happiness, him I hold to be the supreme Yogin.

अर्जुन उवाच —
योऽयं योगस्त्वया प्रोक्तः साम्येन मधुसूदन ।
एतस्याहं न पश्यामि चञ्चलत्वात् स्थितिं स्थिराम् ॥३३॥

33. Arjuna said: This[2] Yoga of the nature of equality which has been described by Thee, O Madhusudana, I see no stable foundation for it owing to restlessness.

चञ्चलं हि मनः कृष्ण प्रमाथि बलवद् दृढम् ।
तस्याहं निग्रहं मन्ये वायोरिव सुदुष्करम् ॥३४॥

34. Restless indeed is the mind, O Krishna; it is vehement, strong and unconquerable; I deem it as hard to control as the wind.

---

[1] By this it is not meant at all that he himself shall fall from the griefless spiritual bliss and feel again worldly unhappiness, even in the sorrow of others, but seeing in others the play of the dualities which he himself has left and surmounted, he shall still see all as himself, his self in all, God in all and, not disturbed or bewildered by the appearances of these things, moved only by them to help and heal, to occupy himself with the good of all beings, to lead men to the spiritual bliss, to work for the progress of the world Godwards, he shall live the divine life, so long as days upon earth are his portion. The God-lover who can do this, can thus embrace all things in God, can look calmly on the lower nature and the works of the Maya of the three gunas and act in them and upon them without perturbation or fall or disturbance from the height and power of the spiritual oneness, free in the largeness of the God-vision, sweet and great and luminous in the strength of the God-nature, may well be declared to be the supreme Yogin. He indeed has conquered the creation, *jitaḥ sargaḥ*.

[2] When Arjuna realises fully the nature of the Yoga which he is bidden to embrace, his pragmatic nature accustomed to act from mental will and preference and desire is appalled by its difficulty and he asks what is the end of the soul which attempts and fails.

श्रीभगवान् उवाच—
असंशयं महाबाहो मनो दुर्निग्रहं चलम् ।
अभ्यासेन तु कौन्तेय वैराग्येण च गृह्यते ॥३५॥

35. The Blessed Lord said: Without doubt, O mighty-armed, the mind is restless and very difficult to restrain; but O Kaunteya, it may be controlled by constant practice and non-attachment.

असंयतात्मना योगो दुष्प्राप इति मे मतिः ।
वश्यात्मना तु यतता शक्योऽवाप्तुमुपायतः ॥३६॥

36. By one who is not self-controlled, this Yoga is difficult to attain; but by the self-controlled, it is attainable by properly directed efforts.

अर्जुन उवाच—
अयतिः श्रद्धयोपेतो योगाच्चलितमानसः ।
अप्राप्य योगसंसिद्धिं कां गतिं कृष्ण गच्छति ॥३७॥

37. Arjuna said: He who takes up Yoga with faith, but cannot control himself with the mind wandering away from Yoga, failing to attain perfection in Yoga, what is his end, O Krishna?

कच्चिन्नोभयविभ्रष्टश्छिन्नाभ्रमिव नश्यति ।
अप्रतिष्ठो महाबाहो विमूढो ब्रह्मणः पथि ॥३८॥

38. Does he not, O mighty-armed, lose both this life (of human activity and thought and emotion which it has left behind) and the Brahmic consciousness to which it aspires and falling from both perish like a dissolving cloud?

एतन्मे संशयं कृष्ण छेत्तुमर्हस्यशेषतः ।
त्वदन्यः संशयस्यास्य छेत्ता न ह्युपपद्यते ॥३९॥

39. This my doubt, O Krishna, please dispel completely

without leaving any residue; for there is none else than Thyself who can destroy this doubt.

श्रीभगवान् उवाच—
> पार्थ नैवेह नामुत्र विनाशस्तस्य विद्यते ।
> न हि कल्याणकृत्कश्चिद् दुर्गतिं तात गच्छति ॥४०॥

40. The Blessed Lord said: O son of Pritha, neither in this life nor hereafter is there destruction for him; never does anyone who practises good, O beloved, come to woe.

> प्राप्य पुण्यकृतां लोकानुषित्वा शाश्वतीः समाः ।
> शुचीनां श्रीमतां गेहे योगभ्रष्टोऽभिजायते ॥४१॥

41. Having attained to the world of the righteous and having dwelt there for immemorial years, he who fell from Yoga is again born in the house of such as are pure and glorious.

> अथवा योगिनामेव कुले भवति धीमताम् ।
> एतद्धि दुर्लभतरं लोके जन्म यदीदृशम् ॥४२॥

42. Or he may be born in the family of the wise Yogin; indeed such a birth is rare to obtain in this world.

> तत्र तं बुद्धिसंयोगं लभते पौर्वदेहिकम् ।
> यतते च ततो भूयः संसिद्धौ कुरुनन्दन ॥४३॥

43. There he recovers the mental state of union (with the Divine) which he had formed in his previous life; and with this he again endeavours for perfection, O joy of the Kurus.

> पूर्वाभ्यासेन तेनैव ह्रियते ह्यवशोऽपि सः ।
> जिज्ञासुरपि योगस्य शब्दब्रह्मातिवर्तते ॥४४॥

44. By that former practice he is irresistibly carried on.

Even the seeker after the knowledge of Yoga goes beyond the range of the Vedas and Upanishads.

प्रयत्नाद्यतमानस्तु योगी संशुद्धकिल्बिषः ।
अनेकजन्मसंसिद्धस्ततो याति परां गतिम् ॥४५॥

45. But the Yogin, endeavouring with assiduity, purified from sin, perfecting himself through many lives attains to the highest goal.

तपस्विभ्योऽधिको योगी ज्ञानिभ्योऽपि मतोऽधिकः ।
कर्मिभ्यश्चाधिको योगी तस्माद्योगी भवार्जुन ॥४६॥

46. The Yogin[1] is greater than the doers of askesis, greater than the men of knowledge, greater than the men of works; become then the Yogin, O Arjuna.

योगिनामपि सर्वेषां मद्गतेनान्तरात्मना ।
श्रद्धावान्भजते यो मां स मे युक्ततमो मतः ॥४७॥

47. Of all Yogins he who with all his inner self given up to me, for me has love and faith, him I hold to be the most united with me in Yoga.

इति श्रीमद्भगवद्गीतासूपनिषत्सु ब्रह्मविद्यायां योगशास्त्रे श्रीकृष्णार्जुनसंवादे
अध्यात्मयोगो नाम षष्ठोऽध्यायः ।

---

[1] The Gita brings in here as always bhakti as the climax of the Yoga, *sarvabhūtasthitaṁ yo māṁ bhajati ekatvam āsthitaḥ*; that may almost be said to sum up the whole final result of the Gita's teaching – whoever loves God in all and his soul is founded upon the divine oneness, however he lives and acts, lives and acts in God. And to emphasize it still more, after an intervention of Arjuna and a reply to his doubt as to how so difficult a Yoga can be at all possible for the restless mind of man, the divine Teacher returns to this idea and makes it his culminating utterance. "The Yogin is greater than the doers of askesis, greater than the men of knowledge, greater than the men of works; become then the Yogin, O Arjuna," the Yogin, one who seeks for and attains, by works and

knowledge and askesis or by whatever other means, not even spiritual knowledge or power or anything else for their own sake, but the union with God alone; for in that all else is contained and in that lifted beyond itself to a divinest significance. But even among Yogins the greatest is the Bhakta. "Of all Yogins he who with all his inner self given up to me, for me has love and faith *śraddhāvān bhajate*, him I hold to be the most united with me in Yoga." It is this that is the closing word of these first six chapters and contains in itself the seed of the rest, of that which still remains unspoken and is nowhere entirely spoken; for it is always and remains something of a mystery and a secret, *rahasyam*, the highest spiritual mystery and the divine secret.

Seventh Chapter

I. THE TWO NATURES

श्रीभगवान् उवाच —
मय्यासक्तमनाः पार्थ योगं युञ्जन्मदाश्रयः ।
असंशयं समग्रं मां यथा ज्ञास्यसि तच्छृणु ॥१॥

1. The Blessed Lord said: Hear, O Partha, how by practising Yoga with a mind attached to me and with me as *āśraya* (the whole basis, lodgement, point of resort of the conscious being and action) thou shalt know me without any remainder of doubt, integrally.[1]

ज्ञानं तेऽहं सविज्ञानमिदं वक्ष्याम्यशेषतः ।
यज्ज्ञात्वा नेह भूयोऽन्यज्ज्ञातव्यमवशिष्यते ॥२॥

2. I will speak to thee without omission or remainder the essential knowledge, attended with all the comprehensive knowledge, by knowing which there shall be no other thing here left to be known.

मनुष्याणां सहस्रेषु कश्चिद्यतति सिद्धये ।
यततामपि सिद्धानां कश्चिन्मां वेत्ति तत्त्वतः ॥३॥

---

[1] The implication of the phrase is that the Divine Being is all, *vasudevah sarvam*, and therefore if he is known integrally in all his powers and principles, then all is known, not only the pure Self, but the world and action and Nature. There is then nothing else here left to be known, because all is that Divine Existence. It is only because our view here is not thus integral, because it rests on the dividing mind and reason and the separative idea of the ego, that our mental perception of things is an ignorance. We have to get away from this mental and egoistic view to the true unifying knowledge, and that has two aspects, the essential, *jñāna*, and the comprehensive, *vijñāna*, the direct spiritual awareness of the supreme Being and the right intimate knowledge of the principles of his existence, Prakriti, Purusha and the rest, by which all that is can be known in its divine origin and in the supreme truth of its nature. That integral knowledge, says the Gita, is a rare and difficult thing.

3. Among thousands of men one here and there strives after perfection, and of those who strive and attain to perfection one here and there knows me in all the principles of my existence.

भूमिरापोऽनलो वायुः खं मनो बुद्धिरेव च ।
अहङ्कार इतीयं मे भिन्ना प्रकृतिरष्टधा ॥४॥

4. The five elements (conditions of material being), mind (with its various senses and organs), reason, ego, this is my eightfold[1] divided Nature.

अपरेयमितस्त्वन्यां प्रकृतिं विद्धि मे पराम् ।
जीवभूतां महाबाहो ययेदं धार्यते जगत् ॥५॥

5. This the lower. But know my other Nature[2] different

---

[1] To start with and in order to found this integral knowledge, the Gita makes that deep and momentous distinction which is the practical basis of all its Yoga, the distinction between the two Natures, the phenomenal and the spiritual Nature. Here is the first new metaphysical idea of the Gita which helps it to start from the notions of the Sankhya philosophy and yet exceed them and give to their terms, which it keeps and extends, a Vedantic significance. An eightfold nature is the Sankhya description of Prakriti. The Sankhya stops there, and because it stops there, it has to set up an unbridgeable division between the soul and Nature; it has to posit them as two quite distinct primary entities. The Gita also, if it stopped there, would have to make the same incurable antinomy between the Self and cosmic Nature which would then be only the Maya of the three gunas and all this cosmic existence would be simply the result of this Maya; it could be nothing else. But there is something else, there is a higher principle, a nature of spirit, *parā prakṛtir me*.

[2] This "I" here is the Purushottama, the supreme Being, the supreme Soul, the transcendent and universal Spirit. The original and eternal nature of the Spirit and its transcendent and originating Shakti is what is meant by the Para Prakriti. For speaking first of the origin of the world from the point of view of the active power of his Nature, Krishna assevers, "This is the womb of all beings." And in the next line of the couplet, again stating the same fact from the point of view of the originating Soul, he continues, "I am the birth of the whole world and so too its dissolution; there is nothing else supreme beyond Me." Here then the supreme Soul,

from this, O mighty-armed, the supreme which becomes the Jiva[1] and by which this world is upheld.

Purushottama, and the supreme Nature, Para Prakiriti, are identified; they are put as two ways of looking at one and the same reality. For when Krishna declares "I am the birth of the world and its dissolution," it is evident that it is this Para Prakriti, supreme Nature, of his being which is both these things. The Spirit is the supreme Being in his infinite consciousness and the supreme Nature is the infinity of power or will of being of the Spirit, – it is his infinite consciousness in its inherent divine energy and its supernal divine action. The birth is the movement of evolution of this conscious Energy out of the Spirit, *parā prakṛtir jīvabhūtā*, its activity in the mutable universe; the dissolution is the withdrawing of that activity by involution of the Energy into the immutable existence and self-gathered power of the Spirit. That then is what is initially meant by the supreme Nature.

[1] The supreme Nature, *parā prakṛtiḥ*, is then the infinite timeless conscious power of the self-existent Being out of which all existences in the cosmos are manifested and come out of timelessness into Time. But in order to provide a spiritual basis for this manifold universal becoming in the cosmos the supreme Nature formulates itself as the Jiva. To put it otherwise, the eternal multiple soul of the Purushottama appears as individual spiritual existence in all the forms of the cosmos. All existences are instinct with the life of the one indivisible Spirit; all are supported in their personality, actions and forms by the eternal multiplicity of the one Purusha. We must be careful not to make the mistake of thinking that this supreme Nature is identical with the Jiva manifested in Time in the sense that there is nothing else or that it is only nature of becoming and not at all nature of being: that could not be the supreme Nature of the Spirit. Even in time it is something more; for otherwise the only truth of it in the cosmos would be nature of multiplicity and there would be no nature of unity in the world. That is not what the Gita says: it does not say that the supreme Prakriti is in its essence the Jiva, *jīvātmikām*, but that it has become the Jiva, *jīvabhūtām*; and it is implied in that expression that behind its manifestation as the Jiva here it is originally something else and higher, it is nature of the one supreme spirit. The Jiva, as we are told later on, is the Lord, *īśvara*, but in his partial manifestation, *mamaivāṁśaḥ*; even all the multiplicity of beings in the universe or in numberless universes could not be in their becoming the integral Divine, but only a partial manifestation of the infinite One. In them Brahman the one indivisible existence resides as if divided, *avibhaktam ca bhūteṣu vibhaktam iva ca sthitam*. The unity is the greater truth, the multiplicity is the

एतद्योनीनि भूतानि सर्वाणीत्युपधारय ।
अहं कृत्स्नस्य जगतः प्रभवः प्रलयस्तथा ॥६॥

6. Know this to be the womb of all beings. I am the birth of the whole world and so too its dissolution.

मत्तः परतरं नान्यत्किञ्चिदस्ति धनञ्जय ।
मयि सर्वमिदं प्रोतं सूत्रे मणिगणा इव ॥७॥

7. There is nothing else supreme beyond Me, O Dhananjaya. On Me[1] all that is here is strung like pearls upon a thread.

lesser truth, though both are a truth and neither of them is an illusion.

It is by the unity of this spiritual nature that the world is sustained, *yayedam dhāryate jagat*, even as it is that from which it is born with all its becomings, *etad-yonīni bhūtāni sarvāṇi*, and that also which withdraws the whole world and its existences into itself in the hour of dissolution, *aham kṛtsnasya jagataḥ prabhavaḥ pralayastathā*. But in the manifestation which is thus put forth in the Spirit, upheld in its action, withdrawn in its periodical rest from action, the Jiva is the basis of the multiple existence; it is the multiple soul, if we may so call it, or, if we prefer, the soul of the multiplicity we experience here. It is one always with the Divine in its being, different from it only in the power of its being, – different not in the sense that it is not at all the same power, but in this sense that it only supports the one power in a partial multiply individualised action. Therefore all things are initially, ultimately and in the principle of their continuance too the Spirit. The fundamental nature of all is nature of the Spirit, and only in their lower differential phenomena do they seem to be something else, to be nature of body, life, mind, reason, ego and the senses. But these are phenomenal derivatives, they are not the essential truth of our nature and our existence.

The supreme nature of spiritual being gives us then both an original truth and power of existence beyond cosmos and a first basis of spiritual truth for the manifestation in the cosmos. But where is the link between this supreme nature and the lower phenomenal nature?

[1] This is only an image which we cannot press very far: for the pearls are only kept in relation to each other by the thread and have no other oneness or relation with the pearl-string except their dependence on it for this mutual connection. Let us go then from the image to that which it images. It is the supreme nature of Spirit, the infinite conscious power of its being, self-conscient, all-conscient, all-wise, which maintains these

SEVENTH CHAPTER

रसोऽहमप्सु कौन्तेय प्रभास्मि शशिसूर्ययो: ।
प्रणव: सर्ववेदेषु शब्द: खे पौरुषं नृषु ॥८॥

8. I am taste[1] in the waters, O son of Kunti, I am the light[2]

phenomenal existences in relation to each other, penetrates them, abides in and supports them and weaves them into the system of its manifestation. This one supreme power manifests not only in all as the One, but in each as the Jiva, the individual spiritual presence; it manifests also as the essence of all quality of Nature. These are therefore the concealed spiritual powers behind all phenomena. This highest quality is not the working of the three gunas, which is phenomenon of quality and not its spiritual essence. It is rather the inherent, one, yet variable inner power of all these superficial variations. It is a fundamental truth of the Becoming, a truth that supports and gives a spiritual and divine significance to all its appearances. The workings of the gunas are only the superficial unstable becomings of reason, mind, sense, ego, life and matter, *sāttvikā bhāva rājāsastāmasāśca*; but this is rather the essential stable original intimate power of the becoming, *svabhāva*. It is that which determines the primary law of all becoming and of each Jiva; it constitutes the essence and develops the movement of the nature. It is a principle in each creature that derives from and is immediately related to a transcendent divine Becoming, that of the Ishvara, *madbhāvaḥ*. In this relation of the divine *bhāva* to the *svabhāva* and of the *svabhāva* to the superficial *bhāvāḥ*, of the divine Nature to the individual self-nature and of self-nature in its pure and original quality to the phenomenal nature in all its mixed and confused play of qualities, we find the link between that supreme and this lower existence. The degraded powers and values of the inferior Prakriti derive from the absolute powers and values of the supreme Shakti and must go back to them to find their own source and truth and the essential law of their operation and movement. So too the soul or Jiva involved here in the shackled, poor and inferior play of the phenomenal qualities, if he would escape from it and be divine and perfect, must by resort to the pure action of his essential quality of *svabhāva* go back to that higher law of his own being in which he can discover the will, the power, the dynamic principle, the highest working of his divine nature.

This is clear from the immediately subsequent passage in which the Gita gives a number of instances to show how the Divine in the power of his supreme Nature manifests and acts within the animate and so-called inanimate existences of the universe.

[1] The Divine himself in his Para Prakriti is energy at the basis of the various sensory relations of which, according to the ancient Sankhya system, the ethereal, the radiant, electric and gaseous, the liquid and the

of sun and moon, I am pranava[1] (the syllable OM) in all the Vedas, sound in ether and manhood in men.

---

other elemental conditions of matter are the physical medium. The five elemental conditions of matter are the quantitative or material element in the lower nature and are the basis of material forms. The five *tanmātras* – taste, touch, scent and the others – are the qualitative element. These *tanmātras* are the subtle energies whose action puts the sensory consciousness in relation to the gross forms of matter, – they are the basis of all phenomenal knowledge. From the material point of view matter is the reality and the sensory relations are derivative; but from the spiritual point of view the truth is the opposite. Matter and the material media are themselves derivative powers and at bottom are only concrete ways or conditions in which the workings of the quality of Nature in things manifest themselves to the sensory consciousness of the Jiva. The one original and eternal fact is the energy of Nature, the power and quality of being which so manifests itself to the soul through the senses. And what is essential in the senses, most spiritual, most subtle is itself stuff of that eternal quality and power. But energy or power of being in Nature is the Divine himself in his Prakriti; each sense in its purity is therefore that Prakriti, each sense is the Divine in his dynamic conscious force.

[2] In each case it is the energy of the essential quality on which each of these becomings depends for what it has become, that is given as the characteristic sign indicating the presence of the divine Power in their nature.

[1] The basic syllable OM is the foundation of all the potent creative sounds of the revealed word; OM is the one universal formulation of the energy of sound and speech, that which contains and sums up, synthesises and releases, all the spiritual power and all the potentiality of *vāk* and *śabda* and of which the other sounds, out of whose stuff words of speech, are woven, are supposed to be the developed evolutions. That makes it quite clear. It is not the phenomenal developments of the senses or of life or of light, intelligence, energy, strength, manhood, ascetic force that are proper to the supreme Prakriti. It is the essential quality in its spiritual power that constitutes the *svabhāva*. It is the force of spirit so manifesting, it is the light of its consciousness and the power of its energy in things revealed in a pure original sign that is the self-nature. That force, light, power is the eternal seed from which all other things are the developments and derivations and variabilities and plastic circumstances. Therefore the Gita throws in as the most general statement in the series, "Know me to be the eternal seed of all existences, O son of Pritha." This eternal seed is the power of spiritual being, the concious will in the being, the seed which, as is said elsewhere, the Divine casts into the great Brahman, into

पुण्यो गन्धः पृथिव्यां च तेजश्चास्मि विभावसौ।
जीवनं सर्वभूतेषु तपश्चास्मि तपस्विषु ॥९॥

9. I am pure scent in earth and energy of light in fire; I am life in all existences, I am the ascetic force of those who do askesis.

बीजं मां सर्वभूतानां विद्धि पार्थ सनातनम्।
बुद्धिर्बुद्धिमतामस्मि तेजस्तेजस्विनामहम् ॥१०॥

10. Know me to be the eternal seed of all existences, O son of Pritha. I am the intelligence of the intelligent, the energy of the energetic.

बलं बलवतां चाहं कामरागविवर्जितम्।
धर्माविरुद्धो भूतेषु कामोऽस्मि भरतर्षभ ॥११॥

11. I am the strength of the strong devoid of desire and liking.[1] I am in beings the desire which is not contrary to dharma, O Lord of the Bharatas.

---

the supramental vastness, and from that all are born into phenomenal existence. It is that seed of Spirit which manifests itself as the essential quality in all becomings and constitutes their *svabhāva*.

[1] The practical distinction between this original power of essential quality and the phenomenal derivations of the lower nature, between the thing itself in its purity and the thing in its lower appearances, is indicated very clearly at the close of the series.

But how can the Divine be desire, *kāma*? for this desire, this Kama has been declared to be our one great enemy who has to be slain. But that desire was the desire of the lower nature of the gunas which has its native point of origin in the rajasic being, *rajoguṇa-samudbhavaḥ*; for this is what we usually mean when we speak of desire. This other, the spiritual, is a will not contrary to the dharma. Dharma in the spiritual sense is not morality or ethics. Dharma, says the Gita elsewhere, is action governed by the swabhava, the essential law of one's nature. And this swabhava is at its core the pure quality of the spirit in its inherent power of conscious will and its characteristic force of action. The desire meant here is therefore the purposeful will of the Divine in us searching for and discovering not the pleasure of the lower Prakriti, but the Ananda of its

ये चैव सात्त्विका भावा राजसास्तामसाश्च ये ।
मत्त एवेति तान् विद्धि न त्वहं तेषु ते मयि ॥१२॥

12. And as for the secondary subjective becomings of Nature, *bhāvāḥ* (states of mind, affections of desire, movements of passion, the reactions of the senses, the limited and dual play of reason, the turns of the feeling and moral sense), which are sattwic, rajasic and tamasic, they are verily from me, but I am not in them, it is they that are in Me.[1]

त्रिभिर्गुणमयैर्भावैरेभिः सर्वमिदं जगत् ।
मोहितं नाभिजानाति मामेभ्यः परमव्ययम् ॥१३॥

own play and self-fulfilling; it is the desire of the divine Delight of existence unrolling its own conscious force of action in accordance with the law of the *svabhāva*.

[1] What again is meant by saying that the Divine is not in the becomings, the forms and affections of the lower nature, even the sattwic, though they all are in his being? In a sense he must evidently be in them, otherwise they could not exist. But what is meant is that the true and supreme spiritual nature of the Divine is not imprisoned there; they are only phenomena in his being created out of it by the action of the ego and the ignorance. The ignorance presents everything to us in an inverted vision and at least a partially falsified experience. We imagine that the soul is in the body, almost a result and derivation from the body; even we so feel it: but it is the body that is in the soul and a result and derivation from the soul. We think of the spirit as a small part of us – the Purusha who is no bigger than the thumb – in this great mass of material and mental phenomena: in reality, the latter for all its imposing appearance is a very small thing in the infinity of the being of the spirit. So it is here; in much the same sense these things are in the Divine rather than the Divine in these things. This lower nature of the three gunas which creates so false a view of things and imparts to them an inferior character is a Maya, a power of illusion, by which it is not meant that it is all non-existent or deals with unrealities, but that it bewilders our knowledge, creates false values, envelops us in ego, mentality, sense, physicality, limited intelligence and there conceals from us the supreme truth of our existence. This illusive Maya hides from us the Divine that we are, the infinite and imperishable spirit. If we could see that the Divine is the real truth of our existence, all else also would change to our vision, assume its true character and our life and action acquire the divine values and move in the law of the divine nature.

13. By these three kinds of becoming which are of the nature of the gunas, this whole world is bewildered and does not recognise Me supreme beyond them and imperishable.

दैवी ह्येषा गुणमयी मम माया दुरत्यया ।
मामेव ये प्रपद्यन्ते मायामेतां तरन्ति ते ॥१४॥

14. This is my divine[1] Maya of the gunas and it is hard to overcome; those cross beyond it who approach Me.

---

[1] It is itself divine and a development from the nature of the Divine, but the Divine in the nature of the gods; it is *daivī*, of the godheads or, if you will, of the Godhead, but of the Godhead in its divided subjective and lower cosmic aspects, sattwic, rajasic and tamasic. It is a cosmic veil which the Godhead has spun around our understanding; Brahma, Vishnu and Rudra have woven its complex threads; the Shakti, the Supreme Nature is there at its base and is hidden in its every tissue. We have to work out this web in ourselves and turn through it and from it leaving it behind us when its use is finished, turn from the gods to the original and supreme Godhead in whom we shall discover at the same time the last sense of the gods and their works and the inmost spiritual verities of our own imperishable existence. "To Me who turn and come, they alone cross over beyond this Maya."

II. THE SYNTHESIS OF DEVOTION AND KNOWLEDGE

(The Gita, after giving us in the first fourteen verses of this chapter a leading philosophical truth of which we stand in need, hastens in the next sixteen verses to make an immediate application of it. It turns it into a first starting-point for the unification of works, knowledge and devotion, – for the preliminary synthesis of works and knowledge by themselves has already been accomplished.

The intrinsic activity of the supreme Nature (Para Prakriti) is always a spiritual, a divine working. It is force of the supreme divine Nature, it is the conscious will of the being of the Supreme that throws itself out in various essential and spiritual power of quality in the Jiva: that essential power is the swabhava of the Jiva. All act and becoming which proceed directly from this spiritual force are a divine becoming and a pure and spiritual action. Therefore it follows that in action the effort of the human individual must be to get back to his true spiritual personality and to make all his works flow from the power of its supernal Shakti, to develop action through the soul and the inmost intrinsic being, not through the mental idea and vital desire, and to turn all his acts into a pure outflowing of the will of the Supreme, all his life into a dynamic symbol of the Divine Nature.)

न मां दुष्कृतिनो मूढाः प्रपद्यन्ते नराधमाः ।
माययापहृतज्ञाना आसुरं भावमाश्रिताः ॥१५॥

15. The evil-doers attain not to Me, souls bewildered,[1] low in the human scale; for their knowledge is reft away from them by Maya and they resort to the nature of being of the Asura.

[1] This bewilderment is a befooling of the soul in Nature by the deceptive ego. The evil-doer cannot attain to the Supreme, because he is for ever trying to satisfy the idol ego on the lowest scale of human nature;

SEVENTH CHAPTER

चतुर्विधा भजन्ते मां जनाः सुकृतिनोऽर्जुन ।
आर्तो जिज्ञासुरर्थार्थीं ज्ञानी च भरतर्षभ ॥१६॥

his real God is this ego. His mind and will, hurried away in the activities of the Maya of the three gunas, are not instruments of the spirit, but willing slaves or self-deceived tools of his desires. The Gita has laid it down from the beginning that the very first precondition of the divine birth, the higher existence is the slaying of rajasic desire and its children, and that means the exclusion of sin. Sin is the working of the lower nature for the crude satisfaction of its own ignorant, dull or violent rajasic and tamasic propensities in revolt against any high self-control and self-mastery of the nature by the spirit. And in order to get rid of this crude compulsion of the being by the lower Prakriti in its inferior modes we must have recourse to the highest mode of that Prakriti, the sattwic, which is seeking always for a harmonious light of knowledge and for a right rule of action. The Purusha, the soul within us which assents in Nature to the varying impulse of the gunas, has to give its sanction to that sattwic impulse and that sattwic will and temperament in our being which seeks after such a rule. The sattwic will in our nature has to govern us and not the rajasic and tamasic will. This is the meaning of all high reason in action as of all true ethical culture; it is the law of Nature in us striving to evolve from her lower and disorderly to her higher and orderly action, to act not in passion and ignorance with the result of grief and unquiet, but in knowledge and enlightened will with the result of inner happiness, poise and peace. We cannot get beyond the three gunas, if we do not first develop within ourselves the rule of the highest guna, sattwa Man, therefore, has first of all to become ethical, *sukṛti*, and then to rise to heights beyond any mere ethical rule of living, to the light, largeness and power of the spiritual nature, where he gets beyond the grasp of the dualities and its delusion, *dvandva-moha*. There he no longer seeks his personal good or pleasure or shuns his personal suffering or pain, for by these things he is no longer affected, nor says any longer, "I am virtuous," "I am sinful," but acts in his own high spiritual nature by the will of the Divine for the universal good.

We have already seen that for this end self-knowledge, equality, impersonality are the first necessities, and that that is the way of reconciliation between knowledge and works, between spirituality and activity in the world, between the ever immobile quietism of the timeless Self and the eternal play of the pragmatic energy of Nature. But the Gita now lays down another and greater necessity for the Karmayogin who has unified his Yoga of works with the Yoga of knowledge. Not knowledge and works alone are demanded of him, but *bhakti* also, devotion to the Divine, love and adoration and the soul's desire of the Highest.

16. Among the virtuous ones who turns towards Me (the Divine) with devotion, O Arjuna, there are four[1] kinds of *bhaktas*; the suffering, the seeker for good in the world, the seeker for knowledge, and those who adore Me with knowledge, O Lord of the Bharatas.

तेषां ज्ञानी नित्ययुक्त एकभक्तिर्विशिष्यते ।
प्रियो हि ज्ञानिनोऽत्यर्थमहं स च मम प्रियः ॥१७॥

17. Of these the knower, who is ever in constant union with the Divine, whose bhakti[2] is all concentrated on Him, is the best; he loves Me perfectly and is My beloved.

उदाराः सर्व एवैते ज्ञानी त्वात्मैव मे मतम् ।
आस्थितः स हि युक्तात्मा मामेवानुत्तमां गतिम् ॥१८॥

18. Noble are all these without exception, but the knower

---

[1] We may say that these forms are successively the bhakti of the vital-emotional and affective nature, that of the practical and dynamic nature, that of the reasoning intellectual nature, and that of the highest intuitive being which takes up all the rest of the nature into unity with the Divine. Practically, however, the others may be regarded as preparatory movements. For the Gita itself here says that it is only at the end of many existences that one can, after possession of the integral knowledge and after working that out in oneself throughout many lives, attain at the long last to the Transcendent. For the knowledge of the Divine as all things that are is difficult to attain and rare on earth is the great soul, *mahātmā*, who is capable of fully so seeing him and of entering into him with his whole being, in every way of his nature, by the wide power of this all-embracing knowledge, *sarvavit sarvabhāvena*.

[2] This single devotion is his whole law of living and he has gone beyond all creeds of religious belief, rules of conduct, personal aims of life. He has no griefs to be healed, for he is in possession of the All-blissful. He has no desires to hunger after, for he possesses the highest and the All and is close to the All-power that brings all fulfilment. He has no doubts or baffled seekings left, for all knowledge streams upon him from the Light in which he lives. He loves perfectly the Divine and is his beloved; for as he takes joy in the Divine, so too the Divine takes joy in him. This is the God-lover who has the knowledge, *jñānī bhakta*.

is verily my self; for as his highest goal he accepts Me, the Purushottama with whom he is in union.

बहूनां जन्मनामन्ते ज्ञानवान्मां प्रपद्यते ।
वासुदेवः सर्वमिति स महात्मा सुदुर्लभः ॥१९॥

19. At the end of many births the man of knowledge attains to Me. Very rare is the great soul who knows[1] that Vasudeva, the omnipresent Being, is all that is.

कामैस्तैस्तैर्हृतज्ञानाः प्रपद्यन्तेऽन्यदेवताः ।
तं तं नियममास्थाय प्रकृत्या नियताः स्वया ॥२०॥

20. Men are led away by various outer desires which take from them the working of the inner knowledge; they resort to other godheads and they set up this or that rule, which satisfies the need of their nature.

यो यो यां यां तनुं भक्तः श्रद्धयार्चितुमिच्छति ।
तस्य तस्याचलां श्रद्धां तामेव विदधाम्यहम् ॥२१॥

21. Whatever form of Me any devotee with faith desires to worship, I make that faith of his firm and undeviating.

स तया श्रद्धया युक्तस्तस्याराधनमीहते ।
लभते च ततः कामान् मयैव विहितान् हि तान् ॥२२॥

22. He endowed with that faith worships that form; and when by the force of that faith in his cult and worship he gets his desires, it is I myself who (in that form) give these fruits.

---

[1] And this knower, says the Godhead in the Gita, is my self; the others seize only motives and aspects in Nature, but he the very self-being and all-being of the Purushottama with which he is in union. His is the divine birth in the supreme Nature, integral in being, completed in will, absolute in love, perfected in knowledge. In him the Jiva's cosmic existence is justified because it has exceeded itself and so found its own whole and highest truth of being.

अन्तवत्तु फलं तेषां तद्भवत्यल्पमेधसाम् ।
देवान्देवयजो यान्ति मद्भक्ता यान्ति मामपि ॥२३॥

23. But these fruits are temporary,[1] sought after by those who are of petty intelligence and unformed reason. To the gods go the worshippers of the gods, but my devotees come to Me.

अव्यक्तं व्यक्तिमापन्नं मन्यन्ते मामबुद्धयः ।
परं भावमजानन्तो ममाव्ययमनुत्तमम् ॥२४॥

24. Petty minds think of Me, the unmanifest, as being limited by manifestation, because they know not my supreme nature of being, imperishable, most perfect.

नाहं प्रकाशः सर्वस्य योगमायासमावृतः ।
मूढोऽयं नाभिजानाति लोको मामजमव्ययम् ॥२५॥

25. Nor am I revealed to all, enveloped in my Yogamaya;[2] this bewildered[3] world knows Me not, the unborn, the imperishable.

[1] So far as there is a spiritual attainment by this way, it is only to the gods; it is only the Divine in formations of mutable nature and as the giver of her results that they realise. But those who adore the transcendent and integral Godhead embrace all this and transform it all, exalt the gods to their highest, Nature to her summits, and go beyond them to the very Godhead, realise and attain to the Transcendent. Still the supreme Godhead does not at all reject these devotees because of their imperfect vision. For the Divine in his supreme transcendent being, unborn, imminuable and superior to all these partial manifestations, cannot be easily known to any living creature.
[2] He is self-enveloped in this immense cloak of Maya, that Maya of his Yoga, by which he is one with the world and yet beyond it, immanent but hidden, seated in all hearts but not revealed to any and every being. Man in Nature thinks that these manifestations in Nature are all the Divine, when they are only his works and his powers and his veils.
[3] If after thus bewildering them with his workings in Nature, he were not to meet them in these at all, there would be no divine hope for man or for any soul in Maya. Therefore according to their nature, as they

वेदाहं समतीतानि वर्तमानानि चार्जुन ।
भविष्याणि च भूतानि मां तु वेद न कश्चन ।।२६।।

26. I know all past and all present and future existences, O Arjuna, but Me none yet knows.

इच्छाद्वेषसमुत्थेन द्वन्द्वमोहेन भारत ।
सर्वभूतानि सम्मोहं सर्गे यान्ति परन्तप ।।२७।।

27. By the delusion[1] of the dualities which arises from wish and disliking, O Bharata, all existences in the creation are led into bewilderment.

---

approach him, he accepts their bhakti and answers to it with the reply of divine love and compassion. These forms are after all a certain kind of manifestation through which the imperfect human intelligence can touch him, these desires are first means by which our souls turn towards him: nor is any devotion worthless or ineffective, whatever its limitations. It has the one grand necessity, faith. "Whatever form of me any devotee with faith desires to worship, I make that faith of his firm and undeviating." By the force of that faith in his cult and worship he gets his desire and the spiritual realisation for which he is at the moment fitted. By seeking all his good from the Divine, he shall come in the end to seek in the Divine all his good. By depending for his joys on the Divine, he shall learn to fix in the Divine all his joy. By knowing the Divine in his forms and qualities, he shall come to know him as the All and the Transcendent who is the source of all things. Thus by spiritual development devotion becomes one with knowledge. The Jiva comes to delight in the one Godhead, – in the Divine known as all being and consciousness and delight and as all things and beings and happenings, known in Nature, known in the self, known for that which exceeds self and Nature. We have now set before us three interdependent movements of our release out of the normal nature and our growth into the divine and spiritual being.

[1] That is the ignorance, the egoism which fails to see and lay hold on the Divine everywhere, because it sees only the dualities of Nature and is constantly occupied with its own separate personality and its seekings and shrinkings. For escape from this circle the first necessity in our works is to get clear of the sin of the vital ego, the fire of passion, the tumult of desire of the rajasic nature, and this has to be done by the steadying sattwic impulse of the ethical being.

येषां त्वन्तगतं पापं जनानां पुण्यकर्मणाम् ।
ते द्वन्द्वमोहनिर्मुक्ता भजन्ते मां दृढव्रताः ॥२८॥

28. But those men of virtuous deeds, in whom sin is come to an end, they, freed from the delusion of the dualities,[1] worship[2] Me, steadfast in the vow of self-consecration.

जरामरणमोक्षाय मामाश्रित्य यतन्ति ये ।
ते ब्रह्म तद्विदुः कृत्स्नमध्यात्मं कर्म चाखिलम् ॥२९॥

29. Those who have resort to Me as their refuge, those who turn to me in their spiritual effort towards release from

[1] When that is done, or rather as it is being done, for after a certain point all growth in the sattwic nature brings an increasing capacity for a high quietude, equality and transcendence, – it is necessary to rise above the dualities and to become impersonal, equal, one self with the Immutable, one self with all existences. This process of growing into the spirit completes our purification.

[2] But while this is being done, while the soul is enlarging into self-knowledge, it has also to increase in devotion. For it has not only to act in a large spirit of equality, but to do also sacrifice to the Lord, to that Godhead in all beings which it does not yet know perfectly, but which it will be able so to know, integrally, when it has firmly the vision of the one self everywhere and in all existences. Equality and vision of unity once perfectly gained, a supreme bhakti, an all-embracing devotion to the Divine, becomes the whole and the sole law of the being. All other law of conduct merges into that surrender, *sarva dharmān parityajya*. The soul then becomes firm in this bhakti and in the vow of self-consecration of all its being, knowledge, works; for it has now for its sure base, its absolute foundation of existence and action the perfect, the integral, the unifying knowledge of the all-originating Godhead.

An integral knowledge in our self-giving is the first condition of its effective force. And therefore we have first of all to know this Purusha in all the powers and principles of his divine existence, *tattvataḥ*, in the whole harmony of it, in its eternal essence and living process. But to the ancient thought all the value of this knowledge, *tattva jñāna*, lay in its power for release out of our mortal birth into the immortality of a supreme existence. The Gita therefore proceeds next to show how this liberation too in the highest degree is a final outcome of its own movement of spiritual self-fulfilment. The knowledge of the Purushottama, it says in effect, is the perfect knowledge of the Brahman.

age and death, (from the mortal being and its limitations), come to know that Brahman and all the integrality of the spiritual nature and the entirety of Karma.

साधिभूताधिदैवं मां साधियज्ञं च ये विदुः ।
प्रयाणकालेऽपि च मां ते विदुर्युक्तचेतसः ॥३०॥

30. Because they know Me and know at the same time the material and the divine nature of being and the truth of the Master of sacrifice, they keep knowledge of Me also in the critical moment of their departure from physical existence and have at that moment their whole consciousness in union with Me[1] (the Purushottama).

इति श्रीमद्भगवद्गीतासूपनिषत्सु ब्रह्मविद्यायां योगशास्त्रे श्रीकृष्णार्जुनसंवादे
ज्ञानविज्ञानयोगो नाम सप्तमोऽध्यायः ।

---

[1] Therefore they attain to Me. No longer bound to the mortal existence, they reach the very highest status of the Divine quite as effectively as those who lose their separate personality in the impersonal and immutable Brahman. Thus the Gita closes this important and decisive seventh chapter.

Eighth Chapter

THE SUPREME DIVINE

(In the last two slokas of the seventh chapter we have certain expressions which give us in their brief sum the chief essential truths of the manifestation of the supreme Divine in the cosmos. All the originative and effective aspects of it are there, all that concerns the soul in its return to integral self-knowledge. First, there is that Brahman, *tad brahma;* *adhyātma,* second, the principle of the self in nature; *adhibhūta* and *adhidaiva* next, the objective phenomenon and subjective phenomenon of being; *adhiyajña* last, the secret of the cosmic principle of works and sacrifice. I, the Purushottama (*mam viduḥ*), says in effect Krishna, I who am above all these things, must yet be sought and known through all together and by means of their relations, – that is the only complete way for the human consciousness which is seeking its path back towards Me. But these terms in themselves are not at first quite clear or at least they are open to different interpretations, they have to be made precise in their connotation, and Arjuna the disciple at once asks for their elucidation. Krishna answers very briefly, – nowhere does the Gita linger very long upon any purely metaphysical explanation; it gives only so much and in such a way as will make their truth just seizable for the soul to proceed on to experience.)

अर्जुन उवाच —
किं तद् ब्रह्म किमध्यात्मं किं कर्म पुरुषोत्तम ।
अधिभूतं च किं प्रोक्तमधिदैवं किमुच्यते ॥१॥

1. Arjuna said: What is *tad brahma*, what *adhyātma*, what *karma*, O Purushottama? And what is declared to be *adhibhuta*, what is called *adhidaiva*?

अधियज्ञः कथं कोऽत्र देहेऽस्मिन्मधुसूदन ।
प्रयाणकाले च कथं ज्ञेयोऽसि नियतात्मभिः ॥२॥

2. What is *adhiyajña* in this body, O Madhusudana? And how, in the critical moment of departure from physical existence, art Thou to be known by the self-controlled?

श्रीभगवान् उवाच —
अक्षरं ब्रह्म परमं स्वभावोऽध्यात्ममुच्यते ।
भूतभावोद्भवकरो विसर्गः कर्मसंज्ञितः ॥३॥

3. The Blessed Lord said: The Akshara is the supreme Brahman: *svabhāva* is called *adhyatama*; Karma is the name given to the creative movement, *visarga*, which brings into existence all beings and their subjective and objective states.[1]

अधिभूतं क्षरो भावः पुरुषश्चाधिदैवतम् ।
अधियज्ञोऽहमेवात्र देहे देहभृतां वर ॥४॥

---

[1] Here we find the universal principles enumerated. By that Brahman, a phrase which in the Upanishads is more than once used for the self-existent as opposed to the phenomenal being, the Gita intends, it appears, the immutable self-existence which is the highest self-expression of the Divine and on whose unalterable eternity all the rest, all that moves and evolves, is founded, *akṣaram paramam*. By adhyatma it means *svabhāva*, the spiritual way and law of being of the soul in the supreme Nature. Karma, it says, is the name given to the creative impulse and energy, *visarga*, which looses out things from this first essential self-becoming, this swabhava, and effects, creates, works out under its influence the cosmic becoming of existences in Prakriti. By *adhibhūta* is to be understood all the result of mutable becoming, *kṣaro bhāvaḥ*. By *adhidaiva* is intended the Purusha, the soul in Nature, the subjective being who observes and enjoys as the object of his consciousness all that is this mutable becoming of his essential existence worked out here by Karma in Nature. By *adhiyajña*, the Lord of works and sacrifice, I mean, says Krishna, myself, the Divine, the Godhead, the Purushottama here secret in the body of all these embodied existences. All that is, therefore, falls within this formula.

4. *Adhibhūta* is *kṣaro bhāva, adhidaiva* is the Purusha; I myself am the Lord of sacrifice, *adhiyajña* here in the body, O best of embodied beings.

अन्तकाले च मामेव स्मरन्मुक्त्वा कलेवरम् ।
यः प्रयाति स मद्भावं याति नास्त्यत्र संशयः ॥५॥

5. Whoever leaves his body and departs remembering Me at his time of end, comes to my *bhāva* (that of the Purushottama, my status of being); there is no doubt of that.

यं यं वापि स्मरन् भावं त्यजत्यन्ते कलेवरम् ।
तं तमेवैति कौन्तेय सदा तद्भावभावितः ॥६॥

6. Whosoever at the end[1] abandons the body, thinking upon any form of being, to that form he attains, O Kaunteya, into which the soul was at each moment growing inwardly during the physical life.

---

[1] Man, born into the world, revolves between world and world in the action of Prakriti and Karma. Purusha in Prakriti is his formula: what the soul in him thinks, contemplates and acts that always he becomes. All that he had been, determined his present birth; and all that he is, thinks, does in this life up to the moment of his death, determines what he will become in the worlds beyond and in lives yet to be. If birth is a becoming, death also is a becoming, not by any means a cessation. The body is abandoned, but the soul goes on its way, *tyaktvā kalevaram*. Much then depends on what he is at the critical moment of his departure. But it is not a death-bed remembrance at variance with or insufficiently prepared by the whole tenor of our life and our past subjectivity that can have this saving power. The thought of the Gita here is not on a par with the indulgences and facilities of popular religion; it has nothing in common with the crude fancies that make the absolution and last unction of the priest an edifying "Christian" death after an unedifying, profane life or the precaution or accident of a death in sacred Benares or holy Ganges a sufficient machinery of salvation. The divine subjective becoming on which the mind has to be fixed firmly in the moment of the physical death, must have been one into which the soul was at each moment growing inwardly during the physical life.

तस्मात्सर्वेषु कालेषु मामनुस्मर युद्ध्य च ।
मय्यर्पितमनोबुद्धिर्मामेवैष्यस्यसंशयम् ॥७॥

7. Therefore at all times remember me and fight; for if thy mind and thy understanding are always fixed on and given up to Me, to Me thou shalt surely come.

अभ्यासयोगयुक्तेन चेतसा नान्यगामिना ।
परमं पुरुषं दिव्यं याति पार्थानुचिन्तयन् ॥८॥

8. For it is by thinking always of him with a consciousness united with him in an undeviating Yoga of constant practice that one comes to the divine and supreme Purusha, O Partha.

कविं पुराणमनुशासितारमणोरणीयांसमनुस्मरेद्यः ।
सर्वस्य धातारमचिन्त्यरूपमादित्यवर्णं तमसः परस्तात् ॥९॥
प्रयाणकाले मनसाचलेन भक्त्या युक्तो योगबलेन चैव ।
भ्रुवोर्मध्ये प्राणमावेश्य सम्यक् स तं परं पुरुषमुपैति दिव्यम् ॥१०॥

9-10. This supreme Self is the Seer,[1] the Ancient of Days, subtler than the subtle and (in his eternal self-vision and wisdom) the Master and Ruler of all existence who sets in their place in his being all things that are; his form is unthinkable, he is refulgent as the sun beyond the darkness; he who thinketh upon this Purusha in the time of departure, with motionless mind, a soul armed with the strength of

---

[1] We arrive here at the first description of this supreme Purusha, – the Godhead who is even more and greater than the Immutable and to whom the Gita gives subsequently the name of Purushottama. He too in his timeless eternity is immutable and far beyond all this manifestation and here in Time there dawn on us only faint glimpses of his being conveyed through many varied symbols and disguises, *avyakto'kṣaraḥ*. Still he is not merely a featureless or indiscernible existence, *anirdeśyam*; or he is indiscernible only because he is subtler than the last subtlety of which the mind is aware and because the form of the Divine is beyond our thought.

Yoga, a union with God in bhakti[1] and the life-force entirely drawn up and set between the brows in the seat of mystic vision, he attains to this supreme divine Purusha.

यदक्षरं वेदविदो वदन्ति विशन्ति यद्यतयो वीतरागाः ।
यदिच्छन्तो ब्रह्मचर्यं चरन्ति तत्ते पदं संग्रहेण प्रवक्ष्ये ॥११॥

11. This supreme Soul[2] is the immutable self-existent Brahman of whom the Veda-knowers speak, and this is that into which the doers of askesis enter when they have passed beyond the affections of the mind of mortality and for the desire of which they practise the control of the bodily passions; that status I will declare to thee with brevity.

सर्वद्वाराणि संयम्य मनो हृदि निरुद्ध्य च ।
मूर्ध्न्याधायात्मनः प्राणमास्थितो योगधारणाम् ॥१२॥
ओमित्येकाक्षरं ब्रह्म व्याहरन्मामनुस्मरन् ।
यः प्रयाति त्यजन्देहं स याति परमां गतिम् ॥१३॥

12-13. All the doors of the senses closed, the mind shut in into the heart, the life-force taken up out of its diffused movement into the head, the intelligence concentrated in the utterance of the sacred syllable OM and its conceptive thought in the remembrance of the supreme Godhead, he who goes forth, abandoning the body, he attains to the highest status.[3]

---

[1] The union by love is not here superseded by the featureless unification through knowledge, it remains to the end a part of the supreme force of the Yoga.

[2] That eternal reality is the highest step, place, foothold of being (*padam*); therefore is it the supreme goal of the soul's movement in Time, itself no movement but a status original, sempiternal and supreme, *paramaṁ sthānam ādyam*.

[3] The Gita describes the last state of the mind of the Yogin in which he passes from life through death to this supreme divine existence. This is the established Yogic way of going, a last offering up of the whole being to the Eternal, the Transcendent. But still that is only a process; the essential

अनन्यचेताः सततं यो मां स्मरति नित्यशः ।
तस्याहं सुलभः पार्थ नित्ययुक्तस्य योगिनः ॥१४॥

14. He who continually remembers Me, thinking of none else, the Yogin, O Partha, who is in constant union with Me, finds Me easy to attain.

मामुपेत्य पुनर्जन्म दुःखालयमशाश्वतम् ।
नाप्नुवन्ति महात्मानः संसिद्धिं परमां गताः ॥१५॥

15. Having come to me, these great souls come not again to birth, this transient and painful condition of our mortal being; they reach the highest perfection.¹

आब्रह्मभुवनाल्लोकाः पुनरावर्तिनोऽर्जुन ।
मामुपेत्य तु कौन्तेय पुनर्जन्म न विद्यते ॥१६॥

16. The highest heavens of the cosmic plan are subject to a return to rebirth, but, O Kaunteya, there is no rebirth imposed on the soul that comes to Me (the Purushottama).

सहस्रयुगपर्यन्तमहर्यद् ब्रह्मणो विदुः ।
रात्रिं युगसहस्रान्तां तेऽहोरात्रविदो जनाः ॥१७॥

---

condition is the constant undeviating memory of the Divine in life, even in action and battle – *mām anusmara yudhya ca* – and the turning of the whole act of living into an uninterrupted Yoga, *nitya-yoga*.

¹ The condition to which the soul arrives when it thus departs from life is supracosmic. Therefore whatever fruit can be had from the aspiration of knowledge to the indefinable Brahman, is acquired also by this other and comprehensive aspiration through knowledge, works and love to the self-existent Godhead who is the Master of works and the Friend of mankind and of all beings. To know him so and so to seek him does not bind to rebirth or to the chain of Karma; the soul can satisfy its desire to escape permanently from the transient and painful condition of our mortal being.

And the Gita here, in order to make more precise to the mind this circling round of births and the escape from it, adopts the ancient theory of the cosmic cycles which became a fixed part of Indian cosmological notions.

17. Those who know the day[1] of Brahma, a thousand ages (Yugas) in duration, and the night, a thousand ages in ending, they are the knowers of day and night.

अव्यक्ताद्व्यक्तयः सर्वाः प्रभवन्त्यहरागमे ।
रात्र्यागमे प्रलीयन्ते तत्रैवाव्यक्तसंज्ञके ॥१८॥

18. At the coming of the Day all manifestations are born into being out of the unmanifest, at the coming of the Night all vanish or are dissolved into it.

भूतग्रामः स एवायं भूत्वा भूत्वा प्रलीयते ।
रात्र्यागमेऽवशः पार्थ प्रभवत्यहरागमे ॥१९॥

19. This multitude of existences helplessly comes into the becoming again and again, is dissolved at the coming of the Night, O Partha, and is born into being at the coming of the Day.

परस्तस्मात्तु भावोऽन्योऽव्यक्तोऽव्यक्तात्सनातनः ।
यः स सर्वेषु भूतेषु नश्यत्सु न विनश्यति ॥२०॥

20. But this unmanifest is not the original divinity of the Being; there is another status of his existence, a supracosmic unmanifest beyond this cosmic non-manifestation (which is eternally self-seated, is not an opposite of this cosmic status of manifestation but far above and unlike it, changeless, eternal), not forced to perish with the perishing of all these existences.

अव्यक्तोऽक्षर इत्युक्तस्तमाहुः परमां गतिम् ।
यं प्राप्य न निवर्तन्ते तद्धाम परमं मम ॥२१॥

---

[1] There is an eternal cycle of alternating periods of cosmic manifestation and non-manifestation, each period called respectively a day and a night of the creator Brahma, each of equal length in Time, the long aeon of his working which endures for a thousand ages, the long aeon of his sleep of another thousand silent ages.

EIGHTH CHAPTER

21. He is called the unmanifest immutable, him they speak of as the supreme soul and status, and those who attain to him return[1] not; that is my supreme place of being.

पुरुषः स परः पार्थ भक्त्या लभ्यस्त्वनन्यया ।
यस्यान्तःस्थानि भूतानि येन सर्वमिदं ततम् ॥२२॥

22. But that supreme Purusha has to be won by a bhakti which turns to him alone in whom all beings exist and by whom all this world has been extended in space.

यत्र काले त्वनावृत्तिमावृत्तिं चैव योगिनः ।
प्रयाता यान्ति तं कालं वक्ष्यामि भरतर्षभ ॥२३॥

---

[1] For the soul attaining to it has escaped out of the cycle of cosmic manifestation and non-manifestation.

Whether we entertain or we dismiss this cosmological notion, – which depends on the value we are inclined to assign to the knowledge of "the knowers of day and night," – the important thing is the turn the Gita gives to it. One might easily imagine that this eternally unmanifested Being whose status seems to have nothing to do with the manifestation or the non-manifestation, must be the ever undefined and indefinable Absolute, and the proper way to reach him is to get rid of all that we have become in the manifestation, not to carry up to it our whole inner consciousness in a combined concentration of the mind's knowledge, the heart's love, the Yogic will, the vital life-force. Especially, bhakti seems inapplicable to the Absolute who is void of every relation, *avyavahārya*. But the Gita insists in the next sloka that although this condition is supracosmic and although it is eternally unmanifest, still that supreme Purusha has to be won by bhakti.

In others words, the supreme Purusha is not an entirely relationless Absolute aloof from our illusions, but he is the Seer, Creator and Ruler of the worlds, *kavim anuśāsitāram, dhātāram*, and it is by knowing and by loving Him as the One and the All, *vāsudevaḥ sarvam iti*, that we ought by a union with him of our whole conscious being in all things, all energies, all actions to seek the supreme consummation, the perfect perfection, the absolute release.

Then there comes a more curious thought which the Gita has adopted from the mystics of the early Vedanta. It gives the different times at which the Yogin has to leave his body according as he wills to seek rebirth or to avoid it.

23. That time[1] wherein departing Yogins do not return, and also that wherein departing they return, that time shall I declare to thee, O foremost of the Bharatas.

अग्निर्ज्योतिरहः शुक्लः षण्मासा उत्तरायणम् ।
तत्र प्रयाता गच्छन्ति ब्रह्म ब्रह्मविदो जनाः ॥२४॥
धूमो रात्रिस्तथा कृष्णः षण्मासा दक्षिणायनम् ।
तत्र चान्द्रमसं ज्योतियोगी प्राप्य निवर्तते ॥२५॥

24-25. Fire and light and smoke or mist, the day and the night, the bright fortnight of the lunar month and the dark, the northern solstice and the southern, these are the opposites. By the first in each pair the knowers of the Brahman go to the Brahman; but by the second the Yogin reaches the "lunar light" and returns subsequently to human birth.

---

[1] Whatever psycho-physical fact or else symbolism there may be behind this notion,* – it comes down from the age of the mystics who saw in every physical thing an effective symbol of the psychological and who traced everywhere an interaction and a sort of identity of the outward with the inward, light and knowledge, the fiery principle and the spiritual energy, – we need observe only the turn by which the Gita closes the passage; "Therefore at all times be in Yoga."

For that is after all the essential, to make the whole being one with the Divine, so entirely and in all ways one as to be naturally and constantly fixed in union, and thus to make all living, not only thought and meditation, but action, labour, battle, a remembering of God. "Remember me and fight," means not to lose the ever-present thought of the Eternal for one single moment in the clash of the temporal which normally absorbs our minds, and that seems sufficiently difficult, almost impossible. It is entirely possible indeed only if the other conditions are satisfied. If we have become in our consciousness one self with all, one

(*Yogic experience shows in fact that there is a real psycho-physical truth, not indeed absolute in its application, behind this idea, viz, that in the inner struggle between the powers of the Light and the powers of the Darkness, the former tend to have a natural prevalence in the bright periods of the day or the year, the latter in the dark periods, and this balance may last until the fundamental victory is won.)

शुक्लकृष्णे गती ह्येते जगतः शाश्वते मते ।
एकया यात्यनावृत्तिमन्ययाऽऽवर्तते पुनः ॥२६॥

26. These are the bright and the dark paths (called the path of the gods and the path of the fathers in the Upanishads); by the one he departs who does not return, by the other he who returns again.

नैते सृती पार्थ जानन् योगी मुह्यति कश्चन ।
तस्मात्सर्वेषु कालेषु योगयुक्तो भवार्जुन ॥२७॥

27. The Yogin who knows them is not misled into any error, therefore at all times be in Yoga, O Arjuna.

वेदेषु यज्ञेषु तपःसु चैव दानेषु यत्पुण्यफलं प्रदिष्टम् ।
अत्येति तत्सर्वमिदं विदित्वा योगी परं स्थानमुपैति चाद्यम् ॥२८॥

28. The fruit of meritorious deeds declared in the Vedas, sacrifices, austerities and charitable gifts, the Yogin passes all these by having known this and attains to the supreme and sempiternal status.

इति श्रीमद्भगवद्गीतासूपनिषत्सु ब्रह्मविद्यायां योगशास्त्रे श्रीकृष्णार्जुनसंवादे
अक्षरब्रह्मयोगो नामाष्टमोऽध्यायः ।

---

self which is always to our thought the Divine, and even our eyes and our other senses see and sense the Divine Being everywhere so that it is impossible for us at any time at all to feel or think of anything as that merely which the unenlightened sense perceives, but only as the Godhead at once concealed and manifested in that form, and if our will is one in consciousness with a supreme will and every act of will, of mind, of body is felt to come from it, to be its movement, instinct with it or identical, then what the Gita demands can be integrally done. The remembrance of the Divine Being becomes no longer an intermittent act of the mind, but the natural condition of our activities and in a way the very substance of the consciousness. The Jiva has become possessed of its right and natural, its spiritual relation to the Purushottama and all our life is a Yoga, an accomplished and yet an eternally self-accomplishing oneness.

Ninth Chapter

WORKS, DEVOTION AND KNOWLEDGE

(All the truth that has developed itself at this length step by step, each bringing forward a fresh aspect of the integral knowledge and founding on it some result of spiritual state and action, has now to take a turn of immense importance. The Teacher therefore takes care first to draw attention to the decisive character of what he is about to say, so that the mind of Arjuna may be awakened and attentive. For he is going to open his mind to the knowledge and sight of the integral Divinity and lead up to the vision of the eleventh book, by which the warrior of Kurukshetra becomes conscious of the author and upholder of his being and action and mission, the Godhead in man and the world, whom nothing in man and world limits or binds, because all proceeds from him, is a movement in his infinite being, continues and is supported by his will, is justified in his divine self-knowledge, has him always for its origin, substance and end. Arjuna is to become aware of himself as existing only in God and as acting only by the power within him, his workings only an instrumentality of the divine action, his egoistic consciousness only a veil and to his ignorance a misrepresentation of the real being within him which is an immortal spark and portion of the supreme Godhead.)

श्रीभगवान् उवाच —
इदं तु ते गुह्यतमं प्रवक्ष्याम्यनसूयवे ।
ज्ञानं विज्ञानसहितं यज्ज्ञात्वा मोक्ष्यसेऽशुभात् ॥१॥

1. The Blessed Lord said: What I am going to tell thee, the uncarping, is the most secret thing of all, the essential knowledge attended with all the comprehensive knowledge, by knowing which thou shalt be released from evil.

राजविद्या राजगुह्यं पवित्रमिदमुत्तमम् ।
प्रत्यक्षावगमं धर्म्यं सुसुखं कर्तुमव्ययम् ॥२॥

2. This is the king-knowledge, the king-secret (the wisdom of all wisdoms, the secret of all secrets), it is a pure and supreme light which one can verify by direct spiritual experience, it is the right and just knowledge, the very law of being. It is easy to practise and is imperishable.

अश्रद्दधानाः पुरुषा धर्मस्यास्य परन्तप ।
अप्राप्य मां निवर्तन्ते मृत्युसंसारवर्त्मनि ॥३॥

3. (But faith[1] is necessary). The soul that fails to get faith in the higher truth and law, O Parantapa, not attaining to Me, must return into the path of ordinary mortal living (subject to death and error and evil.)

---

[1] For this is a truth which has to be lived, – and lived in the soul's growing light, not argued out in the mind's darkness. One has to grow into it, one has to become it, – that is the only way to verify it. It is only by an exceeding of the lower self that one can become the real divine self and live the truth of our spiritual existence. All the apparent truths one can oppose to it are appearances of the lower Nature. The release from the evil and the defect of the lower Nature, *aśubham*, can only come by accepting a higher knowledge in which all this apparent evil becomes convinced of ultimate unreality, is shown to be a creation of our darkness. But to grow thus into the freedom of the divine Nature one must accept and believe in the Godhead secret within our present limited nature. For the reason why the practice of this Yoga becomes possible and easy is that in doing it we give up the whole working of all that we naturally are into the hands of that inner divine Purusha. The Godhead works out the divine birth in us progressively, simply, infallibly, by taking up our being into his and by filling it with his own knowledge and power, *jñānadīpena bhāsvatā*; he lays hands on our obscure ignorant nature and transforms it into his own light and wideness. What with entire faith and without egoism we believe in and impelled by him will to be, the God within will surely accomplish. But the egoistic mind and life we now and apparently are must first surrender itself for transformation into the hands of that inmost secret Divinity within us.

मया ततमिदं सर्वं जगदव्यक्तमूर्तिना ।
मत्स्थानि सर्वभूतानि न चाहं तेष्ववस्थितः ॥४॥

4. By Me,[1] all this universe has been extended in the ineffable mystery of My being; all existences are situated in Me, not I in them.

न च मत्स्थानि भूतानि पश्य मे योगमैश्वरम् ।
भूतभृन्न च भूतस्थो ममात्मा भूतभावनः ॥५॥

5. And yet all existences are not situated in Me, behold My divine Yoga;[2] Myself is that which supports all being and constitutes their existence.

यथाकाशस्थितो नित्यं वायुः सर्वत्रगो महान् ।
तथा सर्वाणि भूतानि मत्स्थानीत्युपधारय ॥६॥

---

[1] The Gita then proceeds to unveil the supreme and integral secret, the one thought and truth in which the seeker of perfection and liberation must learn to live and the one law of perfection of his spiritual members and of all their movements. This supreme secret is the mystery of the transcendent Godhead who is all and everywhere, yet so much greater and other than the universe and all its forms that nothing here contains him, nothing expresses him really, and no language which is borrowed from the appearances of things in space and time and their relations can suggest the truth of his unimaginable being. The consequent law of our perfection is an adoration by our whole nature and its self-surrender to its divine source and possessor. Our one ultimate way is the turning of our entire existence in the world, and not merely of this or that in it, into a single movement towards the Eternal. By the power and mystery of a divine Yoga we have come out of his inexpressible secrecies into this bounded nature of phenomenal things. By a reverse movement of the same Yoga we must transcend the limits of phenomenal nature and recover the greater consciousness by which we can live in the Divine and the Eternal.

[2] There is a Yoga of divine Power, *me yoga aiśvaraḥ*, by which the Supreme creates phenomena of himself in a spiritual, not a material, self-formulation of his own extended infinity, an extension of which the material is only an image.

6. It is as the great, the all-pervading[1] aerial principle dwells in the etheric that all existences dwell in Me, that is how you have to conceive of it.

सर्वभूतानि कौन्तेय प्रकृतिं यान्ति मामिकाम् ।
कल्पक्षये पुनस्तानि कल्पादौ विसृजाम्यहम् ॥७॥

7. All existences, O Kaunteya, return into My divine Nature (out of her action into her immobility and silence) in the lapse of the cycle; at the beginning of the cycle again I loose them forth.

प्रकृतिं स्वामवष्टभ्य विसृजामि पुनः पुनः ।
भूतग्राममिमं कृत्स्नमवशं प्रकृतेर्वशात् ॥८॥

8. Leaning – pressing down upon my own Nature (Prakriti) I create (loose forth into various being) all this multitude of existences, all helplessly[2] subject to the control of Nature.

[1] The universal existence is all-pervading and infinite and the Self-existent too is all-pervading and infinite; but the self-existent infinity is stable, static, immutable, the universal is an all-pervading movement. The Self is one, not many; but the universal expresses itself as all existence and is, as it seems, the sum of all existences. One is Being; the other is Power of Being which moves and creates and acts in the existence of the fundamental, supporting, immutable Spirit. The Self does not dwell in all these existences or in any of them; that is to say, he is not contained by any, – just as the ether here is not contained in any form, though all forms are derived ultimately from the ether. Nor is he contained in or constituted by all existences together – any more than the ether is contained in the mobile extension of the aerial principle or is constituted by the sum of its forms or its forces. But still in the movement also is the Divine; he dwells in the many as the Lord in each being. Both these relations are true of him at one and the same time.

[2] Ignorant, the Jiva is subject to her cyclic whirl, not master of itself, but dominated by her; only by return to the divine consciousness can it attain to mastery and freedom. The Divine too follows the cycle, not as subject to it, but as its informing Spirit and guide, not with his whole being involved in it, but with his power of being accompanying and shaping it.

न च मां तानि कर्माणि निबध्नन्ति धनञ्जय ।
उदासीनवदासीनमसक्तं तेषु कर्मसु ॥९॥

9. Nor do these works bind me, O Dhananjaya, for I am seated as if indifferent[1] above, unattached to those actions.

मयाध्यक्षेण प्रकृतिः सूयते सचराचरम् ।
हेतुनानेन कौन्तेय जगद्विपरिवर्तते ॥१०॥

10. I am the presiding control of my own action of Nature, (not a spirit born in her, but) the creative spirit who causes her to produce all that appears in the manifestation. Because of this, O Kaunteya, the world proceeds in cycles.

अवजानन्ति मां मूढा मानुषीं तनुमाश्रितम् ।
परं भावमजानन्तो मम भूतमहेश्वरम् ॥११॥

11. Deluded[2] minds despise me lodged in the human body because they know not my supreme nature of being, Lord of all existences.

[1] If in his power he accompanies her and causes all her workings, he is outside it too, as if one seated above her universal action in the supracosmic mastery, not attached to her by any involving and mastering desire and not therefore bound by her works, because he infinitely exceeds them and precedes them, is the same before, during and after all their procession in the cycles of Time. But also since this action is the action of the divine Nature, *sva prakṛtiḥ*, and the divine Nature can never be separate from the Divine, in everything she creates the Godhead must be immanent. That is a relation which is not the whole truth of his being, but neither is it a truth which we can at all afford to ignore.

[2] Mortal mind is bewildered by its ignorant reliance upon veils and appearances; it sees only the outward human body, human mind, human way of living and catches no liberating glimpse of the Divinity who is lodged in the creature. It ignores the divinity within itself and cannot see it in other men, and even though the Divine manifest himself in humanity as Avatar and Vibhuti, it is still blind and ignores or despises the veiled Godhead. And if it ignores him in the living creature, still less can it see him in the objective world on which it looks from its prison of separative ego through the barred windows of the finite mind. It does not see God in the universe; it knows nothing of the supreme Divinity who is master of

NINTH CHAPTER

मोघाशा मोघकर्माणो मोघज्ञाना विचेतसः ।
राक्षसीमासुरीं चैव प्रकृतिं मोहिनीं श्रिताः ॥१२॥

12. All their hope, action, knowledge are vain things (when judged by the Divine and eternal standard); they dwell in the Rakshasic and Asuric nature which deludes the will and the intelligence.

महात्मानस्तु मां पार्थ दैवीं प्रकृतिमाश्रिताः ।
भजन्त्यनन्यमनसो ज्ञात्वा भूतादिमव्ययम् ॥१३॥

13. The great-souled,[1] O Partha, who dwell in the divine

---

these planes full of various existences and dwells within them; it is blind to the vision by which all in the world grows divine and the soul itself awakens to its own inherent divinity and becomes of the Godhead, godlike. What it does see readily, and to that it attaches itself with passion, is only the life of the ego hunting after finite things for their own sake and for the satisfaction of the earthly hunger of the intellect, body, senses. Those who have given themselves up too entirely to this outward drive of the mentality, fall into the hands of the lower nature, cling to it and make it their foundation. They become a prey to the nature of the Rakshasa in man who sacrifices everything to a violent and inordinate satisfaction of his separate vital ego and makes that the dark godhead of his will and thought and action and enjoyment. Or they are hurried onward in a fruitless cycle by the arrogant self-will, self-sufficient thought, self-regarding act, self-satisfied and yet ever unsatisfied intellectualised appetite of enjoyment of the Asuric nature. But to live persistently in this separative ego-consciousness and make that the centre of all our activities is to miss altogether the true self-awareness. The charm it throws upon the misled instruments of the spirit is an enchantment that chains life to a profitless circling. All its hope, action, knowledge are vain things when judged by the divine and eternal standard, for it shuts out the great hope, excludes the liberating action, banishes the illuminating knowledge. It is a false knowledge that sees the phenomenon but misses the truth of the phenomenon, a blind hope that chases after the transient but misses the eternal, a sterile action whose every profit is annulled by loss and amounts to a perennial labour of Sisyphus.

[1] The great-souled who open themselves to the light and largeness of the diviner nature of which man is capable, are alone on the path narrow in the beginning, inexpressibly wide in the end that leads to liberation and

nature know Me (the Godhead lodged in human body) as the Imperishable from whom all existences originate and so knowing they turn to Me with a sole and entire love.

सततं कीर्तयन्तो मां यतन्तश्च दृढव्रताः ।
नमस्यन्तश्च मां भक्त्या नित्ययुक्ता उपासते ॥१४॥

14. Always adoring Me, steadfast in spiritual endeavour, bowing down to Me with devotion, they worship Me ever in Yoga.

ज्ञानयज्ञेन चाप्यन्ये यजन्तो मामुपासते ।
एकत्वेन पृथक्त्वेन बहुधा विश्वतोमुखम् ॥१५॥

15. Others also seek Me out by the sacrifice of knowledge and worship Me in My oneness and in every separate being

---

perfection. The growth of the god in man is man's proper business; the steadfast turning of this lower Asuric and Rakshasic into the divine nature is the carefully hidden meaning of human life. As this growth increases, the veil falls and the soul comes to see the greater significance of action and the real truth of existence. The eye opens to the Godhead in man, to the Godhead in the world; it sees inwardly and comes to know outwardly the infinite Spirit, the Imperishable from whom all existences originate and who exists in all and by him and in him all exist always. Therefore when this vision, this knowledge seizes on the soul, its whole life-aspiration becomes a surpassing love and fathomless adoration of the Divine and Infinite. The mind attaches itself singly to the eternal, the spiritual, the living, the universal, the Real; it values nothing but for its sake, it delights only in the all-blissful Purusha. All the word and all the thought become one hymning of the universal greatness, Light, Beauty, Power and Truth that has revealed itself in its glory to the human spirit and a worship of the one supreme Soul and infinite Person. All the long stress of the inner self to break outward becomes a form now of spiritual endeavour and aspiration to possess the Divine in the soul and realise the Divine in the nature. All life becomes a constant Yoga and unification of that Divine and this human spirit. This is the manner of the integral devotion; it creates a single uplifting of our whole being and nature through sacrifice by the dedicated heart to the eternal Purushottama.

and in all My million universal faces (fronting them in the world and its creatures).[1]

अहं क्रतुरहं यज्ञः स्वधाहमहमौषधम् ।
मन्त्रोऽहमहमेवाज्यमहमग्निरहं हुतम् ॥१६॥

16. I the ritual action, I the sacrifice, I the food-oblation, I the fire-giving herb, the mantra I, I also the butter, I the flame, the offering I.

पिताहमस्य जगतो माता धाता पितामहः ।
वेद्यं पवित्रमोङ्कार ऋक् साम यजुरेव च ॥१७॥

17. I the Father of this world, the Mother, the Ordainer, the first Creator, the object of Knowledge, the sacred syllable OM and also the Rik, Sama and Yajur (Vedas).

गतिर्भर्ता प्रभुः साक्षी निवासः शरणं सुहृत् ।
प्रभवः प्रलयः स्थानं निधानं बीजमव्ययम् ॥१८॥

---

[1] This knowledge becomes easily an adoration, a large devotion, a vast self-giving, an integral self-offering because it is the knowledge of a Spirit, the contact of a Being, the embrace of a supreme and universal Soul which claims all that we are even as it lavishes on us when we approach it all the treasures of its endless delight of existence.

The way of works too turns into an adoration and a devotion of self-giving because it is an entire sacrifice of all our will and its activities to the one Purushottama. The outward Vedic rite is a powerful symbol, effective for a slighter though still a heavenward purpose; but the real sacrifice is that inner oblation in which the Divine All becomes himself the ritual action, the sacrifice and every single circumstance of the sacrifice. All the working and forms of that inner rite are the self-ordinance and self-expression of his power in us mounting by our aspiration towards the source of its energies. The Divine Inhabitant becomes himself the flame and the offering, because the flame is the Godward will and that will is God himself within us. And the offering too is form and force of the constituent Godhead in our nature and being; all that has been received from him is given up to the service and the worship of its own Reality, its own supreme Truth and Origin.

18. I the path and goal, the upholder, the master, the witness, the house and country, the refuge, the benignant friend; I the birth and status and destruction of apparent existence, I the imperishable seed of all and their eternal resting-place.

तपाम्यहमहं वर्षं निगृह्णाम्युत्सृजामि च ।
अमृतं चैव मृत्युश्च सदसच्चाहमर्जुन ॥१९॥

19. I give heat, I withhold and send forth the rain; immortality and also death, existent and non-existent am I, O Arjuna.

त्रैविद्या मां सोमपाः पूतपापा यज्ञैरिष्ट्वा स्वर्गतिं प्रार्थयन्ते ।
ते पुण्यमासाद्य सुरेन्द्रलोकमश्नन्ति दिव्यान् दिवि देवभोगान् ॥२०॥

20. The Knowers of the triple Veda, who drink the soma-wine, purify themselves from sin, worshipping Me with sacrifice, pray of Me the way to heaven; they ascending to the heavenly worlds by their righteousness enjoy in paradise the divine feasts of the gods.

ते तं भुक्त्वा स्वर्गलोकं विशालं क्षीणे पुण्ये मर्त्यलोकं विशन्ति ।
एवं त्रयीधर्ममनुप्रपन्ना गतागतं कामकामा लभन्ते ॥२१॥

21. They, having enjoyed heavenly worlds of larger felicities, the reward of their good deeds exhausted, return to mortal existence. Resorting to the virtues enjoined by the three Vedas, seeking the satisfaction of desire, they follow the cycle of birth and death.

अनन्याश्चिन्तयन्तो मां ये जनाः पर्युपासते ।
तेषां नित्याभियुक्तानां योगक्षेमं वहाम्यहम् ॥२२॥

22. To those men who worship Me making Me alone the whole object of their thought, to those constantly in Yoga

with Me, I spontaneously bring every good.¹

येऽप्यन्यदेवता भक्ता यजन्ते श्रद्धयाऽन्विताः ।
तेऽपि मामेव कौन्तेय यजन्त्यविधिपूर्वकम् ॥२३॥

23. Even those who sacrifice to other godheads with devotion and faith, they also sacrifice to Me, O son of Kunti, though not according to the true law.

अहं हि सर्वयज्ञानां भोक्ता च प्रभुरेव च ।
न तु मामभिजानन्ति तत्त्वेनातश्च्यवन्ति ते ॥२४॥

24. It is I myself who am the enjoyer and the Lord of all

---

¹ Thus the Vedic ritualist of old learned the exoteric sense of the triple Veda, purified himself from sin, drank the wine of communion with the gods and sought by sacrifice and good deeds the rewards of heaven. This firm belief in a Beyond and this seeking of a diviner world secures to the soul in its passing the strength to attain to the joys of heaven on which its faith and seeking were centred: but the return to mortal existence imposes itself because the true aim of that existence has not been found and realised. Here and not elsewhere the highest Godhead has to be found, the soul's divine nature developed out of the imperfect physical human nature and through unity with God and man and universe the whole large truth of being discovered and lived and made visibly wonderful. That completes the long cycle of our becoming and admits us to a supreme result; that is the opportunity given to the soul by the human birth and, until that is accomplished, it cannot cease. The God-lover advances constantly towards this ultimate necessity of our birth in cosmos through a concentrated love and adoration by which he makes the supreme and universal Divine the whole object of his living – not either egoistic terrestrial satisfaction or the celestial worlds – and the whole object of his thought and his seeing. To see nothing but the Divine, to be at every moment in union with him, to love him in all creatures and have the delight of him in all things is the whole condition of his spiritual existence. His God-vision does not divorce him from life, nor does he miss anything of the fulness of life; for God himself becomes the spontaneous bringer to him of every good and of all his inner and outer getting and having. The joy of heaven and the joy of earth are only a small shadow of his possessions; for as he grows into the Divine, the Divine too flows out upon him with all the light, power and joy of an infinite existence.

sacrifices, but they do not know Me in the true principles and hence they fall.

यान्ति देवव्रता देवान् पितॄन् यान्ति पितृव्रताः ।
भूतानि यान्ति भूतेज्या यान्ति मद्याजिनोऽपि माम् ॥२५॥

25. They who worship[1] the gods go to the gods, to the (divinised) Ancestors go the Ancestor-worshippers, to elemental spirits go those who sacrifice to elemental spirits; but My worshippers come to Me.

[1] All sincere religious belief and practice is really a seeking after the one supreme and universal Godhead; for he always is the sole master of man's sacrifice and askesis and infinite enjoyer of his effort and aspiration. However small or low the form of the worship, however limited the idea of the godhead, however restricted the giving, the faith, the effort to get behind the veil of one's own ego-worship and limitation by material Nature, it yet forms a thread of connection between the soul of man and the All-soul and there is a response. Still the response, the fruit of the adoration and offering is according to the knowledge, the faith and the work and cannot exceed their limitations, and therefore from the point of view of the greater God-knowledge, which alone gives the entire truth of being and becoming, this inferior offering is not given according to the true and highest law of the sacrifice. It is not founded on a knowledge of the supreme Godhead in his integral existence and the true principle of his self-manifestation, but attaches itself to external and partial appearances. Therefore its sacrifice too is limited in its object, largely egoistic in its motive, partial and mistaken in its action and giving. An entire seeing of the Divine is the condition of an entire conscious self-surrender; the rest attains to things that are incomplete and partial and has to fall back from them and return to enlarge itself in a greater seeking and wider God-experience. But to follow after the supreme and universal Godhead alone and utterly is to attain to all knowledge and result which other ways acquire while yet one is not limited by any aspect, though one finds the truth of him in all aspects. This movement embraces all forms of divine being on its way to the supreme Purushottama. This absolute self-giving, this one-minded surrender is the devotion which the Gita makes the crown of its synthesis. All action and effort are by this devotion turned into an offering to the supreme and universal Godhead.

पत्रं पुष्पं फलं तोयं यो मे भक्त्या प्रयच्छति ।
तदहं भक्त्युपहृतमश्रामि प्रयतात्मनः ॥२६॥

26. He who offers to Me with devotion a leaf,[1] a flower, a fruit, a cup of water, that offering of love from the striving soul, is acceptable to Me.

यत्करोषि यदश्रासि यज्जुहोषि ददासि यत् ।
यत्तपस्यसि कौन्तेय तत्कुरुष्व मदर्पणम् ॥२७॥

27. Whatever thou doest, whatever thou enjoyest, whatever thou sacrificest, whatever thou givest, whatever energy of *tapasyā*, of the soul's will or effort, thou puttest forth, make it an offering unto Me.

शुभाशुभफलैरेवं मोक्ष्यसे कर्मबन्धनैः ।
संन्यासयोगयुक्तात्मा विमुक्तो मामुपैष्यसि ॥२८॥

28. Thus shalt thou be liberated from good and evil results which constitute the bonds of action; with thy soul in union with the Divine through renunciation, thou shalt become free and attain to Me.

---

[1] Here the least, the slightest circumstance of life, the most insignificant gift out of oneself or what one has, the smallest action assumes a divine significance and it becomes an acceptable offering to the Godhead who makes it a means for his possession of the soul and life of the God-lover. The distinctions made by desire and ego then disappear. As there is no straining after the good result of one's action, no shunning of unhappy result, but all action and result are given up to the Supreme to whom all work and fruit in the world belong for ever, there is no further bondage. For by an absolute self-giving all egoistic desire disappears from the heart and there is a perfect union between the Divine and the individual soul through an inner renunciation of its separate living. All will, all action, all result become that of the Godhead, work divinely through the purified and illumined nature and no longer belong to the limited personal ego. The finite nature thus surrendered becomes a free channel of the Infinite; the soul in its spiritual being, uplifted out of ignorance and the limitation, returns to its oneness with the Eternal.

समोऽहं सर्वभूतेषु न मे द्वेष्योऽस्ति न प्रियः ।
ये भजन्ति तु मां भक्त्या मयि ते तेषु चाप्यहम् ॥२९॥

29. I (the Eternal Inhabitant) am equal[1] in all existences, none is dear to Me, none hated; yet those who turn to Me with love and devotion, they are in Me and I also in them.

अपि चेत्सुदुराचारो भजते मामनन्यभाक् ।
साधुरेव स मन्तव्यः सम्यग्व्यवसितो हि सः ॥३०॥

30. If even a man of very evil conduct turns to Me with a sole and entire love, he must be regarded as a saint, for the settled will of endeavour in him is a right and complete will.

क्षिप्रं भवति धर्मात्मा शश्वच्छान्तिं निगच्छति ।
कौन्तेय प्रतिजानीहि न मे भक्तः प्रणश्यति ॥३१॥

31. Swiftly[2] he becomes a soul of righteousness and

---

[1] He is the enemy of none and he is the partial lover of none; none has he cast out, none has he eternally condemned, none has he favoured by any despotism of arbitrary caprice: all at last equally come to him through their circlings in the ignorance. But it is only this perfect adoration that can make this indwelling of God in man and man in God a conscious thing and an engrossing and perfect union. Love of the Highest and a total self-surrender are the straight and swift way to this divine oneness.

[2] A will of entire self-giving opens wide all the gates of the spirit and brings in response an entire descent and self-giving of the Godhead to the human being, and that at once reshapes and assimilates everything in us to the law of the divine existence by a rapid transformation of the lower into the spiritual nature. The will of self-giving forces away by its power the veil between God and man; it annuls every error and annihilates every obstacle. Those who aspire in their human strength by effort of knowledge or effort of virtue or effort of laborious self-discipline, grow with much anxious difficulty towards the Eternal; but when the soul gives up its ego and its works to the Divine, God himself comes to us and takes up our burden. To the ignorant he brings the light of divine knowledge, to the feeble the power of the divine will, to the sinner the liberation of the divine purity, to the suffering the infinite spiritual joy and Ananda. Their weakness and the stumblings of their human strength make no difference.

obtains eternal peace. This is my word of promise, O Arjuna, that he who loves me shall not perish.

मां हि पार्थ व्यपाश्रित्य येऽपि स्यु: पापयोनय: ।
स्त्रियो वैश्यास्तथा शूद्रास्तेऽपि यान्ति परां गतिम् ॥३२॥

32. Those who take refuge with Me, O Partha, though outcastes, born from a womb of sin, women, Vaishyas, even Shudras, they also[1] attain to the highest goal.

किं पुनर्ब्राह्मणा: पुण्या भक्ता राजर्षयस्तथा ।
अनित्यमसुखं लोकमिमं प्राप्य भजस्व माम् ॥३३॥

33. How much rather then holy Brahmins and devoted king-sages; thou who hast come to this transient and unhappy world, love and turn to Me.

मन्मना भव मद्भक्तो मद्याजी मां नमस्कुरु ।
मामेवैष्यसि युक्त्वैवमात्मानं मत्परायण: ॥३४॥

34. Become my minded, my lover and adorer, a sacrificer to me, bow thyself to me, thus united with me in the Self

---

[1] Previous effort and preparation, the purity and the holiness of the Brahmin, the enlightened strength of the king-sage great in works and knowledge have their value, because they make it easier for the imperfect human creature to arrive at this wide vision and self-surrender; but even without this preparation all who take refuge in the divine Lover of man, the Vaishya once preoccupied with the narrowness of wealth-getting and the labour of production, the Shudra hampered by a thousand hard restrictions, woman shut in and stunted in her growth by the narrow circle society has drawn around her self-expansion, those too, *pāpa-yonayaḥ*, on whom their past Karma has imposed even the very worst of births, the outcaste, the Pariah, the Chandala, find at once the gates of God opening before them. In the spiritual life all the external distinctions of which men make so much because they appeal with an oppressive force to the outward mind, cease before the equality of the divine Light and the wide omnipotence of an impartial Power.

thou shalt come to me, having me as thy supreme goal.[1]

इति श्रीमद्भगवद्गीतासूपनिषत्सु ब्रह्मविद्यायां योगशास्त्रे श्रीकृष्णार्जुनसंवादे
राजविद्याराजगुह्ययोगो नाम नवमोऽध्यायः ।

[1] The earthly world preoccupied with the dualities and bound to the immediate transient relations of the hour and the moment is for man, so long as he dwells here attached to these things and while he accepts the law they impose on him for the law of his life, a world of struggle, suffering and sorrow. The way to liberation is to turn from the outward to the inward, from the appearance created by the material life which lays its burden on the mind and imprisons it in the grooves of the life and the body to the divine Reality which waits to manifest itself through the freedom of the spirit.

Love of the world, the mask, must change into the love of God, the Truth. Once this secret and inner Godhead is known and is embraced, the whole being and the whole life will undergo a sovereign uplifting and a marvellous transmutation. In place of the ignorance of the lower Nature absorbed in its outward works and appearances the eye will open to the vision of God everywhere, to the unity and universality of the spirit. The world's sorrow and pain will disappear in the bliss of the All-blissful; our weakness and error and sin will be changed into the all-embracing and all-transforming strength, truth and purity of the Eternal. To make the mind one with the divine consciousness, to make the whole of our emotional nature one love of God everywhere, to make all our works one sacrifice to the Lord of the worlds and all our worship and aspiration one adoration of him and self-surrender, to direct the whole self Godwards in an entire union is the way to rise out of a mundane into a divine existence. This is the Gita's teaching of divine love and devotion, in which knowledge, works and the heart's longing become one in a supreme unification, a merging of all their divergences, an intertwining of all their threads, a high fusion, a wide identifying movement.

Tenth Chapter

I. THE SUPREME WORD OF THE GITA

श्रीभगवान् उवाच —
भूय एव महाबाहो शृणु मे परमं वचः ।
यत्तेऽहं प्रीयमाणाय वक्ष्यामि हितकाम्यया ॥१॥

1. The Blessed Lord said: Again,[1] O mighty-armed, hearken to my supreme word, that I will speak to thee from my will for thy soul's good, now that thy heart is taking delight[2] in me.

न मे विदुः सुरगणाः प्रभवं न महर्षयः ।
अहमादिर्हि देवानां महर्षीणां च सर्वशः ॥२॥

2. Neither the gods nor the great Rishis know any birth[3] of Me, for I am altogether and in every way the origin[4] of the gods[5] and the great Rishis.

---

[1] The divine Avatar declares, in a brief reiteration of the upshot of all that he has been saying, that this and no other is his supreme word which he had promised to reveal.

[2] This delight of the heart in God is the whole constituent and essence of true bhakti, *bhajanti prītipūrvakam*; this is put as a condition for the further development by which the final command to action comes at last to be given to the human instrument, Arjuna. The supreme word of the Lord contains the declaration of a unified knowledge and bhakti as the supreme Yoga.

[3] The Gita harmonises the pantheistic, the theistic and the highest transcendental terms of our spiritual conception and spiritual experience. The Divine is the unborn Eternal, the transcendental Being, who has no origin.

[4] But at the same time the divine Transcendence is not a negation, nor is it an Absolute empty of all relation to the universe. All cosmic relations derive from this Supreme; all cosmic existences return to it and find in it alone their true and immeasurable existence.

[5] The gods are the great undying Powers and immortal Personalities who consciously inform, constitute, preside over the subjective and

यो मामजमनादिं च वेत्ति लोकमहेश्वरम् ।
असम्मूढः स मर्त्येषु सर्वपापैः प्रमुच्यते ॥३॥

3. Whosoever knows Me as the Unborn, without origin, mighty Lord of the worlds[1] and peoples, lives unbewildered[2] among mortals and is delivered[3] from all sin and evil.

बुद्धिर्ज्ञानमसम्मोहः क्षमा सत्यं दमः शमः ।
सुखं दुःखं भवोऽभावो भयं चाभयमेव च ॥४॥
अहिंसा समता तुष्टिस्तपो दानं यशोऽयशः ।
भवन्ति भावा भूतानां मत्त एव पृथग्विधाः ॥५॥

4-5. Understanding and knowledge and freedom from the bewilderment of the Ignorance, forgiveness and truth and self-government and calm of inner control, grief and pleasure, coming into being and destruction, fear and fearless-

---

objective forces of the cosmos. The gods are spiritual forms of the eternal and original Deity who descend from him into the many processes of the world. All their own existence, nature, power, process proceeds in every way, in every principle, in its every strand from the truth of the transcendent Ineffable.

[1] The Supreme who becomes all creation, yet infinitely transcends it, is not a will-less cause aloof from his creation. He is the mighty lord of the worlds and peoples, and governs all not only from within but from above, from his supreme transcendence. This is the theistic seeing of the universe.

[2] All the perplexity of man's mind and action, all the stumbling, insecurity and affliction of his mind can be traced back to the groping and bewildered cognition and volition natural to his sense obscured mortal mind in the body, *sammoha*. But when he sees the divine Origin of all things, when he looks steadily from the cosmic appearance to its transcendent Reality and back from that Reality to the appearance, he is then delivered from this bewilderment of the mind, will, heart and senses.

[3] Assigning to everything its supernal and real and not any longer only its present and apparent value, he finds the hidden links and connections; he consciously directs all life and acts to their high and true object and governs them by the light and power which comes to him from the Godhead within him. Thus he escapes from the wrong cognition, the wrong mental and volitional reaction, the wrong sensational reception and impulse which here originate sin and error and suffering.

ness, glory and ingloriousness, non-injuring and equality, contentment and austerity and giving, all here in their separate diversities are subjective becomings[1] of existences, and they all proceed from Me.[2]

महर्षयः सप्त पूर्वे चत्वारो मनवस्तथा ।
मद्भावा मानसा जाता येषां लोक इमाः प्रजाः ॥६॥

6. The great Rishis,[3] the seven Ancients of the world, and also the four Manus,[4] are my mental becomings; from them[5] are all these living creatures in the world.

[1] We must observe here the emphatic collocation of the three worlds from the verb *bhū* to become, *bhavanti, bhāvāḥ, bhūtānām*. All existences are becomings of the Divine, *bhutani*; all subjective states and movements are his and their psychologial becomings, *bhāvāḥ*. These even, our lesser subjective conditions and their apparent results no less than the highest spiritual states, are all becomings from the supreme Being, *bhavanti matta eva*.

[2] The theism of the Gita is no shrinking and gingerly theism afraid of the world's contradictions, but one which sees God as the omniscient and omnipotent, the sole original Being, who manifests in himself all, whatever it may be, good and evil, pain and pleasure, light and darkness as stuff of his own existence, and governs himself what in himself he has manifested. Unaffected by its oppositions, unbound by his creation, exceeding, yet intimately related to this Nature and closely one with her creatures, their Spirit, Lord, Lover, Friend, Refuge, he is ever leading them from within them and from above through the mortal appearances of ignorance and suffering and sin and evil towards a supreme light and bliss and immortality and transcendence. This is the fullness of the liberating knowledge, the character of which is emphasised in three separate verses of promise in this chapter, 3, 7 and 11.

[3] The great Rishis, called here as in the Veda the seven original Seers, are intelligence powers of that divine Wisdom which has evolved all things out of its own self-conscious infinitude, *prajñā purāṇī*, – developed them down the range of the seven principles of its own essence.

[4] Along with these are coupled the four eternal Manus, the spiritual fathers of every human mind and body, – for the active nature of the Godhead is fourfold* and humanity expresses this nature in its fourfold character. These also, as their name implies, are mental beings.

(* In its aspects as Knowlege, Power, Harmony and Work.)

[5] These are the creators of all this life that depends on manifest or latent mind for its action; all are their children and offspring.

एतां विभूतिं योगं च मम यो वेत्ति तत्त्वतः ।
सोऽविकम्पेन योगेन युज्यते नात्र संशयः ॥७॥

7. Whosoever knows in its right principles this my pervading lordship[1] and this my Yoga,[2] unites himself to me by an untrembling[3] Yoga; of this there is no doubt.

अहं सर्वस्य प्रभवो मत्तः सर्वं प्रवर्तते ।
इति मत्वा भजन्ते मां बुधा भावसमन्विताः ॥८॥

8. I am the birth of everything and from Me[4] all proceeds into development of action and movement; understanding thus, the wise adore Me in rapt emotion.[5]

---

[1] The wisdom of the liberated man is not, in the view of the Gita, a consciousness of abstracted and unrelated impersonality, a do-nothing quietude. His mind and soul are firmly settled in a constant sense, an integral feeling of the pervasion of the world by the actuating and directing presence of the divine Master of the universe.

[2] He is aware of his spirit's transcendence of the cosmic order, but he is aware also of his oneness with it by the divine Yoga. And he sees each aspect of the transcendent, the cosmic and the individual existence in its right relation to the supreme Truth and puts all in their right place in the unity of the divine Yoga.

[3] By this Yoga once perfected, undeviating and fixed, he is able to take up whatever poise of nature, assume whatever human condition, do whatever world-action without any fall from his oneness with the divine Self, without any loss of his constant communion with the Master of existence.

[4] God does not create out of a void, out of a Nihil or out of an unsubstantial matrix of dream. Out of himself he creates, in himself he becomes; all are in his being and all is of his being. This truth admits and exceeds the pantheistic seeing of things. Vasudeva is all, *vāsudevaḥ sarvam*, but Vasudeva is all that appears in the cosmos because he is too all that does not appear in it, all that is never manifested.

[5] This knowledge translated into the affective, emotional, temperamental plane becomes a calm love and intense adoration of the original and transcendental Godhead above us, the ever-present Master of all things here, God in man, God in Nature. It is at first a wisdom of the intelligence, the *buddhi*; but that is accompanied by a moved spiritualised

मच्चित्ता मद्गतप्राणा बोधयन्तः परस्परम् ।
कथयन्तश्च मां नित्यं तुष्यन्ति च रमन्ति च ॥९॥

9. Their consciousness full of Me, their life wholly given up to Me, illumining each other, mutually talking about Me, they are ever contented and joyful.

तेषां सततयुक्तानां भजतां प्रीतिपूर्वकम् ।
ददामि बुद्धियोगं तं येन मामुपयान्ति ते ॥१०॥

10. To these who are thus in a constant union with Me, and adore Me with an intense delight of love,[1] I give the Yoga of understanding[2] by which they come to Me.

---

state of the affective nature, *bhāva*. This change of the heart and mind is the beginning of a total change of all the nature. A new inner birth and becoming prepares us for oneness with the supreme object of our love and adoration, *madbhāvāya*. There is an intense delight of love in the greatness and beauty and perfection of the divine Being now seen everywhere in the world and above it, *prīti*. That deeper ecstasy assumes the place of the scattered and external pleasure of the mind in existence or rather it draws all other delight into it and transforms by a marvellous alchemy the mind's and the heart's feelings and all sense movements.

[1] From the moment that this inner state begins, even in the stage of imperfection, the Divine confirms it by the perfect Yoga of the will and intelligence. He uplifts the blazing lamp of knowledge within us, he destroys the ignorance of the separative mind and will, he stands revealed in the human spirit.

[2] By the Yoga of the will and intelligence founded on an illumined union of works and knowledge the transition was effected from our lower troubled mind-ranges to the immutable calm of the witnessing Soul above the active nature. But now by this greater Yoga of the Buddhi founded on an illumined union of love and adoration with an all-comprehending knowledge the soul rises in a vast ecstasy to the whole transcendental truth of the absolute and all-originating Godhead. The Eternal is fulfilled in the individual spirit and individual nature; the individual spirit is exalted from birth in time to the infinitudes of the Eternal.

तेषामेवानुकम्पार्थमहमज्ञानजं तमः ।
नाशयाम्यात्मभावस्थो ज्ञानदीपेन भास्वता ॥११॥

11. Out of compassion for them, I, lodged in their self, lift the blazing lamp of knowledge and destroy the darkness which is born of the ignorance.

II. GOD IN POWER OF BECOMING

अर्जुन उवाच —
परं ब्रह्म परं धाम पवित्रं परमं भवान् ।
पुरुषं शाश्वतं दिव्यमादिदेवमजं विभुम् ॥१२॥

12. Arjuna[1] said: Thou[2] art the supreme Brahman, the supreme Abode, the supreme Purity, the one Permanent, the divine Purusha, the original Godhead, the Unborn, the all-pervading Lord.

आहुस्त्वामृषयः सर्वे देवर्षिर्नारदस्तथा ।
असितो देवलो व्यासः स्वयं चैव ब्रवीषि मे ॥१३॥

13. All the Rishis[3] say this of Thee and the divine seer Narada, Asita, Devala, Vyasa; and Thou Thyself[4] sayest it to me.

[1] Arjuna accepts the entire knowledge that has thus been given to him by the divine Teacher. His mind is already delivered from its doubts and seekings; his heart, turned now from the outward aspect of the world, from its baffling appearance to its supreme sense and origin and its inner realities, is already released from sorrow and affliction and touched with the ineffable gladness of a divine revelation. The language in which Arjuna voices his acceptance emphasises again the profound integrality of this knowledge and its all-embracing finality and fullness.

[2] He accepts first the Avatar, the Godhead in man who is speaking to him as the supreme Brahman, as the supracosmic All and Absolute of existence in which the soul can dwell when it rises out of this manifestation and this partial becoming to its source. He accepts him as the supreme purity of the ever free Existence to which one arrives through the effacement of ego in the self's immutable impersonality calm and still for ever. He accepts him next as the one Permanent, the eternal Soul, the divine Purusha. He acclaims in him the original Godhead, adores the Unborn who is the pervading, indwelling, self-extending master of all existence.

[3] This is a secret wisdom which one must hear from the seers who have seen the face of this Truth, have heard its word and have become one with it in self and spirit.

[4] Or else one must receive it from within by revelation and inspiration from the inner Godhead who lifts in us the blazing lamp of knowledge.

सर्वमेतदृतं मन्ये यन्मां वदसि केशव ।
न हि ते भगवन् व्यक्तिं विदुर्देवा न दानवाः ॥१४॥

14. All this that Thou sayest, my mind[1] holds for the truth, O Keshava. Neither the Gods nor the Titans, O blessed Lord, know Thy manifestation.

स्वयमेवात्मनात्मानं वेत्थ त्वं पुरुषोत्तम ।
भूतभावन भूतेश देवदेव जगत्पते ॥१५॥

15. Thou alone knowest Thyself by Thyself, O Purushottama; Source[2] of beings, Lord of beings, God of gods, Master of the world!

वक्तुमर्हस्यशेषेण दिव्या ह्यात्मविभूतयः ।
याभिर्विभूतिभिर्लोकानिमांस्त्वं व्याप्य तिष्ठसि ॥१६॥

16. Thou shouldst tell me of Thy divine self-manifestations,[3] all without exception, Thy Vibhutis by which Thou standest pervading these worlds.

कथं विद्यामहं योगिंस्त्वां सदा परिचिन्तयन् ।
केषु केषु च भावेषु चिन्त्योऽसि भगवन्मया ॥१७॥

---

[1] Once revealed, it has to be accepted by the assent of the mind, the consent of the will and the heart's delight and submission, the three elements of the complete mental faith, *śraddhā*. It is so that Arjuna has accepted it. But still there will remain the need of that deeper possession in the very self of our being and out from its most intimate psychic centre, the soul's demand for that permanent inexpressible spiritual realisation of which the mental is only a preliminary or a shadow and without which there cannot be a complete union with the Eternal. Now the way to arrive at that realisation has been given to Arjuna.

[2] Arjuna accepts him not only as that Wonderful who is beyond expression of any kind, for nothing is sufficient to manifest him, – "neither the Gods nor the Titans, O blessed Lord, know Thy manifestation," – but as the lord of all existences and the one divine efficient cause of all their becoming, God of the gods from whom all godheads have sprung, master of the universe who manifests and governs it from above by the power of his supreme and his universal Nature.

[3] Lastly Arjuna accepts him as that Vasudeva in and around us who is

17. How shall I know[1] Thee, O Yogin, by thinking of Thee everywhere at all moments and in what pre-eminent becomings should I think of Thee, O Blessed Lord?

विस्तरेणात्मनो योगं विभूतिं च जनार्दन ।
भूयः कथय तृप्तिर्हि शृण्वतो नास्ति मेऽमृतम् ॥१८॥

18. In detail tell me of Thy Yoga and Vibhuti, O Janardana; and tell me ever more of it; it is nectar[2] of immortality to me, and however much of it I hear, I am not satiated.

श्रीभगवान् उवाच —
हन्त ते कथयिष्यामि दिव्या ह्यात्मविभूतयः ।
प्राधान्यतः कुरुश्रेष्ठ नास्त्यन्तो विस्तरस्य मे ॥१९॥

19. The Blessed Lord said: Yes, I will tell thee of my divine Vibhutis, but only in some of My principal pre-

---

all things here by virtue of the world-pervading, all-inhabiting, all-constituting master powers of his becoming, *vibhūtayaḥ*.

[1] Arjuna, though he accepts the revelation of Vasudeva as all and though his heart is full of the delight of it, yet feels it difficult to see him in the apparent truths of existence, to detect him in this fact of Nature and in these disguising phenomena of the world's becoming; for here all is opposed to the sublimity of this unifying conception. How can we consent to see the Divine as man and animal being and inanimate object, in the noble and the low, the sweet and the terrible, the good and the evil? At least some compelling indications are needed, some links and bridges, some supports to the difficult effort at oneness. So Arjuna requires guiding indications, asks Krishna even for a complete and detailed enumeration of the sovereign powers of his becoming and desires that nothing shall be left out of the vision, nothing remain to baffle him.

[2] Here we get an indication in the Gita of something which the Gita itself does not bring out expressly, but which occurs frequently in the Upanishads and was developed later on by Vaishnavism and Shaktism in a greater intensity of vision, man's possible joy of the Divine in the world-existence, the universal Ananda, the play of the Mother, the sweetness and beauty of God's Lila.

eminences,[1] O best of the Kurus; for there is no end to the detail of My self-extension in the universe.

अहमात्मा गुडाकेश सर्वभूताशयस्थितः ।
अहमादिश्च मध्यं च भूतानामन्त एव च ॥२०॥

20. I, O Gudakesha, am the Self,[2] which abides within all beings. I am the beginning and middle and end of all beings.

आदित्यानामहं विष्णुर्ज्योतिषां रविरंशुमान् ।
मरीचिर्मरुतामस्मि नक्षत्राणामहं शशी ॥२१॥

21. Among the Adityas[3] I am Vishnu; among lights[4] and splendours I am the radiant Sun; I am Marichi among the Maruts; among the stars the Moon am I.

[1] Throughout the rest of the chapter we get a summary description of these principal indications, these pre-eminent signs of the divine force present in the things and persons of the universe. It seems at first as if they were given pell-mell, without any order, but still we can disengage a certain principle in the enumeration. The chapter has been called the Vibhuti-Yoga, – an indispensable Yoga. For while we must identify ourselves impartially with the universal divine Becoming in all its extension, we must at the same time realise that there is an ascending evolutionary power in it, an increasing intensity of its revelation in things, a hierarchic secret something that carries us upward from the first concealing appearances through higher and higher forms towards the large ideal nature of the universal Godhead.

[2] This summary enumeration begins with a statement of the primal principle that underlies all the power of this manifestation in the universe. It is this that in every being and object God dwells concealed and discoverable. It is this inner divine Self hidden from the mind and heart which he inhabits, who is all the time evolving the mutations of our personality in Time and our sensational existence in Space, – Time and Space that are the conceptual movement and extension of the Godhead in us.

[3] Among all these living beings, cosmic godheads, superhuman and human and subhuman creatures, and amid all these qualities, powers and objects, the chief, the head, the greatest in quality of each class is a special power of the becoming of the Godhead.

[4] At the other end of the scale he is the sun among radiances, Meru among the peaks of the world, Ganges among the rivers and so forth.

वेदानां सामवेदोऽस्मि देवानामस्मि वासवः ।
इन्द्रियाणां मनश्चास्मि भूतानामस्मि चेतना ॥२२॥

22. Among the Vedas I am the Sama-Veda; among the gods I am Vasava; I am mind among the senses; in living beings I am consciousness.

रुद्राणां शङ्करश्चास्मि वित्तेशो यक्षरक्षसाम् ।
वसूनां पावकश्चास्मि मेरुः शिखरिणामहम् ॥२३॥

23. I am Shiva among the Rudras, the lord of wealth among the Yakshas and Rakshasas, Agni among the Vasus; Meru among the peaks of the world am I.

पुरोधसां च मुख्यं मां विद्धि पार्थ बृहस्पतिम् ।
सेनानीनामहं स्कन्दः सरसामस्मि सागरः ॥२४॥

24. And know Me, O Partha, of the high priests of the world the chief, Brihaspati; I am Skanda, the war-god, leader of the leaders of battle; among the flowing waters I am the ocean.

महर्षीणां भृगुरहं गिरामस्म्येकमक्षरम् ।
यज्ञानां जपयज्ञोऽस्मि स्थावराणां हिमालयः ॥२५॥

25. I am Bhrigu among the great Rishis; I am the sacred syllable OM among words; among acts of worship I am the worship called Japa (silent repetitions of sacred names etc.); among the mountain-ranges I am Himalaya.

अश्वत्थः सर्ववृक्षाणां देवर्षीणां च नारदः ।
गन्धर्वाणां चित्ररथः सिद्धानां कपिलो मुनिः ॥२६॥

26. I am the Aswattha among all plants and trees; and I am Narada among the divine sages, Chitraratha among the Gandharvas, the Muni Kapila among the Siddhas.

उच्चैःश्रवसमश्वानां विद्धि माममृतोद्भवम् ।
ऐरावतं गजेन्द्राणां नराणां च नराधिपम् ॥२७॥

27. Uchchaisravas among horses know me, nectar-born; Airavata among lordly elephants; and among men the king of men.

आयुधानामहं वज्रं धेनूनामस्मि कामधुक् ।
प्रजनश्चास्मि कन्दर्पः सर्पाणामस्मि वासुकिः ॥२८॥

28. Among weapons I am the divine thunderbolt; I am Kamadhuk the cow of plenty among cattle; I am Kandarpa the love-god among the progenitors; among the serpents Vasuki am I.

अनन्तश्चास्मि नागानां वरुणो यादसामहम् ।
पितृणामर्यमा चास्मि यमः संयमतामहम् ॥२९॥

29. And I am Ananta among the Nagas, Varuna among the peoples of the sea, Aryaman among the Fathers, Yama (lord of the Law) among those who maintain rule and law.

प्रह्लादश्चास्मि दैत्यानां कालः कलयतामहम् ।
मृगाणां च मृगेन्द्रोऽहं वैनतेयश्च पक्षिणाम् ॥३०॥

30. And I am Prahlada among the Titans; I am Time the head of all reckoning to those who reckon and measure; and among the beasts of the forest I am the king of the beasts, and Vainateya among birds.

पवनः पवतामस्मि रामः शस्त्रभृतामहम् ।
झषाणां मकरश्चास्मि स्रोतसामस्मि जाह्नवी ॥३१॥

31. I am the wind among purifiers; I am Rama among warriors; and I am the alligator among fishes; among the rivers Ganges am I.

---

[1] Divinised ancestors.

सर्गाणामादिरन्तश्च मध्यं चैवाहमर्जुन ।
अध्यात्मविद्या विद्यानां वादः प्रवदतामहम् ॥३२॥

32. Of creation[1] I am the beginning and the end and also the middle, O Arjuna. I am spiritual knowledge among the many philosophies, arts and sciences; I am the logic of those who debate.

अक्षराणामकारोऽस्मि द्वन्द्वः सामासिकस्य च ।
अहमेवाक्षयः कालो धाताहं विश्वतोमुखः ॥३३॥

33. I am the letter A among letters, the dual among compounds. I am imperishable Time;[2] I am the Master and Ruler (of all existences), whose faces are everywhere.

मृत्युः सर्वहरश्चाहमुद्भवश्च भविष्यताम् ।
कीर्तिः श्रीर्वाक् च नारीणां स्मृतिर्मेधा धृतिः क्षमा ॥३४॥

34. And I am all-snatching Death,[3] and I am too the birth[4] of all that shall come into being. Among feminine qualities I

---

[1] All things are his powers and effectuations in his self-Nature, Vibhutis. He is the origin of all they are, their beginning; he is their support in their ever-changing status, their middle; he is their end too, the culmination or the disintegration of each created thing in its cessation or its disappearance.

[2] God is imperishable, beginningless, unending Time; this is his most evident Power of becoming and the essence of the whole universal movement. In that movement of Time and Becoming God appears to our conception or experience of him by the evidence of his works as the divine Power who ordains and sets all things in their place in the movement. In his form of space it is he who fronts us in every direction, million-bodied, myriad-minded, manifest in each existence; we see his faces on all sides of us.

[3] He appears to us too in the universe as the universal spirit of Destruction, who seems to create only to undo his creations in the end.

[4] And yet his Power of becoming does not cease from its workings, for the rebirth and force of new creation ever keeps pace with the force of death and destruction.

am glory and beauty and speech and memory and intelligence and steadfastness and forgiveness.

बृहत्साम तथा साम्नां गायत्री छन्दसामहम् ।
मासानां मार्गशीर्षोऽहमृतूनां कुसुमाकरः ॥३५॥

35. I am also the great Sama among mantras, the Gayatri among metres; among the months I am Margasirsha, first of the months; I am spring, the fairest of seasons.

द्यूतं छलयतामस्मि तेजस्तेजस्विनामहम् ।
जयोऽस्मि व्यवसायोऽस्मि सत्त्वं सत्त्ववतामहम् ॥३६॥

36. I am the gambling of the cunning, and the strength of the mighty; I am resolution and perseverance and victory; I am the sattwic quality of the good.

वृष्णीनां वासुदेवोऽस्मि पाण्डवानां धनञ्जयः ।
मुनीनामप्यहं व्यासः कवीनामुशना कविः ॥३७॥

37. I am Krishna[1] among the Vrishnis, Arjuna among the Pandavas; I am Vyasa among the sages; I am Ushanas among the seer-poets.

दण्डो दमयतामस्मि नीतिरस्मि जिगीषताम् ।
मौनं चैवास्मि गुह्यानां ज्ञानं ज्ञानवतामहम् ॥३८॥

38. I am the mastery and power of all who rule and tame and vanquish and the policy of all who succeed and conquer; I am the silence of things secret and the knowledge of the knower.

यच्चापि सर्वभूतानां बीजं तदहमर्जुन ।
न तदस्ति विना यत्स्यान्मया भूतं चराचरम् ॥३९॥

[1] Krishna who in his divine inner being is the Godhead in a human form, is in his outer human being the leader of his age, the great man of the Vrishnis. The Avatar is at the same time the Vibhuti.

39. And whatsoever is the seed[1] of all existences, that am I, O Arjuna; nothing[2] moving or unmoving, animate or inanimate in the world can be without me.

नान्तोऽस्ति मम दिव्यानां विभूतीनां परन्तप ।
एष तूद्देशतः प्रोक्तो विभूतेर्विस्तरो मया ॥४०॥

40. There is no numbering or limit to My divine Vibhutis, O Parantapa; what I have spoken, is nothing more than a summary development and I have given only the light of a few leading indications.

यद्यद्विभूतिमत्सत्त्वं श्रीमदूर्जितमेव वा ।
तत्तदेवावगच्छ त्वं मम तेजोंऽशसम्भवम् ॥४१॥

41. Whatever beautiful and glorious creature thou seest in the world, whatever being is mighty and forceful (among men and above man and below him), know to be a very splendour, light, and energy of Me and born of a potent portion and intense power of my existence.

अथवा बहुनैतेन किं ज्ञातेन तवार्जुन ।
विष्टभ्याहमिदं कृत्स्नमेकांशेन स्थितो जगत् ॥४२॥

42. But what need is there of a multitude of details for this knowledge, O Arjuna? Take it thus,[3] that I am here in

---

[1] The Divine is the seed of all existences, and of that seed they are the branches and flowers; what is in the seed of self, that only they can develop in Nature.

[2] With whatever variety of degree in manifestation, all beings are in their own way and nature powers of the Godhead.

[3] All classes, general species, individuals are vibhutis of the One. But since it is through power in his becoming that he is apparent to us, he is

this world and everywhere, I support this entire universe with an infinitesimal portion of Myself.

इति श्रीमद्भगवद्गीतासूपनिषत्सु ब्रह्मविद्यायां योगशास्त्रे श्रीकृष्णार्जुनसंवादे
विभूतियोगो नाम दशमोऽध्यायः

especially apparent in whatever is of a pre-eminent value or seems to act with a powerful and pre-eminent force. And therefore in each kind of being we can see him most in those in whom the power of nature of that kind reaches its highest, its leading, its most effectively self-revealing manifestation. These are in a special sense Vibhutis. Yet the highest power and manifestation is only a very partial revelation of the Infinite; even the whole universe is informed by only one degree of his greatness, illumined by one ray of his splendour, glorious with a faint hint of his delight and beauty. This is in sum the gist of the enumeration, the result we carry away from it, the heart of its meaning.

Eleventh Chapter

I. TIME THE DESTROYER

अर्जुन उवाच —
मदनुग्रहाय परमं गुह्यमध्यात्मसंज्ञितम् ।
यत्त्वयोक्तं वचस्तेन मोहोऽयं विगतो मम ॥१॥

1. Arjuna said: This word of the highest spiritual secret of existence, Thou hast spoken out of compassion for me; by this my delusion[1] is dispelled.

भवाप्ययौ हि भूतानां श्रुतौ विस्तरशो मया ।
त्वत्तः कमलपत्राक्ष माहात्म्यमपि चाव्ययम् ॥२॥

2. The birth and passing away of existences have been heard by me in detail from Thee, O Lotus-eyed, and also the imperishable greatness of the divine conscious Soul.[2]

---

[1] The illusion which so persistently holds man's sense and mind, the idea that things at all exist in themselves or for themselves apart from God or that anything subject to Nature can be self-moved and self-guided, has passed from Arjuna, – that was the cause of his doubt and bewilderment and refusal of action.

[2] All is a Yoga of this great eternal Spirit in things and all happenings are the result and expression of that Yoga; all Nature is full of the secret Godhead and in labour to reveal him in her. But Arjuna would see too the very form and body of this Godhead, if that be possible. The vision of the universal Purusha is one of the best known and most powerfully poetic passages in the Gita, but its place in the thought is not altogether on the surface. It is evidently intended for a poetic and revelatory symbol and we must see how it is brought in and for what purpose and discover to what it points in its significant aspects before we can capture its meaning. It is invited by Arjuna in his desire to see the living image, the visible greatness of the unseen Divine, the very embodiment of the Spirit and Power that governs the universe. For this greatest all-comprehending vision he is made to ask because it is so, from the Spirit revealed in the universe, that he must receive the command to his part in the world-action.

एवमेतद्यथात्थ त्वमात्मानं परमेश्वर ।
द्रष्टुमिच्छामि ते रूपमैश्वरं पुरुषोत्तम ॥३॥

3. So it is, as Thou hast declared Thyself, O Supreme Lord; I desire to see Thy divine form and body, O Purushottama.

मन्यसे यदि तच्छक्यं मया द्रष्टुमिति प्रभो ।
योगेश्वर ततो मे त्वं दर्शयात्मानमव्ययम् ॥४॥

4. If Thou thinkest that it can be seen by me, O Lord, O Master of Yoga, then show me Thy imperishable Self.

श्रीभगवान् उवाच —
पश्य मे पार्थ रूपाणि शतशोऽथ सहस्रशः ।
नानाविधानि दिव्यानि नानावर्णाकृतीनि च ॥५॥

5. The Blessed Lord said: Behold, O Partha, my hundreds and thousands of divine forms, various in kind, various in shape and hue.

पश्यादित्यान् वसून् रुद्रानश्विनौ मरुतस्तथा ।
बहून्यदृष्टपूर्वाणि पश्याश्चर्याणि भारत ॥६॥

6. Behold the Adityas, the Vasus, the Rudras, the two Aswins and also the Maruts; behold many wonders that none has beheld, O Bharata.

इहैकस्थं जगत्कृत्स्नं पश्याद्य सचराचरम् ।
मम देहे गुडाकेश यच्चान्यद् द्रष्टुमिच्छसि ॥७॥

7. Here, to-day, behold the whole world, with all that is moving and unmoving, unified[1] in my body, O Gudakesha, and whatever else thou willest to see.

---

[1] This then is the keynote, the central significance. It is the vision of the One in the Many, the Many in the One, – and all are the One. It is this vision that to the eye of the divine Yoga liberates, justifies, explains all

न तु मां शक्यसे द्रष्टुमनेनैव स्वचक्षुषा ।
दिव्यं ददामि ते चक्षुः पश्य मे योगमैश्वरम् ॥८॥

8. What thou hast to see, this thy human[1] eye cannot grasp; but there is a divine eye (an inmost seeing) and that eye I now give to thee. Behold Me in My divine Yoga.

सञ्जय उवाच—
एवमुक्त्वा ततो राजन्महायोगेश्वरो हरिः ।
दर्शयामास पार्थाय परमं रूपमैश्वरम् ॥९॥
अनेकवक्त्रनयनमनेकाद्भुतदर्शनम् ।
अनेकदिव्याभरणं दिव्यानेकोद्यतायुधम् ॥१०॥
दिव्यमाल्याम्बरधरं दिव्यगन्धानुलेपनम् ।
सर्वाश्चर्यमयं देवमनन्तं विश्वतोमुखम् ॥११॥
दिवि सूर्यसहस्रस्य भवेद्युगपदुत्थिता ।
यदि भाः सदृशी सा स्याद् भासस्तस्य महात्मनः ॥१२॥
तत्रैकस्थं जगत्कृत्स्नं प्रविभक्तमनेकधा ।
अपश्यद्देवदेवस्य शरीरे पाण्डवस्तदा ॥१३॥
ततः स विस्मयाविष्टो हृष्टरोमा धनञ्जयः ।
प्रणम्य शिरसा देवं कृताञ्जलिरभाषत ॥१४॥

9-14. Sanjaya said: Having thus spoken, O King, the Master of the great Yoga, Hari, showed to Partha His supreme Form. It is that of the infinite Godhead whose faces are everywhere and in whom are all the wonders of existence, who multiplies unendingly all the many marvellous revelations of His being, a world-wide Divinity seeing with innumerable eyes, speaking from innumerable mouths,

---

that is and was and shall be. Once seen and held, it lays the shining axe of God at the root of all doubts and perplexities and annihilates all denials and oppositions. If the soul can arrive at unity with the Godhead in this vision, – Arjuna has not yet done that, therefore we find that he has fear when he sees, – all even that is terrible in the world loses its terror.

[1] For the human eye can see only the outward appearances of things or make out of them separate symbol forms, each of them significant of only a few aspects of the eternal Mystery.

armed for battle with numberless divine uplifted weapons, glorious with divine ornaments of beauty, robed in heavenly raiment of deity, lovely with garlands of divine flowers, fragrant with divine perfumes. Such is the light of this body of God as if a thousand suns had risen at once in heaven. The whole world multitudinously divided and yet unified is visible in the body of the God of Gods. Arjuna sees him (God magnificent and beautiful and terrible, the Lord of souls who has manifested in the glory and greatness of his spirit this wild and monstrous and orderly and wonderful and sweet and terrible world) and overcome with marvel and joy and fear he bows down and adores with words of awe and with clasped hands the tremendous vision.

अर्जुन उवाच —
पश्यामि देवांस्तव देव देहे सर्वांस्तथा भूतविशेषसङ्घान् ।
ब्रह्माणमीशं कमलासनस्थमृषींश्च सर्वानुरगांश्च दिव्यान् ॥१५॥

15. Arjuna said: I see all the gods in Thy body, O God, and different companies of beings, Brahma the creating Lord seated in the Lotus, and the Rishis and the race of the divine Serpents.

अनेकबाहूदरवक्त्रनेत्रं पश्यामि त्वां सर्वतोऽनन्तरूपम् ।
नान्तं न मध्यं न पुनस्तवादिं पश्यामि विश्वेश्वर विश्वरूप ॥१६॥

16. I see numberless arms and bellies and eyes and faces, I see Thy infinite forms on every side, but I see not Thy end nor Thy middle nor Thy beginning, O Lord of the universe, O Form universal.

किरीटिनं गदिनं चक्रिणं च तेजोराशिं सर्वतो दीप्तिमन्तम् ।
पश्यामि त्वां दुर्निरीक्ष्यं समन्ताद्दीप्तानलार्कद्युतिमप्रमेयम् ॥१७॥

17. I see Thee crowned and with Thy mace and Thy discus, hard to discern because Thou art a luminous mass of energy on all sides of me, an encompassing blaze, a sun-bright fire-bright Immeasurable.

त्वमक्षरं परमं वेदितव्यं त्वमस्य विश्वस्य परं निधानम् ।
त्वमव्ययः शाश्वतधर्मगोप्ता सनातनस्त्वं पुरुषो मतो मे ॥१८॥

18. Thou art the supreme Immutable whom we have to know, Thou art the high foundation and abode of the universe, Thou art the imperishable guardian of the eternal laws. Thou art the sempiternal soul of existence.

अनादिमध्यान्तमनन्तवीर्यमनन्तबाहुं शशिसूर्यनेत्रम् ।
पश्यामि त्वां दीप्तहुताशवक्त्रं स्वतेजसा विश्वमिदं तपन्तम् ॥१९॥

19. I behold Thee without end or middle or beginning, of infinite force, of numberless arms, Thy eyes are suns and moons, Thou hast a face of blazing fire and thou art ever burning[1] up the whole universe with the flame of Thy energy.

द्यावापृथिव्योरिदमन्तरं हि व्याप्तं त्वयैकेन दिशश्च सर्वाः ।
दृष्ट्वाद्भुतं रूपमुग्रं तवेदं लोकत्रयं प्रव्यथितं महात्मन् ॥२०॥

20. The whole space between earth and heaven is occupied by Thee alone; when is seen this Thy fierce and astounding form, the three worlds are all in pain and suffer, O Thou mighty Spirit.

अमी हि त्वां सुरसङ्घा विशन्ति केचिद् भीताः प्राञ्जलयो गृणन्ति ।
स्वस्तीत्युक्त्वा महर्षिसिद्धसङ्घाः स्तुवन्ति त्वां स्तुतिभिः पुष्कलाभिः ॥२१॥

21. The companies of the gods enter Thee, afraid, adoring; the Rishis and the Siddhas crying "May there be peace and weal" praise Thee with many praises.

रुद्रादित्या वसवो ये च साध्या विश्वेऽश्विनौ मरुतश्चोष्मपाश्च ।
गन्धर्वयक्षासुरसिद्धसङ्घा वीक्षन्ते त्वां विस्मिताश्चैव सर्वे ॥२२॥

---

[1] In the greatness of this vision there is too the terrific image of the Destroyer. This Immeasurable without end or middle or beginning is He in whom all things begin and exist and end. This Godhead embraces the worlds with His numberless arms and destroys with his million hands.

22. The Rudras, Adityas, Vasus, Sadhyas, Vishvas, the two Ashwins and the Maruts and the Ushmapas, the Gandharvas, Yakshas, Asuras, Siddhas, all have their eyes fixed on Thee in amazement.

रूपं महत्ते बहुवक्त्रनेत्रं महाबाहो बहुबाहूरुपादम् ।
बहूदरं बहुदंष्ट्राकरालं दृष्ट्वा लोकाः प्रव्यथितास्तथाहम् ॥२३॥

23. Seeing Thy great form of many mouths and eyes, O Mighty-armed, of many arms, thighs and feet and bellies, terrible with many teeth, the world and its nations are shaken and in anguish, as also am I.

नभःस्पृशं दीप्तमनेकवर्णं व्यात्ताननं दीप्तविशालनेत्रम् ।
दृष्ट्वा हि त्वां प्रव्यथितान्तरात्मा धृतिं न विन्दामि शमं च विष्णो ॥२४॥

24. I see Thee, touching heaven, blazing, of many hues, with opened mouths and enormous burning eyes; troubled and in pain is the soul within me and I find no peace or gladness.

दंष्ट्राकरालानि च ते मुखानि दृष्ट्वैव कालानलसन्निभानि ।
दिशो न जाने न लभे च शर्म प्रसीद देवेश जगन्निवास ॥२५॥

25. As I look upon Thy mouths terrible with many tusks of destruction, Thy faces like the fires of Death and Time, I lose sense of the directions and find no peace. Turn Thy heart to grace, O God of gods! refuge of all the worlds!

अमी च त्वां धृतराष्ट्रस्य पुत्राः सर्वे सहैवावनिपालसङ्घैः ।
भीष्मो द्रोणः सूतपुत्रस्तथासौ सहास्मदीयैरपि योधमुख्यैः ॥२६॥
वक्त्राणि ते त्वरमाणा विशन्ति दंष्ट्राकरालानि भयानकानि ।
केचिद्विलग्ना दशनान्तरेषु सन्दृश्यन्ते चूर्णितैरुत्तमाङ्गैः ॥२७॥

26-27. The sons of Dhritarashtra, all with the multitude of kings and heroes, Bhishma and Drona and Karna along with the foremost warriors on our side too, are hastening into Thy tusked and terrible jaws and some are seen with crushed and bleeding heads caught between Thy teeth of power.

यथा नदीनां बहवोऽम्बुवेगाः समुद्रमेवाभिमुखा द्रवन्ति ।
तथा तवामी नरलोकवीरा विशन्ति वक्त्राण्यभिविज्वलन्ति ॥२८॥

28. As is the speed of many rushing waters racing towards the ocean, so all these heroes of the world of men are entering into Thy many mouths of flame.

यथा प्रदीप्तं ज्वलनं पतङ्गा विशन्ति नाशाय समृद्धवेगाः ।
तथैव नाशाय विशन्ति लोकास्तवापि वक्त्राणि समृद्धवेगाः ॥२९॥

29. As a swarm of moths with ever-increasing speed fall to their destruction into a fire that some one has kindled, so now the nations with ever-increasing speed are entering into Thy jaws of doom.

लेलिह्यसे ग्रसमानः समन्ताल्लोकान् समग्रान् वदनैर्ज्वलद्भिः ।
तेजोभिरापूर्य जगत्समग्रं भासस्तवोग्राः प्रतपन्ति विष्णो ॥३०॥

30. Thou lickest the regions all around with Thy tongues and Thou art swallowing up all the nations in Thy mouths of burning; all the world is filled with the blaze of Thy energies; fierce and terrible are Thy lustres and they burn us, O Vishnu.

आख्याहि मे को भवानुग्ररूपो नमोऽस्तु ते देववर प्रसीद ।
विज्ञातुमिच्छामि भवन्तमाद्यं न हि प्रजानामि तव प्रवृत्तिम् ॥३१॥

31. Declare[1] to me who Thou art that wearest this form of

---

[1] This last cry of Arjuna indicates the double intention in the vision. This is the figure of the supreme and universal Being, this is he who forever creates, for Brahma the Creator is one of the Godheads seen in his body, he who keeps the world always in existence, for he is the

fierceness. Salutation to Thee, O Thou great Godhead, turn Thy heart to grace. I would know who Thou art who wast from the beginning, for I know not the will of Thy workings.

---

guardian of the eternal laws, but who is always too destroying in order that he may new-create, who is Time, who is Death, who is Rudra the Dancer of the calm and awful dance, who is Kali with her garland of skulls trampling naked in battle and flecked with the blood of the slaughtered Titans, who is the cyclone and the fire and the earthquake and pain and famine and revolution and ruin and the swallowing ocean. And it is this last aspect of him which he puts forward at the moment. It is an aspect from which the mind in men willingly turns away and ostrich-like its head so that perchance, not seeing, it may not be seen by the Terrible. The weakness of the human heart wants only fair and comforting truths or in their absence pleasant fables; it will not have the truth in its entirety because there there is much that is not clear and pleasant and comfortable, but hard to understand and harder to bear.

To put away the responsibility for all that seems to us evil or terrible on the shoulders of a semi-omnipotent Devil, or to put it aside as part of Nature, making an unbridgeable oppostion between world-nature and God-Nature, as if Nature were independent of God, or to throw the responsibility on man and his sins, as if he had preponderant voice in the making of this world or could create anything against the will of God, are clumsily comfortable devices in which the religious thought of India has never taken refuge. We have to look courageously in the face of the reality and see that it is God and none else who has made this world in his being and that so he has made it. The torment of the couch of pain and evil on which we are racked is his touch as much as happiness and sweetness and pleasure. The discords of the worlds are God's discords and it is only by accepting and proceeding through them that we can arrive at the greater concords of his supreme harmony, the summits and thrilled vastnesses of his transcendent and his cosmic Ananda.

The problem raised by the Gita and the solution it gives demand this character of the vision of the World-Spirit. Why should it be thus that the All-Spirit manifests himself in Nature? What is the significance of this creating and devouring flame that is mortal existence, this world-wide struggle, these constant disastrous revolutions, this labour and anguish and travail and perishing of creatures? Arjuna here puts the ancient question and breathes the eternal prayer.

श्रीभगवान् उवाच—
कालोऽस्मि लोकक्षयकृत्प्रवृद्धो लोकान् समाहर्तुमिह प्रवृत्तः ।
ऋतेऽपि त्वां न भविष्यन्ति सर्वे येऽवस्थिताः प्रत्यनीकेषु योधाः ।।३२।।

32. The Blessed Lord said: I am the Time-Spirit,[1] destroyer of the world, arisen huge-statured for the destruction of the nations. Even without[2] thee all these warriors shall be not, who are ranked in the opposing armies.

तस्मात्त्वमुत्तिष्ठ यशो लभस्व जित्वा शत्रून् भुङ्क्ष्व राज्यं समृद्धम् ।
मयैवैते निहताः पूर्वमेव निमित्तमात्रं भव सव्यसाचिन् ।।३३।।

33. Therefore arise, get thee glory, conquer thy enemies and enjoy an opulent kingdom. By me and none other already even are they slain, do thou become the occasion only, O Savyasachin.

द्रोणं च भीष्मं च जयद्रथं च कर्णं तथान्यानपि योधवीरान् ।
मया हतांस्त्वं जहि मा व्यथिष्ठा युद्ध्यस्व जेतासि रणे सपत्नान् ।।३४।।

---

[1] The Godhead does not mean either that he is the Time-Spirit alone or that the whole essence of the Time-Spirit is destruction.* But it is this which is the present will of his workings, *pravṛtti*.

(* Indian spirituality knows that God is Love and Peace and calm Eternity, – the Gita which presents us with these terrible images, speaks of the Godhead who embodies himself in them as the lover and friend of all creatures, *suhṛdaṁ sarvabhūtānām*.)

[2] I have a foreseeing purpose, says the Godhead in effect, which fulfils itself infallibly and no participation or abstention of any human being can prevent, alter or modify it; all is done by me already in my eternal eye of will before it can at all be done by man upon earth. I as Time have to destroy the old structures and to build up a new, mighty and splendid kingdom. Thou as a human instrument of the divine Power and Wisdom hast, in this struggle which thou canst not prevent, to battle for the right and slay and conquer its opponents. Thou too, the human soul in Nature, hast to enjoy in Nature the fruit given by me, the empire of right and justice. Let this be sufficient for thee, – to be one with God in thy soul, to receive his command, to do his will, to see calmly a supreme purpose fulfilled in the world.

34. Slay, by me who are slain, Drona, Bhishma, Jayadratha, Karna and other heroic fighters; be not pained and troubled. Fight, thou shalt[1] conquer the adversary in the battle.

---

[1] The fruit of the great and terrible work is promised and prophesied, not as a fruit hungered for by the individual, – for to that there is to be no attachment, – but as the result of the divine will, the glory and success of the thing to be done accomplished, the glory given by the Divine to himself in his Vibhuti. Thus is the final and compelling command to action given to the protagonist of the world-battle.

II. THE DOUBLE ASPECT

संजय उवाच —
एतच्छ्रुत्वा वचनं केशवस्य कृताञ्जलिर्वेपमानः किरीटी ।
नमस्कृत्वा भूय एवाह कृष्णं सगद्गदं भीतभीतः प्रणम्य ॥३५॥

35. Sanjaya said: Having heard these words of Keshava, Kiriti (Arjuna), with clasped hands and trembling, saluted again and spoke to Krishna in a faltering voice very much terrified and bowing down.

अर्जुन उवाच —
स्थाने हृषीकेश तव प्रकीर्त्या जगत्प्रहृष्यत्यनुरज्यते च ।
रक्षांसि भीतानि दिशो द्रवन्ति सर्वे नमस्यन्ति च सिद्धसङ्घाः ॥३६॥

36. Arjuna said: Rightly and in good place, O Krishna, does the world rejoice[1] and take pleasure in Thy name; the Rakshasas are fleeing from Thee in terror to all the quarters and the companies of the Siddhas bow down before Thee in adoration.[2]

[1] Even while the effects of the terrible aspect of this vision are still upon him, the first words uttered by Arjuna after the Godhead has spoken are eloquent of a greater uplifting and reassuring reality behind this face of death and this destruction. There is something that makes the heart of the world to rejoice and take pleasure in the name and nearness of the Divine. It is the profound sense of that which makes us see in the dark face of Kali the face of the Mother and to perceive even in the midst of destruction the protecting arms of the Friend of creatures, in the midst of evil the presence of a pure unalterable Benignity and in the midst of death the Master of Immortality.

[2] From the terror of the King of the divine action the Rakshasas, the fierce giant powers of darkness, flee destroyed, defeated and overpowered. But the Siddhas, the complete and perfect who know and sing the names of the Immortal and live in the truth of his being, bow down before every form of Him and know what every form enshrines and signifies. Nothing has real need to fear except that which is to be destroyed, the evil, the ignorance, the veilers in Night, the Rakshasa powers. All the movement and action of Rudra the Terrible is towards perfection and divine height and completeness.

कस्माच्च ते न नमेरन्महात्मन् गरीयसे ब्रह्मणोऽप्यादिकर्त्रे ।
अनन्त देवेश जगन्निवास त्वमक्षरं सदसत्तत्परं यत् ॥३७॥

37. How should they not do Thee homage, O great Spirit? For Thou art the original Creator[1] and Doer of works and greater even than creative Brahma. O Thou Infinite, O Thou Lord of the gods, O Thou abode of the universe, Thou art the Immutable and Thou art what is and is not, and Thou art that which is the Supreme.

त्वमादिदेवः पुरुषः पुराणस्त्वमस्य विश्वस्य परं निधानम् ।
वेत्तासि वेद्यं च परं च धाम त्वया ततं विश्वमनन्तरूप ॥३८॥

38. Thou art the ancient Soul and the first and original Godhead and the supreme resting-place of this All; Thou art the knower[2] and that which is to be known and the highest status; O infinite in form, by Thee was extended[3] the universe.

वायुर्यमोऽग्निर्वरुणः शशाङ्कः प्रजापतिस्त्वं प्रपितामहश्च ।
नमो नमस्तेऽस्तु सहस्रकृत्वः पुनश्च भूयोऽपि नमो नमस्ते ॥३९॥
नमः पुरस्तादथ पृष्ठतस्ते नमोऽस्तु ते सर्वत एव सर्व ।
अनन्तवीर्यामितविक्रमस्त्वं सर्वं समाप्नोषि ततोऽसि सर्वः ॥४०॥

---

[1] The real divine creation is eternal; it is the Infinite manifested sempiternally in finite things, the Spirit who conceals and reveals himself for ever in his innumerable infinity of souls and in the wonder of their actions and in the beauty of their forms. But what he is beyond all these is That, the Supreme, who holds all things mutable in the single eternity of a Time to which all is ever present.

[2] He is the Knower who develops in man the knowledge of himself and world and God; he is the one Object of all knowing who reveals himself to man's heart and mind and soul, so that every new opening form of our knowledge is a partial unfolding of him up to the highest by which he is intimately, profoundly and integrally seen and discovered.

[3] By him in his own existence the world is extended, by his omnipotent power, by his miraculous self-conception and energy and Ananda of never-ending creation.

39-40. Thou art Yama and Vayu and Agni and Soma and Varuna and Prajapati, father of creatures, and the great-grandsire. Salutation to Thee a thousand times over and again and yet again salutation, in front and behind and from every side, for Thou art each[1] and all that is. Infinite in might and immeasurable in strength of action Thou pervadest all and art everyone.

सखेति मत्वा प्रसभं यदुक्तं हे कृष्ण हे यादव हे सखेति ।
अजानता महिमानं तवेदं मया प्रमादात्प्रणयेन वापि ॥४१॥
यच्चावहासार्थमसत्कृतोऽसि विहारशय्यासनभोजनेषु ।
एकोऽथवाऽप्यच्युत तत्समक्षं तत्क्षामये त्वामहमप्रमेयम् ॥४२॥

41-42. For whatsoever I have spoken to Thee in rash vehemence, thinking of Thee only as my human friend and companion, 'O Krishna, O Yadava, O Comrade,' not knowing this Thy greatness,[2] in negligent error or in love, and for whatsoever disrespect was shown by me to Thee in

---

[1] He is all the many gods from the least to the greatest, he is the father of creatures and all are his children and his people. On this truth there is a constant insistence. Again it is repeated that he is the All, he is each and every one, *sarvaḥ*. He is the infinite Universal and he is each individual and everything that is, the one Force and Being in everyone of us, the infinite Energy that throws itself out in these multitudes, the immeasurable Will and mighty Power of motion and action that forms out of itself all the courses of Time and all the happenings of the Spirit in Nature. And from that insistence the thought naturally turns to the presence of this one great Godhead in man.

[2] This supreme universal Being has lived here before him with the human face, in the mortal body, the divine man, the embodied Godhead, the Avatar, and till now he has not known him. He has seen the humanity only and has treated the Divine as a mere human creature. He has not pierced through the earthly mask to the Godhead of which the humanity was a vessel and a symbol, and he prays now for that Godhead's forgiveness of his unseeing carelessness and his negligent ignorance. Now only he sees this tremendous, infinite, immeasurable Reality of all these apparent things, this boundless universal Form which so exceeds every individual form and yet of whom each individual thing is a house for his dwelling.

jest, at play, on the couch and the seat and in the banquet, alone or in Thy presence, O faultless One, I pray forgiveness from Thee, the immeasurable.

पितासि लोकस्य चराचरस्य त्वमस्य पूज्यश्च गुरुर्गरीयान् ।
न त्वत्समोऽस्त्यभ्यधिकः कुतोऽन्यो लोकत्रयेऽप्यप्रतिमप्रभाव ॥४३॥

43. Thou art the father of all this world of the moving and unmoving; Thou art one to be worshipped and the most solemn object of veneration. None is equal to Thee, how then another greater in all the three worlds, O incomparable in might?

तस्मात्प्रणम्य प्रणिधाय कायं प्रसादये त्वामहमीशमीड्यम् ।
पितेव पुत्रस्य सखेव सख्युः प्रियः प्रियायार्हसि देव सोढुम् ॥४४॥

44. Therefore I bow down before Thee and prostrate my body and I demand grace of Thee the adorable Lord. As a father[1] to his son, as a friend to his friend and comrade, as one dear with him he loves, so shouldst Thou, O Godhead, bear with me.

अदृष्टपूर्वं हृषितोऽस्मि दृष्ट्वा भयेन च प्रव्यथितं मनो मे ।
तदेव मे दर्शय देव रूपं प्रसीद देवेश जगन्निवास ॥४५॥

---

[1] What was figured in the human manifestation and the human relation is also a reality. The transcendence and cosmic aspect have to be seen, for without that seeing the limitations of humanity cannot be exceeded. But the infinite presence in its unmitigated splendour would be too overwhelming for the separate littleness of the limited, individual and natural man. A link is needed by which he can see this universal Godhead in his own individual and natural being, close to him, not only omnipotently there to govern all he is by universal and immeasurable Power, but humanly figured to support and raise him to unity by an intimate individual relation. The Divine inhabits the human soul and body; he draws around him and wears like a robe the human mind and figure. He assumes the human relations which the soul affects in the mortal body and they find in God their own fullest sense and greatest realisation. This is the Vaishnava bhakti of which the seed is here in the Gita's words, but which received afterwards a more deep, ecstatic and significant extension.

45. I have seen what never was seen before and I rejoice, but my mind is troubled with fear. O Godhead, show me that other[1] form of Thine; turn Thy heart to grace, O Thou Lord of the gods, O Thou abode of this universe.

किरीटिनं गदिनं चक्रहस्तमिच्छामि त्वां द्रष्टुमहं तथैव ॥
तेनैव रूपेण चतुर्भुजेन सहस्रबाहो भव विश्वमूर्ते ॥४६॥

46. I would see Thee even as before crowned and with Thy mace and discus. Assume Thy four-armed shape, O thousand-armed, O Form universal.

श्रीभगवान् उवाच —
मया प्रसन्नेन तवार्जुनेदं रूपं परं दर्शितमात्मयोगात् ।
तेजोमयं विश्वमनन्तमाद्यं यन्मे त्वदन्येन न दृष्टपूर्वम् ॥४७॥

47. The Blessed Lord said: This that thou now seest by my favour, O Arjuna, is my supreme shape, my form of luminous energy, the universal, the infinite, the original which none but thou amongst men has yet seen. I have shown it by my self-Yoga.[2]

---

[1] The form of the transcendent and universal Being is to the strength of the liberated spirit a thing mighty, encouraging and fortifying, a source of power, an equalising, sublimating, all-justifying vision; but to the normal man it is overwhelming, appalling, incommunicable. But there is too the gracious mediating form of divine Narayana, the God who is so close to man and in man, the Charioteer of the battle and the journey, with his four arms of helpful power, a humanised symbol of Godhead, not this million-armed universality. It is this mediating aspect which man must have for his support constantly before him. For it is this figure of Narayana which symbolises the truth that reassures. It makes close, visible, living, seizable the vast spiritual joy in which for the inner spirit and life of man the universal workings behind all their stupendous circling, retrogression, progression sovereignly culminate, their marvellous and auspicious upshot.

[2] For it is an image of my very Self and Spirit, it is the very Supreme self-figured in cosmic existence and the soul in perfect Yoga with Me sees it without any trembling of the nervous parts or any bewilderment and

न वेदयज्ञाध्ययनैर्न दानैर्न च क्रियाभिर्न तपोभिरुग्रैः ।
एवंरूपः शक्य अहं नृलोके द्रष्टुं त्वदन्येन कुरुप्रवीर ॥४८॥

48. Neither by the study of Vedas and sacrifices, nor by gifts or ceremonial rites or severe austerities, this form of mine can be seen by any other than thyself, O foremost of Kurus.

मा ते व्यथा मा च विमूढभावो दृष्ट्वा रूपं घोरमीदृङ्ममेदम् ।
व्यपेतभीः प्रीतमनाः पुनस्त्वं तदेव मे रूपमिदं प्रपश्य ॥४९॥

49. Thou shouldst envisage this tremendous vision without pain, without confusion of mind, without any sinking of the members. Cast away fear and let thy heart rejoice, behold again this other[1] form of mine.

सञ्जय उवाच —
इत्यर्जुनं वासुदेवस्तथोक्त्वा स्वकं रूपं दर्शयामास भूयः ।
आश्वासयामास च भीतमेनं भूत्वा पुनः सौम्यवपुर्महात्मा ॥५०॥

50. Sanjaya said: Vasudeva, having thus spoken to Arjuna, again manifested his normal (Narayana) image; the Mahatman again assuming the desired form of grace and love and sweetness consoled the terrified one.

अर्जुन उवाच —
दृष्ट्वेदं मानुषं रूपं तव सौम्यं जनार्दन ।
इदानीमस्मि संवृत्तः सचेताः प्रकृतिं गतः ॥५१॥

51. Arjuna said: Beholding again Thy gentle human

---

confusion of the mind, because he descries not only what is terrible and overwhelming in its appearance, but also its high and reassuring significance.

[1] But since the lower nature in thee is not yet prepared to look upon it with that high strength and tranquillity, I will reassume again for thee my Narayana figure in which the human mind sees isolated and toned to its humanity the calm, helpfulness and delight of a friendly Godhead.

form, O Janardana, my heart is filled with delight and I am restored to my own nature.

श्रीभगवान् उवाच —
सुदुर्दर्शमिदं रूपं दृष्टवानसि यन्मम ।
देवा अप्यस्य रूपस्य नित्यं दर्शनकाङ्क्षिणः ॥५२॥
नाहं वेदैर्न तपसा न दानेन न चेज्यया ।
शक्य एवंविधो द्रष्टुं दृष्टवानसि मां यथा ॥५३॥
भक्त्या त्वनन्यया शक्य अहमेवंविधोऽर्जुन ।
ज्ञातुं द्रष्टुं च तत्त्वेन प्रवेष्टुं च परन्तप ॥५४॥

52-54. The Blessed Lord said: The greater Form that thou hast seen is only for the rare highest souls. The gods themselves ever desire to look upon it. Nor can I be seen[1] as thou hast seen Me by Veda or austerities or gifts or sacrifice, it can be seen, known, entered into only by that bhakti which regards, adores and loves Me alone in all things.

मत्कर्मकृन्मत्परमो मद्भक्तः सङ्गवर्जितः ।
निर्वैरः सर्वभूतेषु यः स मामेति पाण्डव ॥५५॥

55. Be a doer of my works, accept Me as the supreme being and object, become my bhakta, be free from attach-

---

[1] Man can know by other means this or that exclusive aspect of the one existence, its individual, cosmic or world-excluding figures, but not this greatest reconciling Oneness of all the aspects of the Divinity in which at one and the same time and in one and the same vision all is manifested, all is exceeded and all is consummated. This vision can be reached only by the absolute adoration, the love, the intimate unity that crowns at their summit the fullness of works and knowledge. There is a supreme consciousness through which it is possible to enter into the glory of the Transcendent and contain in him the immutable Self and all mutable Becoming, – it is possible to be one with all, yet above all, to exceed world and yet embrace the whole nature at once of the cosmic and the supracosmic Godhead. This is difficult indeed for limited man imprisoned in his mind and body; but the Godhead shows the way in the next sloka.

ment and without enmity to all existences; for such a man comes to Me, O Pandava.[1]

इति श्रीमद्भगवद्गीतासूपनिषत्सु ब्रह्मविद्यायां योगशास्त्रे श्रीकृष्णार्जुनसंवादे
विश्वरूपदर्शनयोगो नामैकादशोऽध्यायः ।

---

[1] In other words, superiority to the lower nature, unity with all creatures, oneness with the cosmic Godhead and the Transcendence, oneness of will with the Divine in works, absolute love for the One and for God in all, – this is the way to that absolute spiritual self-exceeding and that unimaginable transformation.

Twelfth Chapter

THE WAY AND THE BHAKTA

अर्जुन उवाच —
एवं सततयुक्ता ये भक्तास्त्वां पर्युपासते ।
ये चाप्यक्षरमव्यक्तं तेषां के योगवित्तमाः ॥१॥

1. Arjuna said: Those devotees who thus by a constant union seek after Thee, and those who seek after the unmanifest Immutable, which of these have the greater[1] knowledge of Yoga?
[To this question Krishna replies with an emphatic decisiveness.]

---

[1] The question raised here by Arjuna points to the difference between the current Vedantic view of liberation and the view propounded in the Gita. The orthodox Yoga of knowledge aims at a fathomless immergence in the one infinite existence, *sāyujya*; it looks upon that alone as the entire liberation. The Yoga of adoration envisages an eternal habitation or nearness as the greater release, *sālokya, sāmīpya*. The Yoga of works leads to oneness in power of being and nature, *sādṛśya*; but the Gita envelops them all in its catholic integrality and fuses them all into one greatest and richest divine freedom and perfection.

Arjuna has been enjoined first to sink his separate personality in the calm impersonality of the one eternal and immutable Self, a teaching which agreed well with his previous notions and offered no difficulties. But now he is confronted with the vision of this greatest transcendent, this widest universal Godhead and commanded to seek oneness with him by knowledge and works and adoration. He is asked to unite himself in all his being, *satata-yukta*, with the Godhead (referred to by the word, *tvam*) manifest in the universe, seated as the Lord of works in the world and in our hearts by his mighty world-Yoga. But what then of this Immutable who never manifests (*akṣaramavyaktam*), never puts on any form, stands back and apart from all action, enters into no relation with the universe or with anything in it, is eternally silent and one and impersonal and immobile? This eternal Self is the greater Principle according to all current notions and the Godhead in the manifestation is an inferior figure: the unmanifest and not the manifest is the eternal Spirit. How then does the union which admits the manifestation, admits the lesser thing, come yet to be the greater Yoga-knowledge?

श्रीभगवान् उवाच —
मय्यावेश्य मनो ये मां नित्ययुक्ता उपासते ।
श्रद्धया परयोपेतास्ते मे युक्ततमा मताः ॥२॥

2. The Blessed Lord said: Those who found their mind in Me and by constant union, possessed of a supreme faith,[1] seek after Me, I hold to be the most perfectly in union of Yoga.

ये त्वक्षरमनिर्देश्यमव्यक्तं पर्युपासते ।
सर्वत्रगमचिन्त्यं च कूटस्थमचलं ध्रुवम् ॥३॥
संनियम्येन्द्रियग्रामं सर्वत्र समबुद्धयः ।
ते प्राप्नुवन्ति मामेव सर्वभूतहिते रताः ॥४॥

3-4. But those who seek after the indefinable unmanifest Immutable omnipresent, unthinkable, self-poised, immobile, constant, they also[2] by restraining all their senses, by the equality of their understanding and by their seeing of one self in all things and by their tranquil benignancy of silent will for the good of all existences, arrive to Me.

[1] The supreme faith is that which sees God in all and to its eye the manifestation and the non-manifestation are one Godhead. The perfect union is that which meets the Divine at every moment, in every action and with all the integrality of the nature.
  The Godhead with whom the soul of man has to enter into this closest oneness, is indeed in his supreme status a transcendent Unthinkable, too great for any manifestation, Parabrahman; but he is at the same time the living supreme Soul of all things. He is the supreme Lord, the Master of works and universal nature. He at once exceeds and inhabits as its self the soul and mind and body of the creature. He is Purushottama, Parameshwara and Paramatman and in all these equal aspects the same single and eternal Godhead. It is an awakening to this integral reconciling knowledge that is the wide gate to the utter release of the soul and an unimaginable perfection of the nature.
[2] For they are not mistaken in their aim, but they follow a more difficult and a less complete and perfect path. The Immutable offers no hold to the mind; it can only be gained by a motionless spiritual impersonality and silence and those who follow after it alone have to restrain altogether and even draw in completely the action of the mind and senses.

क्लेशोऽधिकतरस्तेषामव्यक्तासक्तचेतसाम् ।
अव्यक्ता हि गतिर्दुःखं देहवद्भिरवाप्यते ॥५॥

5. The difficulty[1] of those who devote themselves to the search of the unmanifest Brahman is greater; it is a thing to which embodied souls can only arrive by a constant mortification, a suffering of all the repressed members, a stern difficulty and anguish of the nature.

ये तु सर्वाणि कर्माणि मयि सन्न्यस्य मत्पराः ।
अनन्येनैव योगेन मां ध्यायन्त उपासते ॥६॥
तेषामहं समुद्धर्ता मृत्युसंसारसागरात् ।
भवामि नचिरात्पार्थ मय्यावेशितचेतसाम् ॥७॥

6-7. But those who giving up all their actions to Me,[2] and wholly devoted to Me, worship meditating on Me with an unswerving Yoga, those who fix on Me all their consciousness, O Partha, speedily I deliver them out of the sea of death-bound existence.

[1] And it must not be thought that because it is more arduous, therefore it is a higher and more effective process. The easier way of the Gita leads more rapidly, naturally and normally to the same absolute liberation. The Yogin of exclusive knowledge imposes on himself a painful struggle with the manifold demands of his nature; he denies them even their highest satisfaction and cuts away from him even the upward impulses of his spirit whenever they imply relations or fall short of a negating absolute. The living way of the Gita on the contrary finds out the most intense upward trend of all our being and by turning it Godwards uses knowledge, will, feeling and the instinct for perfection as so many puissant wings of a mounting liberation.
[2] The indefinable Oneness accepts all that climb to it, but offers no help of relation and gives no foothold to the climber. All has to be done by a severe austerity and a stern and lonely individual effort. How different is it for those who seek after the Purushottama in the way of the Gita! When they meditate on him with a Yoga which sees none else, because it sees all to be Vasudeva, he meets them at every point, in every moment, at all times, with innumerable forms and faces, holds up the lamp of knowledge within and floods with its divine and happy lustre the whole of existence. The other method of a difficult relationless stillness

मय्येव मन आधत्स्व मयि बुद्धिं निवेशय ।
निवसिष्यसि मय्येव अत ऊर्ध्वं न संशय: ॥८॥

8. On Me repose all thy mind and lodge all thy understanding in Me; doubt not that thou shalt dwell in Me above this mortal existence.

अथ चित्तं समाधातुं न शक्नोषि मयि स्थिरम् ।
अभ्यासयोगेन ततो मामिच्छाप्तुं धनञ्जय ॥९॥

9. And if thou art not[1] able to keep the consciousness fixed steadily in Me, then by the Yoga of practice seek after Me, O Dhananjaya.

अभ्यासेऽप्यसमर्थोऽसि मत्कर्मपरमो भव ।
मदर्थमपि कर्माणि कुर्वन् सिद्धिमवाप्स्यसि ॥१०॥

10. If thou art unable even to seek by practice, then be it

---

tries to get away from all action even though that is impossible to embodied creatures. Here the actions are all given up to the supreme Master of action and he as the supreme Will meets the will of sacrifice, takes from it its burden and assumes himself the charge of the works of the divine Nature in us. And when too in the high passion of love the devotee of the Lover and Friend of man and of all creatures casts upon him all his heart of consciousness and yearning of delight, then swiftly the Supreme comes to him as the saviour and exalts him by a happy embrace of his mind and heart and body out of the waves of the sea of death in this mortal nature into the secure bosom of the Eternal.

This then is the swiftest, largest and greatest way.

[1] No doubt, on this way too there are difficulties; for there is the lower nature with its fierce or dull downward gravitation which resists and battles against the motion of ascent and clogs the wings of the exaltation and the upward rapture. There are nights of long exile from the Light, there are hours or moments of revolt, doubt or failure. But still by the practice of union and by constant repetition of the experience, the divine consciousness grows upon the being and takes permanent possession of the nature.

thy supreme aim to do My work;[1] doing all actions for My sake, thou shalt attain perfection.

अथैतदप्यशक्तोऽसि कर्तुं मद्योगमाश्रित: ।
सर्वकर्मफलत्यागं तत: कुरु यतात्मवान् ॥११॥

11. But if even this constant remembering of Me and lifting up of your works to Me is felt beyond[2] your power, then renounce all fruit of action with the self controlled.

श्रेयो हि ज्ञानमभ्यासाज्ज्ञानाद् ध्यानं विशिष्यते ।
ध्यानात्कर्मफलत्यागस्त्यागाच्छान्तिरनन्तरम् ॥१२॥

12. Better indeed is knowledge than practice;[3] than knowledge, meditation is better; than meditation, renunciation of the fruit of action; on renunciation follows peace.

---

[1] Is this also found too difficult because of the power and persistence of the outward-going movement of the mind? Then the way is simple, to do all actions for the sake of the Lord of the action, so that every outward-going movement of the mind shall be associated with the inner spiritual truth of the being and called back even in the very movement to the eternal reality and connected with its source. Then the presence of the Purushottama will grow upon the natural man, till he is filled with it and becomes a Godhead and a spirit.

[2] The limited mind in its forgetfulness turns to the act and its outward object and will not remember to look within and lay our every movement on the divine altar of the Spirit. Then the way is to control the lower self in the act and do works without desire of the fruit. All fruit has to be renounced, to be given up to the Power that directs the work, and yet the work has to be done that is imposed by It on the nature. For by this means the obstacle steadily diminishes and easily disappears, the mind is left free to remember the Lord and to fix itself in the liberty of the divine consciousness. And here the Gita gives an ascending scale of potencies and assigns the palm of excellence to this Yoga of desireless action.

[3] *Abhyāsa*, practice of a method, repetition of an effort and experience is a great and powerful thing; but better than this is knowledge, the successful and luminous turning of the thought to the Truth behind things. This thought knowledge too is excelled by a silent complete concentration on the Truth so that the consciousness shall eventually live in it and be

अद्वेष्टा सर्वभूतानां मैत्रः करुण एव च।
निर्ममो निरहङ्कारः समदुःखसुखः क्षमी ॥१३॥
सन्तुष्टः सततं योगी यतात्मा दृढनिश्चयः।
मय्यर्पितमनोबुद्धिर्यो मद्भक्तः स मे प्रियः ॥१४॥

13-14. He who has no egoism, no I-ness and my-ness, who has friendship and pity for all beings and hate for no living thing, who has a tranquil equality to pleasure and pain, and is patient and forgiving, he who has a desireless content, the steadfast control of self and the firm unshakable will and resolution of the Yogin and a love and devotion which gives up the whole mind and reason to Me, he is dear to Me.

यस्मान्नोद्विजते लोको लोकान्नोद्विजते च यः।
हर्षामर्षभयोद्वेगैर्मुक्तो यः स च मे प्रियः ॥१५॥

15. He by whom the world is not afflicted or troubled, who also is not afflicted or troubled by the world, who is freed from the troubled agitated lower nature and from its waves of joy and fear and anxiety and resentment, he is dear to Me.

अनपेक्षः शुचिर्दक्ष उदासीनो गतव्यथः।
सर्वारम्भपरित्यागी यो मद्भक्तः स मे प्रियः ॥१६॥

16. He who desires nothing, is pure, skilful in all actions,

---

always one with it. But more powerful still is the giving up of the fruit of one's works, because that immediately destroys all causes of disturbance and brings and preserves automatically an inner calm and peace, and calm and peace are the foundation on which all else becomes perfect and secure in possession by the tranquil spirit.

What then will be the divine nature, what will be the greater state of consciousness and being of the bhakta who has followed this way and turned to the adoration of the Eternal? The Gita in a number of verses rings the changes on its first insistent demand, on equality, on desirelessness, on freedom of spirit. Several formulas of this fundamental equal consciousness are given here.

indifferent to whatever comes, not pained or afflicted by any result or happening, who has given up all initiative[1] of action, he, My devotee, is dear to Me.

यो न हृष्यति न द्वेष्टि न शोचति न काङ्क्षति ।
शुभाशुभपरित्यागी भक्तिमान् यः स मे प्रियः ॥१७॥

17. He who neither desires the pleasant and rejoices at its touch nor abhors the unpleasant and sorrows at its touch, who has abolished the distinction between fortunate and unfortunate happenings (because his devotion receives all things equally as good from the hands of his eternal Lover and Master), he is dear to Me.

समः शत्रौ च मित्रे च तथा मानापमानयोः ।
शीतोष्णसुखदुःखेषु समः सङ्गविवर्जितः ॥१८॥
तुल्यनिन्दास्तुतिर्मौनी सन्तुष्टो येन केनचित् ।
अनिकेतः स्थिरमतिर्भक्तिमान्मे प्रियो नरः ॥१९॥

18-19. Equal[2] to friend and enemy, equal to honour and insult, pleasure and pain, praise and blame, grief and

---

[1] He has flung away from him all egoistic, personal and mental initiative whether of the inner or the outer act, one who lets the divine will and divine knowledge flow through him undeflected by his own resolves, preferences and desires, and yet for that very reason is swift and skilful in all action of his nature, because this flawless unity with the supreme will, this pure instrumentation is the condition of the greatest skill in works.

[2] Equality, desirelessness and freedom from the lower egoistic nature and its claims are always the one perfect foundation demanded by the Gita for the great liberation. There is to the end an emphatic repetition of its first fundamental teaching and original desideratum, the calm soul of knowledge that sees the one self in all things, the tranquil ego-less equality that results from this knowledge, the desireless action offered in that equality to the Master of works, the surrender of the whole mental nature of man into the hands of the mightier indwelling spirit. And the crown of this equality is love founded on knowledge, fulfilled in instrumental action, extended to all things and beings, a vast absorbing and all-containing love for the divine Self who is Creator and Master of the universe, *suhṛdaṁ sarva-bhūtānāṁ sarva-loka-maheśvaram.*

happiness, heat and cold (to all that troubles with opposite affections the normal nature), silent, content and well-satisfied with anything and everything, not attached to person or thing, place or home, firm in mind (because it is constantly seated in the highest self and fixed for ever on the one divine object of his love and adoration), that man is dear to Me.

ये तु धर्म्यामृतमिदं यथोक्तं पर्युपासते ।
श्रद्दधाना मत्परमा भक्तास्तेऽतीव मे प्रियाः ॥२०॥

20. But exceedingly dear to Me are those devotees who make Me (the Purushottama) their one supreme aim and follow out with a perfect faith and exactitude the immortalising Dharma[1] described in this teaching.

इति श्रीमद्भगवद्गीतासूपनिषत्सु ब्रह्मविद्यायां योगशास्त्रे श्रीकृष्णार्जुनसंवादे
भक्तियोगो नाम द्वादशोऽध्यायः ।

[1] Dharma in the language of the Gita means the innate law of the being and its works and an action proceeding from and determined by the inner nature, *svabhāvaniyataṁ karma*. In the lower ignorant consciousness of mind, life and body there are many dharmas, many rules, many standards and laws, because there are many varying determinations and types of the mental, vital and physical nature. The immortal Dharma is one; it is that of the highest spiritual divine consciousness and its powers, *parā prakṛtiḥ*. It is beyond the three gunas, and to reach it all these lower dharmas have to be abandoned, *sarva-dharmān parityajya*. Alone in their place the one liberating unifying consciousness and power of the Eternal has to become the infinite source of our action, its mould, determinant and exemplar. To rise out of our lower personal egoism, to enter into the impersonal and equal calm of the immutable eternal all-pervading Akshara Purusha, to aspire from that calm by a perfect self-surrender of all one's nature and existence to that which is other and higher than the Akshara, is the first necessity of this Yoga. In the strength of that aspiration one can rise to the immortal Dharma. There, made one in being, consciousness and divine bliss with the greatest *uttama puruṣa*, made one with this supreme dynamic nature-force, *svāprakṛtiḥ*, the liberated spirit can know infinitely, love illimitably, act unfalteringly in the authentic power of a highest immortality and a perfect freedom. The rest of the Gita is written to throw a fuller light on this immortal Dharma.

Thirteenth Chapter

THE FIELD AND ITS KNOWER

अर्जुन उवाच —
प्रकृतिं पुरुषं चैव क्षेत्रं क्षेत्रज्ञमेव च ।
एतद्वेदितुमिच्छामि ज्ञानं ज्ञेयं च केशव ॥१॥

1. Arjuna[1] said: Prakriti and Purusha, the Field and the Knower of the Field, Knowledge and the object of Knowledge, these I fain would learn, O Keshava.

श्रीभगवान् उवाच —
इदं शरीरं कौन्तेय क्षेत्रमित्यभिधीयते ।
एतद्यो वेत्ति तं प्राहुः क्षेत्रज्ञ इति तद्विदः ॥२॥

2. The Blessed Lord said: This body,[2] O son of Kunti, is called the Field; that which takes cognizance of the Field is called the Knower of the Field by the sages.

क्षेत्रज्ञं चापि मां विद्धि सर्वक्षेत्रेषु भारत ।
क्षेत्रक्षेत्रज्ञयोर्ज्ञानं यत्तज्ज्ञानं मतं मम ॥३॥

[1] Arjuna has been asked to do divine work as the instrument of the divine Will in the cosmos. As a pragmatic and practical man he asks to learn the actual difference between Purusha and Prakriti, the Field of being and the Knower of the Field, so important for the practice of desireless action under the drive of the divine Will. How does this way practically affect the great object of spiritual life, the rising from the lower into the higher nature, from mortal into immortal being?

The Gita in its last six chapters, in order to found on a clear and complete knowledge the way of the soul's rising out of the lower into the divine nature, restates in another form the enlightenment the Teacher has already imparted to Arjuna. Essentially it is the same knowledge, but details and relations are now made prominent and assigned their entire significance, thoughts and truths brought out in their full value that were alluded to only in passing or generally stated in the light of another purpose.

[2] It is evident from the definitions that succeed that it is not the physical body alone which is the Field (kṣetra), but all too that the body supports, the working of nature, the mentality, the natural action of the

3. Understand Me as the Knower of the Field in all[1] Fields, O Bharata; it is the knowledge at once of the Field and its Knower which is the real illumination and only wisdom.

तत् क्षेत्रं यच्च यादृक्च यद्विकारि यतश्च यत् ।
स च यो यत्प्रभावश्च तत्समासेन मे शृणु ॥४॥

4. What[2] that Field is and what are its character, nature, source, deformations, and what He is and what His powers, hear that now briefly from Me.

ऋषिभिर्बहुधा गीतं छन्दोभिर्विविधैः पृथक् ।
ब्रह्मसूत्रपदैश्चैव हेतुमद्भिर्विनिश्चितैः ॥५॥

5. It has been sung by the Rishis[3] in manifold ways in various inspired verses; and also by the Brahma Sutras which give us the rational and philosophic analysis.

---

objectivity and subjectivity of our being.* This wider body too is only the individual field; there is a larger, a universal, a world-body, a world-field of the same Knower. For in each embodied creature there is this one Knower.

(* The Upanishad speaks of a fivefold body or sheath of Nature, a physical, vital, mental, ideal and divine body; this may be regarded as the totality of the Field, *kṣetra*.)

[1] The world exists to us as it is seen in our single mind; even this seemingly small embodied consciousness can so enlarge itself that it contains in itself the whole universe, *ātmani viśvadarśanam*. But, physically, it is a microcosm in a macrocosm, and the macrocosm too, the large world too, is a body and field inhabited by the spiritual knower.

[2] From the description which follows it becomes evident that it is the whole working of the lower Prakriti that is meant by the *kṣetra*. That totality is the field of action of the embodied spirit here within us, the field of which it takes cognizance.

[3] For a varied and detailed knowledge of all this world of Nature in its essential action as seen from the spiritual point of view we are referred to the Veda and Upanishads and to the Brahma Sutras. The Gita contents itself with a brief practical statement of the lower nature of our being in the terms of the Sankhya thinkers.

THIRTEENTH CHAPTER

महाभूतान्यहङ्कारो बुद्धिरव्यक्तमेव च ।
इन्द्रियाणि दशैकं च पञ्च चेन्द्रियगोचराः ॥६॥

6. The indiscriminate unmanifest Energy; the five elemental states of matter; the ten senses and the one (mind), intelligence and ego; the five objects of the senses. (This is the constitution of the Kshetra.)

इच्छा द्वेषः सुखं दुःखं संघातश्चेतना धृतिः ।
एतत् क्षेत्रं समासेन सविकारमुदाहृतम् ॥७॥

7. Liking and disliking, pleasure[1] and pain (these are the principal deformations of the Kshetra); consciousness,[2] collocation, persistence; these,[3] briefly described, constitute the Field and its deformations.

अमानित्वमदम्भित्वमहिंसा क्षान्तिरार्जवम् ।
आचार्योपासनं शौचं स्थैर्यमात्मविनिग्रहः ॥८॥

---

[1] From the Vedantic point of view we may say that pleasure and pain are the vital or sensational deformations given by the lower energy to the spontaneous Ananda or delight of the spirit when brought into contact with her workings. These dualities are the positive and negative terms in which the ego soul of the lower nature enjoys the universe.

[2] There is a general consciousness that first informs and then illumines the Energy in its works; there is a faculty of that consciousness by which the Energy holds together the relations of objects; there is too a continuity, a persistence of the subjective and objective relations of our consciousness with its objects. These are the necessary powers of the field; all these are common and universal powers at once of the mental, vital and physical Nature.

[3] All these things taken together constitute the fundamental character of our first transactions with the world of Nature, but it is evidently not the whole description of our being; it is our actuality but not the limit of our possibilities. There is something beyond to be known, *jñeyam*, and it is when the knower of the field turns from the field itself to learn of himself within it and of all that is behind its appearances that real knowledge begins, *jñānam*, – the true knowledge of the field no less than of the knower. For both soul and nature are the Brahman, but the true truth of the world of Nature can only be discovered by the liberated sage

8. A total absence of wordly pride and arrogance, harmlessness, a candid soul, a tolerant, long-suffering and benignant heart, purity of mind and body, tranquil firmness and steadfastness, self-control and a masterful government of the lower nature and the heart's worship given to the Teacher.[1]

इन्द्रियार्थेषु वैराग्यमनहङ्कार एव च ।
जन्ममृत्युजराव्याधिदुःखदोषानुदर्शनम् ॥९॥
असक्तिरनभिष्वङ्गः पुत्रदारगृहादिषु ।
नित्यं च समचित्तत्वमिष्टानिष्टोपपत्तिषु ॥१०॥

9-10. A firm removal of the natural being's attraction to the objects of the senses, a radical freedom from egoism, absence of clinging to the attachment and absorption of family and home, a keen perception of the defective nature of the ordinary life of physical man with its aimless and painful subjection to birth and death and disease and age, a constant equalness to all pleasant or unpleasant happenings.[2]

मयि चानन्ययोगेन भक्तिरव्यभिचारिणी ।
विविक्तदेशसेवित्वमरतिर्जनसंसदि ॥११॥
अध्यात्मज्ञाननित्यत्वं तत्त्वज्ञानार्थदर्शनम् ।
एतज्ज्ञानमिति प्रोक्तमज्ञानं यदतोऽन्यथा ॥१२॥

---

who possesses also the truth of the Spirit. One Brahman, one reality in Self and Nature is the object of all knowledge.

The Gita then tells us what is the spiritual knowledge or rather it tells us what are the conditions of knowledge, the marks, the signs of the man whose soul is turned towards the inner wisdom. First, there comes a certain moral condition, a sattwic government of the natural being.

[1] Whether to the divine Teacher within or to the human Master in whom the divine Wisdom is embodied, − for that is the sense of the reverence given to the Guru.

Then there is a nobler and freer attitude of perfect detachment and equality.

[2] For the soul is seated within and impervious to the shocks of external events.

Finally, there is a strong turn within towards the things that really matter.

11-12. A meditative mind turned towards solitude and away from the vain noise of crowds and the assemblies of men, a philosophic perception of the true sense and large principles of existence, a tranquil continuity of inner spiritual knowledge and light, the Yoga of an unswerving devotion, love of God, the heart's deep and constant adoration of the universal and eternal Presence; that is declared to be the knowledge; all against it is ignorance.

ज्ञेयं यत्तत्प्रवक्ष्यामि यज्ज्ञात्वाऽमृतमश्नुते ।
अनादिमत्परं ब्रह्म न सत्तन्नासदुच्यते ॥१३॥

13. I will declare the one object to which the mind of spiritual knowledge must be turned, by fixity in which the soul clouded here recovers and enjoys its nature and original consciousness of immortality,[1] – the eternal supreme Brahman[2] called neither Sat (existence) nor Asat (non-existence).

---

[1] The soul, when it allows itself to be tyrannised over by the appearances of Nature, misses itself and goes whirling about in the cycle of the births and deaths of its bodies. There, passionately following without end the mutations of personality and its interests, it cannot draw back to the possession of its impersonal and unborn self-existence. To be able to do that is to find oneself and get back to one's true being, that which assumes these births but does not perish with the perishing of its forms. To enjoy the eternity to which birth and life are only outward circumstances, is the soul's true immortality and transcendence.

[2] That Eternal or that Eternity is the Brahman. Brahman is That which is transcendent and That which is universal: it is the free spirit who supports in front the play of soul with nature and assures behind their imperishable oneness; it is at once the mutable and the immutable, the All that is the One. In his highest supracosmic status Brahman is a transcendent Eternity without origin or change far above the phenomenal oppositions of existence and non-existence, persistence and transience between which the outward world moves. But once seen in the substance and light of this eternity, the world also becomes other than it seems to the mind and senses; for then we see the universe no longer as a whirl of mind and life and matter or a mass of the determinations of energy and substance, but as no other than this eternal Brahman.

सर्वतः पाणिपादं तत्सर्वतोऽक्षिशिरोमुखम् ।
सर्वतः श्रुतिमल्लोके सर्वमावृत्य तिष्ठति ॥१४॥

14. His hands and feet are on every side of us, his heads and eyes and faces are those innumerable visages which we see wherever we turn, his ear is everywhere, he immeasurably fills and surrounds all this world with himself, he is the universal Being in whose embrace we live.

सर्वेन्द्रियगुणाभासं सर्वेन्द्रियविवर्जितम् ।
असक्तं सर्वभृच्चैव निर्गुणं गुणभोक्तृ च ॥१५॥

15. All[1] the senses and their qualities reflect him but he is without any senses; he is unattached, yet all-supporting; he is enjoyer of the gunas, though not limited by them.

बहिरन्तश्च भूतानामचरं चरमेव च ।
सूक्ष्मत्वात्तदविज्ञेयं दूरस्थं चान्तिके च तत् ॥१६॥

16. That which is in us is he and all that we experience outside ourselves is he. The inward and the outward, the far and the near, the moving and the unmoving, all this he is at once. He is the subtlety of the subtle which is beyond our knowledge.

अविभक्तं च भूतेषु विभक्तमिव च स्थितम् ।
भूतभर्तृ च तज्ज्ञेयं ग्रसिष्णु प्रभविष्णु च ॥१७॥

17. He is indivisible and the One, but seems to divide himself in forms and creatures and appears as all the

---

[1] All relations of Soul and Nature are circumstances in the eternity of Brahman; sense and quality, their reflectors and constituents, are this supreme Soul's devices for the presentation of the workings that his own energy in things constantly liberates into movement. He is himself beyond the limitation of the senses, sees all things but not with the physical eye, hears all things but not with the physical ear, is aware of all things but not with the limiting mind – which represents but cannot truly know.

separate existences. All things are eternally born from him, upborne in his eternity, taken eternally back into his oneness.

ज्योतिषामपि तज्ज्योतिस्तमसः परमुच्यते ।
ज्ञानं ज्ञेयं ज्ञानगम्यं हृदि सर्वस्य विष्ठितम् ॥१८॥

18. He is the light of all lights and luminous beyond all the darkness of our ignorance. He is knowledge[1] and the object of knowledge. He is seated in the hearts[2] of all.

इति क्षेत्रं तथा ज्ञानं ज्ञेयं चोक्तं समासतः ।
मद्भक्त एतद्विज्ञाय मद्भावायोपपद्यते ॥१९॥

19. Thus the Field, Knowledge and the Object of Knowledge, have been briefly told. My devotee, thus knowing,[3] attains to My *bhāva* (the divine being and divine nature).

प्रकृतिं पुरुषं चैव विद्ध्यनादी उभावपि ।
विकारांश्च गुणांश्चैव विद्धि प्रकृतिसम्भवान् ॥२०॥

20. Know thou that Purusha (the Soul) and Prakriti

---

[1] The spiritual supramental knowledge that floods the illumined mind and transfigures it is this spirit manifesting himself in light to the force-obscured soul which he has put forth into the action of Nature.

[2] This eternal Light is in the heart of every being; it is he who is the secret knower of the field, *kṣetrajña*, and presides as the Lord in the heart of things over this province and over all these kingdoms of his manifested becoming and action.

[3] When man sees this eternal and universal Godhead within himself, when he becomes aware of the soul in all things and discovers the spirit in Nature, when he feels all the universe as a wave mounting in this Eternity and all that is as the one existence, he puts on the light of Godhead and stands free in the midst of the worlds of Nature. A divine knowledge and a perfect turning with adoration to this Divine is the secret of the great spiritual liberation. Freedom, love and spiritual knowledge raise us from mortal nature to immortal being.

(Nature) are both without origin and eternal[1]; but the modes of Nature and the lower forms she assumes to our conscious experience have an origin in Prakriti (in the transactions of these two entities).

कार्यकारणकर्तृत्वे हेतुः प्रकृतिरुच्यते ।
पुरुषः सुखदुःखानां भोक्तृत्वे हेतुरुच्यते ॥२१॥

21. The chain[2] of cause and effect and the state of being the doer are created by Prakriti; Purusha enjoys pleasure and pain.

पुरुषः प्रकृतिस्थो हि भुङ्क्ते प्रकृतिजान् गुणान् ।
कारणं गुणसङ्गोऽस्य सदसद्योनिजन्मसु ॥२२॥

22. Purusha involved[3] in Prakriti enjoys the qualities born of Prakriti; attachment to the qualities is the cause of his birth in good and evil wombs.

उपद्रष्टानुमन्ता च भर्ता भोक्ता महेश्वरः ।
परमात्मेति चाप्युक्तो देहेऽस्मिन् पुरुषः परः ॥२३॥

---

[1] The Soul and Nature are only two aspects of the eternal Brahman, an apparent duality which founds the operations of his universal existence. These operations, the modes of Nature and their derivative formations, constantly change and the Soul and Nature seem to change with them, but in themselves these two powers are eternal and always the same.

[2] Nature creates and acts, the Soul enjoys her creation and action; but in this inferior form of her action she turns this enjoyment into the obscure and petty figures of pain and pleasure.

[3] Forcibly the soul, the individual Purusha, is attracted by her qualitative workings and this attraction of her·qualities draws him constantly to births of all kinds in which he enjoys the variation and vicissitudes, the good and evil of birth in Nature.

But this is only the outward experience of the soul mutable in conception by identification with mutable Nature. Seated in this body is her and our Divinity, the supreme Self, Paramatman, the supreme Soul, Para Purusha.

23. Witness, source of the consent, upholder of the work of Nature, her enjoyer, almighty Lord and supreme Self is the Supreme Soul[1] seated in this body.

य एवं वेत्ति पुरुषं प्रकृतिं च गुणै: सह ।
सर्वथा वर्तमानोऽपि न स भूयोऽभिजायते ॥२४॥

24. He who thus knows Purusha and Prakriti with her qualities, howsoever he lives and acts, he shall not be born again.

ध्यानेनात्मनि पश्यन्ति केचिदात्मानमात्मना ।
अन्ये साङ्ख्येन योगेन कर्मयोगेन चापरे ॥२५॥

25. This knowledge comes by an inner meditation through which the eternal Self becomes apparent to us in our self-existence. Or it comes by the Yoga of the Sankhyas (the separation of the soul from nature). Or it comes by the Yoga of works.[2]

अन्ये त्वेवमजानन्त: श्रुत्वान्येभ्य उपासते ।
तेऽपि चातितरन्त्येव मृत्युं श्रुतिपरायणा: ॥२६॥

26. Others, who are ignorant of these paths of Yoga, may hear of the truth from others and mould the mind into the sense of that to which it listens with faith and concentration.

---

[1] That is the self-knowledge to which we have to accustom our mentality before we can truly know ourselves as an eternal portion of the Eternal. Once that is fixed, no matter how the soul in us may comport itself outwardly in its transactions with Nature, whatever it may seem to do or however it may seem to assume this or that figure of personality and active force and embodied ego, it is in itself free, no longer bound to birth because one through impersonality of self with the inner unborn spirit of existence. That impersonality is our union with the supreme egoless I of all that is in cosmos.

[2] In which the personal will is dissolved through the opening up of our mind and heart and all our active forces to the Lord who assumes to himself the whole of our works in nature.

But however arrived at, it carries us beyond death to immortality.

यावत्सञ्जायते किञ्चित्सत्त्वं स्थावरजङ्गमम् ।
क्षेत्रक्षेत्रज्ञसंयोगात्तद्विद्धि भरतर्षभ ॥२७॥

27. Whatever[1] being, moving or unmoving, is born, know thou, O best of the Bharatas, that it is from the union between the Field and the Knower of the Field.

समं सर्वेषु भूतेषु तिष्ठन्तं परमेश्वरम् ।
विनश्यत्स्वविनश्यन्तं यः पश्यति स पश्यति ॥२८॥

28. Seated equally in all beings, the supreme Lord, unperishing within the perishing – he who thus sees, he sees.[2]

समं पश्यन् हि सर्वत्र समवस्थितमीश्वरम् ।
न हिनस्त्यात्मनात्मानं ततो याति परां गतिम् ॥२९॥

29. Perceiving the equal Lord as the spiritual inhabitant in all forces, in all things and in all beings, he does not injure

---

[1] The whole of existence must be regarded as a field of the soul's construction and action in the midst of Nature. All life, all works are a transaction between the soul and Nature.

[2] Knowledge shows us high above the mutable transactions of the soul with the mortality of nature our highest Self as the supreme Lord of her actions, one and equal in all objects and creatures, not born in the taking up of a body, not subject to death in the perishing of all these bodies. That is the true seeing, the seeing of that in us which is eternal and immortal. As we perceive more and more this equal spirit in all things, we pass into that equality of the spirit; as we dwell more and more in this universal being, we become ourselves universal beings, as we grow more and more aware of this eternal, we put on our own eternity and are for ever. We identify ourselves with the eternity of the self and no longer with the limitation and distress of our mental and physical ignorance.

Then we see that all our works are an evolution and operation of Nature and our real self not the executive doer, but the free witness and lord and unattached enjoyer of the action.

himself (by casting his being into the hands of desire and passions), and thus he attains to the supreme status.

प्रकृत्यैव च कर्माणि क्रियमाणानि सर्वशः ।
यः पश्यति तथात्मानमकर्तारं स पश्यति ॥३०॥

30. He who sees that all action is verily done by Prakriti, and that the Self is the inactive witness, he sees.

यदा भूतपृथग्भावमेकस्थमनुपश्यति ।
तत एव च विस्तारं ब्रह्म संपद्यते तदा ॥३१॥

31. When he perceives the diversified[1] existence of beings abiding in the one eternal Being, and spreading forth from it, then he attains to Brahman.

अनादित्वान्निर्गुणत्वात्परमात्मायमव्ययः ।
शरीरस्थोऽपि कौन्तेय न करोति न लिप्यते ॥३२॥

32. Because it is without origin and eternal, not limited by the qualities, the imperishable supreme Self, though seated in the body, O Kaunteya, does not[2] act, nor is affected.

यथा सर्वगतं सौक्ष्म्यादाकाशं नोपलिप्यते ।
सर्वत्रावस्थितो देहे तथात्मा नोपलिप्यते ॥३३॥

---

[1] All this surface of cosmic movement is a diverse becoming of natural existences in the one eternal Being, all is extended, manifested, rolled out by the universal Energy from the seeds of her Idea deep in his existence; but the spirit even though it takes up and enjoys her workings in this body of ours, is not affected by its mortality.

[2] It does not act even in action *kartāram api akartāram*, because it supports natural action in a perfect spiritual freedom from its effects, it is the originator indeed of all activities, but in no way changed or affected by the play of its Nature.

33. As the all-pervading ether[1] is not affected by reason of its subtlety, so seated everywhere in the body, the Self is not affected.

यथा प्रकाशयत्येकः कृत्स्नं लोकमिमं रविः ।
क्षेत्रं क्षेत्री तथा कृत्स्नं प्रकाशयति भारत ॥३४॥

34. As the one sun illumines the entire earth, so the Lord[2] of the Field illumines the entire Field, O Bharata.

क्षेत्रक्षेत्रज्ञयोरेवमन्तरं ज्ञानचक्षुषा ।
भूतप्रकृतिमोक्षं च ये विदुर्यान्ति ते परम् ॥३५॥

35. They who with the eye of knowledge perceive this difference between the Field and the Knower of the Field and the liberation of beings from Prakriti, they attain to the Supreme.

इति श्रीमद्भगवद्गीतासूपनिषत्सु ब्रह्मविद्यायां योगशास्त्रे श्रीकृष्णार्जुनसंवादे
क्षेत्रक्षेत्रज्ञविभागयोगो नाम त्रयोदशोऽध्यायः ।

[1] As the ether is not affected or changed by the multiple forms it assumes, but remains always the same pure subtle original substance, even so this spirit when it has done and become all possible things, remains through it all the same pure immutable subtle infinite essence. That is the supreme status of the soul, *para gatih*, that is the divine being and nature, *madbhava*, and whoever arrives at spiritual knowledge, rises to that supreme immortality of the Eternal.

[2] This Brahman, this eternal and spiritual knower of the field of his own natural becoming, this Nature, his perpetual energy, which converts herself into that field, this immortality of the soul in mortal nature, – these things together make the whole reality of our existence. The spirit within, when we turn to it, illumines the entire field of Nature with his own truth in all the splendour of its rays. In the light of that sun of knowledge the eye of knowledge opens in us and we live in that truth and no longer in this ignorance. Then we perceive that our limitation to our present mental and physical nature was an error of the darkness, then we are liberated from the law of the lower Prakriti, the law of the mind and body, then we attain to the supreme nature of the spirit. That splendid and lofty change is the last, the divine and infinite becoming, the putting off of mortal nature, the putting on of an immortal existence.

Fourteenth Chapter
ABOVE THE GUNAS

श्रीभगवान् उवाच —
परं भूयः प्रवक्ष्यामि ज्ञानानां ज्ञानमुत्तमम् ।
यज्ज्ञात्वा मुनयः सर्वे परां सिद्धिमितो गताः ॥१॥

1. The Blessed Lord said: I will again declare the supreme[1] Knowledge, the highest of all knowings, which having known, all the sages have gone hence to the highest perfection.

इदं ज्ञानमुपाश्रित्य मम साधर्म्यमागताः ।
सर्गेऽपि नोपजायन्ते प्रलये न व्यथन्ति च ॥२॥

2. Having taken refuge in this knowledge and become of like[2] nature and law of being with Me, they are not born[3] in the creation, nor troubled by the anguish of the universal dissolution.

[1] The distinctions between the Soul and Nature rapidly drawn in the verses of the thirteenth chapter by a few decisive epithets, especially the distinction between the embodied soul subject to the action of Nature by its enjoyment of her gunas, qualities or modes and the Supreme Soul who dwells enjoying the gunas, but not subject because it is itself beyond them, are the basis on which the Gita rests its whole idea of the liberated being made one in the conscious law of its existence with the Divine. That liberation, that oneness, that putting on of the divine nature, *sādharmya*, it declares to be the very essence of spiritual freedom and the whole significance of immortality. Therefore, says the Gita, this is the supreme knowledge because it leads to the highest perfection, and brings the soul to likeness with the Divine. This supreme importance assigned to *sādharmya* is a capital point in the teaching of the Gita.

[2] Mark that nowhere in the Gita is there any indication that dissolution of the individual spiritual being into the unmanifest, indefinable or absolute Brahman, *avyaktam anirdeśyam*, is the true meaning or condition of Immortality or the true aim of Yoga. On the contrary it describes Immortality later on as an indwelling in the Ishwara in his supreme status, *mayi nivasisyasi, param dhāma*, and here as *sādharmya, param siddhim*, a

मम योनिर्महद् ब्रह्म तस्मिन् गर्भं दधाम्यहम् ।
संभव: सर्वभूतानां ततो भवति भारत ।।३।।

3. My womb is the Mahat Brahman; into that I cast the seed; thence[1] spring all beings, O Bharata.

---

supreme perfection, a becoming of one law of being and nature with the Supreme, persistent still in existence and conscious of the universal movement but above it, as all the sages still exist, *munayaḥ sarve*, not bound to birth in the creation, not troubled by the dissolution of the cycles.

[3] To be immortal was never held in the ancient spiritual teaching to consist merely in a personal survival of death of the body: all beings are immortal in that sense and it is only the forms that perish. The souls that do not arrive at liberation, live through the returning aeons; all exist involved or secret in the Brahman during the dissolution of the manifest worlds and are born again in the appearance of a new cycle. To be immortal in the deeper sense is something different from this survival of death and this constant recurrence. Immortality is that supreme status in which the Spirit knows itself to be superior to death and birth, not conditioned by the nature of its manifestation, infinite, imperishable, immutably eternal, – immortal, because never being born it never dies. The divine Purushottama, who is the supreme Lord and supreme Brahman, possesses for ever this immortal eternity and is not affected by his taking up a body or by his continuous assumption of cosmic forms and powers because he exists always in this self-knowledge. His very nature is to be unchangeably conscious of his own eternity; he is self-aware without end or beginning. He is here the Inhabitant of all bodies, but as the unborn in every body, not limited in his consciousness by that manifestation, not identified with the physical nature which he assumes; for that is only a minor circumstance of his universal activised play of existence. Liberation, Immortality is to live in this unchangeably conscious eternal being of the Purushottama. But to arrive here at this greater spiritual Immortality the embodied soul must cease to live according to the law of the lower nature; it must put on the law of the Divine's supreme way of existence which is in fact the real law of its own eternal essence. In the spiritual evolution of its becoming, no less than in its secret original being, it must grow into the likeness of the Divine.

[1] The soul of man could not grow into the likeness of the Divine if it were not in its secret essence imperishably one with the Divine and part and parcel of his divinity: it could not be or become immortal if it were merely a creature of mental, vital and physical Nature. All existence is a manifestation of the divine existence and that which is within us is spirit of the eternal Spirit.

FOURTEENTH CHAPTER 213

सर्वयोनिषु कौन्तेय मूर्तयः संभवन्ति याः ।
तासां ब्रह्म महद्योनिरहं बीजप्रदः पिता ॥४॥

4. Whatever forms are produced in whatsoever wombs, O Kaunteya, the Mahat Brahman is their womb, and I am the Father who[1] casts the seed.

सत्त्वं रजस्तम इति गुणाः प्रकृतिसम्भवाः ।
निबध्नन्ति महाबाहो देहे देहिनमव्ययम् ॥५॥

5. The three gunas born of Prakriti, sattwa, rajas and tamas, bind[2] in the body, O great-armed one, the imperishable dweller in the body.

तत्र सत्त्वं निर्मलत्वात्प्रकाशकमनामयम् ।
सुखसङ्गेन बध्नाति ज्ञानसङ्गेन चानघ ॥६॥

6. Of these sattwa is by the purity of its quality a cause of

---

[1] He is at once the Father and Mother of the universe; the substance of the infinite Idea, *vijñāna*, the Mahat Brahman, is the womb into which he casts the seed of his self-conception. As the Over-Soul he casts the seed; as the Mother, the Nature-Soul, the Energy filled with his conscious power, he receives it into this infinite substance of being made pregnant with his illimitable, yet self-limiting Idea. He receives into this Vast of self-conception and develops there the divine embryo into mental and physical form of existence born from the original act of conceptive creation. All we see springs from that act of creation.

What is it then that makes the difference, what is it that gets the soul into the appearance of birth and death and bondage, – for this is patent that it is only an appearance?

[2] It is a subordinate act or state of consciousness, it is a self-oblivious identification with the modes of Nature in the limited workings of this lower motivity and with this self-wrapped ego-bounded knot of action of the mind, life and body that gets the soul into the appearance of birth and death and bondage. To rise above the modes of Nature, to be *traiguṇyātīta*, is indispensable, if we are to get back into our fully conscious being away from the obsessing power of the lower action and to put on the free nature of the spirit and its eternal Immortality. That condition of the *sādharmya* is what the Gita next proceeds to develop.

light and illumination, and by virtue of that purity produces no disease or morbidity or suffering in the nature; it binds[1] by attachment to knowledge and attachment to happiness, O sinless one.

रजो रागात्मकं विद्धि तृष्णासङ्गसमुद्भवम् ।
तन्निबध्नाति कौन्तेय कर्मसङ्गेन देहिनम् ॥७॥

7. Rajas, know thou, has for its essence attraction of liking and longing; it is a child of the attachment of the soul to the desire of objects; O Kaunteya, it binds the embodied spirit by attachment to works.

तमस्त्वज्ञानजं विद्धि मोहनं सर्वदेहिनाम् ।
प्रमादालस्यनिद्राभिस्तन्निबध्नाति भारत ॥८॥

8. But tamas, know thou, born of ignorance, is the deluder of all embodied beings; it binds by negligence, indolence and sleep, O Bharata.

सत्त्वं सुखे सञ्जयति रजः कर्मणि भारत ।
ज्ञानमावृत्य तु तमः प्रमादे सञ्जयत्युत ॥९॥

9. Sattwa attaches to happiness, rajas to action, O

---

[1] Sattwa binds, as much as the other gunas and binds just in the same way by desire, by ego; a nobler desire, a purer ego, – but so long as in any form these two hold the being, there is no freedom. The man of virtue, of knowledge, has his ego of the virtuous man, his ego of knowledge, and it is that sattwic ego which he seeks to satisfy; for his own sake he seeks virtue and knowledge. Only when we cease to satisfy the ego, to think and to will from the ego, the limited "I" in us, then is there a real freedom. In other words, freedom, highest self-mastery begins when above the natural self we see and hold the supreme Self of which the ego is an obstructing veil and a blinding shadow. And that can only be when we see the one Self in us seated above Nature and make our individual being one with it in being and consciousness and in its individual nature of action only an instrument of a supreme Will, the one Will that is really free. For that we must rise high above the three gunas, become *triguṇātīta*.

Bharata; tamas covers up the knowledge and attaches to negligence of error and inaction.¹

रजस्तमश्चाभिभूय सत्त्वं भवति भारत ।
रजः सत्त्वं तमश्चैव तमः सत्त्वं रजस्तथा ॥१०॥

10. Now sattwa leads, having overpowered rajas and tamas, O Bharata; now rajas, having overpowered sattwa and tamas; and now tamas, having overpowered sattwa and rajas.

सर्वद्वारेषु देहेऽस्मिन् प्रकाश उपजायते ।
ज्ञानं यदा तदा विद्याद्विवृद्धं सत्त्वमित्युत ॥११॥

11. When into all the doors in the body there comes a flooding of light,² a light of understanding, perception and

¹ The soul by attachment to the enjoyment of the gunas and their results concentrates its consciousness on the lower and outward action of life, mind and body in Nature, imprisons itself in the form of these things and becomes oblivious of its own greater consciousness behind in the spirit, unaware of the free power and scope of the liberating Purusha. Evidently, in order to be liberated and perfect we must get back from these things, away from the gunas and above them and return to the power of that free spiritual consciousness above Nature.

These three qualities of Nature are evidently present and active in all human beings and none can be said to be quite devoid of one and another or free from any one of the three; but they are not constant in any man in the quantitative action of their force or in the combination of their elements; for they are variable and in a continual state of mutual impact, displacement and interaction. Only by a general and ordinary predominance of one or other of the qualities can a man be said to be either sattwic or rajasic or tamasic in his nature; but this can only be a general and not an exclusive or absolute description.

² The intelligence is alert and illumined, the senses quickened, the whole mentality satisfied and full of brightness and the nervous being calmed and filled with an illumined ease and clarity, *prasāda*. Knowledge and a harmonious ease and pleasure and happiness are the characteristic results of sattwa.

But how does sattwa, the power of knowledge and happiness, become a chain? It so becomes because it is a principle of mental nature, a knowledge, one should understand that there has been a great increase and uprising of the sattwic guna in the nature.

लोभ: प्रवृत्तिरारम्भ: कर्मणामशम: स्पृहा ।
रजस्येतानि जायन्ते विवृद्धे भरतर्षभ ॥१२॥

12. Greed, seeking impulsions,[1] initiative of actions, unrest, desire – all this mounts in us when rajas increases.

अप्रकाशोऽप्रवृत्तिश्च प्रमादो मोह एव च ।
तमस्येतानि जायन्ते विवृद्धे कुरुनन्दन ॥१३॥

13. Nescience,[2] inertia, negligence and delusion – these are born when tamas predominates, O joy of the Kurus.

---

principle of limited and limiting knowledge and of a happiness which depends upon right following or attainment of this or that object or else on particular states of the mentality, on a light of mind which can be only a more or less clear twilight. Its pleasure can only be a passing intensity or a qualified ease. Other is the infinite spiritual knowledge and the free self-existent delight of our spiritual being.
[1] It is the force of desire which motives all ordinary personal initiative of action and all that movement of stir and seeking and propulsion in our nature which is the impetus towards action and works, *pravṛtti*. Rajas, then, is evidently the kinetic force in the modes of Nature. Its fruit is the lust of action, but also grief, pain, all kinds of suffering; for it has no right possession of its object – desire in fact implies non-possession – and even its pleasure of acquired possession is troubled and unstable because it has not clear knowledge and does not know how to possess nor can it find the secret of accord and right enjoyment. All the ignorant and passionate seeking of life belongs to the rajasic mode of Nature.
[2] It is the darkness of tamas which obscures knowledge and causes all confusion and delusion. Therefore it is the opposite of sattwa, for the essence of sattwa is enlightenment, *prakāśa*, and the essence of tamas is absence of light, nescience, *aprakāśa*. But tamas brings incapacity and negligence of action as well as the incapacity and negligence of error, inattention and misunderstanding or non-understanding; indolence, languor and sleep belong to this guna. Therefore it is the opposite too of rajas; for the essence of rajas is movement and impulsion and kinesis, *pravṛtti*, but the essence of tamas is inertia, *apravṛtti*. Tamas is inertia of nescience and inertia of inaction, a double negative.

यदा सत्त्वे प्रवृद्धे तु प्रलयं याति देहभृत् ।
तदोत्तमविदां लोकानमलान् प्रतिपद्यते ॥१४॥

14. If sattwa prevails when the embodied goes to dissolution,[1] then he attains to the spotless worlds of the knowers of the highest principles.

रजसि प्रलयं गत्वा कर्मसङ्गिषु जायते ।
तथा प्रलीनस्तमसि मूढयोनिषु जायते ॥१५॥

15. Going to dissolution when rajas prevails, he is born among those attached to action; if dissolved during the increase of tamas, he is born in the wombs of beings involved in nescience.

कर्मणः सुकृतस्याहुः सात्त्विकं निर्मलं फलम् ।
रजसस्तु फलं दुःखमज्ञानं तमसः फलम् ॥१६॥

16. It is said the fruit of works[2] rightly done is pure and sattwic; pain[3] is the consequence of rajasic works, ignorance is the result of tamasic action.

[1] Our physical death is also a *pralaya*, the soul bearing the body comes to a pralaya, to a disintegration of that form of matter with which its ignorance identified its being and which now dissolves into the natural elements. But the soul itself persists and after an interval resumes in a new body formed from those elements, its round of births in the cycle, just as after the interval of pause and cessation the universal Being resumes his endless round of the cyclic aeons.

[2] All natural action is done by the gunas, by Nature through her modes. The soul cannot act by itself, it can only act through Nature and her modes. And yet the Gita, while it demands freedom from the modes, insists upon the necessity of action. Here comes in the importance of its insistence on the abandonment of the fruits; for it is the desire of the fruits which is the most potent cause of the soul's bondage and by abandoning it the soul can be free in action.

[3] Ignorance is the result of tamasic action, pain the consequence of rajasic works, pain of reaction, disappointment, dissatisfaction or transience, and therefore in attachment to the fruits of this kind of activity attended as they are with these undesirable accompaniments there is no

सत्त्वात्सञ्जायते ज्ञानं रजसो लोभ एव च ।
प्रमादमोहौ तमसो भवतोऽज्ञानमेव च ॥१७॥

17. From sattwa[1] knowledge is born, and greed from rajas; negligence and delusion are of tamas, and also ignorance.

ऊर्ध्वं गच्छन्ति सत्त्वस्था मध्ये तिष्ठन्ति राजसाः ।
जघन्यगुणवृत्तिस्था अधो गच्छन्ति तामसाः ॥१८॥

profit. But of works rightly done the fruit is pure and sattwic, the inner result is knowledge and happiness. Yet attachment even to these pleasurable things must be entirely abandoned, first, because in the mind they are limited and limiting forms and, secondly, because, since sattwa is constantly entangled with and besieged by rajas and tamas which may at any moment overcome it, there is a perpetual insecurity in their tenure. But, even if one is free from any clinging to the fruit, there may be an attachment to the work itself, either for its own sake, the essential rajasic bond, or owing to a lax subjection to the drive of Nature, the tamasic, or for the sake of the attracting rightness of the thing done, which is the sattwic attaching cause powerful on the virtuous man or the man of knowledge. And here evidently the resource is in that other injunction of the Gita, to give up the action itself to the Lord of works and be only a desireless and equal-minded instrument of his will. (See sloka 19.)

[1] The three modes of Nature, *sattwa, rajas, tamas* are described in the Gita only by their psychological action in man, or incidentally in things such as food according as they produce a psychological or vital effect on human beings. If we look for a more general definition, we shall perhaps catch a glimpse of it in the symbolic idea of Indian religion which attributes each of these qualities respectively to one member of the cosmic Trinity, sattwa to the preserver Vishnu, rajas to the creator Brahma, tamas to the destroyer Rudra. Looking behind this idea for the rationale of the triple ascription, we might define the three modes or qualities in terms of the motion of the universal Energy as Nature's three concomitant and inseparable powers of equilibrium, kinesis and inertia. But that is only their appearance in terms of the external action of Force. Since consciousness is always there even in an apparently inconscient Force, we must find a corresponding psychological power of these three modes which informs their more outward executive action. On their psychological side the three qualities may be defined, tamas as Nature's power of nescience, rajas as her power of active seeking ignorance enlightened by desire and impulsion, sattwa as her power of possessing and harmonising knowledge.

FOURTEENTH CHAPTER

18. They rise upwards who are in sattwa; those in rajas remain in the middle;[1] those enveloped in ignorance and inertia, the effect of the lowest quality, the tamas, go downwards.

नान्यं गुणेभ्यः कर्तारं यदा द्रष्टानुपश्यति ।
गुणेभ्यश्च परं वेत्ति मद्भावं सोऽधिगच्छति ॥१९॥

19. When the seer perceives that the modes of Nature are the whole agency and cause of works and knows and turns to That which is supreme above the gunas, he attains to *madbhāva* (the movement and status of the Divine).

गुणानेतानतीत्य त्रीन् देही देहसमुद्भवान् ।
जन्ममृत्युजरादुःखैर्विमुक्तोऽमृतमश्नुते ॥२०॥

20. When the soul thus rises above the three gunas born

---

[1] The ordinary human soul takes a pleasure in the customary disturbances of its nature-life; it is because it has this pleasure and because, having it, it gives a sanction to the troubled play of the lower nature that the play continues perpetually; for the Prakriti does nothing except for the pleasure and with the sanction of its lover and enjoyer, the Purusha. The joy of the soul in the dualities is the secret of the mind's pleasure in living. Ask it to rise out of all this disturbance to the unmingled joy of the pure bliss-soul which all the time secretly supports its strength in the struggle and makes its own continued existence possible, – it will draw back at once from the call. The true cause of its unwillingness is that it is asked to rise above its own atmosphere and breathe a rarer and purer air of life, whose bliss and power it cannot realise and hardly even conceives as real, while the joy of this lower turbid nature is to it the one thing familiar and palpable. Nor is this lower satisfaction in itself a thing evil and unprofitable; it is rather the condition for the upward evolution of our human nature out of the tamasic ignorance and inertia to which its material being is most subject; it is the rajasic stage of the graded ascent of man towards the supreme self-knowledge, power and bliss. But if we rest eternally on this plane, the *madhyamā gatiḥ* of the Gita, our ascent remains unfinished, the evolution of the soul incomplete. Through the sattwic being and nature to that which is beyond the three gunas lies the way of the soul to its perfection.

of the embodiment in Nature, he is freed from subjection to birth and death and their concomitants, decay, old age and suffering, and enjoys in the end the Immortality of its self-existence.

अर्जुन उवाच —
कैर्लिङ्गैस्त्रीन् गुणानेतानतीतो भवति प्रभो ।
किमाचारः कथं चैतांस्त्रीन् गुणानतिवर्तते ॥२१॥

21. Arjuna[1] said: What are the signs of the man who has risen above the three gunas, O Lord? What his action and how does he surmount the gunas?

श्रीभगवान् उवाच —
प्रकाशं च प्रवृत्तिं च मोहमेव च पाण्डव ।
न द्वेष्टि संप्रवृत्तानि न निवृत्तानि काङ्क्षति ॥२२॥

22. The Blessed Lord said: He, O Pandava, who does not abhor or shrink from the operation of enlightenment (the result of rising sattwa) or impulsion to works (the result of rising rajas) or the clouding over of the mental and nervous being (the result of rising tamas), nor longs after them, when they cease;

उदासीनवदासीनो गुणैर्यो न विचाल्यते ।
गुणा वर्तन्त इत्येव योऽवतिष्ठति नेङ्गते ॥२३॥

23. He who, established in a position[2] as of one seated

---

[1] This question again reveals the pragmatic and practical nature of Arjuna. How can one live and act in the world and yet be above the gunas? The sign, says Krishna, is that equality of which I have so constantly spoken.

[2] He has seated himself in the conscious light of another principle than the nature of the gunas and that greater consciousness remains steadfast in him, above these powers and unshaken by their motions like the sun above clouds to one who has risen into a higher atmosphere. He from that height sees that it is the gunas that are in process of action and that their storm and calm are not himself but only a movement of Prakriti; his self is

high above, is unshaken by the gunas; who seeing that it is the gunas that are in process of action stands apart immovable;

समदुःखसुखः स्वस्थः समलोष्टाश्मकाञ्चनः ।
तुल्यप्रियाप्रियो धीरस्तुल्यनिन्दात्मसंस्तुतिः ॥२४॥
मानापमानयोस्तुल्यस्तुल्यो मित्रारिपक्षयोः ।
सर्वारम्भपरित्यागी गुणातीतः स उच्यते ॥२५॥

24-25. He who regards happiness and suffering alike, gold and mud and stone as of equal value, to whom the pleasant and the unpleasant, praise and blame, honour and insult, the faction of his friends and the faction of his enemies are equal things; who is steadfast in a wise imperturbable and immutable inner calm and quietude; who initiates no action (but leaves all works to be done by the gunas of Nature) – he is said to be above the gunas.

मां च योऽव्यभिचारेण भक्तियोगेन सेवते ।
स गुणान् समतीत्यैतान् ब्रह्मभूयाय कल्पते ॥२६॥

26. He also who loves and strives after Me with an undeviating love and adoration, passes beyond the three gunas and he too is prepared for becoming the Brahman.

---

immovable above and his spirit does not participate in that shifting mutability of things unstable. This is the impersonality of the Brahmic status; for that higher principle, that greater wide high-seated consciousness, *kūṭastha*, is the immutable Brahman.

But still there is evidently here a double status, there is a scission of the being between two opposites; a liberated spirit in the immutable Self or Brahman watches the action of an unliberated mutable Nature, – Akshara and Kshara. Is there no greater status, is it the end of Yoga to drop the mutable nature and the gunas born of the embodiment in Nature and disappear into the impersonality and everlasting peace of the Brahman? There is, it would seem, something else; the Gita refers to it at the close of this chapter, always returning to this one final note.

ब्रह्मणो हि प्रतिष्ठाहममृतस्याव्ययस्य च ।
शाश्वतस्य च धर्मस्य सुखस्यैकान्तिकस्य च ॥२७॥

27. I[1] (the Purushottama) am the foundation of the silent Brahman and of Immortality and imperishable spiritual existence and of the eternal dharma and of an utter bliss of happiness.

इति श्रीमद्भगवद्गीतासूपनिषत्सु ब्रह्मविद्यायां योगशास्त्रे श्रीकृष्णार्जुनसंवादे
गुणत्रयविभागयोगो नाम चतुर्दशोऽध्यायः ।

[1] There is a status then which is greater than the peace of the Akshara as it watches unmoved the strife of the gunas. There is a highest spiritual experience and foundation above the immutability of the Brahman, there is an eternal dharma greater than the rajasic impulsion to works, *pravṛtti*, there is an absolute delight which is untouched by rajasic suffering and beyond the sattwic happiness, and these things are found and possessed by dwelling in the being and power of the Purushottama. But since it is acquired by bhakti, its status must be that divine delight, Ananda, in which is experienced the union of utter love* and possessing oneness, the crown of bhakti. And to rise into that Ananda, into that inexpressible oneness must be the completion of spiritual perfection and the fulfilment of the eternal immortalising dharma.

(* *niratiśayapremāspadatvam ānandatattvam*.)

Fifteenth Chapter

THE THREE PURUSHAS

श्रीभगवान् उवाच —
ऊर्ध्वमूलमधःशाखमश्वत्थं प्राहुरव्ययम् ।
छन्दांसि यस्य पर्णानि यस्तं वेद स वेदवित् ॥१॥

1. The Blessed Lord said: With its original source above (in the Eternal), its branches stretching below, the Ashwattha[1] is said to be eternal and imperishable; the leaves of it are the hymns of the Veda; he who knows it is the Veda-knower.[2]

अधश्चोर्ध्वं प्रसृतास्तस्य शाखा गुणप्रवृद्धा विषयप्रवालाः ।
अधश्च मूलान्यनुसन्ततानि कर्मानुबन्धीनि मनुष्यलोके ॥२॥

---

[1] Here is a description of cosmic existence in the Vedantic image of the Ashwattha tree.

[2] The knowledge the Veda gives us is a knowledge of the gods, of the principles and powers of the cosmos, and its fruits are the fruits of a sacrifice which is offered with desire, fruits of enjoyment and lordship in the nature of the three worlds, in earth and heaven and the world between earth and heaven. The branches of this cosmic tree extend both below and above, below in the material, above in the supraphysical planes; they grow by the gunas of Nature, for the triple guna is all the subject of the Vedas, *traigunya-viṣayā vedāḥ*. The Vedic rhythms are the leaves and the sensible objects of desire supremely gained by a right doing of sacrifice are the constant budding of the foliage. Man, therefore, so long as he enjoys the play of the gunas and is attached to desire, is held in the coils of Pravritti, in the movement of birth and action, turns about constantly between the earth and the middle planes and the heavens and is unable to get back to his supreme spiritual infinitudes. This was perceived by the sages. To achieve liberation they followed the path of Nivritti or cessation from the original urge to action, and the consummation of this way is the cessation of birth itself and a transcendent status in the highest supracosmic reach of the Eternal.

But for this purpose it is necessary to cut these long-fixed roots of desire by the strong sword of detachment.

2. The branches of this cosmic tree extend both below and above (below in the material, above in the supraphysical planes), they grow by the gunas of Nature; the sensible objects are its foliage, downward here into the world of men it plunges its roots of attachment and desire with their consequences of an endlessly developing action.

न रूपमस्येह तथोपलभ्यते नान्तो न चादिर्न च संप्रतिष्ठा ।
अश्वत्थमेनं सुविरूढमूलमसङ्गशस्त्रेण दृढेन छित्त्वा ॥३॥
ततः पदं तत्परिमार्गितव्यं यस्मिन् गता न निवर्तन्ति भूयः ।
तमेव चाद्यं पुरुषं प्रपद्ये यतः प्रवृत्तिः प्रसृता पुराणी ॥४॥

3-4. The real form of it cannot be perceived by us in this material world of man's embodiment, nor its beginning nor its end, nor its foundation; having cut down this firmly rooted Ashwattha by the strong sword of detachment, one should seek for that highest goal whence, once having reached it, there is no compulsion of return to mortal life; I turn away (says the Vedantic verse) to seek that original Soul alone from whom proceeds the ancient sempiternal urge to action.

निर्मानमोहा जितसङ्गदोषा अध्यात्मनित्या विनिवृत्तकामाः ।
द्वन्द्वैर्विमुक्ताः सुखदुःखसंज्ञैर्गच्छन्त्यमूढाः पदमव्ययं तत् ॥५॥

5. To be free from the bewilderment of this lower Maya, without egoism, the great fault of attachment conquered, all desires stilled, the duality of joy and grief cast away, always to be fixed in a pure spiritual consciousness, these are the steps of the way to that supreme Infinite.

न तद्भासयते सूर्यो न शशाङ्को न पावकः ।
यद्गत्वा न निवर्तन्ते तद्धाम परमं मम ॥६॥

6. There we find the timeless being which is not illumined by sun or moon or fire (but is itself the light of the presence of the eternal Purusha); having gone thither they return not;

that is the highest eternal status¹ of My Being.

ममैवांशो जीवलोके जीवभूतः सनातनः ।
मनःषष्ठानीन्द्रियाणि प्रकृतिस्थानि कर्षति ॥७॥

7. It is an eternal portion² of Me that becomes the Jiva in the world of living creatures and cultivates the subjective powers of Prakriti, mind and the five senses.

¹ But it would seem that this can be attained very well, best even, pre-eminently, directly, by the quiesence of Sannyasa. Its appointed path would seem to be the way of the Akshara, a complete renunciation of works and life, an ascetic seclusion, an ascetic inaction. Where is the room here, or at least where is the call, the necessity, for the command to action, and what has all this to do with the maintenance of the cosmic existence, *lokasamgraha*, the slaughter of Kurukshetra, the ways of the Spirit in Time, the vision of the million-bodied Lord and his high-voiced bidding, "Arise, slay the foe, enjoy a wealthy kingdom"? And what then is this soul in Nature? The spirit, too, this Kshara, this enjoyer of our mutable existence is the Purushottama; it is he in his eternal multiplicity, that is the Gita's answer.

² This is an epithet, a statement of immense bearing and consequence. For it means that each soul, each being in its spiritual reality is the very Divine, however partial its actual manifestation of him in Nature. And it means too, if words have any sense, that each manifesting spirit, each of the many, is an eternal individual, an eternal unborn undying power of the one Existence. We call this manifesting spirit the Jiva, because it appears here as if a living creature in a world of living creatures, and we speak of this spirit in man as the human soul and think of it in the terms of humanity only. But in truth it is something greater than its present appearance and not bound to its humanity: it was a lesser manifestation than the human in its past, it can become something much greater than mental man in its future. And when this soul rises above all ignorant limitation, then it puts on its divine nature of which its humanity is only a temporary veil, a thing of partial and incomplete significance. The individual spirit exists and ever existed beyond in the Eternal, for it is itself everlasting, *sanātana*. It is evidently this idea of the eternal individual which leads the Gita to avoid any expression at all suggestive of a complete dissolution, *laya*, and to speak rather of the highest state of the soul as a dwelling in the Purushottama, *nivasiṣyasi mayyeva*.

शरीरं यदवाप्नोति यच्चाप्युत्क्रामतीश्वरः ।
गृहीत्वैतानि संयाति वायुर्गन्धानिवाशयात् ॥८॥

8. When the Lord[1] takes up this body (he brings in with him the mind and the senses) and in his going forth too (casting away the body) he goes taking them as the wind takes the perfumes from a vase.

श्रोत्रं चक्षुः स्पर्शनं च रसनं घ्राणमेव च ।
अधिष्ठाय मनश्चायं विषयानुपसेवते ॥९॥

9. The ear, the eye, the touch, the taste and the smell, using these and the mind also, he enjoys the objects of mind and sense as the indwelling and over-dwelling Soul.

उत्क्रामन्तं स्थितं वापि भुञ्जानं वा गुणान्वितम् ।
विमूढा नानुपश्यन्ति पश्यन्ति ज्ञानचक्षुषः ॥१०॥

10. The deluded do not perceive him in his coming in and his going forth or in his staying and enjoying and assumption of quality;[2] they perceive who have the eye of knowledge.

यतन्तो योगिनश्चैनं पश्यन्त्यात्मन्यवस्थितम् ।
यतन्तोऽप्यकृतात्मानो नैनं पश्यन्त्यचेतसः ॥११॥

11. The Yogins who strive, see the Lord in themselves;

---

[1] This eternal individual is not other than or in any way really separate from the Divine Purusha. It is the Lord himself, the Ishwara who by virtue of the eternal multiplicity of his oneness – is not all existence a rendering of that truth of the Infinite? – exists for ever as the immortal soul within us and has taken up this body and goes forth from the transient framework when it is cast away to disappear into the elements of Nature. But the identity of the Lord and the soul in mutable Nature is hidden from us by outward appearance and lost in the crowding mobile deceptions of that Nature. And those who allow themselves to be governed by the figures of Nature, the figure of humanity or any other form, will never see it, but will ignore and despise the Divine lodged in the human body.

[2] They see only what is there visible to the mind and senses, not the greater truth which can only be glimpsed by the eye of knowledge.

but though they strive to do so, the ignorant[1] perceive Him not, as they are not formed in the spiritual mould.

यदादित्यगतं तेजो जगद् भासयतेऽखिलम् ।
यच्चन्द्रमसि यच्चाग्नौ तत्तेजो विद्धि मामकम् ॥१२॥

12. The light of the sun that illumines all this world, that which is in the moon and in fire, that light know as from Me.

गामाविश्य च भूतानि धारयाम्यहमोजसा ।
पुष्णामि चौषधीः सर्वाः सोमो भूत्वा रसात्मकः ॥१३॥

13. I have entered into this form of earth (and am the spirit of its material force) and sustain by My might these multitudes. I am the godhead of Soma who by the *rasa* (the sap in the earth-mother) nourishes all plants and trees.

अहं वैश्वानरो भूत्वा प्राणिनां देहमाश्रितः ।
प्राणापानसमायुक्तः पचाम्यन्नं चतुर्विधम् ॥१४॥

14. I, having become the flame of life, sustain the physical body of living creatures, and united with Prana and Apana, digest the four kinds[2] of food.[3]

[1] Never can they have sight of him, even if they strive to do so, until they learn to put away the limitations of the outward consciousness and build in themselves their spiritual being, create for it, as it were, a form in their nature. Man, to know himself, must be *kṛtātmā*, formed and complete in the spiritual mould, enlightened in the spiritual vision. The Yogins who have this eye of knowledge, see the Divine Being we are in their own endless reality, their own eternity of spirit. Illumined, they see the Lord in themselves and are delivered from the crude material limitation, from the form of mental personality, from the transient life formulation: they dwell immortal in the truth of the self and spirit. But they see him too not only in themselves, but in all the cosmos.
[2] In other words, the Divine is at once the Soul of matter and the Soul of life and Soul of mind as well as the Soul of the supramental light that is beyond mind and its limited reasoning intelligence.
[3] Namely, that which is chewed, that which is sucked, that which is licked and that which is drunk.

सर्वस्य चाहं हृदि सन्निविष्टो मत्त: स्मृतिर्ज्ञानमपोहनं च ।
वेदैश्च सर्वैरहमेव वेद्यो वेदान्तकृद्वेदविदेव चाहम् ॥१५॥

15. I am lodged in the heart of all; from Me are memory and knowledge and their absence. And that which is known by all the Vedas (and by all forms of knowing) am I; and I indeed the knower of Veda and the maker of Vedanta.

द्वाविमौ पुरुषौ लोके क्षरश्चाक्षर एव च ।
क्षर: सर्वाणि भूतानि कूटस्थोऽक्षर उच्यते ॥१६॥

16. There are two Purushas[1] (spiritual beings) in this world, the immutable (and impersonal) and the mutable (and personal); the mutable is all these existences, the

[1] These two are the two spirits we see in the world; one emerges in front in its action, the other remains behind it steadfast in that perpetual silence from which the action comes and in which all actions cease and disappear into timeless being, Nirvana. The difficulty which baffles our intelligence is that these two seem to be irreconcilable opposites with no real nexus between them or any transition from the one to the other except by an intolerant movement of separation. The Kshara acts, or at least motives action, separately in the Akshara; the Akshara stands apart self-centred, separate in its inactivity from the Kshara. When we live in the mobility of the becoming, we may be aware of but hardly live in the immortality of timeless self-existence. And when we fix ourselves in timeless being, Time and Space and circumstance fall away from us and begin to appear as a troubled dream in the Infinite. The most persuasive conclusion would be, at first sight, that the mobility of the spirit in Nature is an illusion, a thing real only when we live in it, but not real in essence, and that is why, when we go back into self, it falls away from our incorruptible essence. That is the familiar cutting of the knot of the riddle, *brahma satyam jaganmithyā.*

The Gita does not take refuge in this explanation which has enormous difficulties of its own, besides its failure to account for the illusion, – for it only says that it is all a mysterious and incomprehensible Maya, and then we might just as well say that it is all a mysterious and incomprehensible double reality, spirit concealing itself from spirit. The Gita speaks of Maya, but only as a bewildering partial consciousness which loses hold of the complete reality, lives in the phenomenon of mobile Nature and has no sight of the Spirit of which she is the active power, *me prakṛtiḥ*. When

Kutastha (the high-seated consciousness of the Brahmic status) is called the immutable.

उत्तमः पुरुषस्त्वन्यः परमात्मेत्युदाहृतः ।
यो लोकत्रयमाविश्य बिभर्त्यव्यय ईश्वरः ॥१७॥

17. But other than these two is that highest spirit called the supreme Self,[1] who enters the three worlds and upbears them, the imperishable Lord.

---

we transcend this Maya, the world does not disappear, it only changes its whole heart of meaning. In the spiritual vision we find not that all this does not really exist, but rather that all is, but with a sense quite other than its present mistaken significance: all is self and soul and nature of the Godhead, all is Vasudeva. The world for the Gita is real, a creation of the Lord, a power of the Eternal, a manifestation from the Parabrahman, and even this lower nature of the triple Maya is a derivation from the supreme divine Nature. Nor can we take refuge altogether in this distinction that there is a double, an inferior active and temporal and a superior calm still and eternal reality beyond action and that our liberation is to pass from this partiality to that greatness, from the action to the silence. For the Gita insists that we can and should, while we live, be conscious in the self and its silence and yet act with power in the world of Nature. And it gives the example of the Divine himself who is not bound by necessity of birth, but free, superior to the cosmos, and yet abides eternally in action, *varta eva ca karmaṇi*. Therefore it is by putting on a likeness of the divine nature in its completeness that the unity of this double experience becomes entirely possible. But what is the principle of that oneness?

The Gita finds it in its supreme vision of the Purushottama; for that is the type, according to its doctrine, of the complete and the highest experience, it is the knowledge of the whole-knowers, *kṛtsna-vidaḥ*.

[1] The Akshara is *para*, supreme in relation to the elements and action of cosmic Nature. It is the immutable Self of all, and the immutable Self of all is the Purushottama. The Akshara is he in the freedom of his self-existence unaffected by the action of his own power in Nature, not impinged on by the urge of his own becoming, undisturbed by the play of his own qualities. But this is only one aspect though a great aspect of the integral knowledge. The Purushottama is at the same time greater than the Akshara, because he is more than this immutability and he is not limited even by the highest eternal status of being, *param dhāma*. Still, it is through whatever is immutable and eternal in us that we arrive at that highest status from which there is no returning to birth, and that was the

यस्मात् क्षरमतीतोऽहमक्षरादपि चोत्तमः ।
अतोऽस्मि लोके वेदे च प्रथितः पुरुषोत्तमः ॥१८॥

18. Since I am beyond the mutable and am greater and higher even than the immutable, in the world and the Veda I am proclaimed as the Purushottama (the supreme Self).

liberation which was sought by the wise of old, the ancient sages. But when pursued through the Akshara alone, this attempt at liberation becomes the seeking of the Indefinable, a thing hard for our nature embodied as we are here in Matter. The Indefinable, to which the Akshara, the pure intangible self here in us rises in its separative urge, is some supreme Unmanifest, *parah avyaktah*, and that highest unmanifest Akshara is still the Purushottama. Therefore, the Gita has said, those also who follow after the Indefinable, come to me, the eternal Godhead. But yet is he more even than a highest unmanifest Akshara, more than any negative Absolute, *neti neti*, because he is to be known also as the supreme Purusha who extends this whole universe in his own existence. He is a supreme mysterious All, an ineffable positive Absolute of all things here. He is the Lord in the Kshara, Purushottama not only there, but here in the heart of every creature, Ishwara. And there too even in his highest eternal status *parah avyaktah*, he is the supreme Lord, Parameshwara, no aloof and unrelated Indefinable, but the origin and father and mother and first foundation and eternal abode of self and cosmos and Master of all existences and enjoyer of askesis and sacrifice. It is by knowing him at once in the Akshara and the Kshara, it is by knowing him as the Unborn who partially manifests himself in all birth and even himself descends as the constant Avatar, it is by knowing him in his entirety, *samagram mām*, that the soul is easily released from the appearances of the lower Nature and returns by a vast sudden growth and broad immeasurable ascension into the divine being and supreme Nature. For the truth of the Kshara too is a truth of the Purushottama. The Purushottama is in the heart of every creature and is manifested in his countless Vibhutis; the Purushottama is the cosmic spirit in Time and it is he that gives the command to the divine action of the liberated human spirit. He is both Akshara and Kshara and yet he is other because he is more and greater than either of these opposites.

The Divine is neither wholly the Kshara, nor wholly the Akshara. He is greater than the immutable Self and he is much greater than the Soul of mutable things. If he is capable of being both at once, it is because he is other than they, *anyah*, the Purushottama above all cosmos and yet extended in the world and extended in the Veda, in self-knowledge and in cosmic experience.

यो मामेवमसम्मूढो जानाति पुरुषोत्तमम् ।
स सर्वविद् भजति मां सर्वभावेन भारत ॥१९॥

19. He[1] who undeluded thus has knowledge of Me as the Purushottama, adores Me (has bhakti for Me) with all-knowledge and in every way of his natural being.

इति गुह्यतमं शास्त्रमिदमुक्तं मयानघ ।
एतद् बुद्ध्वा बुद्धिमान् स्यात्कृतकृत्यश्च भारत ॥२०॥

20. Thus by Me the most secret shastra (the supreme teaching and science) has been told, O sinless one. Absolutely to know it is to be perfected in understanding and successful in the supreme sense, O Bharata.

इति श्रीमद्भगवद्गीतासूपनिषत्सु ब्रह्मविद्यायां योगशास्त्रे श्रीकृष्णार्जुनसंवादे
पुरुषोत्तमयोगो नाम पञ्चदशोऽध्यायः ।

---

[1] He sees the entire sense both of the self and of things; he restores the integral reality of the Divine; he unites the Kshara and the Akshara in the Purushottama. He loves, worships, cleaves to and adores the supreme Self of his and all existence, the one Lord of his and all energies, the close and far-off Eternal in and beyond the world. And he does this too with no single side or portion of himself, exclusive spiritualised mind, blinding light of the heart intense but divorced from largeness, or sole aspiration of the will in works, but in all the perfectly illumined ways of his being and his becoming, his soul and his nature. Divine in the equality of his imperturbable self-existence, one in it with all objects and creatures, he brings that boundless equality, that deep oneness down into his mind and heart and life and body and founds on it in an indivisible integrality the trinity of divine love, divine works and divine knowledge. This is the Gita's way of salvation.

SIXTEENTH CHAPTER

DEVA AND ASURA

(The Gita has insisted on doing all actions, *sarvāṇi karmāṇi, kṛtsnakṛt*; it has said that in whatever way the perfected Yogin lives and acts, he lives and acts in God. This can only be, if the nature also in its dynamics and workings becomes divine, a power imperturbable, intangible, inviolate, pure and untroubled by the reactions of the inferior Prakriti. How and by what steps is this most difficult transformation to be effected? What is this last secret of the soul's perfection? What the principle or the process of this transmutation of our human and earthly nature?

The sattwic quality is a first mediator between the higher and the lower nature. It must indeed at a certain point transform or escape from itself and break up and dissolve into its source; its conditioned derivative seeking light and carefully constructed action must change into the free direct dynamic and spontaneous light of the spirit. But meanwhile a high increase of sattwic power delivers us largely from the tamasic and the rajasic disqualification; and its own disqualification, once we are not pulled too much downward by rajas and tamas, can be surmounted with a greater ease. To develop sattwa till it becomes full of spiritual light and calm and happiness is the first condition of this preparatory discipline of the nature.

That, we shall find, is the whole intention of the remaining chapters of the Gita. But first it prefaces the consideration of this enlightening movement by a distinction between two kinds of being, the Deva and the Asura; for the Deva is capable of a high self-transforming sattwic action, the Asura incapable. We must see what is the object of this preface and the precise bearing of this distinction. The general nature of all human beings is the same, it is a mixture of the three gunas; it would seem then that in all there must be the capacity to develop and strengthen the sattwic element and turn it upward towards the heights of the divine transformation. That our ordinary turn is actually towards making our reason and will the servants of our rajasic or tamasic egoism, the ministers of our restless and ill-balanced kinetic desire or our self-indulgent indolence and static inertia, can only be, one would imagine, a temporary characteristic of our undeveloped spiritual being, a rawness of its imperfect evolution and must disappear when our consciousness rises in the spiritual scale. But we actually see that men, at least men above a certain level, fall very largely into two classes, those who have a dominant force of sattwic nature turned towards knowledge, self-control, beneficence, perfection and those who have a dominant force of rajasic nature turned towards egoistic greatness, satisfaction of desire, the indulgence of their own strong will and personality which they seek to impose on the world, not for the service of man or God, but for their own pride, glory and pleasure. These are the human representatives of the Devas and Danavas or Asuras, the Gods and the Titans.

The ancient mind, more open than ours to the truth of things behind the physical veil, saw behind the life of man great cosmic Powers or beings representative of certain turns or grades of the universal Shakti, divine, titanic, gigantic, demoniac, and men who strongly represented in themselves these types of nature were themselves considered as Devas, Asuras, Rakshasas, Pisachas. The Gita for its own purposes takes up this distinction and develops the difference between these two kinds of beings, *dvau bhūtasargau*. It has spoken previously of the nature which is Asuric and Rakshasic and obstructs God-knowledge, salvation and perfection; it now contrasts it with the Daivic nature which is turned to these things.)

श्रीभगवान् उवाच —
अभयं सत्त्वसंशुद्धिर्ज्ञानयोगव्यवस्थितिः ।
दानं दमश्च यज्ञश्च स्वाध्यायस्तप आर्जवम् ॥१॥

अहिंसा सत्यमक्रोधस्त्याग: शान्तिरपैशुनम् ।
दया भूतेष्वलोलुप्त्वं मार्दवं ह्रीरचापलम् ॥२॥
तेज: क्षमा धृति: शौचमद्रोहो नातिमानिता ।
भवन्ति सम्पदं दैवीमभिजातस्य भारत ॥३॥

1-3. The Blessed Lord said: Fearlessness, purity of temperament, steadfastness in the Yoga of Knowledge, giving, self-control, sacrifice, the study of Scripture, askesis, candour and straightforwardness, harmlessness, truth, absence of wrath, self-denial, calm, absence of fault-finding, compassion to all beings, absence of greed, gentleness,[1] modesty, freedom from restlessness, energy, forgiveness, patience, cleanness, absence of envy and pride – these are the wealth of the man born into the Deva nature.

दम्भो दर्पोऽभिमानश्च क्रोध: पारुष्यमेव च ।
अज्ञानं चाभिजातस्य पार्थ सम्पदमासुरीम् ॥४॥

4. Pride, arrogance, excessive self-esteem, wrath, harshness, ignorance, these, O Partha, are the wealth of the man born into the Asuric nature.

दैवी सम्पद्विमोक्षाय निबन्धायासुरी मता ।
मा शुच: सम्पदं दैवीमभिजातोऽसि पाण्डव ॥५॥

5. The Daivic qualities lead towards liberation, the Asuric towards bondage. Grieve[2] not, thou art born in the Deva-nature, O Pandava.

[1] Its gentleness and self-denial and self-control are free from all weakness: it has energy and soul-force, strong resolution, the fearlessness of the soul that lives in the right and according to the truth as well as its harmlessness, *tejaḥ, abhayaṁ, dhṛti, ahiṁsā, satyam*. The whole being, the whole temperament is integrally pure; there is a seeking for knowledge and a calm and fixed abiding in knowledge.

[2] He need not grieve with the thought that by acceptance of battle and slaughter he will be yielding to the impulses of the Asura. The action on which all turns, the battle which Arjuna has to fight with the incarnate Godhead as his charioteer at the bidding of the Master of the world in the

द्वौ भूतसर्गौ लोकेऽस्मिन् दैव आसुर एव च ।
दैवो विस्तरशः प्रोक्त आसुरं पार्थ मे शृणु ॥६॥

6. There are two creations[1] of beings in this material world, the Daivic and the Asuric; the Daivic hath been described at length: hear from Me, O Partha, the Asuric.

प्रवृत्तिं च निवृत्तिं च जना न विदुरासुराः ।
न शौचं नापि चाचारो न सत्यं तेषु विद्यते ॥७॥

7. Asuric men have no true knowledge of the way of action or the way of abstention; truth is not in them, nor clean doing, nor faithful observance.

---

form of the Time-Spirit, is a struggle to establish the kingdom of the Dharma, the empire of Truth, Right and Justice. He himself is born in the Deva kind, he has developed in himself the sattwic being, until he has now come to a point at which he is capable of a high transformation and liberation from the *traigunya* and therefore even from the sattwic nature.

[1] The distinction between the Deva and the Asura is not comprehensive of all humanity, not rigidly applicable to all its individuals, neither is it sharp and definite in all stages of the moral or spiritual history of the race or in all phases of the individual evolution. The tamasic man who makes so large a part of the whole, falls into neither category as it is here described, though he may have both elements in him in a low degree and for the most part serves tepidly the lower qualities. The normal man is ordinarily a mixture; but one or the other tendency is more pronounced, tends to make him predominantly rajaso-tamasic or sattwo-rajasic and can be said to be preparing him for either culmination, for the divine clarity or the titanic turbulence. For here what is in question is a certain culmination in the evolution of the qualitative nature, as will be evident from the descriptions given in the text. On one side there can be a sublimation of the sattwic quality, the culmination or manifestation of the unborn Deva, on the other a sublimation of the rajasic turn of the soul in nature, the entire birth of the Asura. The one leads towards that movement of liberation on which the Gita is about to lay stress; it makes possible a high self-exceeding of the sattwa quality and a transformation into the likeness of the divine being. The other leads away from that universal potentiality and precipitates towards an exaggeration of our bondage to the ego. This is the point of distinction.

असत्यमप्रतिष्ठं ते जगदाहुरनीश्वरम् ।
अपरस्परसम्भूतं किमन्यत्कामहैतुकम् ॥८॥

8. "The world is without God", they say, "not true, not founded in truth, brought about by a mutual union, with Desire for its sole cause, a world of Chance."

एतां दृष्टिमवष्टभ्य नष्टात्मानोऽल्पबुद्धयः ।
प्रभवन्त्युग्रकर्माणः क्षयाय जगतोऽहिताः ॥९॥

9. Leaning on that way of seeing life, and by its falsehood ruining their souls and their reason, the Asuric men become the centre or instrument of a fierce, Titanic, violent action, a power of destruction in the world, a fount of injury and evil.

काममाश्रित्य दुष्पूरं दम्भमानमदान्विताः ।
मोहाद् गृहीत्वाऽसद्ग्राहान् प्रवर्तन्तेऽशुचिव्रताः ॥१०॥

10. Resorting to insatiable desire, arrogant, full of self-esteem and the drunkenness of their pride, these misguided souls delude themselves, persist in false and obstinate aims and pursue the fixed impure resolution of their longings.

चिन्तामपरिमेयां च प्रलयान्तामुपाश्रिताः ।
कामोपभोगपरमा एतावदिति निश्चिताः ॥११॥

11. They imagine that desire and enjoyment are all the aim of life and (in their inordinate and insatiable pursuit of it) they are the prey of a devouring, a measurelessly unceasing care and thought and endeavour and anxiety till the moment of their death.

आशापाशशतैर्बद्धाः कामक्रोधपरायणाः ।
ईहन्ते कामभोगार्थमन्यायेनार्थसञ्चयान् ॥१२॥
इदमद्य मया लब्धमिमं प्राप्स्ये मनोरथम् ।
इदमस्तीदमपि मे भविष्यति पुनर्धनम् ॥१३॥

असौ मया हतः शत्रुर्हनिष्ये चापरानपि ।
ईश्वरोऽहमहं भोगी सिद्धोऽहं बलवान् सुखी ॥१४॥
आढ्योऽभिजनवानस्मि कोऽन्योऽस्ति सदृशो मया ।
यक्ष्ये दास्यामि मोदिष्य इत्यज्ञानविमोहिताः ॥१५॥

12-15. Bound by a hundred bonds, devoured by wrath and lust, unweariedly occupied in amassing unjust gains which may serve their enjoyment and the satisfaction of their craving, always they think, "To-day I have gained this object of desire, to-morrow I shall have that other; to-day I have so much wealth, more I will get to-morrow. I have killed this my enemy, the rest too I will kill. I am a lord and king of men, I am perfect, accomplished, strong, happy, fortunate, a privileged enjoyer of the world; I am wealthy, I am of high birth; who is there like unto me? I will sacrifice, I will give, I will enjoy."

अनेकचित्तविभ्रान्ता मोहजालसमावृताः ।
प्रसक्ताः कामभोगेषु पतन्ति नरकेऽशुचौ ॥१६॥

16. Thus occupied by many egoistic ideas, deluded, addicted to the gratification of desire (doing works, but doing them wrongly, acting mightily, but for themselves, for desire, for enjoyment, not for God in themselves and God in man), they fall into the unclean hell of their own evil.

आत्मसम्भाविताः स्तब्धा धनमानमदान्विताः ।
यजन्ते नामयज्ञैस्ते दम्भेनाविधिपूर्वकम् ॥१७॥

17. They sacrifice and give not in the true order, but from a self-regarding ostentation, from vanity and with a stiff and foolish pride.

अहङ्कारं बलं दर्पं कामं क्रोधं च संश्रिताः ।
मामात्मपरदेहेषु प्रद्विषन्तोऽभ्यसूयकाः ॥१८॥

18. In the egoism of their strength and power, in the

violence of their wrath and arrogance they hate, despise and belittle the God hidden in themselves and the God in man.

तानहं द्विषतः क्रूरान् संसारेषु नराधमान् ।
क्षिपाम्यजस्रमशुभानासुरीष्वेव योनिषु ॥१९॥

19. These proud haters (of good and of God), evil, cruel, vilest among men in the world, I cast down continually into more and more Asuric births.

आसुरीं योनिमापन्ना मूढा जन्मनि जन्मनि ।
मामप्राप्यैव कौन्तेय ततो यान्त्यधमां गतिम् ॥२०॥

20. Cast into Asuric wombs, deluded birth after birth, they find Me not (as they do not seek Me) and sink down into the lowest status of soul-nature.[1]

[1] This graphic description, even giving its entire value to the distinction it implies, must not be pressed to carry more in it than it means. When it is said that there are two creations of beings in this material world, Deva and Asura,* it is not meant that human souls are so created by God from the beginning each with its own inevitable career in Nature, nor is it meant that there is a rigid spiritual predestination and those rejected from the beginning by the Divine are blinded by him so that they may be thrust down to eternal perdition and the impurity of Hell. All souls are eternal portions of the Divine; the Asura as well as the Deva, all can come to salvation: even the greatest sinner can turn to the Divine. But the evolution of the soul in Nature is an adventure of which Swabhava and the Karma governed by the Swabhava are ever the chief powers; and if an excess in the manifestation of the Swabhava, the self-becoming of the soul, a disorder in its play turns the law of being to the perverse side, if the rajasic qualities are given the upper hand, cultured to the diminution of sattwa, then the trend of Karma and its results necessarily culminate not in the sattwic height which is capable of the movement of liberation, but

(* The distinction between the two creations has its full truth in supraphysical planes where the law of spiritual evolution does not govern the movement. There are worlds of the Devas; worlds of the Asuras, and there are in these worlds behind us constant types of beings which support the complete divine play of creation indispensable to the march of the universe and cast their influence also on the earth and on the life and nature of man in this physical plane of existence.)

त्रिविधं नरकस्येदं द्वारं नाशनमात्मनः ।
कामः क्रोधस्तथा लोभस्तस्मादेतत्त्रयं त्यजेत् ॥२१॥

21. Threefold are the doors of Hell, destructive of the soul – desire, wrath and greed: therefore let man renounce these three.

एतैर्विमुक्तः कौन्तेय तमोद्वारैस्त्रिभिर्नरः ।
आचरत्यात्मनः श्रेयस्ततो याति परां गतिम् ॥२२॥

22. A man liberated from these doors of darkness, O son of Kunti, follows his own higher good and arrives at the highest soul-status.

यः शास्त्रविधिमुत्सृज्य वर्तते कामकारतः ।
न स सिद्धिमवाप्नोति न सुखं न परां गतिम् ॥२३॥

23. He who, having cast aside the rules of the Shastra, followeth the promptings of desire, attaineth not to perfection, nor happiness, nor the highest soul-status.

तस्माच्छास्त्रं प्रमाणं ते कार्याकार्यव्यवस्थितौ ।
ज्ञात्वा शास्त्रविधानोक्तं कर्म कर्तुमिहार्हसि ॥२४॥

---

in the highest exaggeration of the perversities of the lower nature. The man, if he does not stop short and abandon his way of error, has eventually the Asura full-born in him, and once he has taken that enormous turn away from the Light and Truth, he can no more reverse the fatal speed of his course because of the very immensity of the misused divine power in him until he has plumbed the depths of which it falls, found bottom and seen where the way has led him, the power exhausted and misspent, himself down in the lowest state of the soul nature, which is Hell. Only when he understands and turns to the Light, does that other truth of the Gita come in, that even the greatest sinner, the most impure and violent evil-doer is saved the moment he turns to adore and follow after the Godhead within him. Then, simply by that turn, he gets very soon into the sattwic way which leads to perfection and freedom.

24. Therefore let the Shastra[1] be thy authority in determining what ought to be done or what ought not to be done. Knowing what hath been declared by the rules of the Shastra, thou oughtest to work in this world.

इति श्रीमद्भगवद्गीतासूपनिषत्सु ब्रह्मविद्यायां योगशास्त्रे श्रीकृष्णार्जुनसंवादे
दैवासुरसंपद्विभागयोगो नाम षोडशोऽध्यायः ।

[1] To follow the law of desire is not the true rule of our nature; there is a higher and juster standard of its works. But where is it embodied or how is it to be found? In the first place, the human race has always been seeking for this just and high Law and whatever it has discovered is embodied in its Shastra, its rule of science and knowledge, rule of ethics, rule of religion, rule of best social living, rule of one's right relations with man and God and Nature. Shastra does not mean a mass of customs, some good, some bad, unintelligently followed by the customary routine mind of the tamasic man. Shastra is the knowledge and teaching laid down by intuition, experience and wisdom, the science and art and ethic of life, the best standards available to the race. The half-awakened man who leaves the observance of its rule to follow the guidance of his instincts and desires, can get pleasure but not happiness, for the inner happiness can only come by right living. He cannot move to perfection, cannot acquire the highest spiritual status. The law of instinct and desire seems to come first in the animal world, but the manhood of man grows by the pursuit of truth and religion and knowledge and a right life. The Shastra, the recognised Right that he has set up to govern his lower members by his reason and intelligent will, must therefore first be observed and made the authority for conduct and works and for what should or should not be done, till the instinctive desire nature is schooled and abated and put down by the habit of self-control and man is ready first for a freer intelligent self-guidance and then for the highest supreme law and supreme liberty of the spiritual nature.

All Shastra is built on a number of preparatory conditions, dharmas; it is a means, not an end. The supreme end is the freedom of the spirit when abandoning all dharmas the soul turns to God for its sole law of action, acts straight from the divine will and lives in the freedom of the divine nature, not in the Law, but in the Spirit. This is the development of the teaching which is prepared by the next question of Arjuna.

Seventeenth Chapter

THE GUNAS, FAITH AND WORKS

(The Gita has made a distinction between action according to the licence of personal desire and action done according to the Shastra. But we see also that there is a freer tendency in man other than the leading of his desires and other than his will to accept the Law, the fixed idea, the safe governing rule of the Shastra. The individual frequently enough, the community at any moment of its life is seen to turn away from the Shastra, becomes impatient of it, loses that form of its will and faith and goes in search of another law which it is now more disposed to accept as the right rule of living and regard as a more vital or higher truth of existence. The Shastra is something impersonal to the individual, and that gives it its authority over the narrow personal law of his members; but at the same time it is personal to the collectivity and is the outcome of its experience, its culture or its nature. It is not in all its form and spirit the ideal rule of fulfilment of the Self or the eternal law of the Master of our nature, although it may contain in itself in small or larger measure indications, preparations, illuminating glimpses of that far greater thing. And the individual may have gone beyond the collectivity and be ready for a greater truth, a wider walk, a deeper intention of the Life-Spirit.

But what then shall be the secure base of an action which departs both from the guidance of desire and from the normal law? For the rule of desire has an authority of its own, no longer safe or satisfactory to us as it is to the animal or as it might have been to a primitive humanity, but still, so far as it goes, founded on a very living part of our nature and fortified by its strong indications; and the law, the Shastra, has behind it all the authority of long-established rule, old successful sanctions and a secure past experience. But this new movement is of the nature of a powerful adventure into the unknown or partly known, a daring development and a new conquest, and what then is the clue to be followed, the guiding light on which it can depend or its strong basis in our being? The answer is that the clue and support is to be found in man's *śraddhā*, his faith, his will to believe, to live what he sees or thinks to be the truth of himself and of existence. In other words this movement is man's appeal to himself or to something potent and compelling in himself or in universal existence for the discovery of his truth, his law of living, his way to fulness and perfection. And everything depends on the nature of his faith, the thing in himself or in the universal soul – of which he is a portion or manifestation – to which he directs it and on how near he gets by it to his real self and the Self or true being of the universe. The Gita deals with this question on its own line of spiritual teaching and self-discipline. For Arjuna puts immediately a suggestive query from which the problem or one aspect of it arises.)

अर्जुन उवाच —
ये शास्त्रविधिमुत्सृज्य यजन्ते श्रद्धयान्विताः ।
तेषां निष्ठा तु का कृष्ण सत्त्वमाहो रजस्तमः ॥१॥

1. Arjuna said: When men sacrifice to God or the gods with faith, but abandon the rule of the Shastra, what is that concentrated will of devotion in them, *niṣṭhā*, which gives them this faith and moves them to this kind of action, O Krishna? Is it sattwa, rajas or tamas?

श्रीभगवान् उवाच —
त्रिविधा भवति श्रद्धा देहिनां सा स्वभावजा ।
सात्त्विकी राजसी चैव तामसी चेति तां शृणु ॥२॥

2. The Blessed Lord said: The faith in embodied beings is of a triple kind like all things in Nature and varies according to the dominating quality of their nature, sattwa, rajas or tamas. Hear thou of these.

SEVENTEENTH CHAPTER

सत्त्वानुरूपा सर्वस्य श्रद्धा भवति भारत ।
श्रद्धामयोऽयं पुरुषो यो यच्छ्रद्धः स एव सः ॥३॥

3. The faith of each man takes the shape given to it by his stuff of being, O Bharata. This Puruṣha,[1] this soul in man, is, as it were, made of shraddha, a faith, a will to be, a belief in itself and existence, and whatever is that will, faith or constituting belief in him, he is that and that is he.

यजन्ते सात्त्विका देवान् यक्षरक्षांसि राजसाः ।
प्रेतान् भूतगणांश्चान्ये यजन्ते तामसा जनाः ॥४॥

4. Sattwic men offer sacrifice to the gods, the rajasic to the Yakshas (the keepers of wealth) and the Rakshasic forces; the others, the tamasic, offer their sacrifice to elemental powers and grosser spirits.[2]

अशास्त्रविहितं घोरं तप्यन्ते ये तपो जनाः ।
दम्भाहङ्कारसंयुक्ताः कामरागबलान्विताः ॥५॥

[1] If we look into this pregnant saying a little closely, we shall find that this single line contains implied in its few forceful words almost the whole theory of the modern gospel of pragmatism. For if a man or the soul in a man consists of the faith which is in him, taken in this deeper sense, then it follows that the truth which he sees and wills to live is for him the truth of his being, the truth of himself that he has created or is creating and there can be for him no other real truth. This truth is a thing of his inner and outer action, a thing of his becoming, of the soul's dynamics, not of that in him which never changes. He is what he is today by some past will of his nature sustained and continued by a present will to know, to believe and to be in his intelligence and vital force, and whatever new turn is taken by this will and faith active in his very substance, that he will tend to become in the future. We create our own truth of existence in our own action of mind and life, which is another way of saying that we create our own selves, are our own makers. But very obviously this is only one aspect of the truth.

[2] The tamasic man does not offer his sacrifice to the gods, but to inferior elemental powers or to those grosser spirits behind the veil who feed upon his works and dominate his life with their darkness. The rajasic man offers his sacrifice to lower godheads or to perverse powers. The sattwic sacrifice is offered as a service to the gods.

कर्षयन्तः शरीरस्थं भूतग्राममचेतसः ।
मां चैवान्तःशरीरस्थं तान् विद्ध्यासुरनिश्चयान् ॥६॥

5-6. The men who perform violent austerities, contrary to the Shastra, with arrogance and egoism, impelled by the force of their desires and passions, men of unripe minds tormenting the aggregated elements forming the body and troubling Me also, seated in the body, know these to be Asuric in their resolves.[1]

आहारस्त्वपि सर्वस्य त्रिविधो भवति प्रियः ।
यज्ञस्तपस्तथा दानं तेषां भेदमिमं शृणु ॥७॥

7. The food[2] also which is dear to each is of triple character, as also sacrifice,[3] askesis and giving. Hear thou the distinction of these.

---

[1] Even if there is ostensibly a more inward and noble object and the faith and will are of a higher kind, yet if any kind of arrogance or pride or any great strength of violent self-will or desire enters into the askesis or if it drives some violent, lawless or terrible action contrary to the Shastra, opposed to the right rule of life and works and afflicting to oneself and to others, or if it is of the nature of self-torture and hurts the mental, vital and physical elements or violates the God within us who is seated in the inner subtle body, then too it is an unwise, an Asuric, a rajasic or rajaso-tamasic *tapasyā*.

[2] Everything here, including physical things, partakes of this triple character. Our food, for example, the Gita tells us, is either sattwic, rajasic or tamasic according to its character and effect on the body.

[3] All dynamic action may be reduced in its essential parts to these three elements. For all dynamic action, all kinesis of the nature involves a voluntary or an involuntary tapasya or askesis, an energism and concentration of our forces or capacities or of some capacity which helps us to achieve, to acquire or to become something, *tapas*. All action involves a giving of what we are or have, an expenditure which is the price of that achievement, acquisition or becoming, *dāna*. All action involves too a sacrifice to elemental or to universal powers or to the supreme Master of our works. The question is whether we do these things inconsciently, passively, or at best with an unintelligent ignorant half-conscient will, or with an unwisely or perversely conscient energism, or with a wisely

आयुःसत्त्वबलारोग्यसुखप्रीतिविवर्धनाः ।
रस्याः स्निग्धाः स्थिरा हृद्या आहाराः सात्त्विकप्रियाः ॥८॥

8. The sattwic temperament in the mental and physical body turns naturally to the things that increase the life, increase the inner and outer strength, nourish at once the mental, vital and physical force and increase the pleasure and satisfaction and happy condition of mind and life and body, all that is succulent and soft and firm and satisfying.

कट्वम्ललवणात्युष्णतीक्ष्णरूक्षविदाहिनः ।
आहारा राजसस्येष्टा दुःखशोकामयप्रदाः ॥९॥

9. The rajasic temperament prefers naturally food that is violently sour, pungent, hot, acrid, rough and strong and burning, the aliments that increase ill-health and the distempers of the mind and body.

यातयामं गतरसं पूति पर्युषितं च यत् ।
उच्छिष्टमपि चामेध्यं भोजनं तामसप्रियम् ॥१०॥

10. The tamasic temperament takes a perverse pleasure in cold, impure, stale, rotten or tasteless food or even accepts like the animals the remnants half-eaten by others.

अफलाकाङ्क्षिभिर्यज्ञो विधिदृष्टो य इज्यते ।
यष्टव्यमेवेति मनः समाधाय स सात्त्विकः ॥११॥

11. The sacrifice[1] which is offered by men without desire for the personal fruit, which is executed according to the right principle, and with a mind concentrated on the idea of the thing to be done as a sacrifice, that is sattwic.

---

conscient will rooted in knowledge, in other words, whether our sacrifice, giving and askesis are tamasic, rajasic or sattwic in nature.

[1] This sattwic sacrifice comes then very near to the ideal and leads directly towards the kind of action demanded by the Gita; but it is not the last and highest ideal, it is not yet the action of the perfected man who

अभिसन्धाय तु फलं दम्भार्थमपि चैव यत् ।
इज्यते भरतश्रेष्ठ तं यज्ञं विद्धि राजसम् ॥१२॥

12. The sacrifice offered with a view to the personal fruit, and also for ostentation, O best of the Bharatas, know thou that to be of a rajasic nature.

विधिहीनमसृष्टान्नं मन्त्रहीनमदक्षिणम् ।
श्रद्धाविरहितं यज्ञं तामसं परिचक्षते ॥१३॥

13. The sacrifice not performed according to the right

---

lives in the divine nature. For it is carried out as a fixed dharma, and it is offered as a sacrifice or service to the gods, to some partial power or aspect of the Divine manifested in ourselves or in the universe. Work done with a disinterested religious faith or selflessly for humanity or impersonally from devotion to the Right or the Truth is of this nature, and action of that kind is necessary for our perfection; for it purifies our thought and will and our natural substance. The culmination of the sattwic action at which we have to arrive is of a still larger and freer kind; it is the high last sacrifice offered by us to the supreme Divine in his integral being and with a seeking for the Purushottama or with the vision of Vasudeva in all that is, the action done impersonally, universally, for the good of the world, for the fulfilment of the divine will in the universe. That culmination leads to its own transcending, to the immortal Dharma. For then comes a freedom in which there is no personal action at all, no sattwic rule of dharma, no limitation of shastra; the inferior reason and will are themselves overpassed and it is not they but a higher wisdom that dictates and guides the work and commands its objective. There is no question of personal fruit; for the will that works is not our own but a supreme Will of which the soul is the instrument. There is no self-regarding and no selflessness; for the Jiva, the eternal portion of the Divine, is united with the highest Self of his existence and he and all are one in that Self and Spirit. There is no personal action, for all actions are given up to the Master of our works and it is he that does the action through the divinised Prakriti. There is no sacrifice, – unless we can say that the Master of sacrifice is offering the works of his energy in the Jiva to himself in his own cosmic form. This is the supreme self-surpassing state arrived at by the action that is sacrifice, this the perfection of the soul that has come to its full consciousness in the divine nature.

rule of the Shastra, without giving of food,[1] without the *mantra*, without gifts, empty of faith, is said to be tamasic.

देवद्विजगुरुप्राज्ञपूजनं शौचमार्जवम् ।
ब्रह्मचर्यमहिंसा च शारीरं तप उच्यते ॥१४॥

14. Worship given to the godhead, to the twice-born, to the spiritual guide, to the wise, cleanness, candid dealing, sexual purity and avoidance of killing and injury to others, are called the askesis of the body.

अनुद्वेगकरं वाक्यं सत्यं प्रियहितं च यत् ।
स्वाध्यायाभ्यसनं चैव वाङ्मयं तप उच्यते ॥१५॥

15. Speech causing no trouble to others, true, kind and beneficial, the study of Scripture, are called the askesis of speech.

मनःप्रसादः सौम्यत्वं मौनमात्मविनिग्रहः ।
भावसंशुद्धिरित्येतत्तपो मानसमुच्यते ॥१६॥

16. A clear and calm gladness of mind, gentleness, silence, self-control, the purifying of the whole temperament – this is called the askesis of the mind.

---

[1] There will be no giving of food in the sacrifice, – and that act in the Indian ritual is symbolic of the element of helpful giving inherent in every action that is real sacrifice, the indispensable giving to others, the fruitful help to others, to the world, without which our action becomes a wholly self-regarding thing and a violation of the true universal law of solidarity and interchange. The work will be done without the Dakshina, the much needed giving or self-giving to the leaders of the sacrificial action, whether to the outward guide and helper of our work or to the veiled or manifest godhead within us. It will be done without the mantra, without the dedicating thought which is the sacred body of our will and knowledge lifted upwards to the godheads we serve by our sacrifice.

The Gita now describes three kinds of sattwic askesis.

श्रद्धया परया तप्तं तपस्तत् त्रिविधं नरै: ।
अफलाकाङ्क्षिभिर्युक्तै: सात्त्विकं परिचक्षते ॥१७॥

17. This threefold askesis, done with a highest enlightened faith, with no desire for fruit, harmonised, is said to be sattwic.[1]

सत्कारमानपूजार्थं तपो दम्भेन चैव यत् ।
क्रियते तदिह प्रोक्तं राजसं चलमध्रुवम् ॥१८॥

18. The askesis which is undertaken to get honour and worship from men, for the sake of outward glory and greatness and for ostentation is said to be rajasic, unstable and fleeting.

---

[1] Here comes in all that quiets or disciplines the rajasic and egoistic nature and all that replaces it by the happy and tranquil principle of good and virtue. This is the askesis of the sattwic dharma so highly prized in the system of the ancient Indian culture. Its greater culmination will be a high purity of the reason and will, an equal soul, a deep peace and calm, a wide sympathy and preparation of oneness, a reflection of the inner soul's divine gladness in the mind, life and body. There at that lofty point the ethical is already passing away into the spiritual type and character. And this culmination too can be made to transcend itself, can be raised into a higher and freer light, can pass away into the settled godlike energy of the supreme nature. And what will remain then will be the spirit's immaculate Tapas, a highest will and luminous force in all the members, acting in a wide and solid calm and a deep and pure spiritual delight, Ananda. There will then be no farther need of askesis, no tapasya, because all is naturally and easily divine, all is that Tapas. There will be no separate labour of the lower energism, because the energy of Prakriti will have found its true source and base in the transcendent will of the Purushottama. Then, because of this high initiation, the acts of this energy on the lower planes also will proceed naturally and spontaneously from an innate perfect will and by an inherent perfect guidance. There will be no limitation by any of the present dharmas; for there will be a free action far above the rajasic and tamasic nature, but also far beyond the too careful and narrow limits of the sattwic rule of action.

As with tapasya, all giving also is of an ignorant tamasic, an ostentatious rajasic or a disinterested and enlightened sattwic character.

मूढग्राहेणात्मनो यत्पीडया क्रियते तपः ।
परस्योत्सादनार्थं वा तत्तामसमुदाहृतम् ॥१९॥

19. That askesis which is pursued under a clouded and deluded idea, performed with effort and suffering imposed on oneself or else with a concentration of the energy in a will to do hurt to others, that is said to be tamasic.

दातव्यमिति यद्दानं दीयतेऽनुपकारिणे ।
देशे काले च पात्रे च तद्दानं सात्त्विकं स्मृतम् ॥२०॥

20. The sattwic way[1] of giving is to do it for the sake of the giving and the beneficence and to one who does no benefit in return; and it is to bestow in the right conditions of time and place and on the right recipient (who is worthy or to whom the gift can be really helpful).

यत्तु प्रत्युपकारार्थं फलमुद्दिश्य वा पुनः ।
दीयते च परिक्लिष्टं तद्दानं राजसं स्मृतम् ॥२१॥

21. The rajasic kind of giving is that which is done with unwillingness or violence to oneself or with a personal and egoistic object or in the hope of a return of some kind.

[1] The culmination of the sattwic way of *dāna* will bring into the action an increasing element of that wide self-giving to others and to the world and to God, *ātma-dāna, ātma-samarpaṇa*, which is the high consecration of the sacrifice of works enjoined by the Gita. And the transcendence in the divine nature will be a greatest completeness of self-offering founded on the largest meaning of existence. All this manifold universe comes into birth and is constantly maintained by God's giving of himself and his powers and the lavish outflow of his self and spirit into all these existences; universal being, says the Veda, is the sacrifice of the Purusha. All the action of the perfected soul will be even such a constant divine giving of itself and its powers, an outflowing of the knowledge, light, strength, love, joy, helpful shakti which it possesses in the Divine and by his influence and effluence on all around it according to their capacity of reception or on all this world and its creatures. That will be the complete result of the complete self-giving of the soul to the Master of our existence.

अदेशकाले यद्दानमपात्रेभ्यश्च दीयते ।
असत्कृतमवज्ञातं तत्तामसमुदाहृतम् ॥२२॥

22. The tamasic gift is offered with no consideration of the right conditions of time, place and object; it is offered without regard for the feelings of the recipient and despised by him even in the acceptance.

ॐ तत्सदिति निर्देशो ब्रह्मणस्त्रिविधः स्मृतः ।
ब्राह्मणास्तेन वेदाश्च यज्ञाश्च विहिताः पुरा ॥२३॥

23. The formula OM,[1] Tat, Sat, is the triple definition of the Brahman, by whom the Brahmanas, the Vedas and sacrifices were created of old.

तस्मादोमित्युदाहृत्य यज्ञदानतपःक्रियाः ।
प्रवर्तन्ते विधानोक्ताः सततं ब्रह्मवादिनाम् ॥२४॥

24. Therefore with the pronunciation[2] of OM the acts of sacrifice, giving and askesis as laid down in the rules are always commenced by the knowers of the Brahman.

तदित्यनभिसंधाय फलं यज्ञतपःक्रियाः ।
दानक्रियाश्च विविधाः क्रियन्ते मोक्षकाङ्क्षिभिः ॥२५॥

25. With the pronunciation of Tat and without desire of fruit are performed the various acts of sacrifice, askesis and giving by the seekers of liberation.

[1] Tat, That, indicates the Absolute. Sat indicates the supreme and universal existence in its principle. OM is the symbol of the triple Brahman, the outward-looking, the inward or subtle and the superconscient causal Purusha. Each letter A, U, M indicates one of these three in ascending order and the syllable as a whole brings out the fourth state, Turiya, which rises to the Absolute.

[2] It is a reminder that our work should be made as expression of the triple Divine in our inner being and turned towards him in the idea and motive.

सद्भावे साधुभावे च सदित्येतत् प्रयुज्यते ।
प्रशस्ते कर्मणि तथा सच्छब्दः पार्थ युज्यते ॥२६॥

26. Sat means good and it means existence; likewise, O Partha, the word Sat is used in the sense of a good work (for all good works prepare the soul for the higher reality of our being).

यज्ञे तपसि दाने च स्थितिः सदिति चोच्यते ।
कर्म चैव तदर्थीयं सदित्येवाभिधीयते ॥२७॥

27. All firm abiding in sacrifice, giving and askesis and all works done with that central view, as sacrifice, as giving, as askesis, are Sat (for they build the basis for the highest truth of our spirit).

अश्रद्धया हुतं दत्तं तपस्तप्तं कृतं च यत् ।
असदित्युच्यते पार्थ न च तत् प्रेत्य नो इह ॥२८॥

28. Whatever is wrought without faith,[1] oblation, giving, askesis or other work, Asat it is called, O Partha; it is nought, here or hereafter.

इति श्रीमद्भगवद्गीतासूपनिषत्सु ब्रह्मविद्यायां योगशास्त्रे श्रीकृष्णार्जुनसंवादे
श्रद्धात्रयविभागयोगो नाम सप्तदशोऽध्यायः

---

[1] Because *śraddhā* is the central principle of our existence, any of these things done without *śraddhā* is a falsity and has no true meaning or true substance on earth or beyond, no reality, no power to endure or create in life here or after the mortal life in greater regions of our conscious spirit. The soul's faith, not a mere intellectual belief, but its concordant will to know, to see, to believe and to do and be according to its vision and knowledge, is that which determines by its power the measure of our possibilities of becoming, and it is this faith and will turned in all our inner and outer self, nature and action towards all that is highest, most divine, most real and eternal that will enable us to reach the supreme perfection.

Eighteenth Chapter

I. THE GUNAS, MIND AND WORKS

अर्जुन उवाच —
संन्याससय महाबाहो तत्त्वमिच्छामि वेदितुम् ।
त्यागस्य च हृषीकेश पृथक्केशिनिषूदन ॥१॥

1. Arjuna said: I desire, O mighty-armed, to know the principle of Sannyasa and the principle of Tyaga, O Hrishikesha, and their difference,[1] O Keshinisudana.

श्रीभगवान् उवाच —
काम्यानां कर्मणां न्यासं संन्यासं कवयो विदुः ।
सर्वकर्मफलत्यागं प्राहुस्त्यागं विचक्षणाः ॥२॥

2. The Blessed Lord said: Sages have known as Sannyasa[2] the physical depositing (or laying aside) of desirable actions; Tyaga is the name given by the wise to an entire abandon-

---

[1] The last question of Arjuna demands a clear distinction between the outer and inner renunciation, Sannyasa and Tyaga. The frequent harping, the reiterated emphasis of the Gita on this crucial distinction has been amply justified by the subsequent history of the later Indian mind, its constant confusion of these two very different things and its strong bent towards belittling any activity of the kind taught by the Gita as at best only a preliminary to the supreme inaction of Sannyasa. As a matter of fact, when people talk of Tyaga, of renunciation, it is always the physical renunciation of the world which they understand by the word or at least on which they lay emphasis, while the Gita takes absolutely the opposite view that the real Tyaga has action and living in the world as its basis and not a flight to the monastery, the cave or the hill-top. The real Tyaga is action with a renunciation of desire and that too is the real Sannyasa.

[2] Sannyasa in the standing terminology of the sages means the laying aside of desirable actions. In that sense Tyaga, not Sannyasa, is the better way. It is not the desirable actions that must be laid aside, but the desire which gives them that character has to be put away from us. The fruit of the action may come in the dispensation of the Master of works, but there is to be no egoistic demand for that as a reward and condition of doing

ment of all attached clinging to the fruit of works.

त्याज्यं दोषवदित्येके कर्म प्राहुर्मनीषिणः ।
यज्ञदानतपःकर्म न त्याज्यमिति चापरे ॥३॥

3. "All action should be relinquished as an evil", declare some learned men; "acts of sacrifice, giving and askesis ought not to be renounced", say others.

निश्चयं शृणु मे तत्र त्यागे भरतसत्तम ।
त्यागो हि पुरुषव्याघ्र त्रिविधः सम्प्रकीर्तितः ॥४॥

4. Hear my conclusions as to renunciation (Tyaga), O best of the Bharatas; since renunciation of works, O tiger of men, has been explained as threefold.

यज्ञदानतपःकर्म न त्याज्यं कार्यमेव तत् ।
यज्ञो दानं तपश्चैव पावनानि मनीषिणाम् ॥५॥

5. Acts of sacrifice, giving and askesis ought not to be renounced at all, but should be performed, for they purify the wise.

एतान्यपि तु कर्माणि सङ्गं त्यक्त्वा फलानि च ।
कर्तव्यानीति मे पार्थ निश्चितं मतमुत्तमम् ॥६॥

---

works. Or the fruit may not at all come and still the work has to be performed as the thing to be done, *kartavyaṁ karma*, the thing which the Master within demands of us. The success, the failure are in his hands and he will regulate them according to his omniscient will and inscrutable purpose. Action, all action has indeed to be given up in the end, not physically by abstention, by immobility, by inertia, but spiritually to the Master of our being by whose power alone can any action be accomplished. There has to be a renunciation of the false idea of ourselves as the doer; for in reality it is the universal Shakti that works through our personality and our ego. The spiritual transference of all our works to the Master and his Shakti is the real Sannyasa in the teaching of the Gita.

6. Even these actions[1] certainly ought to be done, O Partha, leaving aside attachment and fruit.

नियतस्य तु संन्यासः कर्मणो नोपपद्यते ।
मोहात्तस्य परित्यागस्तामसः परिकीर्तितः ॥७॥

7. Verily, renunciation of rightly regulated actions is not proper, to renounce them from ignorance is a tamasic renunciation.

दुःखमित्येव यत्कर्म कायक्लेशभयात्त्यजेत् ।
स कृत्वा राजसं त्यागं नैव त्यागफलं लभेत् ॥८॥

8. He who gives up works because they bring sorrow or

---

[1] Some would have it that all works must be excised from our life, as if that were possible. But it is not possible so long as we are in the body and alive; nor can salvation consist in reducing our active selves by trance to the lifeless immobility of the clod and the pebble. The silence of Samadhi does not abrogate the difficulty, for as soon as the breath comes again into the body, we are once more in action and have toppled down from the heights of this salvation by spiritual slumber. But the true salvation, the release by an inner renunciation of the ego and union with the Purushottama remains steady in whatever state, persists in this world or out of it or in whatever world or out of all world, is self-existent, *sarvathā vartamano'pi*, and does not depend upon inaction or action. What then are the actions to be done? The thoroughgoing ascetic answer, not noted by the Gita – it was perhaps not altogether current at the time – might be that solely begging, eating and meditation are to be permitted among voluntary activities and otherwise only the necessary actions of the body. But the more liberal and comprehensive solution was evidently to continue the three most sattwic activities, sacrifice, giving and askesis. And these certainly are to be done, says the Gita, for they purify the wise. But more generally, and understanding these three things in their widest sense, it is the rightly regulated action, *niyataṁ karma*, that has to be done, action regulated by the Shastra, the science and art of right knowledge, right works, right living, or regulated by the essential nature, *svabhāvaniyataṁ karma*, or, finally and best of all, regulated by the will of the Divine within and above us. The last is the true and only action of the liberated man, *muktasya karma*.

are a trouble to the flesh, thus doing rajasic renunciation, obtaineth not the fruit of renunciation.

कार्यमित्येव यत् कर्म नियतं क्रियतेऽर्जुन ।
सङ्गं त्यक्त्वा फलं चैव स त्यागः सात्त्विको मतः ॥९॥

9. He who performs a rightly regulated action, because it has to be done, without any attachment either to the action or to the fruit of the action, that renunciation is regarded as sattwic.[1]

न द्वेष्ट्यकुशलं कर्म कुशले नानुषज्जते ।
त्यागी सत्त्वसमाविष्टो मेधावी छिन्नसंशयः ॥१०॥

10. The wise man with doubts cast away, who renounces in the light of the full sattwic mind, has no aversion to unpleasant action, no attachment to pleasant action.

न हि देहभृता शक्यं त्यक्तुं कर्माण्यशेषतः ।
यस्तु कर्मफलत्यागी स त्यागीत्यभिधीयते ॥११॥

---

[1] The sattwic principle of renunciation is to withdraw not from action, but from the personal demand, the ego factor behind it. It is to do works not dictated by desire but by the law of right living or by the essential nature, its knowledge, its ideal, its faith in itself and the Truth it sees, its *śraddhā*. Or else, on a higher spiritual plane, they are dictated by the will of the Master and done with the mind in Yoga, without any personal attachment either to the action or to the fruit of the action. There must be a complete renunciation of all desire and of all self-regarding egoistic choice and impulse and finally of that much subtler egoism of the will which either says, "The work is mine, I am the doer", or even "The work is God's but I am the doer". There must be no attachment to pleasant, desirable, lucrative or successful work and no doing of it because it has that nature; but that kind of work too has to be done, – done totally, selflessly, with the assent of the spirit, – when it is the action demanded from above and from within us, *kartavyaṁ karma*. There must be no aversion to unpleasant, undesirable or ungratifying action or work that brings or is likely to bring with it suffering, danger, harsh conditions, inauspicious consequences; for that too has to be accepted, totally, selflessly, with a deep understanding of its need and meaning, when it is the work that should be done, *kartavyaṁ karma*.

11. Nor indeed can embodied beings renounce all works; verily he who gives up the fruit of action, he is said to be a renouncer.[1]

अनिष्टमिष्टं मिश्रं च त्रिविधं कर्मणः फलम् ।
भवत्यत्यागिनां प्रेत्य न तु संन्यासिनां क्वचित् ॥१२॥

12. The three kinds of result, pleasant, unpleasant and mixed, in this or other worlds, in this or another life are for the slaves of desire and ego; these things do not cling to the free spirit.

पञ्चैतानि महाबाहो कारणानि निबोध मे ।
सांख्ये कृतान्ते प्रोक्तानि सिद्धये सर्वकर्मणाम् ॥१३॥

13. These five causes, O mighty-armed, learn of Me as laid down by the Sankhya for the accomplishment of all works.

अधिष्ठानं तथा कर्ता करणं च पृथग्विधम् ।
विविधाश्च पृथक्चेष्टा दैवं चैवात्र पञ्चमम् ॥१४॥

14. These five are the body,[2] the doer, the various instruments, the many kinds of efforts, and last, the Fate.[3]

---

[1] The liberated worker who has given up his works by the inner sannyasa to a greater Power is free from Karma. Action he will do, for some kind of action, less or more, small or great, is inevitable, natural, right for the embodied soul, – action is part of the divine law of living, it is the high dynamics of the Spirit. The essence of renunciation, the true Tyaga, the true Sannyasa is not any rule of thumb of inaction but a disinterested soul, a selfless mind, the transition from ego to the free impersonal and spiritual nature. The spirit of this inner renunciation is the first mental condition of the highest culminating sattwic discipline.

[2] The frame of body, life and mind is the basis or standing-ground of the soul in nature, *adhiṣṭhāna*.

[3] Fate, *daivam*, that is to say, the influence of the Power or powers other than the human factors, other than the visible mechanism of Nature, that stand behind these and modify the work and dispose its fruits in the steps of act and consequence.

शरीरवाङ्मनोभिर्यत्कर्म प्रारभते नरः ।
न्याय्यं वा विपरीतं वा पञ्चैते तस्य हेतवः ॥१५॥

15. These five elements make up among them all the efficient causes, *kāraṇa*, that determine the shaping and outcome of whatever work man undertakes with mind and speech and body.

तत्रैवं सति कर्तारमात्मानं केवलं तु यः ।
पश्यत्यकृतबुद्धित्वान्न स पश्यति दुर्मतिः ॥१६॥

16. That being so, he verily who, owing to ignorant understanding, looketh on the pure Self as the doer, he, of perverted intelligence, seeth not.

यस्य नाहङ्कृतो भावो बुद्धिर्यस्य न लिप्यते ।
हत्वापि स इमांल्लोकान्न हन्ति न निबध्यते ॥१७॥

17. He who is free from the ego-sense,[1] whose intelligence is not affected, though he slay these peoples, he slayeth not, nor is bound.

[1] The doer is ordinarily supposed to be our surface personal ego, but that is the false idea of the understanding that has not arrived at knowledge. The ego is the ostensible doer, but the ego and its will are creations and instruments of Nature with which the ignorant understanding wrongly identifies our self and they are not the only determinants even of human action, much less of its turn and consequence. When we are liberated from ego, our real self behind comes forward, impersonal and universal, and it sees in its self-vision of unity with the universal Spirit universal Nature as the doer of the work and the Divine Will behind as the master of universal Nature. Only so long as we have not this knowledge, are we bound by the character of the ego and its will as the doer and do good and evil and have the satisfaction of our tamasic, rajasic or sattwic nature. But once we live in this greater knowledge, the character and consequences of the work can make no difference to the freedom of the spirit. The work may be outwardly a terrible action like this great battle and slaughter of Kurukshetra; but although the liberated man takes his part in the struggle and though he slay all these peoples, he slays no man and he is not bound by his work, because the work is that of the Master of

ज्ञानं ज्ञेयं परिज्ञाता त्रिविधा कर्मचोदना ।
करणं कर्म कर्तेति त्रिविधः कर्मसंग्रहः ॥१८॥

18. Knowledge, the object of knowledge and the knower, these three things constitute the mental impulsion to work; there are again three things, the doer, the instrument and the work done, that hold the action together and make it possible.

ज्ञानं कर्म च कर्ता च त्रिधैव गुणभेदतः ।
प्रोच्यते गुणसंख्याने यथावच्छृणु तान्यपि ॥१९॥

19. Knowledge, work and doer are of three kinds, says the Sankhya, according to the difference in the Gunas (qualities); hear thou duly these also.

---

the Worlds and it is he who has already slain in his hidden omnipotent will all these armies. This work of destruction was needed that humanity might move forward to another creation and a new purpose, might get rid as in a fire of its past Karma of unrighteousness and oppression and injustice and move towards a kingdom of the Dharma. The liberated man does his appointed work as the living instrument one in spirit with the universal spirit. And knowing that all this must be and looking beyond the outward appearance he acts not for self but for God and man and the human and cosmic order,* not in fact himself acting, but conscious of the presence and power of the divine force in his deeds and their issue. He knows that the supreme Shakti is doing in his mental, vital and physical body, *adhiṣṭhāna*, as the sole doer the thing appointed by a Fate which is in truth not Fate, not a mechanical dispensation, but the wise and all-seeing Will that is at work behind human Karma. This 'terrible work' on which the whole teaching of the Gita turns, is an extreme example of action inauspicious in appearance, *akuśalam*, though a great good lies beyond the appearance. Impersonally has it to be done by the divinely appointed man for the holding together of the world purpose, *loka-saṁgrahārtham*, without personal aim or desire, because it is the appointed service. It is clear then that the work is not the sole thing that matters; the knowledge in which we do works makes an immense spiritual difference.

(* The cosmic order comes into question, because the triumph of the Asura in humanity means to that extent the triumph of the Asura in the balance of the world-forces.)

EIGHTEENTH CHAPTER

सर्वभूतेषु येनैकं भावमव्ययमीक्षते ।
अविभक्तं विभक्तेषु तज्ज्ञानं विद्धि सात्त्विकम् ॥२०॥

20. That by which one imperishable being is seen in all becoming, one indivisible whole in all these divisions, know thou that knowledge as sattwic.

पृथक्त्वेन तु यज्ज्ञानं नानाभावान् पृथग्विधान् ।
वेत्ति सर्वेषु भूतेषु तज्ज्ञानं विद्धि राजसम् ॥२१॥

21. But that knowledge which sees the multiplicity of things only in their separateness and variety of operation in all these existences, that knowledge know thou as rajasic.

यत्तु कृत्स्नवदेकस्मिन् कार्ये सक्तमहैतुकम् ।
अतत्त्वार्थवदल्पं च तत्तामसमुदाहृतम् ॥२२॥

22. The tamasic[1] knowledge is a small and narrow way of

---

[1] The tamasic mind does not look for real cause and effect, but absorbs itself in one movement or one routine with an obstinate attachment to it, can see nothing but the little section of personal activity before its eyes and does not know in fact what it is doing but blindly lets natural impulsion work out through its deed results of which it has no conception, foresight or comprehending intelligence. The rajasic knowledge is unable to discover a true principle of unity or rightly co-ordinate its will and action, but follows the bent of ego and desire, the activity of its many-branching egoistic will and various and mixed motive in response to the solicitation of internal and environing impulsions and forces. This knowing is a jumble of sections of knowledge, often inconsistent knowledge, put forcefully together by the mind in order to make some kind of pathway through the confusion of our half-knowledge and half-ignorance. Or else it is a restless kinetic multiple action with no firm governing higher ideal and self-possessed law of true light and power within it. The sattwic knowledge, on the contrary, sees existence as one indivisible whole in all these divisions, one imperishable being in all becomings; it masters the principle of its action and the relation of the particular action to the total purpose of existence; it puts in the right place each step of the complete process. At the highest top of knowledge this seeing becomes the knowledge of the one spirit in the world, one in all these many existences,

looking at things which has no eye for the real nature of the world; it clings to one movement or one routine as if it were the whole (without foresight or comprehending intelligence).

नियतं सङ्गरहितमरागद्वेषतः कृतम् ।
अफलप्रेप्सुना कर्म यत्तत्सात्त्विकमुच्यते ॥२३॥

23. An action which is rightly regulated, performed without attachment, without liking or disliking (for its spur or its drag), done by one undesirous of fruit, that is called sattwic.[1]

यत्तु कामेप्सुना कर्म साहङ्कारेण वा पुनः ।
क्रियते बहुलायासं तद्राजसमुदाहृतम् ॥२४॥

24. But that action which a man undertakes under the dominion of desire, or with an egoistic sense of his own personality in the action, and which is done with inordinate effort (with a great heaving and straining of the personal will to get at the object of desire), that is declared to be rajasic.

अनुबन्धं क्षयं हिंसामनवेक्ष्य च पौरुषम् ।
मोहादारभ्यते कर्म यत्तत्तामसमुच्यते ॥२५॥

---

of the one Master of all works, of the forces of cosmos as expressions of the Godhead and of the work itself as the operation of his supreme will and wisdom in man and his life and essential nature.

[1] Sattwic action is that which a man does calmly in the clear light of reason and knowledge and with an impersonal sense of right or duty or the demand of an ideal, as the thing that ought to be done whatever may be the result to himself in this world or another. At the line of culmination of sattwa it will be transformed and become a highest impersonal action dictated by the spirit within us and no longer by the intelligence, an action moved by the highest law of the nature, free from the lower ego and its light or heavy baggage and from limitation even by best opinion, noblest desire, purest personal will or loftiest mental ideal. There will be none of these impedimenta; in their place there will stand a clear spiritual self-knowledge and illumination and an imperative intimate sense of an infallible power that acts and of the work to be done for the world and for the world's Master.

25. The action undertaken from delusion (in mechanical obedience to the instincts, impulsions and unseeing ideas), without regarding the strength or capacity, without regarding the consequences, the waste of effort or injury to others, that is declared to be tamasic.

मुक्तसङ्गोऽनहंवादी धृत्युत्साहसमन्वितः ।
सिद्ध्यसिद्ध्योर्निर्विकारः कर्ता सात्त्विक उच्यते ॥२६॥

26. Free from attachment, free from egoism, full of a fixed (impersonal) resolution and a calm rectitude of zeal, unelated by success, undepressed by failure, that doer is called sattwic.[1]

रागी कर्मफलप्रेप्सुर्लुब्धो हिंसात्मकोऽशुचिः ।
हर्षशोकान्वितः कर्ता राजसः परिकीर्तितः ॥२७॥

27. Eagerly attached to the work, passionately desirous of fruit, greedy, impure, often violent and cruel and brutal in the means he uses, full of joy (in success) and grief (in failure) such a doer is known as rajasic.

अयुक्तः प्राकृतः स्तब्धः शठो नैष्कृतिकोऽलसः ।
विषादी दीर्घसूत्री च कर्ता तामस उच्यते ॥२८॥

28. One who acts with a mechanical mind (who does not put himself really into the work), is stupid, obstinate, cunning, insolent, lazy, easily depressed, procrastinating, that doer is called tamasic.

---

[1] The sattwic doer is full of a high and pure and selfless enthusiasm in the work that has to be done. At and beyond the culmination of sattwa this resolution, zeal, enthusiasm become the spontaneous working of the spiritual Tapas and at last a highest soul-force, the direct God-power, the mighty and steadfast movement of a divine energy in the human instrument, the self-assured steps of the seer-will, the gnostic intelligence and with it the wide delight of the free spirit in the works of the liberated nature.

बुद्धेर्भेदं धृतेश्चैव गुणतस्त्रिविधं शृणु ।
प्रोच्यमानमशेषेण पृथक्त्वेन धनञ्जय ॥२९॥

29. Reason[1] as also persistence are of three kinds according to the qualities; hear them related, unreservedly and severally, O Dhananjaya.

प्रवृत्तिं च निवृत्तिं च कार्याकार्ये भयाभये ।
बन्धं मोक्षं च या वेत्ति बुद्धिः सा पार्थ सात्त्विकी ॥३०॥

30. That which sees the law of action and the law of abstention from action, the thing that is to be done and the thing that is not to be done, what is to be feared and what is not to be feared, what binds the spirit of man and what sets it free, that understanding[2] is sattwic, O Partha.

[1] The reason armed with the intelligent will works in man in whatever manner or measure he may possess these human gifts and it is accordingly right or perverted, clouded or luminous, narrow and small or large and wide like the mind of its possessor. It is the understanding power of his nature, *buddhi*, that chooses the work for him or, more often, approves and sets its sanction on one or other among the many suggestions of his complex instincts, impulsions, ideas and desires. It is that which determines for him what is right or wrong, to be done or not to be done, Dharma or Adharma. And the persistence of the will is that continuous force of mental Nature which sustains the work and gives it consistence and persistence. Here again there is the incidence of the gunas.

[2] The culmination of the sattwic intelligence is found by a high persistence of the aspiring buddhi when it is settled on what is beyond the ordinary reason and mental will, pointed to the summits, turned to a steady control of the senses and the life and a union by Yoga with man's highest Self, the universal Divine, the transcendent Spirit. It is there that arriving through the sattwic guna one can pass beyond the gunas, can climb beyond the limitations of the mind and its will and intelligence and sattwa itself disappear into that which is above the gunas and beyond this instrumental nature. There the soul is enshrined in light and enthroned in firm union with the Self and Spirit and Godhead. Arrived upon that summit we can leave the Highest to guide Nature in our members in the free spontaneity of a divine action: for there there is no wrong or confused working, no element of error or impotence to obscure or distort the

यया धर्ममधर्मं च कार्यं चाकार्यमेव च ।
अयथावत्प्रजानाति बुद्धिः सा पार्थ राजसी ॥३१॥

31. That by which one knows awry right and wrong and also what should or should not be done, that understanding, O Partha, is rajasic.

अधर्मं धर्ममिति या मन्यते तमसावृता ।
सर्वार्थान् विपरीतांश्च बुद्धिः सा पार्थ तामसी ॥३२॥

32. That which, enveloped in darkness, takes what is not the true law and upholds it as the law and sees all things in a cloud of misconceptions, that understanding, O Partha, is tamasic.

धृत्या यया धारयते मनःप्राणेन्द्रियक्रियाः ।
योगेनाव्यभिचारिण्या धृतिः सा पार्थ सात्त्विकी ॥३३॥

33. That unwavering persistence by which, through Yoga, one controls the mind, the senses and the life, that persistence, O Partha, is sattwic.

यया तु धर्मकामार्थान् धृत्या धारयतेऽर्जुन ।
प्रसङ्गेन फलाकाङ्क्षी धृतिः सा पार्थ राजसी ॥३४॥

34. But that, O Arjuna, by which one holdeth fast right and justice (Dharma), interest (Artha) and pleasure (Kama), and with great attachment desires for the fruits, that persistence, O Partha, is rajasic.[1]

---

luminous perfection and power of the Spirit. All these lower conditions, laws, dharmas cease to have any hold on us; the Infinite acts in the liberated man and there is no law but the immortal truth and right of the free spirit, no Karma, no kind of bondage.

[1] The rajasic will fixes its persistent attention on the satisfaction of its own attached clingings and desires in its pursuit of interest and pleasure and of what it thinks or chooses to think right and justice, Dharma. Always it is apt to put on these things the construction which will most flatter and justify its desires and to uphold as right or legitimate the means

यया स्वप्नं भयं शोकं विषादं मदमेव च ।
न विमुञ्चति दुर्मेधा धृतिः सा पार्थ तामसी ॥३५॥

35. That by which one from ignorance doth not abandon sleep, fear, grief, depression, and also pride, that persistence, O Partha, is tamasic.

सुखं त्विदानीं त्रिविधं शृणु मे भरतर्षभ ।
अभ्यासाद्रमते यत्र दुःखान्तं च निगच्छति ॥३६॥
यत्तदग्रे विषमिव परिणामेऽमृतोपमम् ।
तत्सुखं सात्त्विकं प्रोक्तमात्मबुद्धिप्रसादजम् ॥३७॥

36-37. And now the threefold kinds of pleasure hear thou from Me, O bull of the Bharatas. That in which one by self-discipline rejoiceth and which putteth an end to pain; which at first is as poison but in the end is as nectar; that pleasure is said to be sattwic, born of the satisfaction of the higher mind and spirit.

विषयेन्द्रियसंयोगाद्यत्तदग्रेऽमृतोपमम् ।
परिणामे विषमिव तत्सुखं राजसं स्मृतम् ॥३८॥

38. That which is born from the contact of the senses with their objects, which at first is as nectar, but in the end is like poison, that pleasure is accounted rajasic.

यदग्रे चानुबन्धे च सुखं मोहनमात्मनः ।
निद्रालस्यप्रमादोत्थं तत्तामसमुदाहृतम् ॥३९॥

39. That pleasure of which delusion is the beginning and

---

which will best help it to get the coveted fruits of its work and endeavour. That is the cause of three-fourths of the falsehood and misconduct of the human reason and will. Rajas with its vehement hold on the vital ego is the great sinner and positive misleader.

delusion is the consequence, which arises from sleep, indolence and ignorance, that is declared tamasic.¹

¹ Happiness is indeed the one thing which is openly or indirectly the universal pursuit of our human nature, – happiness or its suggestion or some counterfeit of it, some pleasure, some enjoyment, some satisfaction of the mind, the will, the passions or the body. Pain is an experience our nature has to accept when it must, involuntarily as a necessity, an unavoidable incident of universal Nature, or voluntarily as a means to what we seek after, but not a thing desired for its own sake, – except when it is so sought in perversity or with an ardour of enthusiasm in suffering for some touch of fierce pleasure it brings or the intense strength it engenders. But there are various kinds of happiness or pleasure according to the guna which dominates in our nature. Thus the tamasic mind can remain well-pleased in its indolence and inertia, its stupor and sleep, its blindness and its error. The mind of the rajasic man drinks of a more fiery and intoxicating cup; the keen, mobile, active pleasure of the senses and the body and the sense-entangled or fiery kinetic will and intelligence are to him all the joy of life and the very siginificance of living. What the sattwic nature seeks is the satisfaction of the higher mind and the spirit and when it once gets this large object of its quest, there comes in a clear, pure happiness of the soul, a state of fullness, an abiding ease and peace. This happiness does not depend on outward things, but on ourselves alone and on the flowering of what is best and most inward within us. But it is not at first our normal possession; it has to be conquered by self-discipline, a labour of the soul, a high and arduous endeavour. At first this means much loss of habitual pleasure, much suffering and struggle, a poison born of the churning of our nature, a painful conflict of forces, much revolt and opposition to the change due to the ill-will of the members or the insistence of vital movements, but in the end the nectar of immortality rises in the place of this bitterness and as we climb to the higher spiritual nature we come to the end of sorrow, the euthanasia of grief and pain. That is the surpassing happiness which descends upon us at the point or line of culmination of the sattwic discipline.

The self-exceeding of the sattwic nature comes when we get beyond the great but still inferior sattwic pleasure, beyond the pleasures of mental knowledge and virtue and peace to the eternal calm of the self and the spiritual ecstasy of the divine oneness. That spiritual joy is no longer the sattwic happiness, *sukham*, but the absolute Ananda. Ananda is the secret delight from which all things are born, by which all is sustained in existence and to which all can rise in the spiritual culmination. Only then can it be possessed when the liberated man, free from ego and its desires, lives at last one with his highest self, one with all beings and one with God in an absolute bliss of the spirit.

II. SWABHAVA AND SWADHARMA

न तदस्ति पृथिव्यां वा दिवि देवेषु वा पुनः ।
सत्त्वं प्रकृतिजैर्मुक्तं यदेभिः स्यात् त्रिभिर्गुणैः ॥४०॥

40. There is not an entity, either on the earth or again in heaven among the gods, that is not subject to the workings of these three qualities (Gunas), born of nature.

ब्राह्मणक्षत्रियविशां शूद्राणां च परन्तप ।
कर्माणि प्रविभक्तानि स्वभावप्रभवैर्गुणैः ॥४१॥

41. The works of Brahmins, Kshatriyas, Vaishyas and Shudras are divided according to the qualities (Gunas) born of their own inner nature.

शमो दमस्तपः शौचं क्षान्तिरार्जवमेव च ।
ज्ञानं विज्ञानमास्तिक्यं ब्रह्मकर्म स्वभावजम् ॥४२॥

42. Calm, self-control, askesis, purity, long-suffering, candour, knowledge, acceptance of spiritual truth are the work of the Brahmin, born of his *svabhāva*.

शौर्यं तेजो धृतिर्दाक्ष्यं युद्धे चाप्यपलायनम् ।
दानमीश्वरभावश्च क्षात्रं कर्म स्वभावजम् ॥४३॥

43. Heroism, high spirit, resolution, ability, not fleeing in the battle, giving, lordship (*īśvara-bhāva*, the temperament of the ruler and leader) are the natural work of the Kshatriya.

कृषिगोरक्ष्यवाणिज्यं वैश्यकर्म स्वभावजम् ।
परिचर्यात्मकं कर्म शूद्रस्यापि स्वभावजम् ॥४४॥

44. Agriculture, cattle-keeping, trade inclusive of the labour of the craftsman and the artisan are the natural work

of the Vaishya. All work of the character of service falls within the natural function of the Shudra.¹

स्वे स्वे कर्मण्यभिरतः संसिद्धिं लभते नरः ।
स्वकर्मनिरतः सिद्धिं यथा विन्दति तच्छृणु ॥४५॥

45. A man who is intent on his own natural work attains perfection. Listen thou how perfection is won by him who is intent on his own natural work.

¹ These verses and the earlier pronouncements of the Gita on the same subject have been seized upon in current controversies on the caste question and interpreted by some as a sanction of the present system, used by others as a denial of the hereditary basis of caste. In point of fact the verses in the Gita have no bearing on the existing caste system, because that is a very different thing from the ancient social ideal of *cāturvarṇya*, the four clear-cut orders of the Aryan community, and in no way corresponds with the description of the Gita. Agriculture, cattle-keeping and trade of every kind are said here to be the work of the Vaishya; but in the later system the majority of those concerned in trade and in cattle-keeping, artisans, small craftsmen and others are actually classed as Shudras – where they are not put altogether outside the pale, – and, with some exceptions, the merchant class is alone and that too not everywhere ranked as Vaishya. Agriculture, government and service are the professions of all classes from the Brahmin down to the Shudra. And if the economical divisions of function have been confounded beyond any possibility of rectification, the law of the Guna or quality is still less a part of the later system. There all is rigid custom, *ācāra*, with no reference to the need of the individual nature. If again we take the religious side of the contention advanced by the advocates of the caste system, we can certainly fasten no such absurd idea on the words of the Gita as that it is a law of a man's nature that he shall follow without regard to his personal bent and capacities the profession of his parents or his immediate or distant ancestors, the son of a milkman be a milkman, the son of a doctor a doctor, the descendants of shoemakers remain shoemakers to the end of measurable time, still less that by doing so, by this unintelligent and mechanical repetition of the law of another's nature without regard to his own individual call and qualities a man automatically farthers his own perfection and arrives at spiritual freedom. The Gita's words refer to the ancient system of *cāturvarṇya*, as it existed or was supposed to exist in its ideal purity, – there is some controversy whether it was ever anything more than an ideal or general norm more or less loosely followed in practice, – and it should be considered in that connection alone.

यतः प्रवृत्तिर्भूतानां येन सर्वमिदं ततम् ।
स्वकर्मणा तमभ्यर्च्य सिद्धिं विन्दति मानवः ॥४६॥

46. He[1] from whom all beings originate, by whom all this

[1] The Gita's philosophy of life and works is that all proceeds from the Divine Existence, the transcendent and universal Spirit. All is a veiled manifestation of the Godhead, Vasudeva, *yataḥ pravṛttir bhūtānāṁ yena sarvam idaṁ tatam,* and to unveil the Immortal within and in the world, to dwell in unity with the Soul of the universe, to rise in consciousness, knowledge, will, love, spiritual delight to oneness with the supreme Godhead, to live in the highest spiritual nature with the individual and natural being delivered from shortcoming and ignorance and made a conscious instrument for the works of the divine Shakti is the perfection of which humanity is capable and the condition of immortality and freedom. But how is this possible when in fact we are enveloped in natural ignorance, the soul shut up in the prison of ego, overcome, beset, hammered and moulded by the environment, mastered by the mechanism of Nature, cut off from our hold on the reality of our own secret spiritual force? The answer is that all this natural action, however now enveloped in a veiled and contrary working, still contains the principle of its own evolving freedom and perfection. A Godhead is seated in the heart of every man and is the Lord of this mysterious action of Nature. And though this Spirit of the universe, this One who is all, seems to be turning us on the wheel of the world as if mounted on a machine by the force of Maya, shaping us in our ignorance as the potter shapes a pot, as the weaver a fabric, by some skilful mechanical principle, yet is this spirit our own greatest self and it is according to the real idea, the truth of ourselves, that which is growing in us and finding always new and more adequate forms in birth after birth, in our animal and human and divine life, in that which we were, that which we are, that which we shall be, – it is in accordance with this inner soul-truth that, as our opened eyes will discover, we are progressively shaped by this spirit within us in its all-wise omnipotence. This machinery of ego, this tangled complexity of the three gunas, mind, body, life, emotion, desire, struggle, thought, aspiration, endeavour, this locked interaction of pain and pleasure, sin and virtue, striving and success and failure, soul and environment, myself and others, is only the outward imperfect form taken by a higher spiritual Force in me which pursues through its vicissitudes the progressive self-expression of the divine reality and greatness I am secretly in spirit and shall overtly become in nature. This action contains in itself the principle of its own success, the principle of the Swabhava and Swadharma.

universe is pervaded, by worshipping Him by his own work, a man reacheth perfection.

श्रेयान् स्वधर्मो विगुणः परधर्मात् स्वनुष्ठितात् ।
स्वभावनियतं कर्म कुर्वन्नाप्नोति किल्बिषम् ॥४७॥

47. Better is one's own law of works, though in itself faulty, than an alien law well wrought out. One does not incur sin when one acts in agreement with the law of one's own nature.[1]

सहजं कर्म कौन्तेय सदोषमपि न त्यजेत् ।
सर्वारम्भा हि दोषेण धूमेनाग्निरिवावृताः ॥४८॥

---

[1] The Jiva is in self-expression a portion of the Purushottama. He represents in Nature the power of the supreme Spirit, he is in his personality that Power; he brings out in an individual existence the potentialities of the Soul of the universe. This Jiva itself is spirit and not the natural ego; the spirit and not the form of ego is our reality and inner soul principle. The true force of what we are and can be is there in that higher spiritual Power and the mechanical Maya of the three gunas is not the inmost and fundamental truth of its movements; it is only a present executive energy, an apparatus of lower convenience, a scheme of outward exercise and practice. The spiritual Nature which has become this multiple personality in the universe, *parā prakṛtir jīvabhūtā*, is the basic stuff of our existence: all the rest is lower derivation and outer formation from a highest hidden activity of the spirit. And in Nature each of us has a principle and will of our own becoming; each soul is a force of self-consciousness that formulates an idea of the Divine in it and guides by that its action and evolution, its progressive self-finding, its constant varying self-expression, its apparently uncertain but secretly inevitable growth to fulness. That is our Swabhava, our own real nature; that is our truth of being which is finding now only a constant partial expression in our various becoming in the world. The law of action determined by this Swabhava is our right law of self-shaping, function, working, our Swadharma.

48. The inborn[1] work, O son of Kunti, though defective, ought not to be abandoned. All actions (in the three Gunas) indeed are clouded by defects as fire by smoke.

[1] The practical basis in ancient times came to be the hereditary principle. A man's social function and position were no doubt determined originally, as they are still in freer, less closely ordered communities by environment, occasion, birth and capacity; but as there set in a more fixed stratification, his rank came practically to be regulated by birth mainly or alone and in the later system of caste birth came to be the sole rule of status. The son of a Brahmin is always a Brahmin in status, though he may have nothing of the typical Brahmin qualities or character, no intellectual training or spiritual experience or religious worth or knowledge, no connection whatever with the right function of his class, no Brahminhood in his work and no Brahminhood in his nature.

This was an inevitable evolution, because the external signs are the only ones which are easily and conveniently determinable and birth was the most handy and manageable in an increasingly mechanised, complex and conventional social order. For a time the possible disparity between the hereditary fiction and the individual's real inborn character and capacity was made up or minimised by education and training; but eventually this effort ceased to be sustained and the hereditary convention held absolute rule. The ancient lawgivers, while recognising the hereditary practice, insisted that quality, character and capacity were the one sound and real basis and that without them the hereditary social status became an unspiritual falsehood because it had lost its true significance. The Gita too, as always, founds its thought on the inner significance. It speaks indeed in one verse of the work born with a man, *sahajam karma*; but this does not in itself imply a hereditary basis. According to the Indian theory of rebirth, which the Gita recognises, a man's inborn nature and course of life are essentially determined by his own past lives, are the self-development already effected by his past actions and mental and spiritual evolution and cannot depend solely on the material factor of his ancestry, parentage, physical birth, which can only be of subordinate moment, one effective sign perhaps, but not the dominant principle. The word *sahaja* means that which is born with us, whatever is natural, inborn, innate; its equivalent in all other passages is *svabhāvaja*. The work or function of a man is determined by his qualities, *karma* is determined by *guṇa*; it is the work born of his Swabhava, *svabhāvajam karma*, and regulated by his Swabhava, *svabhāvaniyatam karma*. This emphasis on an inner quality and spirit which finds expression in work, function and action is the whole sense of the Gita's idea of Karma. And from this emphasis on the inner truth and not on the outer form arises the spiritual significance and power which the Gita assigns to the following of the Swadharma. That is the really important bearing of the passage.

It is true that in this birth men fall very largely into one of four types, the man of knowledge, the man of power, the productive vital man, the man of rude labour and service. These are not fundamental divisions, but stages of self-development in our manhood. There is always in human nature something of all these four personalities developed or undeveloped, wide or narrow, suppressed or rising to the surface, but in most men one or the other tends to predominate and seems to take up sometimes the whole space of action in the nature. And in any society we should have all four types, – even, for an example, if we could create a purely productive and commercial society such as modern times have attempted, or for that matter a Shudra society of labour, of the proletariate such as attracts the most modern mind and is now being attempted in one part of Europe and advocated in others. There would still be the thinkers moved to find the law and truth and guiding rule of the whole matter, the captains and leaders of industry who would make all this productive activity an excuse for the satisfaction of their need of adventure and battle and leadership and dominance, the many typical purely productive and wealth-getting men, the average workers satisfied with a modicum of labour and the reward of their labour. But these are quite outward things, and if that were all, this economy of human type would have no spiritual significance. Or it would mean at most, as has been sometimes held in India, that we have to go through these stages of development in our births; for we must perforce proceed progressively through the tamasic, the rajaso-tamasic, the rajasic or rajaso-sattwic to the sattwic nature, ascend and fix ourselves in an inner Brahminhood, *brāhmaṇya*, and then seek salvation from that basis. But in that case there would be no logical room for the Gita's assertion that even the Shudra or Chandala can by turning his life Godwards climb straight to spiritual liberty and perfection.

The fundamental truth is not this outward thing, but a force of our inner being in movement, the truth of the fourfold active power of the spiritual nature. Each Jiva possesses in his spiritual nature these four sides, is a soul of knowledge, a soul of strength and of power, a soul of mutuality and interchange, a soul of works and service, but one side or other predominates in the action and expressive spirit and tinges the dealings of the soul with its embodied nature; it leads and gives its stamp to the other powers and uses them for the principal strain of action, tendency, experience. The Swabhava then follows, not crudely and rigidly as put in the social demarcation, but subtly and flexibly the law of this strain and develops in developing it the other three powers. Thus the pursuit of the impulse of works and service rightly done develops knowledge, increases power, trains closeness or balance of mutuality and skill and order of relation. Each front of the fourfold godhead moves through the enlargement of its own dominant principle of nature and enrichment by the other three towards a total perfection. This development undergoes the law of the three gunas. There is possible a tamasic and rajasic way of following even the dharma of the soul of knowledge, a brute tamasic and a high sattwic way of following the dharma of power, a forceful rajasic or a beautiful and noble sattwic way of following the dharma of works and service. To arrive at the sattwic way of the inner individual Swadharma and of the works to which it moves us on the ways of life is a preliminary condition of perfection. And it may be noted that the inner Swadharma is not bound to any outward social or other form of action, occupation or function. The soul of works that is satisfied to serve or that element in us can, for example, make the life of the pursuit of knowledge, the life of struggle and power or the life of mutuality, production and interchange a means of satisfying its divine impulse to labour and to service.

And in the end to arrive at the divinest figure and most dynamic soul-power of this fourfold activity is a wide doorway to swiftest and largest reality of the most high spiritual perfection. This we can do if we turn the action of the Swadharma into a worship of the inner Godhead, the universal Spirit, the transcendent Purushottama and, eventually, surrender the whole action into his hands, *mayi samnyasya karmāṇi*. Then as we get beyond the limitation of the three gunas, so also do we get beyond the division of the fourfold law and beyond the limitation of all distinctive dharmas, *sarvadharmān parityajya*. The Spirit takes up the individual into the universal Swabhava, perfects and unifies the fourfold soul of nature in us and does its self-determined works according to the divine will and the accomplished power of the godhead in the creature.

III. TOWARDS THE SUPREME SECRET

(The teacher has completed all else that he needed to say, he has worked out all the central principles and the supporting suggestions and implications of his message and elucidated the principal doubts and questions that might rise around it, and now all that rests for him to do is to put into decisive phrase and penetrating formula the one last word, the heart itself of the message, the very core of his gospel. And we find that this decisive, last and crowning word is not merely the essence of what has been already said on the matter, not merely a concentrated description of the needed self-discipline, the Sadhana, and of that greater spiritual consciousness which is to be the result of all its efforts and askesis; it sweeps out, as it were, yet farther, breaks down every limit and rule, canon and formula and opens into a wide and illimitable spiritual truth with an infinite potentiality of significance. And that is a sign of the profundity, the wide reach, the greatness of spirit of the Gita's teaching.

First the Gita restates the body of its message. It summarises the whole outline and essence in the short space of fifteen verses, lines of a brief and concentrated expression and significance that miss nothing of the kernel of the matter, couched in phrases of the most lucid precision and clearness. And they must therefore be scanned with care, must be read deeply in the light of all that has gone before, because here it is evidently intended to extract what the Gita itself considers to be the central sense of its own teaching. The statement sets out from the original starting-point of the thought in the book, the enigma of human action, the apparently insuperable difficulty of living in the highest self and spirit while yet we continue to do the works of the world. The easiest way is to give up the problem as insoluble, life and action as an illusion or an inferior movement of existence to be abandoned as soon as we can rise out of the snare of the world into the truth of spiritual being. That is the ascetic solution, if it can be called a solution; at any rate it is a decisive and effective way out of the enigma, a way to which ancient Indian thought of the highest and most meditative kind, as soon as it commenced to turn at a sharp incline from its first large and free synthesis, had moved always with an increasing preponderance. The Gita like the Tantra, and on certain sides the later religions, attempts to preserve the ancient balance: it maintains the substance and foundation of the original synthesis, but the form has been changed and renovated in the light of a developing spiritual experience. This teaching does not evade the difficult problem of reconciling the full active life of man with the inner life in the highest self and spirit; it advances what it holds to be the real solution. It does not at all deny the efficacy of the ascetic renunciation of life for its own purpose, but it sees that that cuts instead of loosening the knot of the riddle and therefore it accounts it an inferior method and holds its own for the better way. The two paths both lead us out of the lower ignorant normal nature of man to the pure spiritual consciousness and so for both must be held to be valid and even one in essence: but where one stops short and turns back, the other advances with a firm subtlety and high courage, opens a gate on unexplored vistas, completes man in God and unites and reconciles in the spirit soul and Nature.

And therefore in the first five of these verses the Gita so phrases its statement that it shall be applicable to both the way of the inner and the way of the outer renunciation and yet in such a manner that one has only to assign to some of their common expressions a deeper and more inward meaning in order to get the sense and thought of the method favoured by the Gita.)

असक्तबुद्धिः सर्वत्र जितात्मा विगतस्पृहः ।
नैष्कर्म्यसिद्धिं परमां संन्यासेनाधिगच्छति ॥४९॥

49. An understanding[1] without attachment in all things, a soul self-conquered and empty of desire, man attains by renunciation a supreme perfection of *naiṣkarmya*.[2]

[1] This ideal of renunciation, of a self-conquered stillness, spiritual passivity and freedom from desire is common to all the ancient wisdom. The Gita gives us its psychological foundation with an unsurpassed completeness and clearness. It rests on the common experience of all seekers of self-knowledge that there are two different natures and as it were two selves in us. There is the lower self of the obscure mental, vital and physical nature subject to ignorance and inertia in the very stuff of its consciousness and especially in its basis of material substance, kinetic and vital indeed by the power of life but without inherent self-possession and self-knowledge in its action, attaining in the mind to some knowledge and harmony, but only with difficult effort and by a constant struggle with its own disabilities. And there is the higher nature and self of our spiritual being, self-possessed and self-luminous but in our ordinary mentality inaccessible to our experience. At times we get glimpses of this greater thing within us, but we are not consciously within it, we do not live in its light and calm and illimitable splendour. The first of these two very different things is the Gita's nature of the three gunas. Its seeing of itself is centred in the ego idea, its principle of action is desire born of ego, and the knot of ego is attachment to the objects of the mind and sense and the life's desire. The inevitable constant result of all these things is bondage, settled subjection to a lower control, absence of self-mastery, absence of self-knowledge. The other greater power and presence is discovered to be nature and being of the pure spirit unconditioned by ego, that which is called in Indian philosophy self and impersonal Brahman. Its principle is an infinite and an impersonal existence one and the same in all: and, since this impersonal existence is without ego, without conditioning quality, without desire, need or stimulus, it is immobile and immutable; eternally the same, it regards and supports but does not share or initiate the action of the universe. The soul when it throws itself out into active Nature is the Gita's kshara, its mobile or mutable Purusha; the same soul gathered back into pure silent self and essential spirit is the Gita's akshara, immobile or immutable Purusha.

[2] Renunciation is the way to this perfection and the man who has thus inwardly renounced all is described by the Gita as the true Sannyasin. But because the word usually signifies as well an outward renunciation or sometimes even that alone, the Teacher uses another word, *tyāga*, to distinguish the inward from the outward withdrawal and says that Tyaga is better than Sannyasa. The ascetic way goes much farther in its recoil from the dynamic Nature. It is enamoured of renunciation for its own sake and

सिद्धिं प्राप्तो यथा ब्रह्म तथाप्नोति निबोध मे ।
समासेनैव कौन्तेय निष्ठा ज्ञानस्य या परा ॥५०॥

50. How, having attained this perfection, one thus attains to the Brahman, hear from me, O son of Kunti, – that which is the supreme concentrated direction of the knowledge.[1]

insists on an outward giving up of life and action, a complete quietism of soul and nature. That, the Gita replies, is not possible entirely so long as we live in the body. As far as it is possible, it may be done, but such a rigorous diminution of works is not indispensable: it is not even really or at least ordinarily advisable. The one thing needed is a complete inner quietism and that is all the Gita's sense of *naiṣkarmya*. If we ask why this reservation, why this indulgence to the dynamic principle when our object is to become the pure self and the pure self is described as inactive, *akartā*, the answer is that that inactivity and divorce of self from Nature are not the whole truth of our spiritual release. Self and Nature are in the end one thing; a total and perfect spirituality makes us one with all the Divine in self and in nature. In fact this becoming Brahman, this assumption into the self of eternal silence, *brahma-bhūya*, is not all our objective, but only the necessary immense base for a still greater and more marvellous divine becoming, *madbhāva*. And to get to that greatest spiritual perfection we have indeed to be immobile in the self, silent in all our members, but also to act in the power, Shakti, Prakriti, the true and high force of the Spirit. And if we ask how a simultaneity of what seem to be two opposites is possible, the answer is that that is the very nature of a complete spiritual being; always it has this double poise of the Infinite.

A completest inner quietism once admitted as our necessary means towards living in the pure impersonal self, the question how practically it brings about that result is the next issue that arises.

[1] The knowledge meant here is the Yoga of the Sankhyas, – the Yoga of pure knowledge accepted by the Gita, *jñānayogena sāṅkhyānām*, so far as it is one with its own Yoga which includes also the way of works of the Yogins, *karmayogena yoginām*. But all mention of works is kept back for the moment. For by Brahman here is meant at first the silent, the impersonal, the immutable. The Brahman indeed is both for the Upanishads and the Gita all that is and lives and moves; it is not solely an impersonal Infinite or an unthinkable and incommunicable Absolute, *acintyam avyavahāryam*. All this is Brahman, says the Upanishad, all this is Vasudeva, says the Gita, – the supreme Brahman is all that moves or is stable and his hands and feet and eyes and heads and faces are on every side of us. But still there are two aspects of this All, – his immutable eternal self that supports existence and his self of active power that moves

बुद्ध्या विशुद्धया युक्तो धृत्यात्मानं नियम्य च ।
शब्दादीन् विषयांस्त्यक्त्वा रागद्वेषौ व्युदस्य च ॥५१॥
विविक्तसेवी लघ्वाशी यतवाक्कायमानसः ।
ध्यानयोगपरो नित्यं वैराग्यं समुपाश्रितः ॥५२॥
अहङ्कारं बलं दर्पं कामं क्रोधं परिग्रहम् ।
विमुच्य निर्ममः शान्तो ब्रह्मभूयाय कल्पते ॥५३॥

51-53. Uniting the purified intelligence (with the pure spiritual substance in us), controlling the whole being by firm and steady will, having renounced sound and the other objects of the senses, withdrawing from all liking and disliking, resorting to impersonal solitude, abstemious, speech, body and mind controlled, constantly united with the inmost self by meditation,[1] completely giving up desire

---

abroad in the world movement. It is only when we lose our limited ego personality in the impersonality of the self that we arrive at the calm and free oneness by which we can possess a true unity with the universal power of the Divine in his world movement. Impersonality is a denial of limitation and division, and the cult of impersonality is a natural condition of true being, an indispensable preliminary of true knowledge and therefore a first requisite of true action. It is very clear that we cannot become one self with all or one with the universal Spirit and his vast self-knowledge, his complex will and his wide-spread world-purpose by insisting on our limited personality of ego; for that divides us from others and it makes us bound and self-centred in our view and in our will to action. Imprisoned in personality we can only get at a limited union by sympathy or by some relative accommodation of ourselves to the view-point and feeling and will of others. To be one with all and with the Divine and his will in the cosmos we must become at first impersonal and free from our ego and its claims and from the ego's way of seeing ourselves and the world and others. And we cannot do this if there is not something in our being other than the personality, other than the ego, an impersonal self one with all existences. To lose ego and be this impersonal self, to become this impersonal Brahman in our consciousness is therefore the first movement of this Yoga.

[1] A continual resort to meditation, *dhyāna-yoga-paro nityam*, is the firm means by which the soul of man can realise its self of power and its self of silence. And yet there must be no abandonment of the active life for a life of pure meditation; action must always be done as a sacrifice to

and attachment, having put away egoism, violence, arrogance, desire, wrath, the sense and instinct of possession, free from all I-ness and my-ness, calm and luminously impassive – one is fit to become the Brahman.

ब्रह्मभूतः प्रसन्नात्मा न शोचति न काङ्क्षति ।
समः सर्वेषु भूतेषु मद्भक्तिं लभते पराम् ॥५४॥

54. When one has become the Brahman, when one, serene in the Self, neither grieves nor desires, when one is equal to all beings, then one gets the supreme love and devotion[1] to Me.

---

the supreme spirit. This movement of recoil in the path of Sannyasa prepares an absorbed disappearance of the individual in the Eternal, and renunciation of action and life in the world is an indispensable step in the process. But in the Gita's path of Tyaga it is a preparation rather for the turning of our whole life and existence and of all action into an integral oneness with the serene and immeasurable being, consciousness and will of the Divine, and it preludes and makes possible a vast and total passing upward of the soul out of the lower ego to the inexpressible perfection of the supreme spiritual nature, *parā prakṛtiḥ*.

This decisive departure of the Gita's thought is indicated in the next two verses, of which the first runs with a significant sequence.

[1] In the narrow path of knowledge bhakti, devotion to the personal Godhead, can be only an inferior and preliminary movement; the end, the climax is the disappearance of personality in a featureless oneness with the impersonal Brahman in which there can be no place for bhakti: for there is none to be adored and none to adore; all else is lost in the silent immobile identity of the Jiva with the Atman. Here there is given to us something yet higher than the Impersonal, – here there is the supreme self who is the supreme Ishwara, here there is the supreme Soul and its supreme nature, here there is the Purushottama who is beyond the personal and impersonal and reconciles them on his eternal heights. The ego personality still disappears in the silence of the Impersonal, but at the same time there remains even with this silence at the back the action of a supreme Self, one greater than the Impersonal. There is no longer the lower blind and limping action of the ego and the three gunas, but instead the vast self-determining movement of an infinite spiritual Force, a free immeasurable Shakti. All nature becomes the power of the one Divine and all action his action through the individual as channel and instrument. In place of the ego there comes forward conscious and manifest the true

भक्त्या मामभिजानाति यावान् यश्चास्मि तत्त्वतः ।
ततो मां तत्त्वतो ज्ञात्वा विशते तदनन्तरम् ॥५५॥

55. By devotion he comes to know[1] Me, who and how much I am and in all the reality and principles of My being; having thus known Me he entereth[2] into That (Purushottama).

spiritual individual in the freedom of his real nature, in the power of his supernal status, in the majesty and splendour of his eternal kinship to the Divine, an imperishable portion of the supreme Godhead, an indestructible power of the supreme Prakriti.

[1] The One who eternally becomes the Many, the Many who in their apparent division are still eternally one, the Highest who displays in us this secret and mystery of existence, not dispersed by his multiplicity, not limited by his oneness, – this is the integral knowledge, this is the reconciling experience which makes one capable of liberated action, *muktasya karma*.

This knowledge comes, says the Gita, by a highest bhakti. It is attained when the mind exceeds itself by a supramental and high spiritual seeing of things and when the heart too rises in unison beyond our more ignorant mental forms of love and devotion to a love that is calm and deep and luminous with widest knowledge, to a supreme delight in God and an illimitable adoration, the unperturbed ecstasy, the spiritual Ananda. When the soul has lost its separative personality, when it has become the Brahman, it is then that it can live in the true Person and can attain to the supreme revealing bhakti for the Purushottama and can come to know him utterly by the power of its profound bhakti, its heart's knowledge.

[2] The soul of the liberated man thus enters by a reconciling knowledge, penetrates by a perfect simultaneous delight of the transcendent Divine, of the Divine in the individual and of the Divine in the universe into the Purushottama, *mām viśate tadanantaram*. He becomes one with him in his self-knowledge and self-experience, one with him in his being and consciousness and will and world-knowledge and world-impulse, one with him in the universe and in his unity with all creatures in the universe and one with him beyond world and individual in the transcendence of the eternal Infinite, *śāśvatam padam avyayam*. This is the culmination of the supreme bhakti that is at the core of the supreme knowledge.

And it then becomes evident how action continual and unceasing and of all kinds without diminution or abandonment of any part of the activities of life can be not only quite consistent with a supreme spiritual experience, but as forceful a means of reaching this highest spiritual condition as bhakti or knowledge. Nothing can be more positive than the Gita's statement in this matter.

सर्वकर्माण्यपि सदा कुर्वाणो मद्व्यपाश्रयः ।
मत्प्रसादादवाप्नोति शाश्वतं पदमव्ययम् ॥५६॥

56. And by doing also all actions[1] always lodged in Me he attains by My grace the eternal and imperishable status.

[1] This liberating action is of the character of works done in a profound union of the will and all the dynamic parts of our nature with the Divine in ourself and the cosmos. It is done first as a sacrifice with the idea still of our self as the doer. It is done next without that idea and with a perception of the Prakriti as the sole doer. It is done last with the knowledge of that Prakriti as the supreme power of the Divine and a renunciation, a surrender of all our actions to him with the individual as a channel only and an instrument. Our works then proceed straight from the Self and Divine within us, are a part of the indivisible universal action, are initiated and performed not by us but by a vast transcendent Shakti. All that we do is done for the sake of the Lord seated in the heart of all, for the Godhead in the individual and for the fulfilment of his will in us, for the sake of the Divine in the world, for the good of all beings, for the fulfilment of the world action and the world-purpose, or in one word for the sake of the Purushottama and done really by him through his universal Shakti. These divine works, whatever their form or outward character, cannot bind, but are rather a potent means for rising out of this lower Prakriti of the three gunas to the perfection of the supreme, divine and spiritual nature. Disengaged from these mixed and limited dharmas, we escape into the immortal Dharma which comes upon us when we make ourselves one in all our consciousness and action with the Purushottama. That oneness here brings with it the power to rise there into the immortality beyond time. There we shall exist in his eternal transcendence.

Thus these eight verses carefully read in the light of the knowledge already given by the Teacher are a brief, but still a comprehensive indication of the whole essential idea, the entire central method, all the kernel of the complete Yoga of the Gita.

IV. THE SUPREME SECRET

(The essence of the teaching and the Yoga has thus been given to the disciple on the field of his work and battle and the divine Teacher now proceeds to apply it to his action, but in a way that makes it applicable to all action. Attached to a crucial example, spoken to the protagonist of Kurukshetra, the words bear a much wider significance and are a universal rule for all who are ready to ascend above the ordinary mentality and to live and act in the highest spiritual consciousness.)

चेतसा सर्वकर्माणि मयि संन्यस्य मत्परः ।
बुद्धियोगमुपाश्रित्य मच्चित्तः सततं भव ॥५७॥

57. Devoting[1] all thyself to Me, giving up in thy conscious

---

[1] These are lines that carry in them the innermost heart of this Yoga and lead to its crowning experience and we must understand them in their innermost spirit and in the whole vastness of that high summit of experience. The words express the most complete, intimate and living relation possible between God and man; they are instinct with the concentrated force of religious feeling that springs from the human being's absolute adoration, his upward surrender of his whole existence, his unreserved and perfect self-giving to the transcendent and universal Divinity from whom he comes and in whom he lives. This stress of feeling is in entire consonance with the high and enduring place that the Gita assigns to bhakti, to the love of God, to the adoration of the Highest, as the inmost spirit and motive of the supreme action and the crown and core of the supreme knowledge. The phrases used and the spiritual emotion with which they vibrate seem to give the most intense prominence possible and an utmost importance to the personal truth and presence of the Godhead. It is no abstract Absolute of the philosopher, no indifferent impersonal Presence or ineffable Silence intolerant of all relations to whom this complete surrender of all our works can be made and this closeness and intimacy of oneness with him in all the parts of our conscious existence imposed as the condition and law of our perfection or of whom this divine intervention and protection and deliverance are the promise. It is a Master of our works, a Friend and Lover of our soul, an intimate Spirit of our life, an indwelling and overdwelling Lord of all our personal and impersonal self and nature who alone can utter to us this near and moving message.

mind all thy actions into Me, resorting to Yoga of the will and intelligence be always one in heart and consciousness with Me.

मच्चित्त: सर्वदुर्गाणि मत्प्रसादात्तरिष्यसि ।
अथ चेत्त्वमहङ्कारान्न श्रोष्यसि विनङ्क्ष्यसि ॥५८॥

58. If thou art one[1] in heart and consciousness with Me at all times, then by My grace thou shalt pass safe through all difficult and perilous passages; but if from egoism[2] thou hear not, thou shalt fall into perdition.

[1] It is by the perpetual unified closeness of our heart-consciousness, mind-consciousness, all-consciousness, *satatam maccittaḥ*, that we get the widest, the deepest, the most integral experience of our oneness with the Eternal. A nearest oneness in all the being, profoundly individual in a divine passion even in the midst of universality, even at the top of transcendence is here enjoined on the human soul as its way to reach the Highest and its way to possess the perfection and the divine consciousness to which it is called by its nature as a spirit. The intelligence and will have to turn the whole existence in all its parts to the Ishwara, to the divine Self and Master of that whole existence, *buddhi-yogam upāśritya*. The heart has to cast all other emotion into the delight of oneness with him and the love of him in all creatures. The sense spiritualised has to see and hear and feel him everywhere. The life has to be utterly his life in the Jiva. All the actions have to proceed from his sole power and sole initiation in the will, knowledge, organs of action, senses, vital parts, body. This way is deeply impersonal because the separateness of ego is abolished for the Soul universalised and restored to transcendence. And yet it is intimately personal because it soars to a transcendent passion and power of indwelling and oneness. A featureless extinction may be a rigorous demand of the mind's logic of self-annulment, it is not the last word of the supreme mystery, *rahasyaṁ uttamam*.

Thus it is not by a nirvana, an exclusion and negating extinction of all that we are here, but by a nirvana, an exclusion and negating extinction of ignorance and ego and a consequent ineffable fulfilment of our knowledge and will and heart's aspiration, an uplifted and limitless living of them in the Divine, in the Eternal, *nivasiṣyasi mayyeva*, a transfiguration and transference of all our consciousness to a greater inner status that there comes this supreme perfection and release in the spirit.

[2] The crux of the spiritual problem, the character of this transition of which it is so difficult for the normal mind of man to get a true

यदहङ्कारमाश्रित्य न योत्स्य इति मन्यसे ।
मिथ्यैष व्यवसायस्ते प्रकृतिस्त्वां नियोक्ष्यति ॥५९॥

59. Vain[1] is this thy resolve, that in thy egoism thou thinkest, saying "I will not fight"; thy nature shall appoint thee to thy work.

---

apprehension, turns altogether upon the capital distinction between the ignorant life of the ego in the lower nature and the large and luminous existence of the liberated Jiva in his own true spiritual nature. The renunciation of the first must be complete, the transition to the second absolute. This is the distinction on which the Gita dwells here with all possible emphasis. On the one side is this poor trepidant braggart egoistic condition of consciousness, *ahaṁkṛta bhāva*, the crippling narrowness of this little helpless separative personality according to whose viewpoint we ordinarily think and act, feel and respond to the touches of existence. On the other are the vast spiritual reaches of immortal fullness, bliss and knowledge into which we are admitted through union with the divine Being, of whom we are then a manifestation and expression in the eternal light and no longer a disguise in the darkness of the ego-nature.

[1] The refusal of Arjuna to persevere in his divinely appointed work proceeded from the ego-sense in him, *ahaṁkāra*. Behind it was a mixture and confusion and tangled error of ideas and impulsions of the sattwic, rajasic, tamasic ego, the vital nature's fear of sin and its personal consequences, the heart's recoil from individual grief and suffering, the clouded reason's covering of egoistic impulses by self-deceptive specious pleas of right and virtue, our nature's ignorant shrinking from the ways of God because they seem other than the ways of man and impose things terrible and unpleasant on his nervous and emotional parts and his intelligence. The spiritual consequences will be infinitely worse now than before, now that a higher truth and a greater way and spirit of action have been revealed to him, if yet persisting in his egoism he perseveres in a vain and impossible refusal. For it is a vain resolution, a futile recoil, since it springs only from a temporary failure of strength, a strong but passing deviation from the principle of energy of his inmost character and is not the true will and way of his nature. If now he casts down his arms, he will yet be compelled by that nature to resume them when he sees the battle and slaughter go on without him, his abstention a defeat of all for which he has lived, the cause for whose service he was born weakened and bewildered by the absence or inactivity of its protagonist, vanquished and afflicted by the cynical and unscrupulous strength of the champions of a self-regarding unrighteousness and injustice. And in this return there will be no spiritual virtue. It was a confusion of the ideas and feelings of the

स्वभावजेन कौन्तेय निबद्ध: स्वेन कर्मणा ।
कर्तुं नेच्छसि यन्मोहात्करिष्यस्यवशोऽपि तत् ॥६०॥

60. What from delusion thou desirest not to do. O Kaunteya, that helplessly thou shalt do bound by thy own work born of thy swabhava.

ईश्वर: सर्वभूतानां हृद्देशेऽर्जुन तिष्ठति ।
भ्रामयन् सर्वभूतानि यन्त्रारूढानि मायया ॥६१॥

61. The Lord,[1] O Arjuna, is seated in the heart of all beings turning all beings mounted upon a machine by his Maya.

---

ego mind that impelled his refusal; it will be his nature working through a restoration of the characteristic ideas and feelings of the ego mind that will compel him to annul his refusal. But whatever the direction, this continued subjection to the ego will mean a worse, a more fatal spiritual refusal, a perdition, *vinaṣṭi*; for it will be a definite falling away from a greater truth of his being than that which he has followed in the ignorance of the lower nature. He has been admitted to a higher consciousness, a new self-realisation, he has been shown the possibility of a divine instead of an egoistic action; the gates have been opened before him of a divine and spiritual in place of a merely intellectual, emotional, sensuous and vital life. He is called to be no longer a great blind instrument, but a conscious soul and an enlightened power and vessel of the Godhead.

[1] When we enter into the inmost self of our existence, we come to know that in us and in all is the one Spirit and Godhead whom all Nature serves and manifests and we ourselves are soul of this Soul, spirit of this Spirit, our body his delegated image, our life a movement of the rhythm of his life, our mind a sheath of his consciousness, our senses his instruments, our emotions and sensations the seekings of his delight of being, our actions a means of his purpose, our freedom only a shadow, suggestion or glimpse while we are ignorant, but when we know him and ourselves a prolongation and effective channel of his immortal freedom. Our masteries are a reflection of his power at work, our best knowledge a partial light of his knowledge, the highest most potent will of our spirit a projection and delegation of the will of this Spirit in all things who is the Master and Soul of the universe. It is the Lord seated in the heart of every creature who has been turning us in all our inner and outer action during the ignorance as if mounted on a machine on the wheel of this Maya of the

तमेव शरणं गच्छ सर्वभावेन भारत ।
तत्प्रसादात्परां शान्तिं स्थानं प्राप्स्यसि शाश्वतम् ॥६२॥

62. In him take refuge in every way of thy being and by his grace thou shalt come to the supreme peace and the eternal status.

इति ते ज्ञानमाख्यातं गुह्याद् गुह्यतरं मया ।
विमृश्यैतदशेषेण यथेच्छसि तथा कुरु ॥६३॥

63. So have I expounded to thee a knowledge more secret than that which is hidden; having reflected on it fully, do as thou wouldst.

सर्वगुह्यतमं भूयः शृणु मे परमं वचः ।
इष्टोऽसि मे दृढमिति ततो वक्ष्यामि ते हितम् ॥६४॥

64. Further hear the most secret, the supreme[1] word that

---

lower Nature. And whether obscure in the ignorance or luminous in the knowledge, it is for him in us and him in the world that we have our existence. To live consciously and integrally in this knowledge and this truth is to escape from ego and break out of Maya. All other highest dharmas are only a preparation for this Dharma, and all Yoga is only a means by which we can come first to some kind of union and finally, if we have the full light, to an integral union with the Master and supreme Soul and Self of our existence. The greatest Yoga is to take refuge from all the perplexities and difficulties of our nature with this indwelling Lord of all Nature, to turn to him with our whole being, with the life and body and sense and mind and heart and understanding, with our whole dedicated knowledge and will and action, *sarvabhāvena*, in every way of our conscious self and our instrumental nature. And when we can at all times and entirely do this, then the divine Light and Love and Power takes hold of us, fills both self and instruments and leads us safe through all the doubts and difficulties and perplexities and perils that beset our soul and our life, leads us to a supreme peace and the spiritual freedom of our immortal and eternal status, *parām śāntim, sthānam śāśvatam.*

[1] After giving out all the laws, the dharmas, and the deepest essence of its yoga, after saying that beyond all the first secrets revealed to the mind of man by the transforming light of spiritual knowledge, *guhyāt*, this is a still deeper more secret truth, *guhyataram*, the Gita suddenly declares

I shall speak to thee; beloved art thou intimately of Me, therefore will I speak for thy good.

मन्मना भव मद्भक्तो मद्याजी मां नमस्कुरु ।
मामेवैष्यसि सत्यं ते प्रतिजाने प्रियोऽसि मे ॥६५॥

65. Become my-minded, my lover and adorer, a sacrificer to Me, bow thyself to Me, to Me thou shalt come, this is my pledge and promise to thee, for dear art thou to Me.

सर्वधर्मान् परित्यज्य मामेकं शरणं व्रज ।
अहं त्वा सर्वपापेभ्यो मोक्षयिष्यामि मा शुचः ॥६६॥

66. Abandon all dharmas and take refuge in Me alone. I will deliver thee from all sin and evil, do not grieve.[1]

---

that there is yet a supreme word that it has to speak, *paramam vacaḥ*, and a most secret truth of all, *sarva-guhyatamam*. This secret of secrets the Teacher will tell to Arjuna as his highest good because he is the chosen and beloved soul, *iṣṭa*. For evidently, as had already been declared by the Upanishad, it is only the rare soul chosen by the Spirit for the revelation of his very body, *tanum svām*, who can be admitted to this mystery, because he alone is near enough in heart and mind and life to the Godhead to respond truly to it in all his being and to make it a living practice. The last, the closing supreme word of the Gita expressing the highest mystery is spoken in two brief, direct and simple slokas and these are left without farther comment or enlargement to sink into the mind and reveal their own fullness of meaning in the soul's experience. For it is alone this inner incessantly extending experience that can make evident the infinite deal of meaning with which are for ever pregnant these words in themselves apparently so slight and simple. And we feel, as they are being uttered, that it was this for which the soul of the disciple was being prepared all the time and the rest was only an enlightening and enabling discipline and doctrine.

Thus runs this secret of secrets, the highest most direct message of the Ishwara.

[1] The Gita throughout has been insisting on a great and well-built discipline of Yoga, a large and clearly traced philosophical system, on the Swabhava and the Swadharma, on the sattwic law of life as leading out of itself by a self-exceeding exaltation to a free spiritual dharma of immortal existence utterly wide in its spaces and high-lifted beyond the limitation of

इदं ते नातपस्काय नाभक्ताय कदाचन ।
न चाशुश्रूषवे वाच्यं न च मां योऽभ्यसूयति ॥६७॥

67. Never is this to be spoken by thee to one without askesis, nor to one that is not devoted and not to him who does no service; nor yet to him who despises and belittles Me (lodged in the human body).

---

even this highest guna, on many rules and means and injunctions and conditions of perfection, and now suddenly it seems to break out of its own structure and says to the human soul, "Abandon all dharmas, give thyself to the Divine alone, to the supreme Godhead above and around and within thee: that is all that thou needest, that is the truest and greatest way, that is the real deliverance." The Master of the worlds in the form of the divine Charioteer and Teacher of Kurukshetra has revealed to man the magnificent realities of God and Self and Spirit and the nature of the complex world and the relation of man's mind and life and heart and senses to the Spirit and the victorious means by which through his own spiritual self-discipline and effort he can rise out of mortality into immortality and out of his limited mental into his infinite spiritual existence. And now speaking as the Spirit and Godhead in man and in all things he says to him, "All this personal effort and self-discipline will not in the end be needed, all following and limitation of rule and dharma can at last be thrown away as hampering encumbrances if thou canst make a complete surrender to Me, depend alone on the Spirit and Godhead within thee and all things and trust to his sole guidance. Turn all thy mind to Me and fill it with the thought of Me and my presence. Turn all thy heart to Me, make thy every action, whatever it be, a sacrifice and offering to Me. That done, leave Me to do my will with thy life and soul and action; do not be grieved or perplexed by my dealings with thy mind and heart and life and works or troubled because they do not seem to follow the laws and dharmas man imposes on himself to guide his limited will and intelligence. My ways are the ways of a perfect wisdom and power and love that knows all things and combines all its movements in view of a perfect eventual result; for it is refining and weaving together the many threads of an integral perfection. I am here with thee in thy chariot of battle revealed as the Master of existence within and without thee and I repeat the absolute assurance, the infallible promise that I will lead thee to myself through and beyond all sorrow and evil. Whatever difficulties and perplexities arise, be sure of this that I am leading thee to a complete divine life in the universal and an immortal existence in the transcendent Spirit."

य इदं परमं गुह्यं मद्भक्तेष्वभिधास्यति ।
भक्तिं मयि परां कृत्वा मामेवैष्यत्यसंशयः ॥६८॥

68. He who with the highest devotion for Me, shall declare this supreme secret among My devotees, without doubt he shall come to Me.

न च तस्मान्मनुष्येषु कश्चिन्मे प्रियकृत्तमः ।
भविता न च मे तस्मादन्यः प्रियतरो भुवि ॥६९॥

The Gita indicates that in order that that may wholly be, the surrender must be without reservations; our Yoga, our life, our state of inner being must be determined freely by this living Infinite, not predetermined by our mind's insistence on this or that dharma or any dharma. The divine Master of the Yoga, *yogeśvaraḥ kṛṣṇaḥ*, will then himself take up our Yoga and raise us to our utmost possible perfection, not the perfection of any external or mental standard or limiting rule, but vast and comprehensive, to the mind incalculable. It will be a perfection developed by an all-seeing Wisdom according to the whole truth, first indeed of our human swabhava, but afterwards of a greater thing into which it will open, a spirit and power illimitable, immortal, free and all-transmuting, the light and splendour of a divine and infinite nature.

This then is the supreme word and most secret thing of all, *guhyatamam*, that the spirit and Godhead is an Infinite free from all dharmas and though he conducts the world according to fixed laws and leads man through his dharmas of ignorance and knowledge, sin and virtue, right and wrong, liking and disliking and indifference, pleasure and pain, joy and sorrow and the rejection of these opposites, through his physical and vital, intellectual, emotional, ethical and spiritual forms and rules and standards, yet the Spirit and Godhead transcends all these things, and if we too can cast away all dependence on dharmas, surrender ourself to this free and eternal Spirit and taking care only to keep ourselves absolutely and exclusively open to him, trust to the light and power and delight of the Divine in us and, unafraid and ungrieving, accept only his guidance, then that is the truest, the greatest release and that brings the absolute and inevitable perfection of our self and nature. This is the way offered to the chosen of the Spirit, – to those only in whom he takes the greatest delight because they are nearest to him and most capable of oneness and of being even as he, freely consenting and concordant with Nature in her highest power and movement, universal in soul consciousness, transcendent in the spirit.

69. And there is none among men that does more than he what is most dear to Me; and there will be none else dearer to Me in the world.

अध्येष्यते च य इमं धर्म्यं संवादमावयो: ।
ज्ञानयज्ञेन तेनाहमिष्ट: स्यामिति मे मति: ॥७०॥

70. And he who shall study this sacred discourse of ours, by him I shall be worshipped with the sacrifice of knowledge.

श्रद्धावाननसूयश्च शृणुयादपि यो नर: ।
सोऽपि मुक्त: शुभांल्लोकान् प्राप्नुयात् पुण्यकर्मणाम् ॥७१॥

71. The man also who, full of faith and uncarping, listens to this, even he, being liberated, attains to the happy worlds of the righteous.

कच्चिदेतच्छ्रुतं पार्थ त्वयैकाग्रेण चेतसा ।
कच्चिदज्ञानसम्मोह: प्रनष्टस्ते धनञ्जय ॥७२॥

72. Hath this been heard by thee, O son of Pritha, with a concentrated mind? Has thy delusion, caused by ignorance, been destroyed, O Dhananjaya?

अर्जुन उवाच —
नष्टो मोह: स्मृतिर्लब्धा त्वत्प्रसादान्मयाच्युत ।
स्थितोऽस्मि गतसन्देह: करिष्ये वचनं तव ॥७३॥

73. Arjuna said: Destroyed[1] is my delusion, I have re-

---

[1] The whole Yoga is revealed, the great word of the teaching is given and Arjuna the chosen human soul is once more turned, no longer in his egoistic mind but in this greatest self-knowledge, to the divine action. The Vibhuti is ready for the divine life in the human, his conscious spirit for the works of the liberated soul, *muktasya karma*. Destroyed is the illusion of the mind; the soul's memory of its self and its truth concealed so long by the misleading shows and forms of our life has returned to it and become its normal consciousness: all doubt and perplexity gone, it can

gained memory through Thy grace, O Infallible One, I am firm, dispelled are my doubts. I will act according to Thy word.

सञ्जय उवाच—

इत्यहं वासुदेवस्य पार्थस्य च महात्मनः ।
संवादमिममश्रौषमद्भुतं रोमहर्षणम् ॥७४॥

74. Sanjaya said: I heard this wonderful discourse of Vasudeva and of the great-souled Partha, causing my hair to stand on end.

व्यासप्रसादाच्छ्रुतवानेतद् गुह्यमहं परम् ।
योगं योगेश्वरात् कृष्णात् साक्षात् कथयतः स्वयम् ॥७५॥

75. Through the grace of Vyasa I heard this supreme secret, this Yoga directly from Krishna, the divine Master of Yoga, who himself declared it.

राजन् संस्मृत्य संस्मृत्य संवादमिममद्भुतम् ।
केशवार्जुनयोः पुण्यं हृष्यामि च मुहुर्मुहुः ॥७६॥

76. O King, remembering, remembering this wonderful and sacred discourse of Keshava and Arjuna, I rejoice again and again.

तच्च संस्मृत्य संस्मृत्य रूपमत्यद्भुतं हरेः ।
विस्मयो मे महान् राजन् हृष्यामि च पुनः पुनः ॥७७॥

77. Remembering, remembering also that most marvellous form of Hari, great is my wonder, O King. I rejoice, again and again.

---

turn to the execution of the command and do faithfully whatever work for God and the world may be appointed and apportioned to it by the Master of our being, the Spirit and Godhead self-fulfilled in Time and Universe.

EIGHTEENTH CHAPTER

यत्र योगेश्वरः कृष्णो यत्र पार्थो धनुर्धरः ।
तत्र श्रीर्विजयो भूतिर्ध्रुवा नीतिर्मतिर्मम ॥७८॥

78. Wherever is Krishna, the Master of Yoga, wherever is Partha, the archer, assured are there glory, victory and prosperity, and there also is the immutable Law of Right.[1]

इति श्रीमद्भगवद्गीतासूपनिषत्सु ब्रह्मविद्यायां योगशास्त्रे श्रीकृष्णार्जुनसंवादे
मोक्षसंन्यासयोगो नामाष्टादशोऽध्यायः ।
श्रीकृष्णार्पणमस्तु ॥ शुभं भवतु ॥

---

[1] Sanjaya was given by the great Vyasa the occult power of directly seeing and hearing from a distance all that transpired on the battlefield of Kurukshetra, so that he might report that to the blind king Dhritarashtra. This is the framework of the Gita and the author concludes by referring to it once more.

"The secret of action", so we might summarise the message of the Gita, the word of its divine Teacher, "is one with the secret of all life and existence. Existence is not merely a machinery of Nature, a wheel of law in which the soul is entangled for a moment or for ages; it is a constant manifestation of the Spirit. Life is not for the sake of life alone, but for God, and the living soul of man is an eternal portion of the Godhead. Action is for self-finding, for self-fulfilment, for self-realisation and not only for its own external and apparent fruits of the moment or the future. There is an inner law and meaning of all things dependent on the supreme as well as the manifested nature of the self; the true truth of works lies there and can be represented only incidentally, imperfectly and disguised by ignorance in the outer appearances of the mind and its action. The supreme, the faultless largest law of action is therefore to find out the truth of your own highest and inmost existence and live in it and not to follow any outer standard and Dharma. All life and action must be till then an imperfection, a difficulty, a struggle and a problem. It is only by discovering your true self and living according to its true truth, its real reality that the problem can be finally solved, the difficulty and struggle overpassed and your doings perfected in the security of the discovered self and spirit turn into a divinely authentic action. Know then your self; know your true self to be God and one with the self of all others; know your soul to be a portion of God. Live in what you know; live in the self, live in your supreme spiritual nature, be united with God and Godlike. Offer, first, all your actions as a sacrifice to the Highest and the One in you and to the Highest and One in the world; deliver last all you are and do into his hands for the supreme and universal Spirit to do through you his own will and works in the world. This is the solution that I present to you and in the end you will find that there is no other."

APPENDIX I

THE STORY OF THE GITA

The Mahabharata, of which the Gita is a part, took its present form from the fifth to the first centuries B.C. The Gita occurs in it as one portion of the "Bhishma Parva".

"Mahabharata" means literally "great India"; it is an epic narrative of the ancient Indians who saw the vision of a great India, one in culture and unified in political life, stretching from the Himalayas to Cape Comorin.

Kuru is the name of a leading *kula* or clan of that time, and Kurukshetra was a vast field near their capital Hastinapur (modern Delhi) where the Kurus used to perform their religious sacrifices. When Dhritarashtra the blind king of the Kurus became old, he decided to give his throne not to his own son Duryodhana but to Yudhishthira, the eldest son of his deceased younger brother Pandu, as Duryodhana, being a man of evil propensities, was not fit to be the ruler of a *dharmarājya* (kingdom based on the principles of righteousness and justice, which was the ideal in ancient India); while Yudhishthira, being an embodiment of virtue and purity, was the fittest man. But Duryodhana by cunning and treachery secured the throne for himself, and sought by every means in his power to annihilate Yudhishthira and his four brothers.

Krishna, the incarnate Godhead, was the head of the Yadava clan, and a friend and relative of the Kurus. He tried to bring about a reconciliation between the two sections of the Kuru family; on behalf of the five Pandava brothers (sons of Pandu) he asked only five villages from Duryodhana, but the latter sternly refused saying that without battle he would not give even so much earth as could be held on the point of a needle. So a war became inevitable for the sake of justice and righteousness. All the princes of India joined one side or the other. Krishna, as an impartial friend, offered the rival parties a choice. Duryodhana chose to take the mighty army of Krishna to his side, while Krishna himself went to the other side alone – and even then not as a fighter, but as the charioteer of Arjuna.

Drona, the common military teacher both of the sons of Dhritarashtra (specially called the Kauravas) and of the sons of Pandu (the Pandavas), went to the side of Duryodhana, as his ancient enemy Drupada had joined the other party. Bhishma, who was related as great-uncle both to the Kauravas and to the Pandavas, had observed lifelong celibacy and even in his old age was the strongest man of his time. He was the leader of the party which had tried to bring about a reconciliation between the Kauravas and the Pandavas. But when all peace efforts failed and war became inevitable, he decided to join the side of Duryodhana after a scrupulous consideration of his duty and obligations. He knew that Duryodhana was in the wrong, and if the battle had been confined simply to the two branches of the family, he would have remained neutral. But when he saw that, taking advantage of a family quarrel, the ancient enemies of the Kuru clan had joined the ranks of the Pandavas, he decided to fight on the side of Duryodhana for ten days only and then to retire for a voluntary death (brought about by non-physical means). Considering only the military strength of the two parties, that of Duryodhana was decidedly superior. But this was more than counter-balanced by the presence of Krishna on the other side.

Sanjaya, the charioteer of the old king Dhritarashtra, reports to him what is happening in the field of Kurukshetra where the two armies have assembled for a grim fight, in magnitude and importance unparalleled in the history of ancient India. This is the beginning of the Bhagavad Gita, literally "the Divine Song," so called because it is delivered by Krishna, the incarnate Godhead, and because it teaches man how to rise out of his ordinary human consciousness to a higher divine consciousness, thus realising the Kingdom of Heaven on earth and in the human body.

Of the five Pandava brothers the eldest Yudhishthira was the most virtuous and pure, sattwic; the second brother Bhima was the most strong, rajasic; while in Arjuna, the third brother, there was a balance of purity and strength, of sattwa and rajas, and he was chosen by the Godhead as His chief instrument in that great war which was to determine a world-cycle, *yugāntara*, and as a disciple to whom was delivered the divine message which was to lead humanity to its destined goal of Immortality on earth.

APPENDIX II

THE HISTORICITY OF KRISHNA

For the fundamental teaching of the Gita as for spiritual life generally, the Krishna who matters to us is the eternal incarnation of the Divine and not the historical teacher and leader of men. The historical Krishna, no doubt, existed. We meet the name first in the Chhandogya Upanishad. We know that Krishna and Arjuna were the object of religious worship in the pre-Christian centuries; and there is some reason to suppose that they were so in connection with a religious and philosophical tradition from which the Gita may have gathered many of its elements and even the foundation of its synthesis of knowledge, devotion and works, and perhaps also that the human Krishna was the founder, restorer or at the least one of the early teachers of this school. The Gita may well in spite of its later form represent the outcome in Indian thought of the teaching of Krishna and the connection of that teaching with the historical Krishna, with Arjuna and with the war of Kurukshetra, may be something more than a dramatic fiction. In the Mahabharata Krishna is represented both as the historical character and the Avatar; his worship and Avatarhood must therefore have been well established by the time – apparently from the fifth to the first centuries B.C. – when the old story and poem or epic tradition of the Bharatas took its present form. There is a hint also in the poem of the story or legend of the Avatar's early life in Vrindavan which, as developed by the Puranas into an intense and powerful spiritual symbol, has exercised so profound an influence on the religious mind of India. We have also in the Harivansha an account of the life of Krishna, very evidently full of legends, which perhaps formed the basis of the Puranic accounts.

But all this, though of considerable historical importance, has none whatever for our present purpose. We are concerned only with the figure of the divine Teacher as it is presented to us in the Gita and with the Power for which it there stands in the spiritual illumination of the human being. The Gita accepts the human Avatarhood; but it is not this upon which stress is laid, but on the transcendent, the cosmic and the internal Divine; it is on the Source of all things and the Master of all and on the Godhead secret in man. It is this internal divinity who is meant when the

Gita speaks of the doer of violent Asuric austerities troubling the God within or of the sin of those who despise the Divine lodged in the human body or of the same Godhead destroying our ignorance by the blazing lamp of knowledge. It is then the eternal Avatar, this God in man, the divine Consciousness always present in the human being who manifested in a visible form speaks to the human soul in the Gita, illumines the meaning of life and the secret of divine action and gives it the light of the divine knowledge and guidance and the assuring and fortifying word of the Master of existence in the hour when it comes face to face with the painful mystery of the world. This is what the Indian religious consciousness seeks to make near to itself in whatever form, whether in the symbolic human image it enshrines in its temples or in the worship of its Avatars or in the devotion to the human Guru through whom the voice of the one world-Teacher makes itself heard. Through these it strives to awaken to that inner voice, unveil that form of the Formless and stand face to face with that manifest divine Power, Love and Knowledge.

APPENDIX III

SOME PSYCHOLOGICAL PRESUPPOSITIONS

A few words technically used in the notes in this edition require some explanation, as also certain metaphysical and psychological presuppositions.

Each plane of our being – mental, vital, physical – has its own consciousness, separate though interconnected and interacting. These can be said to be interconnected because there is a continuity from one end to the other, and interacting because all the psychological processes in man – mental, vital, physical – are mixed up with one another. To our outer mind and sense they are all confused together; for the purpose of analysis, however, they may be distinguished thus:

MIND PROPER

The Mind proper is divided into three parts – thinking Mind, dynamic Mind, externalising Mind – the former concerned with ideas and knowledge in their own right, the second with the putting out of mental forces for realisation of the idea, the third with the expresson of them in life (not only by speech, but by any form it can give). The word "physical mind" is rather ambiguous, because it can mean this externalising mind and the mental in the physical taken together.

VITAL MIND

A similar ambiguity arises when one has to speak of the "vital mind"; for this is a comprehensive term for the mental vital and the vital mental. Vital Mind proper is a sort of mediator between vital emotion, desire, impulsion etc. and the mental proper. It expresses the desires, feelings, emotions, passions, ambitions, possessive and active tendencies of the vital and throws them into mental forms (the pure imaginations or dreams in which men indulge of greatness, happiness etc. are one peculiar form of the vital mind activity). There is a still lower stage of the mental in the vital which merely expresses the vital stuff without subjecting it to any play of intelligence. It is through this mental vital that the vital passions, impulses, desires rise up and get into the Buddhi and either cloud or distort it.

Mental Physical

As the vital Mind is limited by the vital view and feeling of things, (while the dynamic Intelligence is not, for it acts by the idea and reason), so the mind in the physical or *mental physical* is limited by the physical view and experience of things, it mentalises the experience brought by the contacts of outward life and things and does not go beyond that (though it can do that much very cleverly), unlike the externalising mind which deals with them more from the reason and its higher intelligence. But in practice these two usually get mixed together. The mechanical mental physical or body-mind is a much lower action of the mental physical which, left to itself, will simply go on repeating the past customary thoughts and movements or will, at the most, add to them such further mechanical reactions to things and reflexes as come in the round of life.

Vital Physical

The lower vital as distinguished from the higher is concerned only with the small greeds, small desires, small passions etc. which made up the daily stuff of life for the ordinary sensational man – while *the vital physical proper* is the nervous being giving vital reflexes to contacts of things with the physical consciousness.

The foregoing are only a selection from among the various possible subdivisions, which might be set out more systematically as follows:–

I. The Mental Plane

The mind proper is concerned with reasoning, formulation of ideas or mental forms, and the activity of the thinking will (the dynamic mind). This is called the Buddhi (at once intelligence and will) as distinguished from the other parts of the mind which are called the Manas or the Sense-mind. Above the mind is the higher mind which organises all these functions; this higher mind again is itself the instrument of the supermind which organises and intuitivises the higher mind.

The mind itself has different levels, the mental proper, the vital in the mind, the physical in the mind. The emotions belong to the vital part of the mind. These are things of the vital plane which pressing upon the mind produce mental forms. They are not created by the mind itself. As examples of things belonging to this vital mental, one might cite imaginations of lust, cinematographic stories told to oneself of great adventures etc. of which one is the hero, and mentalisation of desires generally.

The physical part of the mind is the receiving and externalising intelligence which has two functions – first, to work upon external things and give them a mental order with a way of practically dealing with them – secondly, to be the channel of materialising and putting into effect whatever the thinking and dynamic mind sends down to it for the purpose.

II. THE VITAL PLANE

The vital plane is a realm of desires, not only sexual or physical desires, but desires for power, activity, ambition, pride. In the vital proper the life-force seeks to realise itself, to possess materials and to put its stamp upon them; but in its crude form this vital urge appears as lust, ambition, desire for possession, for money, for enjoyment of all kinds.

The mental part of the vital is the mental activity which accompanies the vital desires, knows and expresses them in mental forms and speech. Thus when Mussolini says, "Italy must have a place in the sun," this is not the result of thinking or reasoning, the desire rises from the vital being, though it may seek to support itself by the reasoning or the Buddhi. As examples of things which belong to the mental vital, one might cite the following: all mentalised impulses and emotions and sensations, thoughts of anger, despair, lust, hatred etc. These have a less imaginative character than the vital mental[1] and are more practical or mechanical, turning about something actual, *e.g.,* some love affair, quarrel, disappointment, – they may be turned towards fulfilment of the feeling or impulse or turn round some memory of something done or enjoyed, try to repeat what has been felt or prolong it, etc.

The physical part of the vital wants to move in grooves and fixed forms, such as habits and instincts. It is necessary for realising the vital impulses in the actual world. There may be the urge but the

---

[1] It is not easy to distinguish mental vital and vital mental unless one has the necessary subtlety of observation or the habit of the differentiated experience.

physical part may not be equal to the task. Thus there are many poets who cannot express themselves well as the physical vital in them is not strong.

III. THE PHYSICAL PLANE

In the physical plane again there is the mental, the vital and the material. The mental part of the physical is that which comes into contact with the physical world and sees only the physical aspect of things and nothing beyond it; it takes matter as being simply matter and nothing more, it does not see the consciousness inherent in matter. It depends on the material structure of the senses and is confined to them and to the material brain. The mind in the physical is thus a very small thing, it does not go far, but it is the thin end which is necessary for the work of the mind upon the physical world.

Sight, hearing, taste, smell, touch are really properties of the mind, not of the body; but the physical mind, which we ordinarily use, limits itself to a translation into sense of so much of the outer impacts as it receives through the nervous system and the physical organs. But the inner Manas has also a subtle sight, hearing, power of contact of its own which is not dependent on the physical organs. And it has, moreover, a power not only of direct communication of mind with object – leading even at a high pitch of action to a sense of the contents of an object within or beyond the physical range, – but direct communication also of mind with mind. Mind is able too to alter, modify, inhibit the incidence, values, intensities of sense impacts. These powers of the mind we do not ordinarily use or develop; they remain subliminal and emerge sometimes in an irregular and fitful action, more readily in some minds than in others, or come to the surface in abnormal states of the being. They are the basis of clairvoyance, clairaudience, transference of thought and impulse, telepathy, most of the more ordinary kinds of occult powers, – so called, though these are better described less mystically as powers of the now subliminal action of the Manas. The phenonena of hypnotism and many others depend upon the action of this subliminal sense-mind; not that it alone constitutes all the elements of the phenomena, but it is the first supporting means of intercourse, communication and response, though much of the actual operation belongs to an inner

Buddhi. Mind physical, mind supra-physical, – we have and can use this double sense-mentality.

The vital in the physical is the vehicle of the nervous responses of our physical nature; it is the field and instrument of the smaller sensations, desires, reactions of all kinds to the impacts of the outer physical and gross material life. This vital part of the physical (supported by the lowest part of the vital proper) is therefore the agent of most of the lesser movements of our external life. It is the life which is bound up with matter, with the nervous system; it cannot exist apart from a material body. But the vital proper is quite independent of matter, it is a universal force. There is force also in matter, but that is not life-force. The real life-force is something apart from the material world, it exists for its own sake and its possibilities are not bound down by material conditions. When Napoleon said that there was nothing impossible, that the term 'impossible' was to be erased from the dictionary, it was the vital which was speaking through Napoleon; to the vital nothing seems impossible.

The vital part of the physical is very important, it gives health and strength to the body. It knows what is beneficial or what is injurious to the system. If left to itself, it would have been the safest guide in regard to health. But in civilized persons it is seldom left unimpaired; the activity of the mind has created great confusion.

Lastly, the material in the physical is the pure material part of it which is the basis of the rest. The characteristics of the physical proper are inertia and conservation.

Thus there are the different planes, the mental, the vital,[1] the physical; the psychic is behind all these. The word "soul", as also the word "psychic", is used very vaguely and in many different senses in the English language. More often than not Europeans in their ordinary parlance make no clear distinction between mind and soul, and often even confuse the true soul, the psychic being, with the vital being of desire – the false soul or desire-soul. The psychic being is quite different from the mind or vital; it stands behind them where they meet in the heart. Its central place is there, but behind the heart rather than in the heart; for what men call usually the heart is the seat of emotion, and human emotions

---

[1] The "astral plane" of the Theosophists would appear to be essentially the same as we have been describing as the "vital plane".

are mental-vital impulses, not ordinarily psychic in their nature. This mostly secret power behind, other than the mind and the life-force, is the true soul, the psychic being in us.

We can speak of a psychic plane also, but it is of a kind which cuts through all the other planes from behind, it enters into the other planes somewhat like rays. There is a direct connection between the psychic being and the higher Truth. There is a psychic consciousness, but it is simple and direct, not like the mental consciousness. The psychic touch helps to bring out the deeper potentialities in the mental, the vital and the physical and make these more fit to receive the higher Truth and Power. Thus mental love is egoistic and depends on mutual interchange and enjoyment. By the psychic touch the love becomes nobler and purer, the egoistic element vanishes.

GLOSSARY

abhayam – fearlessness.
abhyāsa – Yogic practice.
ācārya (Acharya) – teacher.
ahaṅkāra – the ego-sense, egoism.
ahiṁsā – non-violence.
akartā – a non-doer.
akṣara (Akshara) – the immobile, the immutable.
ānanda – spiritual delight, the bliss of the Spirit.
anīśa – not lord, not master of but subject to the nature.
anumantā – giver of sanction.
apāna – the incoming breath.
artha – self-interest.
asura – a hostile being of the mental world.
Asuric – relating to, of the nature of the Asuras.
ātman – the Self or Spirit.
avatāra (Avatar) – descent or incarnation of God.
avikārya – free from all change.
avyaktam – the unmanifest.
bhakti – emotional devotion felt for the Divine.
bhartā – upholder, maintainer of the nature.
bhāva – subjective state or feeling; becoming.
bhūta – any one of the five elements – earth, water, fire, air, ether – which form part of the list of *tattva*s.
bhūtāni – becomings, existences.
brahmacarya (Brahmacharya) – sexual purity.
brahman – the Supreme Reality that is one and indivisible and infinite, besides which nothing else really exists.
Brahmic – relating to Brahman.
buddhi – the reason, intelligence, mental power of understanding.
caṇḍāla (Chandala) – pariah, outcaste.
cāturvarṇya (Chaturvarnya) – the four orders – Brahmin, Kshatriya, Vaishya, Shudra – of the old Indian social culture.
Daivic – relating to, of the nature of the Devas.
dakṣiṇā – giving.
dānava – a Titan.
deva – a god.
dhāmā – status, place.
dharma – action governed by the essential law of one's nature; right moral law.
dhīraḥ – the self-composed.
dhṛti – spiritual patience, persistence.
dhyāna – meditation.

GLOSSARY

dvaita – dualism.
dvandva (Dwandwa) – duality, pair of opposites.
Gudakesha – an epithet applied to Arjuna which means 'one who has conquered sleep'.
guṇa – any one of the three essential modes of energy, of the three primal qualities that form the nature of things.
guru – spiritual guide and teacher.
Hrishikesha – an epithet applied to Krishna which means 'Lord of the senses'.
indriya – any one of the ten senses (five of knowledge and five of action).
īśvara (Ishwara) – Lord; God, as lord of Nature.
jagat – world, universe (lit. "the moving").
Janardana – an epithet applied to Krishna which means 'one who has no birth and puts an end to the birth of other beings'.
jīva – the individual soul.
jñāna – knowledge.
jñātā – knower.
kāma – desire.
kāraṇa – cause.
karma – action entailing its consequences.
kartā – a doer.
Kaunteya – an epithet applied to Arjuna which means 'son of Kunti' (one of his mother's names).
Keshava – an epithet applied to Krishna which means 'one who has long hair.'
kṣara (Kshara) – the mobile, the mutable.
kūṭastha – stable; high-seated.
laya – dissolution of the individual being in the Brahman.
līlā – creation as the play of God.
manas – the sense-mind as opposed to the reason.
mantra – the revealing word.
māyā – the lower Prakriti (as distinguished from the Para Prakriti).
māyāvāda – the doctrine which holds that the world is unreal and that it is created by the power of illusion.
moha – delusion.
mokṣa (Moksha) – liberation from *māyā*.
naiṣkarmya – actionlessness.
Narayana – an epithet applied to Krishna which means 'one who has made the water his abode'.
nigraha – coercion of the nature.
nirguṇa – without qualities.
niṣkāma – free from desire, desireless.
nivṛtti (Nivritti) – inaction.
niyamya – controlling.

niyata – controlled, regulated.
param – supreme.
Parantapa – an epithet applied to Arjuna which means 'subjugator of all enemies'.
Partha – an epithet applied to Arjuna which means 'son of Pritha' (one of his mother's names).
piśāca (Pishacha) – a hostile being of the lower vital world.
prabhu – master.
prakāśa (Prakasha) – light, illumination.
prakṛti (Prakriti) – Nature, creative energy (being more or less a synonym for Shakti).
pralaya – dissolution.
prāṇa – the nervous energy, the vital breath, the half-mental, half-material dynamism which links mind and matter; the outgoing breath.
prāṇāyāma – the Yogic exercise of the control of the respiration.
prasāda – clearness and happy tranquillity.
pravṛtti (Pravritti) – impulsion to works.
puruṣa (Purusha) – Being or Soul as opposed to Prakriti which is Becoming.
puruṣottama (Purushottama) – the Supreme Personality.
rahasyam – a secret.
rajas – the *guṇa* that drives to action.
rajasic – belonging to the *guṇa* of action and passion.
rākṣasa (Rakshasa) – a hostile being of the middle vital world.
rasa – affection of the senses (especially of pleasure).
ṛṣi (Rishi) – Seer.
sādhanā – spiritual self-training and exercise.
sādharmya – becoming of one law of being with the Divine; oneness in nature with the Divine.
sādṛśya – a synonym for *sādharmya*.
saguṇa – with the qualities.
sahaja – inborn, innate.
sākṣī (Sakshi) – a witness, the soul as a detached witness of the actions of the nature.
sālokya – dwelling in the Divine.
samādhi – the Yogic trance.
samagra – integral.
samatā – equality of soul and mind to all things and happenings.
sāmīpya – nearness to the Divine.
sannyāsa – (outward) renunciation.
saṁyama – a spiritual control of the nature; a concentration or directing of the consciousness.
sat – Being, existence, good.

GLOSSARY

sattva (Sattwa) – the *guṇa* that illumines, clarity, intelligence.
sattwic – belonging to the *guṇa* of light and happiness.
satyam – truth.
sāyujya – contact with the Divine.
śabda – sound, word.
śakti (Shakti) – force, energy; the divine or cosmic Energy (being more or less a synonym for Prakriti).
śāstra (Shastra) – the scriptures, theory, prescribed rule.
śraddhā (Shraddha) – faith.
siddhi – Yogic perfection.
śloka(Shloka) – verse.
śruti (Shruti) – revealed scripture (a general term for the Vedas and the Upanishads).
sthiti – status.
sukha – happiness, pleasure.
svabhāva (Swabhava) – the nature proper to each being.
svadharma (Swadharma) – one's own law of action.
tamas – the *guṇa* that hides or darkens, inertia, non-intelligence.
tamasic – belonging to the *guṇa* of ignorance and inertia.
tanmātra – any one of the five subtle energies which underlie the respective sense-experiences of smell, taste, sight, touch, hearing.
tapas – concentration of spiritual will force.
tapasyā – a synonym for *tapas*.
tat – That.
tattva (Tattwa) – any one of the twenty-four principles of the cosmic Energy which are enumerated by Sankhya.
tejaḥ – force, energy.
traiguṇya – the state of being bound to the three *guṇa*s.
triguṇātīta – beyond the control of the three *guṇa*s.
turīya – the superconscient state.
tyāga – (inner) renunciation.
uttama – highest.
vairāgya – distaste for the world and life.
vāk – speech.
Vasudeva – an epithet applied to Krishna which means 'son of Vasudeva'.
vedānta – a general term for all the Upanishads; a monistic philosophy based on the Upanishads.
vedavāda – traditional lore of the Vedic hymns and the Vedic sacrifice.
vibhu – the all-pervading Impersonal.
vibhūti – divine power as manifested in the world.
vicāra – reflective thought.
vidhi – order, rule.
vijñāna – comprehensive knowledge.

vikāra – deformation, distortion.
viveka – direct intuitive discrimination.
yajña – sacrifice.
yoga – union or oneness of the whole subjective being with the Supreme.
   Aishwara Yoga (the divine Yoga) – that by which the Transcendent is one with all existences even while more than them all and dwells in them and contains them as becomings of His own Nature.
yuga – a cycle, age.